Measuring Identity
A Guide for Social Scientists

The concept of identity has taken an increasingly prominent place in the social sciences and humanities. Scholars using social identities as the building blocks of social, political, and economic life have attempted to account for a number of discrete outcomes by treating identities as causal factors. The dominant implication of the literature on identity is that social identities are among the most important social facts of the world in which we live.

This book brings together leading scholars from a variety of disciplines to consider the conceptual and methodological challenges associated with treating identity as a variable, to offer a synthetic theoretical framework, and to demonstrate the possibilities offered by various methods of measurement. The book is thus a collection of empirically grounded theoretical discussions of a wide range of methodological techniques for the study of identities.

Rawi Abdelal is the Joseph C. Wilson Professor of Business Administration at Harvard Business School. He is the author of *National Purpose in the World Economy: Post-Soviet States in Comparative Perspective* (2001) and *Capital Rules: The Construction of Global Finance* (2007).

Yoshiko M. Herrera is Associate Professor in the Department of Political Science at the University of Wisconsin, Madison, and author of *Imagined Economies: The Sources of Russian Regionalism* (Cambridge University Press, 2005) and *Transforming Bureaucracy: Conditional Norms and the International Standardization of Statistics in Russia* (forthcoming).

Alastair Iain Johnston is the Laine Professor of China in World Affairs in the Government Department at Harvard University. He is the author of *Cultural Realism: Strategic Culture and Grand Strategy in Chinese History* (1995) and *Social States: China in International Institutions, 1980–2000* (2008), and coeditor of *Engaging China: The Management of an Emerging Power* (1999), *New Directions in the Study of China's Foreign Policy* (2006), and *Crafting Cooperation: Regional Institutions in Comparative Perspective* (Cambridge University Press, 2007).

Rose McDermott is Professor of Political Science at Brown University. She is the author of *Risk Taking in International Relations* (1998), *Political Psychology in International Relations* (2004), and *Presidential Leadership, Illness, and Decision Making* (Cambridge University Press, 2008).

Measuring Identity

A Guide for Social Scientists

Edited by

RAWI ABDELAL
Harvard University

YOSHIKO M. HERRERA
University of Wisconsin, Madison

ALASTAIR IAIN JOHNSTON
Harvard University

ROSE MCDERMOTT
Brown University

 CAMBRIDGE
UNIVERSITY PRESS

CAMBRIDGE UNIVERSITY PRESS
Cambridge, New York, Melbourne, Madrid, Cape Town, Singapore, São Paulo, Delhi

Cambridge University Press
32 Avenue of the Americas, New York, NY 10013-2473, USA

www.cambridge.org
Information on this title: www.cambridge.org/9780521732093

First published 2009

Printed in the United States of America

A catalog record for this publication is available from the British Library.

Library of Congress Cataloging in Publication Data

Measuring identity: a guide for social scientists / edited by Rawi Abdelal ... [et al.].
    p. cm.
    Includes bibliographical references.
    ISBN 978-0-521-51818-5 (hardback) – ISBN 978-0-521-73209-3 (pbk.)
    1. Group identity. I. Abdelal, Rawi, 1971– II. Title.
    HM753.M43 2008
    305.072'3–dc22   2008022023

ISBN 978-0-521-51818-5 hardback
ISBN 978-0-521-73209-3 paperback

Contents

Contributors

Rawi Abdelal is the Joseph C. Wilson Professor of Business Administration at Harvard Business School.

Laura L. Adams is Lecturer on Sociology and Co-director of the Program on Central Asia and the Caucasus at Harvard University.

Henry E. Brady is Class of 1941 Monroe Deutsch Professor of Political Science and Public Policy at the University of California, Berkeley, and Director of the University of California Survey Research Center.

Kanchan Chandra is Associate Professor in the Wilf Family Department of Politics at New York University.

Jack Citrin is Heller Professor of Political Science and Director of the Institute of Governmental Studies at the University of California, Berkeley.

Michael Dawson is the John D. MacArthur Professor of Political Science and the College at the University of Chicago.

Yoshiko M. Herrera is Associate Professor in the Department of Political Science at the University of Wisconsin, Madison.

Ted Hopf is Associate Professor in the Department of Political Science, Ohio State University.

Alastair Iain Johnston is the Laine Professor of China in World Affairs in the Government Department at Harvard University.

Cynthia S. Kaplan is Professor of Political Science at the University of California, Santa Barbara.

Taeku Lee is Associate Professor of Political Science at the University of California, Berkeley.

Rose McDermott is Professor of Political Science at Brown University.

Amanda K. Metskas is Executive Director of Camp Quest, Inc., and holds an M.A. in Political Science from Ohio State University.

Kimberly A. Neuendorf is Professor in the School of Communication at Cleveland State University.

David O. Sears is Professor of Psychology and Political Science at the University of California, Los Angeles.

Paul D. Skalski is Assistant Professor in the School of Communication at Cleveland State University.

Robalyn Stone is a lead analyst and is in charge of all the text analysis tool development at Social Science Automation, Inc.

Donald A. Sylvan is President of the Jewish Education Service of North America and Professor Emeritus of Political Science at Ohio State University.

Michael Young is President of Social Science Automation, Inc.

Introduction

Rawi Abdelal, Yoshiko M. Herrera, Alastair Iain
Johnston, and Rose McDermott

This volume outlines a variety of definitions and methodologies for studying social identities in a diverse set of contexts within American politics, comparative politics, and international relations. As such, we hope it will serve as a primer on the analysis and methodology of identity scholarship for a wide range of interested researchers. Political scientists have long enjoyed access to many excellent guides to mainstream theories and methods, yet those wanting to do research on social identities have had to synthesize enormous literatures on their own, with no practical guide to the alternatives they might employ in their scholarship. This volume aims to be such a road map, both analytically and methodologically. The chapters include a broad array of definitions as well as methodological options available for scholarly research on identity, including methods currently in use and some promising newer ones.

The chapters of this volume demonstrate concretely how to conduct identity research using several different methodological options. Each chapter shows how the ideas that underlie identity are applied in the context of individual research and what sorts of insights such projects can yield. In this way, the combined chapters create a whole greater than the sum of its parts; by aggregating the various specific methodological approaches, the text provides a coherent basis for the general examination of identity in the study of political science.

Support for this edited volume was made possible by the Weatherhead Initiative of the Weatherhead Center for International Affairs at Harvard University. We are grateful to David Laitin and one anonymous reviewer who commented generously on the entire manuscript. In addition, Lew Bateman of Cambridge University Press has been especially helpful in bringing the project to fruition. Finally, the volume has benefited greatly from comments and suggestions by colleagues too numerous to name individually over the past several years – we thank them sincerely.

IDENTITY

Comparison to Previous Work in Other Fields

Political science is not the only field that has examined and attempted to define and measure identities rigorously. Other disciplines, most prominently psychology, have long invoked, measured, and tested various models of identity in their attempts to create and establish internally valid and reliable instruments and hypotheses about human behavior.[1] Many important conceptualizations have evolved from this tradition, some of which focus on adolescent development, where various aspects of identity are often assumed to remain in flux until later consolidation.[2] Most adult identity measurement scales, however, have focused predominantly, if not exclusively, on measures of ethnic or cultural identification, and several measures have been devised.[3] Many of these attempts to develop identity scales have been designed for specific utility in assessing and treating various clinical populations.[4]

In this volume, we build and expand on this work in identity in three important ways. First, rather than restricting ourselves to an individual or intrapsychic definition, we examine identity as a collective concept. In this way, we hope to explore how individuals establish social and political identities, which can overlap between and among different people and groups. Second, we explore established identities in adults. Although our investigations can easily be applied to younger members of society, we do not focus on the developmental aspects of

[1] Numerous studies of identity can also be found in psychiatry, management, and substance abuse research.
[2] These include the Extended Objective Identity measure of Ego Identity States (EOM-EIS-II) (Bennion and Adams 1986). This measure is typically used to assess identity in late adolescence and appears best utilized to take repeated or continuous measures of identity statuses over time. The Utrecht-Groningen Identity development scale (Meeus, Iedema, and Maassen 2002), for example, focuses on how teens explore various relational and social identities before making identity commitments.
[3] For example, the Orthogonal Cultural Identification Scale (OCIS) (Oetting and Beauvais 1990–1991) allows an individual to demonstrate independent identification with more than one culture – for example, minority and white American cultures. Similar attempts at such assessments are presented in the Citrin and Sears and Lee chapters in this volume.
[4] One of these, the Sun-Lew Asian Self-Identity Acculturation Scale (Ownbey and Horridge 1998), is based on a successful earlier scale designed to help assess underserved Hispanic populations. In another example, some intriguing work examining the interaction between cognitive, emotional, and situational factors in explaining attributions for success among African American students has also used identity scales, in this case the African American Acculturation Scale (Smith and Hopkins 2004), to help assess educational outcomes. Interestingly, even white identity has been examined from this perspective, using implicit association measures (Knowles and Peng 2005) to measure response latency to predict the degree of in-group identification. This model of dominant group identification sheds light on the way in which individuals link evaluations of themselves to evaluations of their in-group.

identity formation and consolidation. Third, we expand the definition of social identity beyond ethnic and cultural identifications to include other forms of social and political identification. While racial and cultural identifications remain central to our concerns, such interests do not exclude other important social identifications, including religious, gender, and class associations.

Identity as Independent and Dependent Variables

Throughout this volume, most of the authors treat identity as an independent variable, a factor to be measured and examined for its impact on other important variables and outcomes. This notion raises at least three important considerations that merit acknowledgment from the outset. First, the assumption of identity as an independent variable rests on a notion that individuals indeed possess certain identities that can be better understood with improved and more accurate measurement techniques and strategies. Even if it is the case that improved measurement can help scholars access identity in a more reliable and valid fashion, it is also theoretically possible that certain individuals do not have clear and stable identities in the way we conventionally suppose. Rather, like individuals who create a response to satisfy a pollster and answer a question without really having a strong opinion, some people may not feel strong identifications with the particular social or political groups we select to interrogate. Certainly, it is likely that many people espouse stronger attachments to certain groups, perhaps racial or gender categories, that are harder to change than others, such as class, which may be more amenable to change over time with education or employment. Nonetheless, we should remain aware of the fact that identity may not always be as real as apparent.

Second, identity often exists as a dependent variable as well as an independent one. In conducting research, scholars must be clear about whether they want to know if identity is causing a person to do a particular thing (an independent variable), or if something else is causing a person to adopt a particular identity (a dependent variable). Certain measures can be used to assess identity as either type of variable, but analysts must be clear about the nature of their causal model in investigating their phenomena of interest.

Identity and Action

Identity, like any form of categorization, proves intrinsically interesting. But the question remains: how does holding an identity translate into a particular type of action or behavior? Just because a person holds a particular identity does not necessarily mean that she will act in a particular way because of it. Motivation remains a key component in the urge for any individual to act on the basis of any given identification. Some differences in motivation may reflect individual temperament; others can indicate strong powers of social persuasion and support; and still others may demonstrate institutional incentives and support. But in any model that examines the impact of identity on particular outcomes, the motivation to transform identity into action cannot be ignored, and many of the chapters in this volume – by empirically and theoretically connecting social identities with outcomes – go some way toward addressing the issue of motivation or the link between identity and action.[5]

METHODS FOR MEASURING IDENTITY

In our survey of the scholarly literature on identity, we found that surveys, content analysis, discourse analysis, and ethnography were the most widely used methods for measuring identity. We did not discover any systematic links between these methods and the types of identity they were used to measure, although nearly all studies of identity included some sort of case study. We also identified two additional methods – cognitive mapping and experiments – that offer great promise to supplement the dominant methods, although the research agendas for their widespread incorporation into identity research are still being formulated. Here we briefly review these methods and offer a few reflections on the tools available to scholars who are interested in measuring identity.

Surveys

Surveys provide the backbone of a great deal of research on public opinion and political behavior. Structured interviews of large numbers of people offer information that may be difficult to extract using alternative methodologies. These techniques can be adapted to great benefit in identity research as well because they allow individuals and groups to offer and establish their own self-definitions.[6] Open-ended survey and interview instruments in particular allow

---

[5] Social identity theory (SIT), discussed in some detail in Chapter 12, is one area of identity research that squarely addresses the question of motivation. SIT presents an advance over previous models of social categorization because it includes notions of motivation and does not rely solely on cognitive biases and processes. Rather, SIT assumes that people are motivated to see both themselves and others in distinct ways and to feel better about themselves as a result of these social comparisons. SIT thus attempts to explain stereotyping and prejudice as not simply the result of cognitive bias or misunderstanding but rather as a motivated process designed to help people feel better about themselves.

[6] For guidance on surveys and interviews related to identity research, see chapters 3–5 in Bauer and Gaskell 2000; on interviews, see Briggs 1986; McCracken 1988; Rubin and Rubin 1995; and Gubrium and Holstein 2002; on surveys more generally, see Fink 2003.

respondents to present their own notions of who they are, what matters to them and why, and how they decide who is or is not included in their group, without being classified according to the researcher's prior biases and interpretations. Surveys and interviews have the obvious advantage of allowing researchers to ask specific questions about identity. These techniques allow interested researchers to address directly questions of content and contestation.

As a general rule, surveys have been fairly straightforward in how they tap into the content of identities. The questions are often a direct inquiry into self-described attributes, attitudes, and practices that respondents believe that they should express as a member of a particular social group. Early work on party identification done by the Social Survey Center at the University of Michigan, for instance, simply asked respondents how important it was to them to think of themselves as members of a political group. This type of question was adapted to the analysis of social identity (Hooper 1976). Other surveys ask equally straight-forward questions. The World Values Survey asks about how proud respondents are to have an identity as, say, a particular nationality.[7] The use of surveys to analyze the content and contestation of identities has since been well established.[8] Not only may surveys be combined with interviews, but experiments may also be embedded in surveys (e.g., Sniderman, Hagendoorn, and Prior 2004). The scholarly record makes it clear that survey research has been and will continue to be a critical method for measurement of social identities.

Content Analysis

Content analysis is, according to Neuendorf (2004a: 33), "a summarizing, quantitative analysis of messages that relies on the scientific method." The "message component" is the unit of analysis, and those components are frequently summarized quantitatively. Whereas discourse analysis relies on the interpretive skills of the scholar to mediate between the reader and the text or practice under study, content analysis is designed to limit mediation. The critical step is the creation of a coding scheme that is written out in great detail in order to ensure reliability among coders of the text.[9]

---

[7] For an application of these questions in developing measures of nationalism and patriotism, see Furia 2002. See also the measures for national identity and pride in Smith and Jarkko 2001; their paper draws on a 1995 cross-national survey on national identity conducted by the International Social Survey Programme (http://www.issp.org/natpride.doc).

[8] For examples, in various subfields of political science, see M. Barnett 1999 for international relations; Citrin et al. 1994 and Jones-Correa and Leal 1996 for American politics; and Laitin 2002 for comparative politics.

[9] Recently there have been advances in computer-aided content analysis, but most research is still based on human coding.

Content analysis can perform two basic functions.[10] Its first function is the provision of frequency counts of both key words and categories of terms. The former is self-evident. The latter allows the virtually unlimited categorization of a text into multiple meanings. Words can be clustered along shared dimensions, and the categories themselves can be analyzed in terms of relative frequency. The content of these categories can be almost anything the researcher requires. Because the researcher is in charge of building these dictionaries, the meanings are, in a sense, imposed by the researcher and his or her dictionary.

The second function entails the provision of concordances, also known as keyword-in-context (KWIC) analysis. A KWIC analysis lists all instances where a particular term is mentioned in a given text. This method can be very useful for examining what the semantic, grammatical, or substantive context of identity language is. The software for performing quantitative analysis has improved substantially in recent years and can now be adapted to texts in multiple languages.[11]

Unlike discourse analysis, which is used to place texts and practices in their intersubjective contexts, content analysis is based on the idea that the individual text is meaningful on its own and that a summary of the messages within it is the desirable outcome (see Hardy, Harley, and Phillips 2004; Neuendorf 2004a). So, whereas scholars employing discourse analysis rely on their close readings, those who undertake content analysis seek to count statements of being and purpose associated with a group identity and the other groups against which it may be defined, as well as to analyze the semantic qualities of such statements of being and purpose (Roberts 1997; Neuendorf 2002). Content analysis has not been used as widely as discourse analysis and surveys for the measurement of identities, but the usefulness of the method has been demonstrated.[12]

Discourse Analysis and Ethnography

Discourse analysis is the qualitative and interpretive recovery of meaning from the language that actors use to describe and understand social phenomena.[13] Most

---

[10] For guidance on conducting quantitative content analysis, see Neuendorf 2002; chapters 8, 16–17 in Bauer and Gaskell 2000; Titscher et al. 2000; Popping 2000; and Wetherell 1987.

[11] For further discussion of the advantages and disadvantages of different content analysis software for the analysis of identity, see Lowe 2002. In addition, see the free software developed by Will Lowe for the Harvard Identity Project at http://www.yoshikoder.org/.

[12] For examples, see Herrera 2005; Eilders and Luter 2000; and Laitin 1998.

[13] We recognize that discourse analysis is a contested notion (Herrera and Braumoeller 2004; Hardy, Harley, and Phillips 2004; Crawford 2004; Hopf 2004; Laffey and Weldes 2004; Neuendorf 2004a; Fierke 2004). Here we offer a broad conception of discourse analysis that inevitably elides some difficult questions of ontology and epistemology but is designed to include all those scholars who explicitly adopt discourse analysis as well as those who implicitly do so by analyzing texts to establish for readers their sense of the intersubjective context.

scholars who employ discourse analysis in their research attempt to contextualize the texts they are studying among other texts or the larger social context.[14] The very notion of discourse is usually understood as a collection of related texts, constituted as speech, written documents, and social practices, that produce meaning and organize social knowledge. Scholars have relied on structured and semistructured interviews and their own informed interpretations of a variety of texts, including policy statements, political party platforms, newspaper articles, classic texts of prominent public intellectuals, speeches of political leaders, and the minutes of government meetings, as well as less explicitly political texts such as popular novels.

As with other methods, discourse analysis places unique demands on the analyst. Rather than statistics, programming, or modeling, deep social knowledge and a familiarity with interrelated texts are required for an analyst to recover meanings from discourse. The critical task is for an author to convince his or her readers that a particular reconstruction of the intersubjective context of some social phenomenon – in our case, a collective identity – is useful for understanding an empirical outcome. For our purposes, scholars who write rich descriptions of cases are engaged in discourse analysis, especially in the sense that they are relying on their own interpretive skills and social knowledge to write convincingly about the content and contestation of an identity. Discourse analysis thus can be considered the qualitative contextualization of texts and practices in order to describe social meanings.

Ethnography can be understood as discourse analysis in its richest, most intensive, and most anthropological form. Because ethnography involves the scholar being situated within a social context to become part of its discourse – its language and its practices – the research that results has the advantage of conveying social meanings as they are experienced. Although many scholars who implicitly or explicitly use discourse analysis to study identity are concerned about the ways in which they themselves mediate the data they extract from texts and practices, ethnographers embrace the challenge of revealing and correcting for their own mediation of the social meanings of the society under study.[15] Discourse analysis and ethnography have been important tools for the study of social identities, and in some disciplines, namely anthropology, have been the dominant method.

Cognitive Mapping

Cognitive mapping is an alternate method to either content or discourse analysis for measurement of social identities. Rather than the subjective

---

[14] For guidance on conducting discourse analysis, see Phillips and Hardy 2002; Wodak and Meyer 2001; chapters 9–12 in Bauer and Gaskell 2000; and Titscher et al. 2000.

[15] For a few examples of ethnographic discourse analysis, see Blee 2002; Field 1999; and Noyes 2003.

interpretation involved in discourse analysis or the calculation in quantitative
content analysis, cognitive mapping entails the description of cause-effect relationships that are both implicit and explicit in a text.

Cognitive mapping entails breaking down selected texts from a decision-
making process into all of their component cause-effect relationships
(Axelrod 1976). The researcher then determines whether these causal relationships are negative or positive – that is, whether a change in direction in the
causal concept leads to a similar or dissimilar change in the effect concept
(e.g., does an increase in arms lead to an increase or decrease of security?).
The technique can help uncover the deep structure of an argument – the
presence or absence of certain cause-effect assumptions, and the consistencies
and inconsistencies across cause-effect arguments. These maps can be compared across actors within an identity group, or aggregated within the group
and compared with the maps of out-groups, to determine what cause-effect
relationships are shared by actors and, if so, the degree to which they are
shared. Cognitive mapping can be done either "by hand" using human coders
or by computer, as discussed in Chapter 8 of this volume. Cognitive mapping
is not yet widely used in identity research, but we think it has great potential.

Experiments

Experiments, another methodology by which to measure identity (Tajfel 1970,
1981a, 1982; Aronson et al. 1990), offer the advantage of unparalleled control
and assessment of causality. They have been used a great deal in psychology to
examine questions related to personal and social identity, including the development of social identity theory, mentioned earlier. Experiments begin with a
particular question that the researcher seeks to answer. A particular experimental protocol that demands the random assignment of subjects to various
conditions is then designed. Each condition typically manipulates only one
variable of central interest or a very few. This allows the experimenter to
determine what caused any observed changes in outcome between individuals
and groups. Random assignment ensures that any differences that emerge
derive from the experimental manipulation and are not merely the consequence
of preexisting or systematic divergences between individuals and groups. In this
way, experimental procedure allows true leverage in making causal arguments.
Because nothing else except the variable of interest shifts in a well-designed
experiment, observers can assume that the manipulation itself caused any
changes that are witnessed.

Social psychology possesses a long tradition of experimental investigation
into various aspects of personal and collective identity. Although political

scientists examining identity have tended not to use experiments as a method, most work on social identity theory (SIT) within social psychology rests on experimental evidence, and SIT has been one of the most successful research paradigms for studying identity, at least in terms of the quantity and quality of research it has generated.

THE ORGANIZATION OF THE VOLUME

Identity scholarship has so far limited itself to a somewhat narrow methodological band, taking little notice of newer, less traditional options. We are proponents of methodological eclecticism, particularly with regard to identity work. Addressing the range of options, this volume advocates use of a variety of methodologies for studying identity and highlights, in particular, surveys, content analysis and cognitive mapping, discourse analysis and ethnography, and experiments. The book's chapters cover this wide range of methodologies, outlining through example the particular benefits of each.

Part I considers identity definition, conceptualization, and measurement alternatives. The first chapter, by Rawi Abdelal, Yoshiko M. Herrera, Alastair Iain Johnston, and Rose McDermott, presents a definition of identity, where identity is a social category that varies in terms of content and contestation. Content describes the meaning of a collective identity, and the content of social identities may take the form of four nonmutually exclusive types: constitutive norms, social purposes, relational comparisons, and cognitive models. Contestation refers to the degree of agreement within a group over the content of the shared category. This analytic framework thus enables social identities to be compared according to the agreement and disagreement about their meanings by members of the group.

The next two chapters demonstrate how various methods can be combined to define and measure identity in useful and creative ways. Chapter 2, by Henry E. Brady and Cynthia S. Kaplan, considers the conceptualization and measurement of politically relevant social identities, such as ethnic identity, which have figured prominently in motivating and shaping political action. They argue that a variety of methods and data – history, demography, surveys, primary source materials, content analysis, and discourse analysis – are necessary in order to fully comprehend the political role of ethnicity at the mass public and elite level. They illustrate the utility of combining methods to construct group-based social identity measures by considering seven groups in four Soviet republics around 1990: Estonians and Russians in Estonia, Tatars and Russians in the Republic of Tatarstan, the Komi and Russians in the Komi Republic, and (to a lesser extent) Russians in Russia.

Similarly, Chapter 3, by Donald A. Sylvan and Amanda K. Metskas, considers a range of methodological options, but in this chapter the focus is on the case of Israeli-Palestinian relations. Focusing on five research projects that used experimental, survey, interview, narrative, and text-based data, Sylvan and Metskas consider the trade-offs between alternative approaches to measuring identity in this context. This chapter argues that the nature of the question and the role of elites can help determine the appropriate measurement strategy to use. As the chapter shows, many real-world identity-related puzzles require multimethod approaches because each approach to measuring identity has its own strengths and weaknesses.

The remaining chapters all proceed by presenting a measurement method that the authors have applied to a particular empirical issue. In essence, these chapters represent extended methodological discussions based on the individual authors' experiences using identity as a variable in larger research projects. Each of these chapters details the workings of a particular definition and method, discussing both its advantages and disadvantages. The chapters are divided into four sections: surveys, content analysis (including cognitive mapping), discourse analysis and ethnography, and experiments.

The first section applying various measurement methods to the definition of identity concentrates on surveys. Chapter 4, by Taeku Lee, examines the conspicuous gap between social theory on race and ethnicity, which stresses its fluidity, multiplicity, and contingency, and quantitative, survey-based studies of race and ethnicity, which remain focused on finding a common, fixed set of categories that reliably and validly reflect how individuals think of themselves in racial or ethnic terms. This chapter proposes a new approach to measuring ethnoracial self-identification. "Identity point allocation" gives respondents latitude over how many groups to identify with and how to weight the strength of their identification with each group. This approach, tested in a 2003 study of adult Californians, shows a demonstrably more graded and multiracial portrait of ethnoracial self-identification than that found in standard survey measures, including the 2000 U.S. Census. Importantly, the chapter argues that the demographic and attitudinal characteristics we infer about a given racial or ethnic group may vary, sometimes quite substantially, by how we ask respondents to self-identify by race or ethnicity.

Chapter 5, by Jack Citrin and David O. Sears, explores the implications of holding multiple identities, concentrating on how individuals balance national and ethnic identities in multiethnic states. Citrin and Sears's case study considers the United States and the current demographic and ideological challenge to the idea of *E pluribus unum*. By reviewing alternative measures of identity and some of the obstacles to systematic measurement, the chapter argues for the need to build upon more qualitative explorations of the content of identities before undertaking survey research. It then uses survey research – both national samples for representativeness and pooled data from Los Angeles – to explore how citizens conceive of and prioritize their national and ethnic identities. The results of Citrin and Sears's study show different patterns of identity choice across ethnic groups and immigrant generations. This chapter also investigates the factors that give rise to different modes of structuring national and ethnic identities and tracks the influence of such identifications on several public policies. The authors also point to the compatibility of national and ethnic identities, in the sense that patriotism and prioritizing one's national identity become the dominant point of view as immigrants assimilate over time.

In Chapter 6, Michael Dawson explores the concept of racial identity in the final contribution to the survey methods section. He examines the empirical and theoretical utility of the conceptualization of black racial identity that has taken root most deeply among students of empirical black politics. Much of the work on black political identity, and increasingly work focused on Latino/a and Asian American political identity as well, has focused on one particular construction of racial identity – that of "linked fate." Empirically, Dawson tests the degree to which racial identity, operationalized by the concept of "linked fate," is still able to shape African Americans' political beliefs. He then theoretically addresses the question of whether the concept of black racial identity is salvageable both as a tool for empirical analysis and as a basis for reconstructing black solidarity.

The next section contains three chapters that use content analysis to measure identity. In Chapter 7, Kimberly A. Neuendorf and Paul D. Skalski consider content analysis in terms of a quantitative investigation based on the coding of message characteristics. They present three main coding possibilities: human coding from a preset scheme; computer text coding from a preset scheme; and "emergent" computer text coding, where dimensions derive from the data at hand. They then break down the messages to be coded into three types based on the nature of the message: response-based; naturally occurring where identity is assumed; and naturally occurring where identity can be extracted. Cross-matching the coding schemes and the message types yields a set of eight possible types of content analysis coding for identity measures. The chapter then presents examples for each, some based on original analyses and others taken from the research of other identity scholars. Advantages and limitations of the various approaches are considered.

Chapter 8, by Robalyn Stone and Michael Young, examines computer-generated cognitive maps as a tool for extracting information about identity concepts in texts. Cognitive maps are a representation of the fundamental underlying belief system expressed in a text. The chapter uses two unique software programs: Profiler Plus parses texts and transforms them into a series of data statements about the relationship between a subject and an object (e.g., one group and another group). Collating the data statements produced by Profiler Plus and the cognitive mapping coding scheme, Worldview generates the network representation of the beliefs extracted from the source documents. This network representation constitutes a cognitive map. WorldView creates a unique node for each unique concept, conjunction, and relationship in the data statements. Each node is associated with both a list of the relationships of which it is the subject and a list of the relationships of which it is an object. Stone and Young show how these applications can be used to examine how different Iraqi leaders conceive of the main traits and characteristics of different ethnic and religious identities. The techniques allow the researcher to compare similarities and differences across these cognitive maps by essentially measuring the number of steps it would take for one text's conceptualization of identity to become perfectly congruent with another. The fewer the number of steps, the closer the identity is. This process can illuminate the conceptual distance across individuals within similar and different identity groups.

Chapter 9, by Kanchan Chandra, presents a constructivist perspective on ethnicity. Chandra discusses the importance of the distinction between ethnic "structure" (the set of potential ethnic identities that characterizes a population) and ethnic "practice" (the set of identities actually activated by that population), while noting that most cross-national datasets on ethnic groups remain primordialist – they do not distinguish between structure and practice, do not accommodate the possibility of multiplicity, and are not sensitive to time and context. This chapter describes a new, constructivist dataset on several concepts related to ethnic identity and institutions – referred to as CDEI (Constructivist Dataset on Ethnicity and Institutions). CDEI, which currently covers 100 countries for the year 1996, generates a range of variables related to ethnicity and institutions. Here, Chandra focuses on one key variable – EVOTE, or the percentage of the vote captured by ethnic parties in each country for the year 1996. EVOTE is based on a content analysis of party rhetoric – that is, what parties actually say to voters rather than what they write in their manifestos – in the election campaign closest to but before 1996. EVOTE has the potential to illuminate a very diverse set of research agendas related to the origins or effects of politically activated ethnic identities, especially when expanded over time.

The next two chapters illustrate how discourse analysis and ethnography can illuminate the measurement of identity. Chapter 10 outlines a constructivist theory of identity that is at once social, structural, and cognitive. The author, Ted Hopf, invokes discourse analysis to explore three logics of social order – consequentialism, appropriateness, and habit – and to relate them to the concept of identity. He then applies this theory to the study of a state's foreign policy choices. He constructs the appropriate methodology for the case of the Sino-Soviet split before going on to assess the empirical validity of a constructivist account for the Sino-Soviet shift from amity to enmity. He concludes with some thoughts about the possibility of a fruitful marriage between, on the one hand, an interpretivist epistemology and ontology and, on the other, positivist methods.

Chapter 11, by Laura Adams, reviews the way that identity has been measured in a select but diverse group of ethnographic studies. The chapter outlines the strengths and weaknesses of ethnographic methods and explores the ways that ethnographers deal with the challenges of their research process. In particular, Adams explains how ethnographers address the following issues: validity and reliability, sampling, gaining access and establishing rapport, data collection and analysis, writing up the research, and theorizing. Adams then illustrates the concrete steps of conducting ethnographic field research using examples from her own work on national identity in post-Soviet Uzbekistan. The chapter makes the case for including ethnographic methods as a component of any study that seeks to understand identity on the level of meaning or in terms of contestation.

The last chapter explores the possibility of employing the experimental method to study and measure social identities. In Chapter 13, Rose McDermott provides an overview of the experimental literature on identity research. This chapter begins with a substantive discussion of the experimental work that has been conducted on social identity, which as it turns out is concerned almost exclusively with the ramifications, implications, and limitations of social identity theory. The chapter discusses limitations of existing experimental work for applications to political science, and the final section examines some of the ways in which the method of experimentation might be expanded to investigate other realms of social identity in political contexts.

It is our hope that this volume helps raise awareness of the various definitions and methods that scholars have used to examine and measure the concept of identity across a wide array of topics and issues. Further, we hope this volume encourages others to build on existing definitions, including some outlined in the individual chapters, and undertake more research into diverse aspects of identity using a variety of methods, thereby enhancing our shared understanding of this important concept.

I

DEFINITION, CONCEPTUALIZATION, AND MEASUREMENT ALTERNATIVES

I

Identity as a Variable

Rawi Abdelal, Yoshiko M. Herrera, Alastair Iain
Johnston, and Rose McDermott

For the past two decades, the attention given to the concept of "identity" –
both in the social sciences and in the world at large – has continued to rise.
Multiple disciplines and subfields are producing an expanding literature on
the definition, meaning, and development of ethnic, national, linguistic,
religious, gender, class, and other identities and their roles in political,
social, and economic outcomes. The ubiquity of identity-based scholarship
suggests an emerging realization that identities, as Rogers Smith (2002: 302)
has observed, are "among the most normatively significant and behaviorally
consequential aspects of politics," yet the literature has remained diffuse.
That is, despite this flurry of activity, the social sciences have not yet witnessed
a commensurate rise in definitional consensus on the concept of identity.

The intense interest in scholarship on identity, as well as the many kinds of
studies this fascination has spawned, has unfortunately helped undermine
the conceptual clarity of identity as a variable. The wide variety of

Research for this chapter was made possible by the generous support of the Weatherhead Initiative of the Weatherhead Center for International Affairs at Harvard University. We are grateful to those who commented on earlier versions of this chapter: Peter Burke, Lars-Erik Cederman,
Jeff Checkel, Michael Dawson, James Fearon, David Frank, Erin Jenne, Michael Jones-Correa,
Cynthia Kaplan, Peter Katzenstein, Herb Kelman, David Laitin, Daniel Posner, Paul Sniderman,
Werner Sollors, Jeff Strabone, Philip Stone, Charles Tilly, Mary Waters, and three anonymous
reviewers. We would also like to thank participants of the 2004 "Identity as a Variable" con-
ference, including Henry Brady, Kanchan Chandra, Jack Citrin, Neta Crawford, Jennifer
Hochschild, Ted Hopf, Jacques Hymans, Cynthia Kaplan, Ulrich Krotz, Taeku Lee, Will Lowe,
Jason Lyall, Kimberly Neuendorf, Roger Petersen, Kevin Quinn, David Rousseau, Rogers Smith,
Ron Suny, Donald Sylvan, Kim Williams, and Michael Young, for comments on this version.
A longer version of this chapter appeared as Rawi Abdelal, Yoshiko Herrera, Alastair Iain
Johnston, and Rose McDermott, "Identity as a Variable," *Perspectives on Politics* 4, no. 4
(December 2006): 695–711.

conceptualizations and definitions of identity has led some to conclude that
identity is so elusive, slippery, and amorphous that it will never prove to be a
useful variable for the social sciences. Rogers Brubaker and Frederick Cooper
(2000) have even argued, in the most important critique of identity scholarship to date, that it is time to let go of the concept of identity altogether and to
move beyond a scholarly language that they suggest is hopelessly vague and
has obscured more than it has revealed. One might conclude that the current
state of the field amounts to definitional anarchy. We believe, however, that
the social sciences should not jettison a generation's worth of scholarship,
much of it provocative and valuable. Instead, it is time to invest identity with
greater definitional and analytical rigor.

Social identity scholarship suffers from two sets of problems: conceptual
issues and coordination gaps. The main conceptual questions that the field needs
to address more clearly consider how we can compare different *types* of identities and how we can exploit theoretical advances in operationalizing identity
as a variable. Among "coordination" problems we include the lack of consistency and clarity in defining and measuring identities and the lack of coordination
of identity research at both the cross-disciplinary and cross-subfield levels.

The progress of scholarly work on social identities depends on further
developing an analytic framework that allows for comparison and
differentiation among the many kinds of identities; being able to differentiate between types of content is the key to such a framework. To this
end, we offer a definition of collective identity as a social category that
varies along two dimensions – content and contestation. Content describes
the *meaning* of a collective identity. The content of social identities may
take the form of four, nonmutually exclusive types: constitutive norms,
social purposes, relational comparisons with other social categories, and
cognitive models. Contestation refers to the degree of *agreement* within a
group over the content of the shared category. Our conceptualization thus
enables collective identities to be compared according to the agreement and
disagreement about their meanings by the members of the group. Our
chapter thus offers one possible path forward for social scientific work
on identity by developing a more rigorous, more precisely defined analytic
framework.

ANALYTIC FRAMEWORK FOR IDENTITY AS VARIABLE

We believe that the lacunae at the heart of identity scholarship are due to the lack
of an analytic framework that is broad enough to serve the majority of scholars
working on identity, yet narrow enough not to include social phenomena that are

distinct from, though related to, identity. Building upon the brush-clearing work already done by others,[1] we suggest an analytic framework that will enable scholars to compare types of identities (e.g., ethnic, national, religious, gender, class, etc.); allow for nuanced operationalization of the theoretical sophistication of identity scholarship; and promote coordination across identity scholarship while providing a conceptualization that is flexible enough to allow researchers to tailor it to their own particular needs. Moreover, we believe the conceptualization of identity in our analytic framework is already implicit in almost all of the research on identity that we have surveyed; what we have to offer is not something new or unusual but rather a conceptual apparatus that allows for the integration not just of future scholarship but especially of the abundance of already existing scholarship on which it is based, and whose implicit assumptions it draws out into the open.

We define a collective identity as a social category that varies along two dimensions – content and contestation. Content describes the meaning of a collective identity. The content of social identities may take the form of four, nonmutually exclusive types:

- *Constitutive norms* refer to the formal and informal rules that define group membership.
- *Social purposes* refer to the goals that are shared by members of a group.
- *Relational comparisons* refer to defining an identity group by what it is not – that is, the way it views *other* identity groups, especially where those views about the other are a defining part of the identity.
- *Cognitive models* refer to the worldviews or understandings of political and material conditions and interests that are shaped by a particular identity.

Contestation refers to the degree of agreement within a group over the content of the shared identity. Far from being understood as fixed or unvarying, collective identities, in this conceptualization, vary in the agreement and disagreement about their meanings. The relevant aspects of the content of

---

[1] Fearon (1999) divides personal from social identities, and then further divides social identities into type and role identities. Brewer and Gardner (1996) distinguish three types of identity: personal, collective, and relational. Our framework considers the relational identity to be one of four types of content of collective identities. Chandra and Laitin (2002) present a general classification scheme for identities. They refer to categories, attributes, and dimensions as the three main components of an identity. Categories are the immediate term used to describe an individual's identity (e.g., working class). Attributes are the qualities individuals are expected to express to meet membership criteria for a social category. Dimensions are the range of categories that make up a typology (working class, middle class, and aristocracy together constitute the typology "class").

collective identities vary a great deal, and it is impossible a priori to specify them all.

We believe that these four types of content encompass the variety of meanings in social identities, while contestation over content addresses the fluidity and contextual nature of identities. Moreover, we argue that every social identity includes all of these types of content, with greater or lesser degrees of contestation over aspects within content types.

Our analytic framework for identity has much in common with definitions and conceptualizations already used implicitly by many scholars, and the words "content" and "contestation" are standard in the scholarly literature. The literature includes many other words for the variation in identities as well, but we hold that such alternative conceptualizations and nomenclatures are either subsets of content and contestation or simply not useful enough to remain part of the lexicon of identity. We developed this typology while surveying the existing literature, where scholars were already measuring identity either implicitly or explicitly along these lines. These four types, each illustrated in detail in the following sections, encompass the range of variation for which the field has so far tried to account.

Constitutive Norms

The normative content of a collective identity specifies its constitutive rules – the practices that define that identity and lead other actors to recognize it. The rules that determine group membership and putative attributes of the group can also be thought of along these lines. This normative content, the set of constitutive rules, may be bundled together into one or more coherent "role" identities. The normative content of an identity derives from a broader set of social norms that emanate from multiple centers of authority. Norms can thus be unwritten or codified – in other words, social or legal – so long as they appear to fix meanings and set collective expectations for members of the group. These practices cause group recognition and are thus, necessarily, obligations of individual members of the group. When practices that lead to recognition are also understood as obligations, they may be valorized by the group as ethical.

Constitutive norms do more than identify the "proper" or "appropriate" behavior for a particular identity, though such a regulatory effect is important, as in role theory (Monroe, Hankin, and van Vechten 2000). The effect that is even more powerful is recognition – constitutive norms are the very actions that lead others to recognize an actor as having a particular identity (Katzenstein 1996; Ruggie 1998a). They are also distinct from social purposes (i.e., shared interests or preferences). Rather than specifying the ends of action, norms help to define social meaning by establishing collective expectations and individual obligations. Thus, constitutive norms do not determine the preferences of a group; rather, they define the boundaries and distinctive practices of a group.

Illustrations of constitutive norms drawn from political science scholarship suggest that practices that lead relevant others to recognize an identity can be either conscious or taken for granted. The degree to which such practices are habituated (Hopf 2002) or internalized (i.e., the degree to which individual members are socialized) is an empirical question. Regardless of the degree to which constitutive practices are unconscious, unquestioned, or taken for granted, such norms are integral parts of the social meaning of an identity. As Price and Tannenwald (1996) have argued, over the course of the late twentieth century the content of the identity "civilized state" evolved a great deal. By the end of the century, "civilized states" did not employ nuclear or chemical weapons in their armed struggles. Klotz (1995a, 1995b) traced the emergence of the norm of racial equality in international society. In security communities, the factors that prevent defection are not institutional per se but are based on the development of shared notions of in-group identification where interaction has literally eliminated defection (war) as a possibility – where there exists the "impossibility of imagining violence."[2] In this conceptualization, the reasons to act in a particular way are found in a decision to perform a role, not in a decision to choose between optimizing paths to some preferred outcome.

Much of the scholarly literature on socialization is also implicitly about the normative content of identities. What is at stake in socialization is ultimately the internalization of constitutive norms – the process by which the collective expectations of the members of an identity group come to feel taken for granted by new members. Checkel's (2001) research on Europe's constitutive norms for citizenship policies falls into this category. Indeed, the European Union's own Copenhagen Criteria for determining the acceptability of potential members – primarily a market economy, a democratic polity, and respect for human rights – represent an explicit assessment of the constitutive norms that define European-ness for current and potential group members.

The process by which constitutive practices are internalized or habituated may be manifested in three ways. First, norms may bias choice, meaning that certain behaviors are consciously ruled out or discounted as inappropriate for one's identity. The commonly used phrase "logic of appropriateness" might

---

[2] On security communities, see Adler and Barnett 1998. On state identities and state practices in general, including national security policies, see Jepperson, Wendt, and Katzenstein 1996.

best describe this level of internalization (March and Olsen 1989). Second, norms may reduce the level of consciousness in choice. Semiconscious choice would mean options are barely considered, or only fleetingly considered, and are dismissed out of hand. "Commonsensible" choice might capture this form of internalization (Weldes et al. 1999). Third, norms may be so deeply internalized that they are acted upon completely unconsciously, out of habit. As Fierke (1996: 473) has written, drawing on Wittgenstein, "rules are lived rather than consciously applied." Hopf (2002) referred to this as the logic of habituation. Options are simply not considered. Practices are just followed.

Social Purposes

The content of a collective identity may be purposive, in the sense that the group attaches specific goals to its identity. This purposive content is analytically similar to the commonsense notion that what groups want depends on who they think they are. Thus, identities can lead actors to endow practices with group purposes and to interpret the world through lenses defined in part by those purposes.[3] Whereas the normative content of an identity refers to practices that lead to individual obligation and social recognition, the purposive content of an identity helps to define group interests, goals, or preferences. Both the normative and purposive content of an identity may impose obligations on members, but in distinctive ways: constitutive norms impose an obligation to engage in practices that reconstitute the group, whereas social purposes create obligations to engage in practices that make the group's achievement of a set of goals more likely.

The notion of the purposive content of identity is already implicit in the literature. The construction that pervades identity scholarship – who we are influences what we want – specifies a shared purpose (Gutmann 2003). Horowitz (1985) similarly has written of the "special missions" ascribed by some members to their groups. Rogers Smith's (2003) theorizing of economic, political, and ethically constitutive "stories of peoplehood" also can be understood in these terms, creating the basis for narratives of purpose. Kelman (1997, 1999) has produced important research on the connection between specific territorial claims and national identities. Yashar (1998) explored the purposive claims to a more equitable form of citizenship of indigenous movements in Latin America. Reus-Smit (1999) found moral purpose to be central to the history of modern statehood and concomitant claims to making citizens and creating justice. For Reus-Smit, societies of states, from ancient Greece to

---

[3] Analogously, see Judith Goldstein and Keohane 1993 on "principled beliefs."

Renaissance Italy, to absolutist Europe, and finally to our modern international system, have been based on fundamental moral purposes that have varied a great deal. These examples cover a wide variety of empirical questions but have in common an emphasis on the purposive meaning derived from an identity.

The scholarly literature on nationalist movements and national identities has identified a variety of purposive claims ranging from the cultivation of an identity as a purpose in itself (B. Anderson 1991) to the creation of a state that is coterminous with the boundaries of the nation and autonomous from a relationally defined other (Prizel 1998). The rise of nationalisms in the former Soviet Union provides a useful example of the purposive content of collective identities. Not all of the nationalist movements that emerged in Eurasia during the 1990s were the same; they proposed different goals for the nations they claimed to represent. Moreover, some post-Soviet societies embraced particular goals putatively connected to their national identities, whereas others rejected them. One of the purposes that was most often linked to the rise of nationalism was these societies' "return to Europe," understood as an escape from the Russian sphere of influence and reentry into the European political and social world from which Soviet authorities had torn them earlier in the century. In the three Baltic republics of Lithuania, Latvia, and Estonia – those that most forcefully asserted their autonomy from post-Soviet Russia – this sense of purpose influenced every aspect of their political-economic transformations. The overriding importance of their return to Europe defined the legitimate ends of policy and also structured the debate about their national interests and identity (Abdelal 2001).

Relational Comparisons

The content of a collective identity is also relational to the extent that it is composed of comparisons and references to other collective identities from which it is distinguished. An identity may be defined by what it is not – that is, by some *other* identities. The relational content of collective identities can be thought of as the discursive formulations of the relations between groups of people that compose social reality. Michael Barnett (1999: 9) provides an excellent relational definition of identity in his work on the Middle East peace process: identity represents "the understanding of oneself in relationship to others. Identities, in short, are not personal or psychological, they are fundamentally social and relational, defined by the actor's interaction with and relationship to others; therefore, identities may be contingent, dependent on the actor's interaction with others and place within an institutional context."

Scholars have already identified a number of relational characteristics of collective identities, including, among others, the extent to which one social identity excludes the holding of another (exclusivity); the relative status of an identity compared to others; and the existence or level of hostility presented by other identities. Examples of the implicit relational theorizing that forms the basis for much identity research are rife in all areas of the social sciences. Klandermans (1997) explored the foundational distinction between a social movement and the "authorities." Neumann (1999) described the importance of a constituting "other" for the creation of European identity. For Bartelson (1998), the relational content of an identity is, following Derrida, more revealing than other putatively self-referential narratives. Bell (2001) described the process of constructing French nationalism with England's barbarianism as a focal point against which to define France. Robert Bailey (1999) examined four cities including San Francisco and Birmingham, Alabama, in order to explore relational aspects of gay identity. Thomas Risse-Kappen (1996) undertook case studies of the 1956 Suez Crisis and the 1962 Cuban Missile Crisis in examining the NATO alliance in his work on shared liberal values and democratic norms as the basis of collective democratic state identities. Our analytic framework makes more explicit the relational component already implicit throughout the literature and seeks to standardize it as one of the four types of identity.

Relational content is also crucial for social identity theory (SIT), which hypothesizes that the creation of in-group identity will tend to produce competitive behavior with out-groups, because the process of in-group identity creation by necessity requires, or leads to, the devaluation of out-groups (Tajfel 1970, 1981a; J. Turner 1985; J. Turner et al. 1987). In social identity theory, the central causal process in behavior derives from in-group and out-group differentiation, not the roles or identity traits per se that are attributed to in-groups and out-groups. In this case, action is in some sense a reaction to, and conditioned by the existence of, those who are different. Some relationships (those with groups socially recognized as similar) will be more cooperative than others (those with groups recognized as different) even if the same issue is at stake (such as territory, power, or status). Under certain scope conditions, SIT-based arguments predict conflict with out-groups regardless of the content of the identity – that is, we are peace-loving, but you are not, and because of this difference you threaten our peace-lovingness; therefore, anything goes in dealing with your disposition to threaten us.

Cognitive Models

There are many ways to think about the cognitive content of social identities, as we find throughout the literature. In the broadest sense, a cognitive model may be thought of as a *worldview*, or a framework that allows members of a group to make sense of social, political, and economic conditions.[4] The cognitive content of a collective identity describes how group membership is associated with explanations of how the world works as well as descriptions of the social reality of the group – a group's ontology and epistemology. Being French, for example, may entail a particular way of interpreting the world (Bell 2001). For some scholars, the "cognitive turn" in the study of identities is critically important. According to Brubaker, Loveman, and Stamatov (2004: 47),

what cognitive perspectives suggest, in short, is that race, ethnicity, and nation are not things in the world but ways of seeing the world. They are ways of understanding and identifying oneself, making sense of one's problems and predicaments, identifying one's interests, and orienting one's action. They are ways of recognizing, identifying, and classifying other people, of construing sameness and difference, and of "coding" and making sense of their actions.

Similarly, a cognitive model may consist of "ways of reasoning" that are specific to particular identity groups. This was Peng and Nisbett's (1999) finding in a survey of Chinese and Americans. This result sparked further debate over the ways in which Eastern versus Western identity affects ways of thinking (Ho 2000; Y. Lee 2000; Peng and Nisbett 2000; Chan 2000). In addition, Gurung (2003) argued that different cultures (Chinese and Western) have different understandings of what constitutes "knowledge" (Li 2003). In an analysis of the 1893 celebration of the Silver Jubilee of Shanghai's Municipal Council of the International Settlement, B. Goodman (2000: 921) argued that different communities taking part in the jubilee (English and Chinese) had different readings of the festivities and indeed "different mental universes."

Identities can strongly affect interpretation and understanding not just of the present but of the past as well. Anthony Smith (1992: 58) argued that "subjective perception and understanding of the communal past by each generation … is a defining element in the concept of cultural identity." More particularly, Azzam (1991) found that Muslim identity may shape memories of shared colonial experience. Identities may also shape conceptions of the future; psychologists have found that cultural differences are associated with different views on what constitutes "the good life" or "well-being" (Ahuvia 2001; Diener, Oishi, and Lucas 2003).

Cognitive models affect not only broad worldviews and temporalities but also understandings of self, group, and other. One of the primary ways that this

---

[4] Some use other terms besides "worldviews." Denzau and North (1994), for example, use "shared mental models."

happens is through language. Mar-Molinero (2000: 8) has argued that "language is a means by which human beings grow to understand themselves and then to understand and share with those who speak the same language." Causal attribution is another cognitive activity affected by identity. Klandermans (1997: 18) has argued that identity "not only emphasizes the commonality of grievances, it also establishes the group's opposition to the actor held responsible.... thus causal attributions are an important element in the identity component.... this element is related to the construction of a cognitive schema which comprises causes and solutions for the adverse situation."[5]

The literature has also produced many cases demonstrating how identities can affect understandings of political and economic interests. In the realm of politics, identities can affect conceptions of legitimacy, shared interests, and policy choices, as well as preferences for political leaders and parties. Kelman (1969) has argued that national identity allows members of a group to see their state as legitimate; Feng (1999) demonstrated that Hainanese groups have different perceptions of political and economic conditions on Hainan Island; Shabad and Slomczynski (1999) found that identity shaped "orientation" toward transition issues in Poland; Adler (1992) explored how being part of a transnational identity group (international arms control specialists) shaped understandings of security concerns; and Valenzuela and Scully (1997) showed that voters from different classes had different values and therefore assessed political leaders and parties differently. Connecting class and gender in the workplace, Canning (1996) argued that identity discourses shape the understanding and meaning of work, which differ by gender.

Identities such as ethnicity and region can also shape interpretations of material conditions and economic interests. Risse et al. (1999: 157) have argued that "collective identities define and shape how actors view their perceived instrumental and material interests and which preferences are regarded as legitimate and appropriate for enacting given identities." Herrera (2005) has explored how regional identities within Russia have led to different views of regional economic conditions. There is also evidence that identities affect understandings of land itself, including understandings of access and rights – see, for example, Tronvoll (1998) and Kelman (2001). Identity may indeed shape perceptions of territory, which also shape perceptions of culture. David Goodman (2002: 849–850) has argued that provincial identity in Shanxi, China, was shaped in concert with a specific "interpretation of the area's centrality to the development of Chinese culture."

---

[5] On worldviews and causal beliefs, see Judith Goldstein and Keohane 1993.

Cognitive content, rather than implying an alternative theory of action, implies a theory of interpretation. The attention to the cognitive shows us both how identity affects how actors understand the world and, consequently, how their material or social incentives for particular actions will be influenced by their identities.

We believe that our analytic framework's four nonexclusive content types, plus the element of contestation discussed in the next section, preserve the restless dynamism that characterizes current identity work. At the same time, by providing more analytical coherence, we hope to move beyond the current crisis of definitional anarchy and toward collaboration and integration of identity scholarship across the social sciences.

Contestation

The content – the collective meaning – of identities is neither fixed nor predetermined. Rather, content is the outcome of a process of social contestation within the group. Indeed, much of identity discourse is the working out of the meaning of a particular collective identity through the contestation of its members. Individuals are continuously proposing and shaping the meanings of the groups to which they belong.

Specific interpretations of the meaning of an identity are sometimes widely shared among members of a group and sometimes less widely shared. At a minimum, then, contestation can be thought of as a matter of degree – the content of collective identities can be more or less contested. Indeed, the further apart the contending interpretations of a collective identity prove to be, the more that identity will be fragmented into conflicting and potentially inconsistent understandings of what the group's purposes or relations should be. Such disputes, occurring within one or more of the four types of content, might be prompted by differences over how exclusive the membership of the group should be, how primordial its traits are considered, or how much status or legitimacy the identity is believed to have in the eyes of out-groups.

We are fully aware of the debates between more "positivist" and more "interpretivist" approaches to the question of the relative stability or constant flux of identity. Although these debates are often cast in terms of fundamental differences in ontology and epistemology, we prefer to take an empirical approach (which we acknowledge is theory-laden as well) – namely, that the degree of stability or flux in identities is an empirical question or, more precisely, that the scope conditions for stability and flux require empirical testing. Describing the level and character of the contestation of a collective identity's meaning at any given moment is difficult particularly because it requires the depiction of a process instead of an outcome. We accept Robert Cox's (1986) implication that even if one assumes the social world is a constructed one, there may be periods and places where intersubjective understandings of these social facts are stable enough that they can be treated as if fixed and can be analyzed with social scientific methods.

Some might argue that this attention to measurement lies in tension with the fluidity of social identities. We would respond by underscoring that we do not assume that identities are fixed, or stable, or uncontested. Precisely because we believe that contestation over content is crucial to the development of the meaning of social groups, we believe it is important to be able to have techniques that can take relatively rapid and easily developed snapshots of identities as they evolve, as they are challenged, and as they are constructed and reconstructed.

In addition, because identities are contested, we are well aware that identity language can be used strategically. However, if language is used strategically, it will be effective only if at least some important portion of the population has internalized the identity cues and responds to their use. That is, the instrumentality and authenticity of identity are two sides of the same coin. This is why, contemporary debates notwithstanding, the need endures for techniques to determine how authentic, or how internalized, these cues need to be in order to achieve their mobilizing effects.

We thus propose to study contestation as a process that occurs *within* groups, because it is the meanings that groups ultimately define for themselves that make up the content of a collective identity (Katzenstein 1996; Kier 1997; Abdelal 2001). We do not mean to imply, however, that these processes of social contestation occur in a vacuum, or that other actors cannot influence their direction or even their outcomes. Indeed, in world politics, for example, the identities of nations and states are formed in constant interaction with other nations and states. Within countries, too, political authorities acting on behalf of the state often attempt to influence the meaning of the range of collective identities within society. The individuals who compose a group often seek the recognition of their identity by others, and that recognition – both formal and informal – clearly influences the particular goals associated with an identity.

The range of behaviors and practices that compose the process of contestation is broad, and, as with other aspects of identity formation and reformation, the study of contestation is most usefully understood as an empirical matter. The potential texts to which scholars have access in measuring and evaluating the process of contestation are many. More important, the process of contestation can be either explicit (and therefore intentional) or implicit (and therefore unplanned).

Explicit debates about the meaning of an identity tend to be self-referential. The controversy that followed the publication of Samuel Huntington's (2004) book *Who Are We? The Challenges to America's National Identity* is rather straightforward: in his book Huntington literally seeks to define, historically, the content of American national identity, and his critics responded with alternate histories and alternate contents. The essence of the debate is clear, however – American intellectuals were contesting the meaning of their national identity in books; in book reviews from the pages of *Foreign Affairs*, *Foreign Policy*, and the *New York Times*; and in articles written for other intellectuals, policy makers, and the educated lay reader. The experience is not unusual in comparative context, as similar explicit debates have emerged in every country.

Even more common is the everyday, implicit contestation of identity, which takes place among members of a group without their consciously seeking to revise or remake the meaning of their identity. If it is a small enough group, this process may take place in conversation or bilateral written communication. In modern societies, journalists and the media play an important role in constructing meanings. Then there are the ongoing claims and counterclaims offered by those who aspire to lead a group, regardless of its size. Thus, political debates, party platforms, and speeches are designed to evoke a sense of collective self and are examples of the process of contestation.

Because the content of an identity is the product of contestation, the very data that a scholar extracts from a group elucidate, in manner and degree, the members' consensus and disagreement about the constitutive norms, social purposes, relational comparisons, and cognitive models of their collective identity. Contestation therefore includes the degree of the within-group's agreement about the constitutive norms of an identity, consensus and congruence of the social purposes ascribed to an identity, agreement about meanings attached to out-groups, and coherence of shared cognitive models.

By considering the level of contestation regarding each type of content within identities, one arrives at a necessarily constructivist approach to identity without having to assume that actors on the ground view their identities as constructed. Where there is little contestation, one might conclude that that part of identity content is taken for granted or considered "natural." Thus, one can appreciate some apparently "primordial" aspects of identity without taking a primordialist theoretical stance that denies the possibility for contextual contestation, that is, contestation at different times and places.

The Question of Salience and Intensity

Finally, let us consider what our framework does not do. We are *not* attempting to account for personal identities or identities of individual persons. Individuals and groups remain analytically distinct objects, each requiring its own concep-tualization.[6] The essential difference lies in the *collective* meaning inherent in social identities. Whereas individual identities are subjective, collective identi-ties are "intersubjective" – comprising shared interpretations of group traits or attributes. Individuals may, and almost always do, ascribe different meanings and purposes to the same collective identity; that is, the meaning of a particular collective identity is defined through a process of contestation among individ-uals who essentially propose alternate collective meanings. In that sense, under-standing the interaction among constituent individuals and their groups – or agents and identity structures – is a crucial part of the analysis of social iden-tities. But it is as members of a group that the practices of individuals are most easily analyzed with social scientific methods. Attempting to impute the iden-tity of the individual *qua* individual is, in other words, a matter more for psychology, whereas social psychology attempts to describe the connections among individual and collective identities (Fiske and Taylor 1991; S. Taylor, Peplau, and Sears 1997).

For this reason, "salience" and "intensity," two terms common in the iden-tity literature, are recast more precisely within our framework for social identities using the concepts of content and contestation. Salience is a critical variable used by psychologists to study the multiple and overlapping identities of individuals as individuals; specific contexts are said to increase the salience of one identity over another. Our framework focuses on the *meaning* of collective identities, a property that salience cannot address. We would further suggest that the sort of variation described by salience is less common than variation in meaning (types of content) and its contestation.

The issue of salience is also related to "groupness," along the lines proposed by Brubaker and Cooper (2000). Groupness describes the degree to which individuals identify with a group (or, in other words, how salient that partic-ular collective identity is to its constituent individuals). Here, again, we find that focusing on the level of attachment to a group bypasses the *meaning* of the group to its members. Identities cannot exist without meanings ascribed to

---

[6] Brubaker and Cooper (2000) move back and forth between personal and social identities in their discussion of alternatives to identity. However, it seems that they are dissatisfied primarily with the use of individuals' identities to explain individuals' behaviors and practices. Had they sep-arated their analysis between individual and social identities, they might not have been as pessimistic regarding prospects for further research on social identities.

them by their members, and we argue that the degree to which members of a group share those meanings is a variable captured by the concept of contestation.

Intensity, like salience, often appears in the literature with regard to individuals, in this case with the idea that some constituent members of groups attach greater importance to a specific collective identity than do others. We argue that, like salience, intensity cannot comprehend the degree to which group understandings are shared. Additionally, the notion of intensity often conflates two analytically distinct variations in identity. The international relations literature on nationalism, for example, regularly includes references to "hyper-nationalism" (Mearsheimer 1990). Scholars generally use this term to describe, without analytical distinction between the two, both the extremeness of the views of a nationalist society and the level of agreement among members of that society about such extreme views. Our analytic framework enables more precise distinctions. In our terms, the first idea concerns the content of an identity, whereas the second is a question of its contestation. Thus, we argue that content and contestation are better ways of getting at the multiple concepts covered by the term intensity.

CONCLUSIONS

Despite the proliferation of identity research in recent years, the social science community has yet to agree on a standardized definition for the concept of identity that has proved widely amenable for measurement across the disciplines and subfields. We have offered in this chapter a new analytic framework that we hope can begin to help move identity research beyond its current impasse, while preserving the dynamism that has characterized the research so far.

We defined collective identity as a social category that varies along two dimensions – content and contestation. We delineated identity content into four, nonmutually exclusive types: constitutive norms, social purposes, relational comparisons with other social categories, and cognitive models. And we argued that there is always some level of in-group contestation over this content, implying that social identities vary in agreement and disagreement about their norms, boundaries, worldviews, analytics, and meanings.

We believe that this framework can help account for the variation in identities that scholars have already been implicitly and explicitly measuring. We hope that our framework provides greater theoretical commensurability among conceptions of identity in political science and the other social sciences, while still recognizing and valorizing a diversity of approaches. Our goal is not to "discipline" identity, or to impose a new, narrow semantic straitjacket on scholars who seek to treat identity as a variable. Rather, by categorizing identity scholarship in a synthetic framework and highlighting complementarities among conceptualizations, we aim to encourage more coordination and explicit comparison among scholars working on identity. In outlining a definition of identity, we also aim to encourage creativity in thinking about identity. We believe any definition of identity must address the issues of content and contestation.

Our framework also helps to clarify differences among types and casual consequences of identities. We also hope that our conceptualization has made a useful contribution to understanding how identities affect the behavior of actors – in other words, the relationship between identity and action. We argue that the definition of identity, that is, content and contestation, can affect predictions about action. Our definition, and in particular the four types of content that we have outlined, specifically addresses theories of action, such as SIT or role theory, as well as models of cognition and the purposive goals of a social group. Our goal in creating this conceptualization has been to encourage more rigorous and replicable studies of identity and overcome some of the reluctance of mainstream political science to incorporate identity variables into explanatory models.

2

Conceptualizing and Measuring Ethnic Identity

Henry E. Brady and Cynthia S. Kaplan

INTRODUCTION

This chapter considers the conceptualization and measurement of politically relevant group-based social identities such as ethnic identity that have figured prominently in motivating and shaping political action. Although we mention some of the substantive findings that can be established using these measures, our primary concern is with different ways to measure and understand ethnic identity – the use of history, demography, surveys, primary source materials, content analysis, and discourse analysis. We argue that a combination of these methods must be used to fully comprehend the political role of ethnicity at the mass public or elite level.

Ethnicity is an intersubjectively agreed-upon categorization of individuals that is widely and publicly understood to have meaning within a society. Consequently, social scientists often use ethnic categories to interpret and explain facts and events. For example, historians and demographers construct narratives or present data using ethnic categories, and survey researchers ask people about their ethnic identity (e.g., African American, Estonian, Tatar) to determine its prevalence and correlates in a society. Because ethnic identity also motivates human activity and matters for people's lives – especially their political activity – even more can be learned by asking people about these activities (or by observing them directly) as well as by asking them about their identity directly. Moreover, because ethnic identity is constructed through social and psychological processes of categorization (there is no primordial periodic table of social identities), much can be learned about it by studying cultural and

This chapter utilizes some material previously published in two articles (Brady and Kaplan 2000; Kaplan 2006), but the focus on definition and measurement of identity is new.

33

social processes, such as the course of political arguments, debates in cultural journals, discussions in the mass media, and social movements that frame, evoke, and memorialize ethnic identities. This chapter considers all these ways of learning about ethnic identity: demography, history, surveys, primary source materials, content analysis of newspapers, and newspaper records of events.

The Seven Features of Group-Based Social Identity

Ethnicity is a type of group-based social identity (Brewer 2001b) that exhibits particular formal properties. The basic cognitive processes of self-categorization and self-schematization (J. Turner 1985; Markus 1977) combine with social interaction (Tajfel 1978; Burke and Reitzes 1981) to produce intersubjective agreement that (almost) every person can be placed into one of the *categories* (A, B, . . ., Z). These categories are described in terms of some easily perceived *attributes* X (e.g., language, race, or religion) such that the attributes can be used for classification (Laitin and Chandra 2002). Moreover, people *attach* themselves to these groups (Brewer 2001b: 118) when asked questions about how they think about themselves, and the strength of these attachments or commitments (Burke and Reitzes 1981) – that is, the salience of the identity (Callero 1985; Stryker and Serpe 1994) – affects people's activities. If a person belongs to a group G, then the person typically *interacts* more with members of G than with members of all other groups (A, B, . . ., F, H, . . . Z), and through the process of self-enhancement or self-verification the person typically *evaluates* members of group G more positively than those of other groups. These five characteristics (categories, attributes, attachments, interactions, and evaluations) are the *relational properties and constitutive norms* of social identity discussed by Abdelal et al. (2006: 697, 698), which they describe as the "rules that determine group membership and putative attributes of the group" and "the comparisons and references to other collective identities from which it is distinguished."

Every group also tells narratives about what it means to be a member and what the group's goals are. This story is typically much more favorable to the in-group than to out-groups. Abdelal et al. (2006) describe these as the *cognitive models and social purposes* of social identities. These cognitive models of ethnicity – how members of ethnic groups perceive, remember, and understand their world – may be developed through processes of social cognition (as in social identity theory; see Hogg and Abrams 1986; Hogg, Terry, and White 1995) or acquired and validated through social interactions (as in identity and role theory; see Burke and Reitzes 1981; Stets and Burke 2000). In either case, they supply a group with *meanings* that are its "ontology and epistemology" (Abdelal et al. 2006: 699) for understanding its place in the world. A teleology for the group is provided by statements of *social purposes* through which "the group attaches specific meanings and goals to its identity" (Abdelal et al. 2006: 698). These social purposes provide motivations for allocations of power, status, and resources that typically favor the in-group against other groups. But the degree to which these social purposes actually lead to activities that press for the group's interests and create what Brewer (2001b: 119) calls collective identities depends upon the salience of group identity and contextual factors that may encourage or inhibit such actions (Burke 1997; Stryker, Owens, and White 2000).[1]

Developers of measures of social identity should consider the following features, which can be grouped into two broad categories. First, there are relational properties and constitutive norms:

- *Categories:* Intersubjectively agreed-upon categories for social identity
- *Attributes:* Attributes that are relatively easy to perceive, such as differences in skin color, ethnicity, language, religion, or income
- *Attachment to categories:* Attachments to these categories by people saying that they are members of some but not others and by people indicating that they are committed to the group
- *Interaction with members of the group:* Typically more interaction with members of the group than with other groups
- *Positive evaluation of the in-group, negative evaluation of the out-group:* In-group members who typically like their in-group and dislike the out-groups

Second, there are aspects of social identity that are cognitive models and social purpose properties:

- *Meanings for each group's social identity:* Each group, especially its elites, constructs meanings about the group's status and relationship to other groups so that belonging to the category says something about how people understand their everyday lives.
- *Social purposes for the group:* Social purposes justify and motivate allocations of power, status, and resources to the in-group so that group members will be willing to discriminate in favor of their own group and against out-groups even if it is costly to them.

---

[1] Horowitz (1985) distinguishes between ranked and unranked social structures that affect the likelihood and nature of physical contact between groups (and hence measurement strategies). Ranked structures involve domination of one group over another (e.g., American South during slavery). Our examples are essentially unranked, and we consider measurement strategies for such situations.

These features should be measured for both the *mass public* and the *elite* for two complementary reasons. First, the properties of ethnicity may be quite different at each level so that a complete picture requires measurement at both levels. Second, elites typically take the lead in constructing and elaborating ethnic identities, so that the dynamics of ethnicity involve an interplay between elites and mass publics that cannot be understood without separate measures at the two levels.

Measuring and Understanding Social Identity

In this chapter we illustrate group-based social identity measures by considering seven groups in four Soviet republics around 1990: Estonians and Russians in Estonia; Tatars and Russians in the Republic of Tatarstan; the Komi and Russians in the Komi Republic; and, to some extent, Russians in Russia. We begin by showing how basic demographic and historical facts about these republics and nationality groups can be used to determine basic features of social identity. Then we turn to methods for understanding how meanings are attached to social identities. These methods include the analysis of articles in cultural journals in Estonia in the mid-1980s, the content analysis of Russian- and Estonian-language newspaper coverage of social movements in Estonia, and the analysis of the nature of political events in Estonia from 1987 to 1993. Then we turn to survey-based methods for measuring social identity, such as self-identification, social distance measures, and a graded ethnicity measure based upon social distance, media use, and the evaluation of groups. We discuss several checks on the graded ethnic identity measure, which show that it appears to capture what we mean by ethnic identity. Table 2.1, discussed in detail at the end of the chapter, summarizes the methods we mention. The table describes each method, shows how each is related to the seven features of group-based social identity, indicates whether the method focuses on elites or the mass public or both, and provides substantiation for the argument that the methods are complementary to one another.

FOUR REPUBLICS AND SEVEN NATIONALITIES: DEMOGRAPHY AND HISTORY

Russia and Estonia were two of the fifteen union republics in the Soviet Union, and each is now a separate country after the breakup of the Soviet Union in 1991. Tatarstan and the Komi Republic were autonomous republics (one level down from union republics) in the Russian Federation in the Soviet Union and are now republics in the Russian Federation. Demographic statistics and

TABLE 2.1. *Measurement Methods for Ethnicity: Major Feature of Ethnicity Measured, Level Measured, and Usefulness for Research*

Type of Measure	Method of Measurement	Major Feature of Ethnicity Measured	Level: Mostly Mass or Elite?	Usefulness for Research
Historical inquiry	Reviewing histories of the area that describe ethnic categories and ethnic group ideas	Categories, attributes, and meanings	Elite and mass	Prima facie case that ethnicity is important; identification of important attributes and meanings in the society over time
Demographic data	Analyzing censuses based upon surveys and administrative records that enumerate membership in categories and relationships between categories and attributes	Categories and attributes	Mass	Description of prevalence of ethnic identity and its association with various attributes; identification of forces that might arouse ethnic concerns (e.g., reduction in fertility rate or in native-language speakers)
Frames	Using discourse analysis to review and analyze political debates, memoirs of leaders, and newspaper articles that describe the ideas and goals of ethnic groups	Evaluations, meanings, and social purposes	Elite	Showing that ethnic appeals are used to give evaluative impact and meaning to political discourse; finding out how they are used to appeal to and mobilize the population

(continued)

TABLE 2.1 *(continued)*

Type of Measure	Method of Measurement	Major Feature of Ethnicity Measured	Level: Mostly Mass or Elite?	Usefulness for Research
Cultural journals	Content analysis of articles in cultural journals that debate the ideas and goals of ethnic groups	Meanings and social purposes	Elite	Showing that elites debate various meanings and social purposes for ethnic identity, especially over time
Mass-media stories	Content analysis of stories to determine the ideas and goals of ethnic groups	Meanings	Mass	Showing that the mass public is exposed to ethnic ideas, especially over time
Events data	Coding of events sponsored by different ethnic groups to see if there is political participation by different ethnic groups demonstrating attachment, interaction, and social purposes for allocation of resources, status, and power	Attachment, interaction, and social purposes	Elite and mass	Showing that elites are able to get the mass public to demonstrate their ethnic attachment to achieve social purposes, especially over time
Passport nationality	Analysis to see if passports describe nationality	Categories	Mass	Description of governmental use of ethnic categories

(continued)

Social distance	Surveying people to see how much they interact with their own versus other ethnic groups	Attachment and interaction	Mass	Measuring strength of attachment through behavioral attachments to family, friends, neighbors, and co-workers
Media usage	Surveying people to see if different ethnic groups use different media	Attachment and interaction	Mass	Measuring strength of attachment through use of ethnically distinct media sources
Evaluation of groups	Surveying people to see if they evaluate their own ethnic group and other groups differently	Evaluations	Mass	Measuring evaluation of ethnic groups in terms of liking or disliking and approving or disapproving
Association with another group	Surveying people to see if they associate with another group	Attachment	Mass	Providing a (weak) measure of salience to see how important ethnic identity is to the person
Parental ethnicity	Using demographic or survey data to see if ethnicity is handed down from generation to generation	Attributes and categories	Mass	Showing that ethnic identity persists over time through socialization
Language usage and knowledge	Using demographic or survey data to see what languages are known and which are spoken at home	Attributes	Mass	Showing how ethnic identity is linked to language knowledge and usage at home

political history tell us a lot about the availability of these groups for ethnically based social identities and for social movements.

In all four areas (as shown in the last row of Table 2.2), the percentage of Slavs plus the Titular nationality is at least 86 percent so that the major ethnic division is between Slavs (mostly Russians) and the titular nationality. The bipolar nature of ethnic relations in these three areas makes them relatively simple cases for comparing measures of social identity and for studying the impact of a Soviet nationalities policy that pursued two contradictory approaches. Through the creation of administrative boundaries encompassing and named for titular nationalities and the promotion of titular cultures, this

TABLE 2.2. *Demographic Characteristics for Four Regions*

	Russian Republic	Estonian Republic	Tatar Republic	Komi Republic
No. of people, 1989	147,021,869	1,565,662	3,641,742	1,250,847
Status in USSR	Union republic	Union republic	Autonomous republic	Autonomous republic
Current status	Independent	Independent	Russian Federation	Russian Federation
Slavs				
Russian in 1989	82%	30%	43%	58%
Slav in 1989	86%	35%	44%	68%
Predominant religion	Orthodox Christian	Orthodox Christian	Orthodox Christian	Orthodox Christian
Titular nationality				
Name of nationality	–	Estonians	Tatars	Komi
Titular nationality	–	62%	48%	23%
Predominant religion	–	Lutheran	Muslim	Orthodox Christian
Population change of group, 1959–1989[a]	–	3.8%	31.2%	19.2%
Type of language	–	Finno-Ugric	Turkic	Finno-Ugric
Rates of ethnic reidentification of group per 1,000[b]	–	2.2	1.9	8.0
TOTALS: Slav + Titular	86%	97%	92%	91%

[a] The figures for Estonia come from Wixman 1993, table 18.2, and they refer to all Estonians in the Soviet Union (almost all of whom lived in Estonia). The remaining figures are calculated from Wixman 1993, table 18.3, and they refer to the titular nationalities in the autonomous republics.
[b] These figures refer to all members of the nationality within the Soviet Union. Most Estonians and Komi in the Soviet Union lived within their respective republics. Only about a quarter of all Tatars live in Tatarstan.
Sources: 1989 Soviet Census; B. A. Anderson and Silver 1990; Wixman 1993.

policy maintained and developed traditional ethnic identification, whereas through the forces of development, including the migration of Slavs into non-Slavic areas and the promotion of Russian-language learning (and the deprecation of the titular language), it promoted Russification. Consequently, the members of titular nationalities in these areas were concerned about "Russification," and Slavs were concerned with policy challenges by the titular nationality. The anxiety about Russification among the titular nationalities was based on real demographic trends. Among Komis, in-migration of outsiders as a result of industrial development and penal colonies located in the region meant that, whereas the Komi constituted 92.2 percent of the population in 1926, by 1989 they represented only 23.3 percent (Lallukka 1990: 127–128; Wixman 1993: 436). Moreover, the Orthodox Christianity of the Komi, their small percentage (23 percent) of the total population, their small absolute number (about 292,000), and Soviet policies of limiting the availability of education in the Komi language made them especially susceptible to assimilation. In our 1993 survey in the Komi Republic (described in Appendix 3), while 53 percent of our ethnically Komi respondents claimed to be fluent in Komi (and another 41 percent claimed to be "good" at speaking it), only about 22 percent of the Komi said they spoke it at home. Barbara Anderson and Brian Silver (1983, 1990) estimated that out of a thousand Komi eight changed their ethnic identification each year from Komi to (probably) Russian between 1959 and 1970 (also see Lallukka 1990). Nevertheless, the Komi did increase, as shown on Table 2.2, by 19.2 percent in the thirty years between 1959 and 1989.

The Tatars and Estonians also faced assimilation but at a much slower rate. Anderson and Silver (1990, 117) describe them as "groups with little net change in ethnic self-identification between 1959 and 1970" and report their halving time as 320 years for Estonians and 370 years for Tatars. Tatars could look back to a long history in which they could lay claim to a larger state encompassing the Middle Volga region, Idel Ural (Iskhaki 1991). Educated Tatars were acculturated to the broader Russian-Soviet culture, but village life continued the traditions of the Tatar people. Islam, for most Tatars, had become a way of life, rather than a religion strictly observed. Yet, as a Muslim people, Tatars had not assimilated, or reidentified as Russians. Moreover, the Tatars enjoyed a plurality in Tatarstan (48 percent) where they numbered almost two million (about seven times the size of the Komi population in the Komi Republic). In our 1993 survey data, 63 percent claimed to speak Tatar fluently and another 27 percent said they are good at speaking it. About 45 percent spoke the Tatar language at home, and 54 percent spoke Russian at home. The Tatars' Muslim religious and cultural heritage provided them (and still provides them within Russia) with a bulwark against Russification, and mostly because of their high birthrates they increased more than 30 percent in Tatarstan between 1959 and 1989.

Estonians were a majority in their republic (62 percent), and they numbered about one million. Estonians enjoyed a national awakening at the end of the nineteenth century, reinforced by independent statehood between the First and Second World Wars. Historical memories were strong and cultural practices were maintained through nonpolitical means, ranging from song festivals to gardening clubs (Aarelaid-Tart 1996). Almost all Estonians spoke their own language (97 percent in our 1991 data), partly because of a Soviet nationalities policy that allowed education in the language of the titular nationality in the Union Republics (B. A. Anderson and Silver 1984). The Estonians' history of national awakening in the nineteenth century, their independence in the interwar period, and their ties with an international diaspora of Estonians provided them with a strong defense against Russification. Nevertheless, because of low fertility rates, the Estonians increased by only 3.8 percent between 1959 and 1989 and less than 1 percent between 1979 and 1989.

Many Slavs in these regions realized for the first time during the 1991 transition that they might be expected to learn the titular language, especially in areas where they lived close to members of the titular nationality. Slavs faced relatively little threat in the Komi Republic where they are the majority and most Komi speak Russian (90 percent in our data). They faced a greater threat in Tatarstan even though 79 percent of the Tatars spoke Russian because Russians are only 43 percent of the population. In Estonia, Slavs faced the most parlous situation because they constituted only 35 percent of the population, few of them knew Estonian, and, although 86 percent of Estonians spoke Russian, they increasingly chose not to do so.

In each instance, both the titular nationality and the Slavs had reasons to be concerned about their position. The Komi were and are most at risk for Russification. The Estonians were being assimilated at a relatively low rate, but their small population size and low birthrates were causes for concern. Finally, although the Tatars were being assimilated at about the same rate as the Estonians, they had both some advantages and disadvantages. Their population was larger, and they had a higher birthrate, but their position as an autonomous republic instead of a union republic disadvantaged them in other ways, including the availability of education in the Tatar language. These demographic and historical facts structured the situations in these three places, and they affected the possibilities for the growth and politicization of social identity. When political opportunities for national expression increased dramatically under Gorbachev's policy of *glasnost*, they led to the efflorescence of ethnic movements that worked to construct meanings for the social identities that they championed.

CONSTRUCTING MEANINGS FOR SOCIAL IDENTITY IN ESTONIA

Cognitive models and social purposes are two of the seven features of social identity mentioned earlier. Our research, in addition to employing survey measures described later, explores how these models and purposes provide meanings by which a social identity can mobilize people to political action. The cognitive content provides group members with "explanations of how the world works" and "descriptions of the social reality of the group" (Abdelal et al. 2006: 699). The social purposes obligate group members "to engage in practices that make the group's achievement of a set of goals more likely" (Abdelal et al. 2006: 698). Elites appealing to ethnic identity to mobilize the public weave these cognitive schemas and social purposes into coherent collective identity frames to activate the mass public.

In general, cultural frames utilize rhetorical devices such as "(1) metaphors, (2) exemplars (i.e., historical examples from which lessons are drawn), (3) catchphrases, (4) depictions, and (5) visual images (e.g., icons)." Frames also use reasoning devices such as appealing to "(1) roots (i.e., a causal analysis), (2) consequences (i.e., a particular type of effect), and (3) . . . principle (i.e., a set of moral claims)" (Gamson and Modigliani 1989: 3–4). In our work on Estonia, we used memoirs, documents, histories, museums, newspaper articles, and interviews to identify competing frames for these social movements. Sometimes these frames link group-based social identities to politicized collective identities to form collective identity frames, and sometimes they downplay social identities to construct other types of frames.

Restorationists. The Restorationist injustice frame argued that the independent Estonian Republic of the interwar years was illegally occupied by the Soviet Union in 1940 and that the republic still had a de jure existence. The era of the first republic (starting in 1918) was viewed as a natural period of independence following the national awakening of the nineteenth century interrupted by the Soviet occupation. The Soviet era was viewed as totally illegitimate without any redeeming qualities. The consequences of Soviet rule, according to the Restorationists, threatened the extinction of the Estonians as a people, making independence essential to their survival. This frame successfully used collective ethnic identity as its primary appeal.

Reformers. While criticizing the Soviet system for the faults of Stalinism, the Popular Front of Estonia did not reject the achievements of the Soviet era. The Reform frame neither concentrated on collective identity nor restricted itself to issues aimed at ethnic mobilization, but rather sought change within the confines of *perestroika*. Edgar Savisaar, the leader of the Popular Front, argued that Estonia had been "annexed" by the Soviet Union rather than "occupied" as the Restorationists argued. He continued to prefer a strategy of "negotiating" with Russia to secure a new status for Estonia. Initially, he and his movement played down an Estonian ethnic identity, and they emphasized economic issues.

Counter-Movement. The Counter-Movement considered the period of the first independent Republic of Estonia (1920–1940) as unnatural. The frame adhered to the idea that the Soviet Union liberated Estonia after World War II and that class interests should dominate any ethnic differences. The frame espoused an orthodox view of the Soviet Union, the role of the Communist Party of the Soviet Union, and the centralized economic system. The aim of the frame was the maintenance of the Soviet Union, and it appealed to a collective Soviet identity meant to resonate with Russians and other Slavs in Estonia, although it was largely unsuccessful.

Describing frames thought to have different relationships to ethnic identity does not, of course, in itself resolve the issue of whether social identities actually exist and have the capacity to mobilize people. We must do more work to see if these frames actually have any widely shared meaning and power. After all, similar kinds of frames existed in Tatarstan and the Komi Republic, but they were not associated with a successful independence movement.

In our research on ethnic mobilization in Estonia during the Soviet transition (1988–1991), we set out three questions. First, did elites such as the Restorationists and the Counter-Movement construct cognitive worlds based upon ethnic identities that they used to justify policy goals such as independence or maintenance of the Soviet state? Second, how was the content of collective identity made available to the mass public? How were common modes of communication created? Third, did these distinct frames lead to ethnically motivated social movements? We address these issues through the analysis of discourse found in literary journals and newspapers, the content analysis of these sources, and the use of events and survey data.

THE INTRODUCTION OF ETHNIC ISSUES

In the USSR, literary journals enjoyed greater freedom of expression than other media sources and thereby were able to play a special role in establishing the new issue agenda. Beginning in 1985 before the emergence of open public discourse, articles in the major literary journals of Estonia reintroduced forbidden topics and began the process by which a mass social movement using a collective identity frame transformed Estonian public opinion to support independence, thereby linking Estonian ethnic identity with the demand for independence. As two leading media scholars, Peter Vihalemm and Marju Lauristin (1997: 106), observe, "More freedom of expression was allowed in the cultural press. . . . On the cultural pages journalists used complicated forms of indirect expression: metaphors, analogies, allusions, parodies. Readers learned to read between the lines, to catch hints and draw parallels."

We utilized literary journals in two ways to determine the nature of the cognitive content of Estonian and Slavic identity. First, we created a database coding all issues appearing in the four journals published during transition (see Appendix 1). This enabled us to confirm the nature of issues initially identified through interviews, memoirs, and documents and to establish a temporal trend. Second, we illustrated the meaning and tone of our findings through the presentation of discourse found in the journals.

Content Analysis of Literary Journals

Figure 2.1 shows how particular issues grew in importance during transition (1985–1991).[2] Discussions of history, culture and values, and independence grew in tandem throughout this period, but they peaked at different moments. Discussions of history that initially challenged what was permissible grew during 1985 through 1989, but they were typically very general. In 1989 the more dangerous discussions of culture and values (language, survival, or citizenship) attained their maximum, and finally in 1990 the most dangerous topic, independence, attained its maximum. By placing these issues at the forefront, literary journals shaped the meaning of collective memories and made them available for competing social movements to use symbolically. Such issues were rarely mentioned in the most widely read Estonian- and Russian-language newspapers during 1987 and began to appear only in the middle of 1988 and were commonplace by 1990.[3] At this point, the literary journals returned to their historic functions of publishing literature and literary criticism.

---

[2] This figure shows the total number of issue mentions, and the same article could have multiple mentions. Independence consists of mentions of such topics as independence, sovereignty, the Soviet occupation, the Molotov-Rippentrop Treaty, or self-determination and democratic values. Culture refers to Estonian culture, language, survival, citizenship, or meetings of the creative unions in April 1988 that dealt with these issues. History refers to any mention of historical events.

[3] *Rahva Hääl* and *Molodezh' Estonii* together during all of 1987 published only five articles on cultural events. During 1988 environmental reporting far surpassed dispatches on events connected with sovereignty and culture.

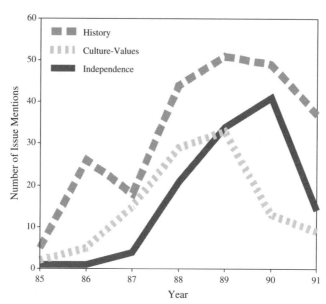

FIGURE 2.1. Absolute Number of Issue Mentions in Estonian Cultural Journals by Year

The four journals had distinctive outlooks and were associated with differ-ent social movements and cultural issues, which in turn were linked with history in different ways. The journals focusing on an ethnic Estonian audience and published in Estonian (*Looming* and *Vikerkaar*) talked a great deal about the National Awakening period (1850–1918) and the Estonian Republic (1918–1940), while *Tallinn* (published in Russian) in particular dealt with the years surrounding World War II. *Raduga* as a conduit for Estonian infor-mation to Russians published fewer articles on the nineteenth century and the Republic of Estonia than Estonian-language journals did, but nonetheless pre-sented substantial material on these issues. Articles about historical periods linked with Estonian ethnic identity and independence were distinct from those concentrating on the "wrongs" of the Stalin years and the incorporation of Estonia into the USSR. Critiques of the Stalinist aspects of the Soviet system typically argued that, once these perversions were removed, socialism could evolve into a new type of democracy. In summary, cultural and historical issues that are closely linked to the cultural frames mobilizing ethnic Estonians were most prominent in *Looming* but also appeared in *Vikerkaar* and even *Raduga*. The journal *Tallinn* looked at issues more clearly linked to *perestroika*, economic autonomy, and nonethnic issues, which also found substantial rep-resentation in *Vikerkaar* and *Raduga*.

Identity Discourse

The differences in discourse can be illustrated through examples drawn from the literary journals *Looming* (a virtual incubator of the Restorationist frame) and *Tallinn*, which sought to undermine Soviet images and stereotypes among non-Estonians. These early efforts at setting the agenda of engagement were critical in drawing activists to the Estonian movements and in providing the basis for appeals to the general public through the mass media.

Looming. Early issues of *Looming* (1985) concentrated on "moral issues" such as the nature of the social contract and freedom as a value. In 1986 a special issue was devoted entirely to a leader of the Estonian National Awakening of the nineteenth century. Additional articles focused on language issues and the philosophical meaning of democracy. In 1988 there was a virtual explosion of articles on history and the founders of the 1920 Republic of Estonia.

Justifications testifying to the value of Estonian culture were common in *Looming.* Rein Ruutsoo noted that as a small nation of just over one million, Estonia was frequently viewed by Russians as not large enough to be a viable nation, and the goal of both German and Russian cultures was assimilation (Ruutsoo 1988: 674–676), but Ruutsoo argued that, despite tsarist Russia's metropole status, Estonia had a more sophisticated professional culture than the Russians in the early twentieth century. Similarly, it was sometimes claimed that Estonia's language and culture could not be sustained, but Mati Hint (1988: 680, 682) argued that by 1914 the Estonian language had begun to develop into a "fully functional and universal cultural language" and that during the period of the Republic of Estonia the power of the German and Russian languages had declined. These articles sought to establish the historical existence, viability, and value of Estonian culture.

Tallinn. Articles in *Tallinn* were concerned with countering the efforts of the Slavic elites to mobilize Russians on the basis of a Soviet identity. To do this, they attempted to redefine Russian and more generally non-Estonian social identity by questioning the assumptions behind Soviet identities, especially by noting that the Soviet emphasis on the Russian language made this rhetoric exclusionary. An article illustrating this aspect noted that Soviets typically referred to "Russian and national languages" or to Russian as "a second native language" (Rebane 1988: 86). Aksel' Tamm pointed out still more instances of this perspective in the use of "national language," "translation into a national language," and "older brother." According to Tamm this "means that 'national' is any language of the people of the USSR in contrast to Russian." He concluded by pronouncing the privileged status of Russian as "absurd" (Tamm and Semenenko 1989: 82) and asking, "Why isn't Russian simply one among many national languages?"

THE COGNITIVE WORLD OF ESTONIANS AND SLAVS: THE MASS MEDIA

An effective collective identity frame explains what it means to live as an Estonian or Russian in Estonia. The messages found in literary journals provided an interpretation of social identity that was communicated to attentive elites, but only newspapers (and the other mass media) could ultimately convey these messages to the mass public to create mass movements. Estonian- and Russian-language newspapers provided different information to their readers who came from different ethnic groups.

Media Coverage of Issues

Content analysis was used to analyze what was reported as well as how frequently issues appeared in the press. The most consistently reported issues were independence, ethnic conflict, economic policies and problems, citizenship, language laws, and voting. The transition that had commenced as a struggle over environmental issues saw this focus quickly fade from the public purview (1.8 percent of Estonian and 1.2 percent of Russian press reports). Table 2.3 shows how the prominence of issues varied in the Estonian- and Russian-language newspapers. Independence dominated reports in both language presses, although such reports were somewhat more numerous in the Estonian press. However, the importance of such differences is clearer when viewed over time. Independence dominated the Estonian press from the end of 1989 through the collapse of the Soviet Union in August 1991, suggesting an intensity absent from the Russian-language press.

Patterns of media consumption along with the factors affecting media choice suggest different worlds of reference. According to our 1991 Estonian survey data, virtually all ethnic Estonians (97 percent) reported that they constantly followed Estonian-language television, radio, and press, whereas only 25 percent of Slavs did so. Only 22 percent of ethnic Estonians constantly followed Russian-language media published in Estonia, whereas 80 percent of Slavs did. And only 34 percent of ethnic Estonians followed Central All-Union media, whereas 92 percent of Slavs did. Estonians focused on life within Estonia and

TABLE 2.3. *Issue Coverage by the Press in Estonia, 1988–1993*

Issues	Press Coverage, %		
	Estonian-Language	Russian-Language	Pravda
Independence	14.8	11.3	16.6
Civil rights	8.1	13.5	2.7
Language law and voting rights	3.2	7.6	2.5
Citizenship	5.9	9.1	0.5
Ethnic conflict	4.0	9.1	26.5
Environment	1.8	1.2	0.4
Economic policy	15.1	16.1	21.6
Right to work	0.4	4.1	6.9
Social welfare	5.8	9.8	16.6
N =	3,095	1,370	1,069

Source: Author's coding of the press. See Appendix 2.

the European world to which they felt historically linked, whereas Slavs viewed their metropole as Moscow and the Soviet Union.

The Tone of Reporting

The content analysis of event reports fails to convey the tone of coverage, although frequency may be a measure of intensity. Here we provide an example of how media coverage differed with regard to the Baltic Chain of August 1989, when a human chain was formed uniting the peoples of Lithuania, Latvia, and Estonia against their occupation by the Soviet Union.

Reede (*Sirp ja Vasar*),[4] a weekly Estonian-language cultural newspaper, devoted its entire cover page to a series of photos showing planes arriving from the West with demonstrators, the line of people at the border with Latvia, and the line in front of the Toompea Castle (the building in which the Estonian parliament meets). At the bottom of the front page was a photo of a demonstrator's sign with the hammer and sickle formed as a swastika. The top banner listed places throughout Estonia, and at the end of the banner it read: "Support Our Plea – Freedom! Freedom!" (*Reede*, 25 August 1989, 1). At the very bottom of the page in large type, a line read: "We Advise: Freedom! Freedom! Freedom!"

The Estonian-language newspaper *Edasi* provided its readers with views ranging from the Estonian National Independence Party to those of the Slavic

[4] *Sirp Ja Vasar* had a circulation in 1989 of 80,000 per week.

Intermovement ("Eesti Tee Iseseisvusele," 23 August 1989, 3). The newspaper (25 August 1989) also published photos of Tartu's Town Hall Square filled with people and noted that 130 buses had left from Tartu filled with people participating in the chain. *Edasi* even provided a map and schedule for those who took chartered buses to different areas of the chain ("MRP kett," 22 August 1989, 2). An article in the official (party and state) Estonian-language paper, *Rahva Hääl,* entitled "Our Road Is a Freedom Road" (Meie Tee on Vabaduse Tee, 24 August 1989, 1) also included photos of the chain and leaders of the Popular Front and the Communist Party of Estonia and noted that the Estonian national hymn, "Mu isamaa on minu arm" was sung by them. However, *Rahva Hääl* (22 August 1989) also reprinted less favorable material from *Pravda.* Indeed, the newspaper noted that *Vremia,* the central nightly news program, in a report on the reaction of the Central Committee of the Communist Party, claimed that "nationalist" and "extremist forces" were involved, with the aim of promoting internal conflict ("Millest mõtleme, millest räägime," *Rahva Hääl,* 30 August 1989, 1).

Coverage in the Russian-language press had a different accent. Just before the demonstration, *Molodezh' Estonii* published an article in which it noted that the Helsinki Accords of 1975 set post–World War II borders and that, although the sovereignty of the Baltic states could be recognized, it did not mean that they could leave the USSR ("Tainye peregovory," 22 August 1989, 1). *Molodezh' Estonii* noted that the sovereignty of the Baltic states could be obtained "only through a parliamentary path" and that all people must be protected without regard to nationality ("Vera, nadezhda, svoboda," 25 August 1989, 1). *Narvskii rabochii* did not publish any photographs or directly mention the Baltic Chain, but it reported on a meeting at which the secretary for ideology of the Communist Party of Estonia spoke. He claimed that, even if the secret protocol to the Molotov-Rippentrop Pact that gave the Soviet Union control over the Baltics was nullified, this was "not a basis for exit from the USSR. Only extremists would take this perspective" (*Narvskii rabochii,* 24 August 1989, 2). On 2 September 1989 *Narvskii rabochii* ("Obrashchenie Biuro TsK Kompartii Estonii," 1) reported that the first secretary of the Communist Party of Estonia Vaino Valjas said that "the fate of the Estonian people and of all residents of Estonia was directly tied to the successful course of renewal of the entire Soviet Union." "I declare directly in the current circumstances a demand to exist [independently] from the USSR is irresponsible and could bring only grief to the Estonian people." Thus, the discussion that ensued around the Baltic Chain in the Russian-language press focused on non-Estonian concerns with much less direct reporting on the event itself and with no sense of the euphoria surrounding the support for a free and independent Estonia evidenced in the Estonian-language press.

By reviewing our content analysis of event reports and the discourse found in newspaper coverage of major events during transition, we found that ethnic Estonians read the Estonian-language press that focused on events inside of Estonia but provided surprisingly limited coverage of events taking place in Eastern Europe and of ethnic conflict occurring in other areas of the Soviet Union. Although most Estonians could read Russian, they chose not to seek out the Russian-language press published in Estonia or the All-Union press. The growing importance of Estonian independence as the dominant issue of political life based on the need to preserve Estonian ethnicity is reflected in the Estonian-language media.

For Russians who could not read Estonian, the Russian press presented a very different world. Eastern Europe and particularly ethnic conflict were omnipresent. When events taking place in Estonia were reported, they were often condemned. None of the enthusiasm for and commitment to change evidenced in our analysis of the Estonian-language press was conveyed by Russian sources. Furthermore, the republic Russian-language press concentrated on protest events, avoiding reports on the emergence of the new Estonian civil society of political organizations and parties. Thus, the cognitive world of non-Estonians was one in which ethnic conflict all too often appeared to lead to violent confrontation.

TESTING THE FRAMING MODEL USING EVENTS DATA

Our content and discourse analyses of literary journals and newspapers help us understand the different appeals to collective identity that were put forth, especially the types of cognitive associations and social purposes that were enumerated as part of those appeals, but they do not tell us about the impact of these appeals on the mass public. Events data coded from newspapers (see Appendix 2) provide a test of these impacts. Using events data, we can determine whether (1) movements sponsored distinct meetings and protests that (2) focused on different issues (e.g., independence versus support for the Soviet Union) and (3) involved distinct sets of people. In the events data, we find that the organizations associated with the Restorationists and Reformers hardly ever sponsored the same events. Moreover, using statistical discriminant analysis (see Table 2.4), we find that speakers or protestors at these events talked about different *issues* that concerned different *targets*. The Restorationists talked about Russian troops in Estonia, independence, and

TABLE 2.4. *Discriminant Function Coefficients for Issues and Targets in Events Data for Each Movement*

	Movement		
	Restore	Reform	Counter
Restorationist issues			
Russian troops in Estonia	**2.209**	.811	.167
Estonian independence	**1.914**	1.065	.362
Estonian culture	**1.673**	1.477	−.210
Civil rights	**1.230**	.724	1.147
Reform issues			
Environmental policies	.263	**2.069**	−1.248
IME/autonomy	.196	**2.644**	.099
Counter-Movement issues			
Support for Soviet symbols	.777	.396	**3.242**
Social welfare policy	.141	.020	**2.996**
Ethnic discrimination	−1.096	−.671	**2.756**
Ethnic tensions	.266	.984	**1.589**
Other issues			
Policies of Estonian government	.988	.711	.597
Criticism of Soviet policies	.754	.989	.766
Economic issues	.744	.332	.829
Targets			
For Estonia	.155	**1.663**	.173
Against Soviets	.607	.750	−.513
Against Estonia	.846	.189	**1.534**
For Soviets	−.613	−.183	**3.423**
Against Russians	.214	.448	**2.735**
For Russians	−.886	.439	**2.815**
(Constant)	−2.072	−1.911	−2.942

Note: Sample size: 775. Method: Discriminant function analysis with three movements as categories and issues and targets as discriminators. The largest coefficient in each row over 1.0 is in bold.
Source: Political Events Dataset in Estonia, 1988–1993.

Estonian culture. The Reformers talked about the environment and economic autonomy for Estonia. The Counter-Movement focused on support for Soviet symbols, social welfare policy, ethnic discrimination, and ethnic tensions. Finally, using survey data, we can show that the events involved distinct sets of people.

In summary, frames provide a method whereby elites can imbue social identities with cognitive meanings and social purposes. Our analysis of cultural journals allowed us to track the development of different frames among elites during the early period of *glasnost*. The analysis of mass-media usage and content demonstrated that different ethnic groups were exposed to different messages, and the analysis of events data provided evidence that political activists from the three major social movements in Estonia were, indeed, motivated to act on the basis of these different frames. Most important, in our work we are able to show that although it started with very little support, between 1988 and 1990 the Restorationist collective identity frame, with its strong appeal to Estonian ethnic identity, managed to surpass the Reformist frame and thereby push Estonia toward independence. This over-time evidence provides support for the notion that the ethnically based Restorationist frame – more than the other frames – had the capacity to mobilize Estonians.

The dynamic nature of social identity, especially in rapidly changing contexts, requires that the researcher focus on the elites' role in establishing cognitive models of identities, connecting them with social purposes, and communicating these meanings to group members. Our research on the transition in Estonia provides examples of how multiple sources (primary documents, events data, and survey data) and methods (content analysis, discourse analysis, and statistical analysis) can be employed to understand this process.

SELF-IDENTIFIED NATIONALITY VERSUS PASSPORT NATIONALITY

We also use surveys to measure ethnic identity in the general population. These measurements are complementary to our analysis of literary journals, newspapers, and events because they tell us about the circumstances of the general public, as different social movements competed for its attention and allegiance. Although our general population surveys fortuitously occurred at two interesting points in time, in 1991 just before the breakup of the Soviet Union and in 1992 (Estonia) and 1993 (Russia, Komi Republic, Tatar Republic) after the breakup of the Soviet Union, they still provide only limited information about the dynamics that occurred during the transitional period, and they must be interpreted in light of the more dynamic time-series data on discourse, the media, and events that were discussed previously. For our purposes, however, they provide very useful examples of methods for measuring ethnic identity.

Most nonexperimental empirical research on ethnic identity has used nominal measures of identity because of their simplicity, utility, and apparent meaningfulness to respondents. In our own survey work in Estonia (see Appendix 3), we have found that respondents have no trouble responding to open-ended questions about their nationality.[5] Moreover, we find that two somewhat different nominal measures of identity lead to practically the same result. On the screener questionnaire, the first of our two waves of interviewing, we asked respondents, "What nationality do you consider yourself?" On our follow-up questionnaire, we asked, "What nationality is recorded on your passport?" Each list included Estonian, Russian, Ukrainian, Byelorussian, Jewish, Finnish and Ingrian, Latvian and Lithuanian, Caucasian, Central Asian, and other. We recoded these responses into three categories: Estonian, Slav (Russian, Ukrainian, Byelorussian), and other.

These two approaches lead to virtually the same identifications in a cross-tabulation of follow-up (passport) nationality and screener (self-identification) nationality. About 96 percent of the cases lie along the diagonal indicating the same identity. The remainder could be errors, or genuine differences in the two measures. These "liminal" respondents and those in the "other" category are interesting in their own right because many of them appear (with other indicators) to be genuinely on the border between nationalities, but the larger lesson is that these two approaches lead to the same result.

SOCIAL SEPARATION AND ETHNIC IDENTITY

Social distance is one of the most fundamental concepts in the study of ethnicity (Levine and Campbell 1971). Social distance scales include items that ask people about their relationships with members of other groups. These relationships, such as acquaintanceship, neighboring, friendship, and marriage, are partly the result of social structures that can be indexed by occupation, neighborhood, and wealth and partly the result of choices made by respondents. People choose friends, for example, but they usually do so from among the people they encounter in their everyday lives. There is less choice in one's allotment of family members, although people can choose spouses from outside their own group. A reliable social distance scale should ask about a range of relationships that involve varying degrees of choice and structure, and on our 1991 surveys in Estonia and Russia we did just that but in somewhat different ways.

Estonia

On our 1991 screener survey, we asked respondents whether they had close relatives, neighbors, co-workers, or friends of another nationality. For each

---

[5] During the Soviet era, nationality was used as a synonym for ethnicity (Tishkov 1997).

kind of relationship, if the respondent reported being connected to another nationality, we asked about the nationality of that person to whom the person was most connected through family, friends, work, or acquaintanceship. We then coded this information for Estonians and Slavs to form four variables, one for each kind of relationship. The variable had the value one if the person had a relationship with someone of "opposite" nationality – Slavs for Estonians and Estonians for Slavs – and it had the value zero otherwise.[6] For each group as defined by the self-identification and passport questions about nationality, we summed the four measures to get a measure of social closeness to the other group ranging from zero to four. A value of zero indicates a member of the group, say an Estonian, who has no contact with Slavs through any of the four relationships. A value of four indicates an Estonian who has contacts with Slavs through all four relationships. Such a person can be said to be socially close to the other group.[7]

Estonians and Slavs are quite separate in Estonia. According to this measure, only about 10 percent of Estonians and 16 percent of Slavs have three or four relationships with the other group. About 41 percent of Estonians have no relationships with Slavs and 31 percent have just one relationship. About 40 percent of Slavs have no relationships with Estonians and 26 percent have just one relationship. In Estonia at the time of transition, there was relatively little intense and intimate contact between the two ethnic groups. This relative lack of personal experience with members of another ethnic group may have made both Estonians and Slavs more open to the elite messages and ethnic images and myths presented by the mass media.

---

[6] When these four measures are factor-analyzed for each group separately, a common pattern emerges. In both cases, all four indicators load heavily on one dimension (with more than 40 percent of the variance explained by this one dimension in both cases), and three of the four items have loadings of more than .48 for both groups. The remaining item regarding family relationships has a smaller loading of between .27 for Slavs and .30 for Estonians.

[7] Of course, a Slav with no relationships with Estonians would also have a value of zero on this scale even though that person is essentially the mirror image of the Estonian with no relationships with Slavs. An obvious way to distinguish between these two situations is to score one group (Estonians) from zero to four and the other group from five to eight with eight indicating a Slav with no relationships with Estonians and five indicating someone with all four kinds of relationships with Estonians. At the low end of this social separation scale, then, are isolated Estonians and at the other end are isolated Slavs. The people at the two ends of the scale are very highly socially separated from one another. In the middle are Estonians and Slavs with multiple relationships with the other group. We use this social separation scale as part of our graded ethnicity measure described later.

Russia, Tatarstan, and the Komi Republic

In Russia we had a weaker version of the social distance question asked in the preceding example.[8] The social distance question asked about the ethnic cast of the person's social structure: "We live with representatives of different nationalities. Do you have: (1) Close relatives, that is, your wife/husband, their parents, etc. of another nationality than you? (2) Friends of another nationality than you? (3) People of another nationality than you among your co-workers, if, of course, you work? (4) Neighbors or acquaintances of another nationality than yours? (5) No one of another nationality?" The instructions on this questionnaire were to take the first "yes" and skip the rest of the questions. This scale was coded with isolated Russians at the one end and isolated members of the titular nationality at the other end.

Discussion of These Social Separation Measures

Although there are some dangers in making comparisons across the measures used in Estonia and Russia, we can compare some of the items across the two surveys because the Estonian social distance scale is constructed from items that are similar to the items described previously for the Russian questionnaire. The Russian version of these social distance items made it easier to score high on the number of relationships because once you said, for example, that you had a friend who was of the opposite nationality, it was assumed that you had a co-worker or neighbor as well. No explicit questions were asked, as in the Estonian survey,

---

[8] We also asked another social distance question that focused on choices made by respondents: "Speaking about the person with whom you socialize most, what is their nationality?" For Russians, this was coded as a minus one if the nationality mentioned was a Russian and a zero if some other nationality was mentioned (which was almost always a member of the titular nationality). For members of the titular nationality, this was coded as a one if the nationality mentioned was the titular nationality and a zero if some other nationality was mentioned (which was almost always Russian). There were also three more social distance questions on the follow-up study that asked more about the ethnic complexion of the social structure in which people were embedded: "We live together with the representatives of various nationalities. Are there people of other than your nationality with whom you work/worked or study?" (Yes, No, Difficult to Answer). "Are there people of other than your nationality among your neighbors or acquaintances?" (Yes, No, Difficult to Answer) "Among your friends and good acquaintances, there are: (1) only people of my nationality, (2) mostly people of my nationality, (3) people of other or various nationalities." Finally, there was a two-question battery of the following questions about helping or having close relationships with other nationalities: "A. I'd sooner help a person of my nationality than a person of another nationality." "B. I wouldn't object if my close relative, son, daughter, brother, sister married a person of another nationality." These questions not only get at people's level of approval for the other group but also suggest the degree they would be motivated, at least on an individual basis, to use social identity distinctions to affect allocations of resources and status.

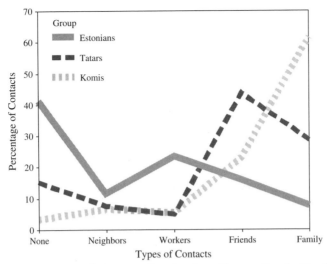

FIGURE 2.2. Percentage with Contacts Ranging from None to Family Ties for Titular Nationalities

about whether you had co-workers or neighbors of the other nationality. But we can construct the first social distance measure on the Russian questionnaire from the responses to the social distance questions on the Estonian questionnaire because the Estonian questionnaire provided more information about social distance as measured by contacts with family, friends, workers, and neighbors.[9]

This social distance measure constituted as on the Russian questionnaire is on the horizontal axis of Figures 2.2 and 2.3, with greater social distance between nationalities on the left (anchored by the "no contact" category) and closer contacts on the right (anchored by "family" contacts). The numbers on the vertical axis indicate the percentage of each group for whom that kind of contact was the closest that they came to the other nationality. Figure 2.2 presents data for the three titular nationalities, and Figure 2.3 does the same for the three Slavic groups in each titular republic. These figures show that among the titular nationalities, Estonians are the most isolated, whereas the Komi are the least isolated and Tatars are in between. About 8 percent of Estonians have family of the other nationality compared to 29 percent of Tatars and 62 percent of Komi.

---

[9] Thus, we can construct a scale in which a yes answer to having family of the other nationality indicates the closest kind of contact. A yes answer to having friends of the other nationality (along with a no to having family of the other nationality) indicates a somewhat less close contact, and so forth through co-workers, neighbors, and no contacts. When we compared the original measure of social distance on the Estonian questionnaire with the one constructed to be similar to the one on the Russian questionnaire, we found that the marginals changed somewhat for each measure but not dramatically. The correlation between the two measures was .86.

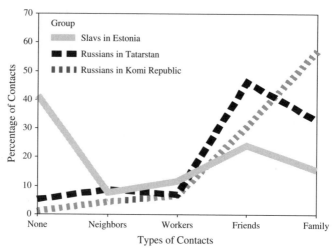

FIGURE 2.3. Percentage with Contacts Ranging from None to Family Ties for Slavs and Russians

And 53 percent of the Estonians have either only neighborhood or no contacts with the other nationality, whereas just 23 percent of the Tatars and 10 percent of the Komi are this isolated. Interestingly, the Slavic and Russian groups in each titular republic have the same pattern as their titular nationalities. About 16 percent of the Slavs in Estonia have family of the other nationality compared to 33 percent of the Russians in Tatarstan and 57 percent of the Russians in the Komi Republic. And 49 percent of Slavs in Estonia have either only neighborhood or no contacts with the other nationality, whereas just 23 percent of the Russians in Tatarstan and 6 percent of the Komi are this isolated.

Because the groups within each republic seem to be mirror images of one another, it makes sense to develop an overall measure of the amount of ethnic separation between groups in each republic. One simple approach is to take the difference between the average percentage of family contacts across the two groups in each republic and the average of no contacts. If 100 percent of the members of each group in a republic have family contacts with the other group, then this measure will be 100. If 100 percent of the members of each group have no contact with the other group, then this measure will be −100. Using this scale, we obtain a value of −30 for the Estonians and Slavs, 21 for the Tatars and Russians, and 57 for the Komi and Russians. These values span a great deal of the possible range of −100 to 100, and they suggest a great deal of interaction between the Komi and Russians in the Komi Republic, less interaction between the Tatars and Russians in Tatarstan, and very little interaction between the Estonians and Slavs in Estonia.

A GRADED ETHNICITY MEASURE FOR ESTONIA

In Estonia we have two other measures that can be used as part of a social identity index. One is media use, and the other is evaluation of groups. We combine these with the Estonian social distance measure to get a "graded measure of ethnic identity."

Media Use

The media that individuals seek out usually reflect their interests and preferences, although in some cases this choice may be structured by language knowledge or the difficulty and cost of obtaining particular media sources. The mass media play a critical role in theories of ethnicity, ranging from those focusing on modernization associated with Karl Deutsch to the "imagined communities" of Benedict Anderson. On the Citizen Participation in Politics in Estonia screener, we asked people about their usage of different media sources including *Estonian-language republic-level* television, radio, and newspapers; *Russian-language* media; *Central (Moscow-based)* media; *new* newspapers and magazines; and *"alternative"* television and radio stations. From research done by others (Lagerspetz 1996; Kirch 1997; Vetik 1999: 198–209; Arutiunian 1992: 392) as well as our own research,[10] we know that these media sources had their own particular perspectives on the events transpiring in Estonia and the USSR and that they offered different views on the issue of ethnicity. Russian-language, Central, and alternative media focused on a Slavic audience. Estonian-language and the new media focused more exclusively on the Estonian audience. The two audiences were offered distinctly different images of themselves and others living within Estonia and the USSR. Our survey respondents were asked to rate their usage of these sources on a one-to-four scale, with four indicating usage "all the time," three indicating "rather often," two indicating "rarely," and one indicating "practically never."

From these indicators, we formed a "Media Usage Index" that took the sum of the three predominantly Slavic sources (Central, Russian, alternative), subtracted off the sum of the two predominantly Estonian sources (Estonian and new), and then "normalized" the index to range from zero to one for each person. Hence, on this index, a value of one would indicate attention solely to Slavic sources with no attention to Estonian ones while a value of zero would indicate attention to only Estonian sources with no attention to Slavic ones.

---

[10] These differences were found in our own analysis of two Estonian- and three Russian-language newspapers from 1988 to 1993; see the Estonian Event Dataset (Brady and Kaplan 1999) described in Appendix 2.

Slavs and Estonians are at quite opposite ends of this index with mean values of .65 and .25, respectively. Estonians are almost all below .60 on this index, and Slavs are almost all above .40, but some Estonians are attentive to Slavic media and vice versa.

Media usage clearly distinguishes between Estonians and Slavs as well as suggesting that some members of each ethnic group attend to what might be considered the other's media. Given our earlier discussion based on a content analysis of some of these media sources, it seems highly likely that the information supplied by the media had a tangible influence on the outlooks and perceptions held by the local communities (and vice versa), so we consider whether media choices and social distance are related. Slavic media usage relative to Estonian media usage increases almost linearly as we go from Estonian isolates on the left-hand side of the social separation scale, through Estonian and Slavic respondents with many relationships to the other ethnic group in the middle of the scale, to Slavic isolates on the right-hand side. Indeed, the correlation between the two indicators is a very high .81 (for a common variance of 66 percent). There can be no doubt that the media usage scale is strongly related to the social distance scale.

Evaluation of Groups

Estonians and Slavs, then, lead largely separate lives, with only a small fraction of each group – something like 10 to 20 percent – having family, friends, neighbors, or co-workers from the other group and following the other group's media. Separation, however, does not necessarily mean that the groups dislike one another or that they even have different political perspectives. Ethnic separation and identity can exist without leading to political differences or to different evaluations by each group of the other.

A tried and true measure of affect or feelings toward another group is the seven-, ten-, or, in our case, the eleven-point rating scale of feelings toward groups that we standardized to run from zero to one. We had both Estonians and Slavs rate two groups on this scale:[11] the "National Radicals," who represented the most nationalist of the Estonian independence groups, and the "nonnative inhabitants" (meaning predominantly Slavs) of Estonia. We expected that Estonians would favor the National Radicals much more than the Slavs and that Slavs would favor nonnative inhabitants much more than the Estonians. It would have been useful to have both groups rate

---

[11] In fact, we had respondents' rate seven groups but we found that the ratings of these two groups capture all of the feelings Slavs had for Estonians and vice versa.

"Estonians," but we deemed this too difficult (and perhaps controversial) to ask in the summer of 1992. We used "National Radicals" as a stand-in for Estonian nationalists.

As we expected, Slavs evaluate nonnative inhabitants much more favorably at .77 than do Estonians at .31. Estonians evaluate the national radicals more favorably at .37 than do Slavs at .16, but both groups dislike national radicals on average. This suggests that the difference of the ratings for nonnative residents and national radicals might be a good summary measure of the evaluation of the two groups. We call this difference the Slavic-Estonian Evaluation scale. This scale is highly correlated with the social separation scale (.67) and with the media usage scale (.65), and when it is factor-analyzed with the Social Separation and Media Usage scale, it yields one dimension that explains 72 percent of the variance and with all loadings above .73.

All Three Scales Together

The question remains, however, about how useful these three scales are in reflecting differences among people within ethnic groups. When we factor-analyze the three scales for each group separately, we still find evidence for only one dimension, but we also find much less coherence with only 24 percent of the variance explained for Slavs and 32 percent for Estonians. Moreover, although the Media Usage scale has a high loading of .90 for Estonians and .77 for Slavs, the loadings for the other two scales range in value from .219 to .285. This suggests that the three indicators still cohere to some extent within each ethnic group but to a much smaller degree than they do across the two groups. It also suggests that media usage, that is, the exposure to consistent and distinct ethnic and political messages heavily influenced by elites, might be the best single measure reflecting ethnic identity.

Despite these caveats, we use the combination of the three scales normalized to range from zero to one to form a scale of "Graded Ethnic Identity," because it allows for a wider variety of factors affecting ethnic identification. This scale measures those factors which place people closer to or farther from the outgroup. It is fair to say, for example, that Estonians and Slavs located at the middle of the scale have the same graded ethnic identity and are equally close to the opposite group, but it is quite possible that the salience of ethnic identity will be much stronger for Estonians at the middle of the scale than for Slavs at this location.

Figure 2.4 depicts the distribution of each nationality in the follow-up sample by the graded ethnic identity measure. Estonians are on the left with a median scale value of .26 and Slavs are on the right with a median value of .79.

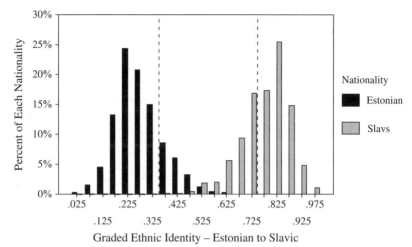

FIGURE 2.4. Percent of Each Nationality by Graded Ethnic Identity Scale

There is some but not a lot of overlap between the two groups in the middle of the histogram that we have demarcated by two dotted vertical lines. About 20 percent of the Estonians and about 36 percent of the Slavs are in this region.

ASSOCIATION WITH ANOTHER NATIONALITY

If our measure of ethnic identity captures gradations in identity, then those in the middle of the scale should be relatively likely to associate themselves with another nationality, while those at each end of the scale should be unlikely to do so. On our follow-up survey, after asking people about the nationality recorded on their passport, we asked them, "Do you associate yourself with another nationality?" and if they answered yes, we asked, "With what nationality do you associate yourself?" Using this question, we constructed a four-category "Nationality Association" measure: Estonians who did not associate themselves with another nationality (scored as a one), Estonians who associated themselves with Slavs (scored as a two), Slavs who associated themselves with Estonians (scored as a two), and Slavs who did not associate themselves with another nationality (scored as a three). About 7 percent of the Estonians associated themselves with a Slavic nationality and about 17 percent of Slavs associated themselves with the Estonian nationality.

Figure 2.5 plots, separately for Estonians and Slavs, the average of this measure versus the graded ethnic identity measure. The shape is exactly

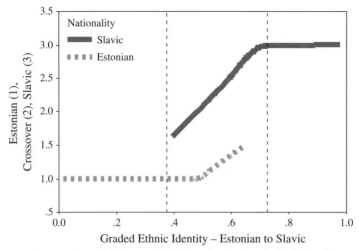

FIGURE 2.5. Association with Opposite Nationality by Graded Ethnic Identity

what we would expect: those on the left and right of the ethnic identity measure almost never associate themselves with another nationality, and the average of the measure is almost identically one on the left and three on the right. Only when we get toward the middle of the graded ethnic identity scale, in the area bounded on the left and right by dotted vertical bars located at the same place as those on Figure 2.4, do we find movements toward the middle of the Nationality Association measure where Estonians associate themselves with Slavs and Slavs with Estonians. Note that Slavs at the middle of the graded ethnicity scale are much more likely to associate themselves with Estonians than are Estonians at the middle of the scale likely to associate themselves with Slavs. Nevertheless, some Estonians do associate themselves with Slavs. This result provides some strong confirmation for the validity of our graded identity measure, and it reveals a pattern of greater identification of Slavs with Estonians. This question about association can be thought of as a measure of attachment to the identity, but because it does not get at the strength of the attachment, it is not really a measure of salience or centrality (Stryker and Serpe 1994). In our conclusions, we discuss the need for more work on measuring salience and related concepts.

WHAT ARE THE ATTRIBUTES BEHIND THESE INDICATORS?

Where do these variations in ethnic identity come from? We examine three possible sources: parental ethnic identity, language use at home, and ability to speak the language of the opposite group. As we noted earlier in this chapter, kinship bonds and language are essential features of most definitions of ethnicity.

Three Attributes: Parental Ethnicity, Language Spoken at Home, and Language Knowledge

Parental ethnicity is an obvious source of ethnic identity as it is for religious, class, and political identity. Parental ethnic identity is measured by a four-point scale constructed from two questions about parents' nationality. We asked, "What is your [mother's; father's] nationality?" We then coded this into Estonian, Slavic, or Other for each parent. There are many ways to code these data, but the following four categories covered almost all but 4 percent of the cases and made it possible to fashion a Parental Ethnic Identity scale:

- Estonian passport identification and both parents Estonian (scored as a one)
- Estonian passport identification and one or two parents Slavic (scored as a two)
- Slavic passport identification and one or two parents Estonian (scored as a three)
- Slavic passport identification and both parents Slavic (scored as a four)

About 95 percent of the cases fell in the first and fourth category, suggesting that parental identity could not explain all of the variation in the graded ethnicity scale, but there is a clear change in the average value of the graded ethnicity from .27 to .38 to .68 to .78 as we move through the four categories on the Parental Ethnic Identity scale.

Using the same approach, we then turned to the language spoken at home. We asked respondents, "In your family do you communicate primarily in Russian, Estonian, or in some other language?" We coded responses as a Estonian, Russian, or both equally. Using passport identity, we then coded people from one to six as follows:

- Estonian passport identification and speak only Estonian (scored as a one)
- Estonian passport identification and speak both Russian and Estonian equally (two)
- Estonian passport identification and speak Russian (three)
- Slavic passport identification and speak Estonian (four)
- Slavic passport identification and speak both Estonian and Russian equally (five)
- Slavic passport identification and speak Russian only (six)

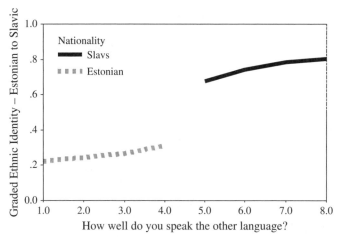

FIGURE 2.6. Graded Ethnic Identity by How Well Respondents Speak Other Language

Even a larger fraction of the population, 97 percent, fits into the first and sixth categories in this case, suggesting that language spoken at home could not fully account for the differences. Once again, however, there is a clear increase in the average value of graded ethnic identity as we move through the categories.[12]

Finally, we constructed a measure of language knowledge from the answers to two questions. "Let us discuss the languages you know [Estonian, Russian]. How well do you know [Estonian, Russian]?" Four answers were possible: "Reads and writes fluently," "daily use," "understands but does not speak," and "not at all." For those whose passport identity was Estonian, we used the response to this question regarding the Russian language. We scored it from one to four with one for those who cannot speak Russian at all (6 percent of Estonians), two for those who understand but do not speak Russian (13 percent), three for those Estonians who can use Russian for daily tasks (50 percent), and four who read and write it fluently (31 percent). For those whose passport identity was Slavic, we used the response to this question regarding the Estonian language. We scored it from five to eight with five for those who read and write it fluently (10 percent of Slavs), six for those Slavs who can use Estonian for daily tasks (22 percent), seven for those who understand but do not speak Estonian (30 percent), and eight for those who cannot speak Estonian at all (38 percent). Answers on this scale are much more spread out than those for parents' nationality or language use at home, and Estonians generally know Russian much better than Russians know Estonian.[13] Figure 2.6 shows

---

[12] The values are .27, .48, .44, .60, .63, and .78 as we go from one to six.
[13] This is to a large degree an artifact of the Soviet educational system.

that there is a strong relationship between graded ethnic identity and knowledge of the other language.

Although none of these factors completely captures ethnic identity, together they provide a good starting place. Table 2.5 reports regressions for Estonians and Slavs of graded ethnic identity on parents' nationality, language at home, and knowledge of the opposite language. Although the adjusted R^2 values are only modest (.136 for Estonians and .218 for Slavs), each of the three factors is statistically significant with beta weights between .126 and .102 for parents' nationality for Estonians and Slavs respectively, .183 and .266 for language at home, and .226 and .238 for language knowledge. Kinship and language, as we would expect, are important determinants of ethnicity.[14]

Graded Ethnic Identity

Graded ethnic identity seems like a sensible measure of ethnicity for the mass public for a number of reasons. First, it combines indicators of important factors that contribute to and reflect ethnicity including social distance, media usage, and evaluation of the opposite group, and these indicators co-vary strongly. Second, it has the expected relationship with responses to a question about associating with another nationality. Third, it is strongly related to the ethnicity of kin and to language use, which are often described as bases of ethnic identity. Fourth, the measure has a strongly bimodal shape, suggesting relatively distinct boundaries between Estonians and Slavs.

CONCLUSIONS: HOW WELL HAVE WE SUCCEEDED IN MEASURING ETHNIC IDENTITY?

At the beginning of this chapter we laid out seven factors that must be considered in measuring ethnic identification, and we argued that these factors must be measured over time at both the elite and mass level to understand fully the dynamics of ethnic identity. Table 2.1 gives the types of measures, listed in the order they are discussed in this chapter. It also summarizes the various

[14] A combined analysis of Estonians and Slavs produces a very substantial adjusted R-squared of .879. This result, however, is suspect because the kinship and language measures employed as independent variables are constructed using passport identity, and the social separation scale, which is part of the dependent variable, also uses passport identity. If we exclude the social separation measure from the dependent variable and just use a combination of media usage and Estonian-Slavic evaluation (which do not use passport identity), then we still get an R-squared of .705 which suggests the real power of kinship and language. In fact, a discriminant analysis for predicting Estonian or Slavic group membership that employs only media usage and Estonian-Slavic evaluation predicts 94 percent of the cases correctly.

TABLE 2.5. *Regression Analysis of Core Ethnic Identity on Parents' Nationality, Language Use at Home, and Knowledge of Other Language for Each Group*

	Regression Coefficients (Standard Errors)	
Explanatory Variables	Estonians	Slavs
Parents' nationality	.063*** (.019)	.042* (.021)
Language use at home	.065*** (.013)	.068*** (.013)
Knowledge of other language	.026*** (.004)	.022*** (.005)
Constant	.521*** (.090)	.526*** (.087)
R^2	.136	.218
N	729	349

*Significant at the .05 level; ***significant at the .001 level.

methods of measurement and the features of ethnicity measured. We have proposed from two to four methods for measuring each feature of ethnicity, described methods for measuring ethnicity at both the mass and elite level, and suggested a variety of purposes ranging from describing ethnicity to determining the dynamics of ethnicity over time.

No doubt many of the measures we have used can be improved, but as we noted earlier, special attention should be paid to improving the measurement of attachment or salience because it is especially important for political action (Brewer 2001b; Huddy 2001; Stryker, Owens, and White 2000). Moreover, in our article on measuring ethnicity (Brady and Kaplan 2000), we argued that ethnicity could be measured nominally for those for whom ethnic identity is highly salient but a graded measure must be used for those for whom ethnic identity is less salient. In that article, we estimated salience as a parameter in a mathematical model, but it would have been much better to measure it directly. Some ways of doing this focus on people's thoughts about the importance of their identity to themselves, and other methods focus on how much respondents want other people to recognize and acknowledge their identity. In Kuhn and McPartland's (1954) "Twenty Statements Test," people are asked to give as many responses as they can in six minutes to the question "Who am I?" Verkuyten (1991) applied this approach and asked respondents to identify the five most important statements. Ethnic identity was considered more salient if it was both mentioned and chosen as one of the five most important statements. Another approach (Callero 1985) asks people about their ethnic identity and then asks them to rate on a nine-point agree-or-disagree scale a series of positive and negative statements about their identity, such as "Being [my ethnic identity] is an important part of who I am," "For me, being [my ethnic identity] means more than just being [my ethnic identity]," "[My ethnic identity] is something I rarely even think about," and "I really don't have any clear feelings about being [my ethnic identity]." Still another approach asks people to indicate how important (in a four-category Likert format) it is to have others (close friends, parents, and people in general) think of them in terms of their ethnicity (White and Burke 1987). All these methods deserve more theoretical development and empirical exploration and use.

Because we are concerned with conceptualizing and measuring ethnic identity, we have largely refrained from describing substantive findings that follow from our measurement methods, but they have made it possible for us to show how ethnicity mattered in Estonia's break with the Soviet Union. Using demographic and historical information, we became familiar with the importance of ethnic identity to Estonians and the threats to that identity. Using political debates, memoirs, and newspaper articles, we were able to identify two collective identity frames (the Restorationist and the Counter-Movement) that emphasized Estonian and Soviet identity respectively and another frame (the Reform) that did not make appeals to ethnic identity. By coding cultural journals over time, we showed how elite discourse about ethnic identity changed from 1986 to 1990: first came an emphasis on historical issues (1986–1988), then a turn to cultural issues (1988–1989), and finally an emphasis upon Estonian independence (1989–1990). A content analysis of media stories confirmed that the Estonian and Slavic mass publics were exposed in different ways to these ideas. Our coding of events data over time then showed that there were palpably different social movements that emphasized different themes, but, most important, over time the Restorationist theme with its appeal to ethnic identity surpassed the Reform theme. Finally, through a variety of survey-based measures (passport nationality, social distance, media usage, and evaluation of groups), we confirmed that Estonians and Slavs in Estonia were estranged from one another and lived in quite different worlds. All of these methods contributed to our understanding of the success of the independence movement in Estonia, and we would have missed important insights if we had dispensed with any one of them. Perhaps, then, our most important message is that no one method alone is adequate for understanding the development, evolution, and impact of ethnic identity in a society.

APPENDIX I: LITERARY JOURNALS

Four literary journals were published in Estonia during the transition: *Looming*, *Tallinn*, *Raduga*, and *Vikerkaar*. Two of these journals, *Looming* (Creation) and *Tallinn* (named for the capital of Estonia), were sponsored by the Writers' Union of the Estonian Soviet Socialist Republic. *Looming* was published only in the Estonian language and *Tallinn* in Russian. *Raduga* (Rainbow) and *Viker-kaar* (Rainbow) were respectively the Russian- and Estonian-language versions of the same journal (although in practice they varied somewhat), sponsored by the Estonian Communist Youth League.

Our analysis is based on coded articles selected from all the articles (except for creative works) published in *Looming* (1985–1991), *Vikerkaar* and *Raduga* (1986–1991), and *Tallinn* (1986–1991) during the reform era. Articles were chosen for coding based on whether they included references to economic, environmental, cultural and ethnic, or political issues. Excluded creative works might have strengthened the trends found. Each of the selected articles was entered in a database with all issues mentioned coded along with the title, author, and publication information for each article. The total number of articles coded from *Looming* was 263, *Vikerkaar* 229, *Raduga* 424, and *Tallinn* 76.

APPENDIX 2: EVENTS DATA – NEWSPAPERS

In creating the events dataset, we took seriously the potential problem of selection bias associated with reliance on newspaper reports (Mueller 1997; McCarthy, McPhail, and Smith 1996; Oliver and Myers 1999; and Oliver and Maney 2000). Consistent with Carol Mueller's (1997: 831) admonition, we rely on "data from local coverage by the most proximate quality newspapers" and code "from more than one newspaper." The political event data project in Estonia draws upon five newspapers. Newspapers were chosen with advice provided by Estonian communications scholars in order to maximize geographical coverage (while still being located in the centers of political activity: Tallinn, Tartu, and Narva) and circulation and to provide variation in the newspapers – in their relationship to the state and communist party, in their political outlook, in the administrative level at which the paper was issued, and in their language of publication. Four newspapers published in Estonia were coded: one republican-level newspaper that was published in Estonian (*Rahva Hääl*), one district-level paper published in Estonian and read throughout Estonia (*Edasi/Postimees*), and one widely read Russian-language republican-level paper (*Molodezh' Estonii*), plus a local Russian paper (*Narvskaia Gazeta/Narvskii Rabochii*) from the third largest city in Estonia (Narva), which is overwhelmingly Slavic. *Pravda*, the official newspaper of the Communist Party of the Soviet Union, published in Moscow was also coded. All newspapers were coded for the period 1988–1993 with the exception of *Pravda*, which was coded only until 1991. *Pravda* briefly stopped publishing after the August 1991 coup and then struggled a bit before disappearing as a daily connected with the Communist Party. *Rahva Hääl* and *Molodezh' Esto-nii* were also coded for 1987 but are not used in our analysis. We extended our coding through 1993 so as to include one year past our survey when the Estonian political agenda had changed and the Slavic response to new Estonian laws on citizenship and the registration of aliens took on importance. The events coded correspond to the fifteen types of political behavior (conventional and unconventional) about which we had asked our survey respondents.

APPENDIX 3: SURVEY DATA

Drawing upon the study of Sidney Verba, Henry E. Brady, Kay Schlozman, and Norman Nie of participation in the United States, the authors of the Citizen Participation in Politics Survey in Russia were Cynthia S. Kaplan, William V. Smirnov, Vladimir G. Andreenkov, and Henry Brady. The first stage of the survey in Russia was supported by the John D. and Catherine T. MacArthur Foundation, the Soviet Academy of Sciences, the Committee on Science and Technology of the Supreme Soviet, USSR, with initial assistance from the International Research and Exchanges Board and the American Council of Learned Societies. Fieldwork was supervised by Vladimir Andreenkov, the Center for Comparative Social Research, Moscow, Russia. Additional assistance was provided by the Center for Political Studies, Institute of State and Law, Moscow, Russia. The second stage of the Russian survey was supported by the National Science Foundation (SES-9122389). The first stage survey in Russia utilized a representative sample of Russia plus an oversample in Tatarstan. Interviews with 12,309 respondents were in person. The second-stage panel included 2,567 politically active respondents chosen from the first panel who were reinterviewed in 1993. Interviews in the first stage were conducted in Russian and the languages of the Autonomous Soviet Socialist Republics (ASSRs). In the second stage, interviews were conducted in the Russian and Tatar languages.

In the current analysis, the sample was divided into the Russian Federation without the autonomous republics, the Tatar Autonomous Republic, and the Komi Autonomous Republic. In the Russian Federation exclusive of ASSRs and the Komi ASSR, the samples were reweighted to correct for gender based on 1989 census data. In the Tatar ASSR, in addition to the gender reweighting, a correction was made to adjust the proportion of ethnic Russians and Tatars based on 1989 census data.

A parallel survey, Citizen Political Participation in Estonia, was prepared by Kaplan and Brady and Andrus Saar, Saar Poll, Ltd., Tallinn, Estonia. Priit Järve, director of the Institute of Philosophy, Sociology, and Law, Estonian

Academy of Sciences, assisted in preparing the screener survey. The first-stage survey in Estonia was supported by the John D. and Catherine T. MacArthur Foundation and the second-stage survey by the National Science Foundation. The survey consisted of two stages: a screener in which 6,884 respondents were interviewed in person during January–February 1991 and a second-stage, long questionnaire, in which 1,120 respondents were reinterviewed during June–July 1992. The screener used a representative sample from Estonia, while the second-stage sample was a weighted sample of political activists drawn from the first stage on the basis of modes of political behavior within the two major ethnic communities, Estonians and Slavs. Slavs were treated as a group after no differences of statistical significance in political behavior were found among ethnic Russians, Ukrainians, and Belorussians. Interviews were conducted in both the Russian and Estonian languages. The fieldwork was conducted by Saar Poll, Ltd., Tallinn, Estonia.

3

Trade-offs in Measuring Identities: A Comparison of Five Approaches

Donald A. Sylvan and Amanda K. Metskas

INTRODUCTION

Which measures of identity are best suited to particular research puzzles and conceptualizations of identity? This chapter considers five measurement strategies – experiments, discourse and content analysis, and open- and closed-ended surveys – employed in work mainly on Israeli and Palestinian identities.[1] The focus of this chapter is on methodological trade-offs and their consequences for identity research, and like other chapters in this volume, we rely largely on our previously published work as a basis for an extended methodological review. The discussion here supplements and complements the second chapter's explication of techniques that can be used to measure identity. This chapter presents the reasons for selecting particular measurement strategies, discusses how measures were constructed, and compares the virtues of the various strategies for answering questions within a research program.

There are clear trade-offs between the measurement approaches discussed in this chapter, including a focus on elites versus the general population, the necessity of direct access to the subjects of research, and the epistemological commitments entailed by the approach. Perhaps the most significant trade-off is whether the approach requires the researcher to rely on preconstructed categories of identity, or whether the researcher inductively defines the relevant identities as a part of the research project itself. Choosing between these trade-offs depends largely on the goals of the research being undertaken. Throughout this chapter, we discuss the trade-offs between these methods by drawing on

---

[1] One of the five works examined deals with a topic other than Israeli-Palestinian relations – Russian and French loss of empire.

the research program of the authors. We find that often there is not one ideal measurement approach; rather, a combination of these approaches can mitigate the weaknesses of any single approach.

Conceptualizing Identity

This chapter relies on a conception of identity that is largely consistent with both Chapters 1 and 2 of this volume. The theoretical approach to identity taken here focuses mostly on the "cognitive models" component of group identification (Abdelal et al., Chapter 1 in this volume). We are most interested in what kind of beliefs go along with holding a particular identity. As it is conceptualized here, identity has problem representation at its core. The concept of problem representation is built upon the assumption that the way in which an individual represents an issue shapes how that individual will reason about and make decisions about that issue (Sylvan and Thorson 1992; Sylvan and Voss 1998). Problem representation is related to the concept of framing, in that it focuses on how people interpret information and represent problems. The term "problem representation" is used here rather than "framing" to emphasize that this is a process in which people engage all the time, often unconsciously; it is not simply a type of spin or marketing that they may use selectively. In order to avoid issues of endogeneity, we have examined *manifestations* of problem representation (e.g., speeches) as variables that might precede (as opposed to "cause") the behaviors we study.

One distinction between the conception of identity used here and that developed in Chapter 1 is that our conception focuses more on individual decision makers. The manner in which individual decision makers represent problems is a cognitive approach to how individuals take on identities. Although the identities they take on are collective identities, they are bringing to those identities their own perspective. The measurement strategies used in our research focus on individuals' representations of their identities and their reactions to members of other groups. Because one of the goals of this kind of research is to assess the linkages between identities and action, we think that it is most useful to find out how individuals represent their identities and then to determine how those individuals act. Through this method, it is possible to learn how different conceptions of what it means to be Israeli or Palestinian, for example, relate to different political attitudes toward members of the other group.

Israeli and Palestinian Identities

Although the primary focus of this chapter is methodological, a little bit of background on Israeli-Palestinian relations, the primary substantive focus of the chapter, may be helpful. There is reason to believe that identity is a key variable in shaping outcomes and relationships in Israeli-Palestinian relations. Perhaps the central debate among international relations scholars studying the Middle East is whether systemic variables that form the core of a realist approach to international relations can account for patterns of Israeli-Palestinian relations. The studies reported here concentrate on a period during which such systemic variables as degree of bipolar power concentration do not vary significantly, thereby controlling for systemic factors and allowing a focus on the influence of other variables on the observed differences in conflictual and cooperative behavior. These studies put forth identity variables as plausible explanatory constructs.

APPROACHES TO MEASUREMENT

In analyzing work on identity employing experimental methods, discourse analysis, content analysis, and open- and closed-ended surveys, we focus on three methodological questions:

1. How do the methodological choices in the study relate to different theories of identity?
2. How are the measurement instruments constructed?
3. What are the trade-offs between different measurement strategies?

Table 3.1 presents an overview of the five articles we analyze. Like Brady and Kaplan in Chapter 2, we contend that identity research is improved by the use of a variety of methods.

Representing Identity Experimentally

Experimental approaches can be employed to both measure and manipulate identification with certain groups. Sylvan and Nadler (2005) employ experiments to capture identities in the context of Israeli-Palestinian relations. They studied the effects of experimental induction of victimhood in the context of a "manufactured" Palestinian-Israeli conflict. Although Israeli subjects were included in the latest phase of this research, their identities were measured rather than manipulated experimentally; thus, this discussion focuses on the methodology used to examine the American subjects. The primary manipulations used in this study were being of Israeli Jewish versus Palestinian Arab identity, high versus low commitment to the in-group, and whether in-group members were portrayed as victims or not. In addition, American subjects'

TABLE 3.1. *Overview of Approaches to Measuring Identity*

Source	Puzzle	Intellectual Roots of Identity Treatment	Technique	Subjects	Operationalization plus Whether Preconstructed	Trade-offs
Sylvan and Nadler 2005	Factors (including identity) leading to willingness to cooperate	Brewer, Berger and Luckmann, Brubaker	Experimental and closed-ended survey for Israeli sample	Israeli and U.S. students	Closed-ended subject response to questions about identity; preconstructed	Allows responses on a scale, but no flexibility to adopt other identity categories; focuses on nonelites
Sylvan and Toronto 2004	Impact of U.S. media on empathy with Palestinians and Israelis	Tilly, Lamont	Closed-ended survey and text coding	Ohio residents, U.S. residents	Questions on empathy with Palestinians and Israelis; preconstructed	Large number of responses; not as many interpretive clues
Metskas, Horowitz, and Sylvan 2006	Interaction between Mizrahi identity and attitudes toward Palestinians	Brewer, Roccas, Marques, Shiloah and Cohen, Reyes-Shramm	Closed- and open-ended survey	Mizrahi Jews in Israel (Ashkenazi as control)	Responses on topic of music preferences and views of other; both preconstructed and not	Need access; allows more free-form answers and approaches to identity
Sylvan, Grove, and Martinson 2005	Cognitive determinants of Israeli-Palestinian conflict and cooperation	Brewer, Tilly, Herrmann	Coding of texts, event data	Palestinian, Israeli, and N. Ireland elites	Statements coded as in-group and out-group inclusivity and exclusivity; preconstructed	Captures psychological dimension; concentrates on elites
Charlick-Paley and Sylvan 2000	Discourses to justify new role (loss of empire)	Brubaker, Hopf	Interviews, coding of texts	Elites – Russian and French military officers	Discourses, coded in a narrative template; not preconstructed	Free-form categories within narrative template; not confined to identity; concentrates on elites

actual identity and views were examined as possible determinants of their choices.

Appendix 1 of this chapter provides the experimental manipulations that were used to assign subjects to conditions in the Sylvan and Nadler (2005) study. The American participants in the study, undergraduates from Ohio State University, received one of eight possible descriptions at the beginning of the study. These descriptions provided subjects with the role that they were playing in the experiment. Subjects were told to imagine that they were either Palestinian Arabs or Israeli Jews and were given descriptions that either included or did not include material that would prime them to feel that their group was the victim of the other group. They were also told that their Israeli Jewish or Palestinian Arab identity either was very important to them or was one of a number of roles they played. These descriptions formed the independent variables in the experiment. For the purposes of the experiment these descriptions were the identities of the subjects.

After subjects read these descriptions, they were asked to answer a few questions about how they felt about their group and the other group. These questions served as manipulation checks to make sure that subjects had read the materials carefully and that they were using the information from the materials to answer the subsequent questions. Following the manipulation checks, subjects read the story about conflict in "Southern Jerusalem." The story was written from a neutral perspective, and all subjects received the same version of the news story. The subjects were then asked to answer questions about how they felt about the two sides in the conflict, who was responsible for the conflict, and their opinions about the future quality of relations between the two groups including the likelihood of the conflict being resolved soon. The final questions in the study asked the subjects to step out of their role in the simulation and give their personal opinions about Arab-Israeli conflict. Lastly, subjects were asked some demographic questions. The questions asked after the story was presented formed the dependent variables for this study.

The experiments with American subjects revealed that the identity manipulations produced a dramatic impact on subjects' assessment of both Israeli Jews and Palestinian Arabs, but very little impact on their assessment of what the future would bring. These results – seemingly pointing out that factors that can affect perceptions of such groups do not necessarily have an impact on overall optimism or pessimism about the future – were consistent with the authors' central proposition. In terms of some possible solutions to the hypothetical Palestinian-Israeli conflict, subjects who were in the high commitment to identity condition rejected integration, while subjects in the low commitment to identity condition recommended it. This shows that this experimental strategy does reveal some variance in attitudes toward the "other."

The experimental manipulations used in Sylvan and Nadler (2005) draw upon Berger and Luckmann (1966). Berger and Luckmann discuss secondary socializations, in a manner consistent with the identity manipulations employed in this chapter, to get at the high or low group commitment (seen as equivalent to identity), as well as victimhood. Berger and Luckmann claim that identities are shaped by social processes and reshaped by social relations. A central part of socialization is language, precisely the instrument used to manipulate identities in this experiment. Furthermore, in-group and out-group behavior is a theme present in much psychological and sociological literature. In Chapter 12 of this volume Rose McDermott provides an in-depth discussion of the use of experimentation in the study of identity, with a particular focus on social identity theory, a major research program in social psychology focused on relations between in-groups and out-groups, how people identify with in-groups, and how their group identifications shape their behavior toward others. This theme is also central to Brewer (2003), and Brubaker, Loveman, and Stamatov (2004) speak to this idea when they talk about the propensity for people to categorize. Categorization is a cognitively complex process that carries with it expectations and knowledge embodied in people, narratives, and memories and encoded in institutions and organizations.

Manipulating the level of identification with a specified in-group was the primary strategy used in that study for testing the impact of aspects of identity on subjects' views of the conflict and the other group. The experimental approach as it is used here has the disadvantage of preordaining identity categories and scales. Subjects are placed in categories that the researcher has defined ahead of time for the purpose of the experiment. However, through the use of scales this approach does allow subjects to express the degree to which they identify with a prespecified group in a manner more nuanced than a dichotomous classification.[2]

One question that is often raised about experimental manipulations of identity is whether the manipulations actually influenced the subjects in a way similar to how people possessing those identity characteristics would be influenced. This question of external validity seems particularly troubling in identity research. It is difficult for people to believe that asking subjects to, in effect, "pretend" to have a particular identity would make them act the same way that

---

[2] An alternative approach in which subjects have the opportunity to communicate their particular social construction of identity is discussed later in this chapter in the discussion of open-ended survey responses used by Metskas, Horowitz, and Sylvan (2006).

people would who were in fact members of that identity group. Although this is a serious concern, several things can be done to mitigate it. The first is the use of manipulation checks.[3] Making sure that participants clearly understand the materials they are presented with and know that they are supposed to use them to answer the questions is a first step toward addressing this issue. Manipulation checks may not address deeper concerns researchers may have that, although subjects are doing their best to respond as though they held the identities in question, their responses still might not be the same as actual members of the identity group. Another way this concern is mitigated is to think about what one should expect if the experiment is not externally valid; in the case of this study, if the subjects were not reacting in the way that actual Israelis and Palestinians would, one would expect to see smaller relationships between the independent and dependent variables, not larger. So if there is a bias presented by external validity problems, it is a bias against finding significant results, not an overestimation of the effects of the variables.

Despite the potential for these tactics to mitigate this concern, it still remains an issue that researchers must consider when doing experimental research on identities. In the case of Sylvan and Nadler, they addressed the external validity issue head on through the inclusion of surveys of Israelis in the study. In future work, they also plan to include Palestinians in their sample. With these populations, the researchers are measuring where people fall on the independent variable questions of ethnic group, level of commitment, and perceived victimization, rather than manipulating those variables. The results from the Israeli portions of the sample were similar to those from the experimental conditions with the American student sample. This indicates that the American students are reacting in similar ways as people who actually belong to these identity groups. This combination of an experiment and a survey of actual identity group members helps to demonstrate how a combination of methods can correct for the weaknesses of any individual method.

The benefits that experiments provide in exchange for these questions about external validity are experimental control and random assignment of subjects to conditions. In the Sylvan and Nadler study, the American participants were randomly assigned to one of the conditions in the study. The benefit of random assignment is that the researcher can be fairly sure that only the experimental manipulation is systematically different between the different groups in the

---

[3] The issues of maturation and bias in the victimhood experiment were handled by affording the aforementioned central position to manipulation checks, which is quite acceptable in social psychology. As evidence for this, two follow-up studies to the Sylvan and Nadler paper (Nadler and Liviatan 2006; Nadler and Halabi 2006) were published in reputable psychology journals using that same approach.

study. Because participants are assigned to conditions randomly, any other variations among participants should show up as random noise in the results of the study, rather than systematically biasing the results. Random assignment is not possible with the Israeli and Palestinian subjects because those subjects are assigned to the condition by their actual identity profile. While that helps with external validity, it poses problems in terms of selection bias – it is possible that there are systematic differences between the groups in the sample of Israelis and Palestinians other than the variables of interest to the researcher. Experimental control also means that subjects are participating in the study in an environment controlled by the experimenter. Unlike participants in a telephone or mail survey, the experimenter can be relatively sure that the conditions under which each subject participated were approximately the same. Along with random assignment, experimental control helps to ensure that only the independent variables of interest are systematically different between the groups in the study.

Examining Identity with Closed-Ended Survey Methods

Although surveys do not allow random assignment or experimental control, they are probably the most similar method to experimental research designs for studying identities. In survey methods, the unit of analysis for identities, as it is in experiments, is typically individuals. This differs from content analysis and discourse analysis, where a text is the unit of analysis. Closed-ended surveys, like experiments, are typically positivist in orientation and take a more psychological approach to identity. Although both surveys and experiments can be done on elites, it is probably more typical for each of them to be used on the general population. One difference between surveys and experimental designs that is highlighted by the Sylvan and Nadler study is that for survey research you need direct access to the population under study, whereas for experiments you can use a different population and simulate the conditions of the group under study.

The two studies examined here that use closed-ended survey research as part of their methodology are by Metskas, Horowitz, and Sylvan (2006) and Sylvan and Toronto (2004). The use of closed-ended survey methods in these two reports differs: Sylvan and Toronto (2004) mostly relied on data from existing surveys, whereas Metskas, Horowitz, and Sylvan (2006) used a survey constructed by the researchers for the purpose of this study. Sylvan and Toronto (2004) asked how substantial the influence of media coverage is on attitudes toward Palestinians and Israelis and tested two hypotheses on this topic. First, they examined the relationship between media representation and empathy with Palestinians and Israelis. Second, they tested for a relationship between the amount of media coverage of Israeli-Palestinian relations and polarization in the views of Israelis and Palestinians. The independent variables were constructed using text analysis of the amount and valence of media coverage, and the hypotheses test the relationship between these factors and the dependent variables of empathy and blame. The data on the dependent variables were gathered through survey research.

This work builds on Tilly's (2003) conceptions of boundaries; the "us versus them" boundary is useful in thinking about how respondents reacted to media representations of victimization, in part because of the pattern that when people were exposed to pro-Palestinian (or pro-Israeli) news they were more likely to identify with the victim. In this respect, Lamont (2001) provides a useful conception of identity for thinking about how groups define themselves in opposition to each other.

Moreover, while the discussion in the American voting literature on media impact does not always explicitly reference the "identity" literature, it has implications for it. Scholars such as Iyengar and Kinder (1987) and Krosnick and Kinder (1990) assumed that priming amounts to manipulation of citizens without their awareness or consent.[4] According to such arguments, primed individuals are "victims swept away by an avalanche of stories and pictures." In short, the content and direction of news media coverage is seen as influencing public opinion. That position is based on identity not playing a central role in this process. In contrast, Miller and Krosnick (2000: 312) find individuals who manifest priming to be "political experts, who apparently *choose* to rely on a source they trust to help them ... make political judgments" (emphasis in original). They tell us that scholars have uniformly presumed that news media attention to a policy issue increases its impact on presidential job evaluations because news coverage enhances the accessibility of beliefs about the issue in citizens' memories, which automatically increases their impact on relevant judgments. Their research demonstrates that media coverage of an issue does indeed increase the cognitive accessibility of related beliefs, but this does not produce priming. Each of these works relates to identity, with the first group implicitly viewing it as more episodic, and the latter seeing it as more stable.

In their paper, Sylvan and Toronto (2004) included six different measures about feelings toward Palestinians and Israelis. They took these measures from different surveys that used slightly different question wordings. One example of a question the researchers used was from The Ohio Political Survey (TOPS), a telephone survey of a random sample of 800 Ohioans, which asked a number

[4] See Miller and Krosnick 2000: 312, for elaboration on this point.

of questions including, "In the ongoing conflict between Israelis and Palestinians, do you agree with the position of the Palestinian Arabs or the Israeli Jews?" The responses were on a seven-point scale, and the survey was administered at eight different time points beginning in May 2000 and ending in November 2003. They also used a question from a Pew Research Center survey of a random sample of the U.S. population that read, "In the dispute between Israel and the Palestinians, which side do you sympathize with more, Israel or the Palestinians?" That question had three response categories and was asked at four different time points. They also included three questions used by Gallup, and one question from Harris that asked about which group respondents blamed for the conflict.

Sylvan and Toronto found support for the more direct relationship between the "bias" of media representations and empathy in attitudes. They also found that more-biased coverage led to less assignment of blame in the short term, but in the long term did lead to polarized empathy. By using questions from different studies that had slightly different wordings, the authors were able to get at nuances in the concepts of empathy and blame that would not have been present with only one measure. The dependent variable questions asked about agreement with each side of the conflict, empathy toward each side of the conflict, favorability toward each side of the conflict, and blame for each side of the conflict. Each of these concepts taps something slightly different, and the results showed that media coverage affects them differently. Additionally, the authors can test for the effects of question wording on the hypothesized relationship to see if their findings are relatively universal, or if they are dependent on very specific framings of the question. For example, the wording of the Gallup empathy question was, "In the Middle East situation, are your sympathies more with the Israelis or more with the Palestinian Arabs?" The wording of the Pew empathy question was "In the dispute between Israel and the Palestinians, which side do you sympathize with more, Israel or the Palestinians?" The Gallup measure performed somewhat differently than the Pew measure in the study, with more significant results for polarization coming from the Gallup measure. Perhaps the inclusion of the word "Arab" in the Gallup measure, as well as the invocation of the "Middle East" led people to respond differently to that question than they did to the Pew question. Although the authors did not get the opportunity to select these question wordings themselves, the authors could compensate to some extent for that limitation by looking at multiple questions that have been asked.

These different survey questions were also used because multiple iterations of the same question through time were required to test the hypothesized relationships that the authors were examining. Each of these surveys asked the same question with the same wording at multiple time points throughout the period under study. A consistent question wording when comparing survey responses across time is important because it allows researchers to know that the changes in responses that exceed the margin of error are due to changes in opinion rather than differences caused by the effects of the question wording. The authors could then compare the findings for each question over time to each other question over time, to look at how change in opinion over time may have differed depending on how the question was asked.

There are advantages and disadvantages to using existing survey questions when conducting research on the subject of identity. Relying on existing survey data limits the ability of the researcher to control question wording and may mean that certain questions that the researcher would really like to see answered were not asked. Existing surveys, on the other hand, can offer researchers access to data they cannot obtain themselves, including data from earlier time periods and from populations the researcher may not be able to access directly. Existing surveys also often have the advantage of being comparable across time because the organization conducting the survey may ask the same sets of questions at certain intervals of time or to different populations.

In contrast to the paper by Sylvan and Toronto (2004), the project of Metskas, Horowitz, and Sylvan (2006) used a survey designed by the authors and administered to Mizrahi and Ashkenazi Jewish populations in Israel by Israeli interviewers who were native speakers of Hebrew. This survey was thus designed to focus specifically on the questions that the authors wanted to answer. Metskas, Horowitz, and Sylvan (2006) examine music listening patterns of Mizrahi Jews (Israeli Jews from Islamic lands) and Ashkenazi Jews to see whether there is a relationship between listening to Mizrahi music, which is stylistically similar to Arabic music, and being more willing to cooperate politically with Palestinians. In their statistical examination of the closed-ended responses the authors found that more listening to Mizrahi music by Mizrahi Jews correlated with less agreement with negotiation with Palestinians, less agreement with recognizing a Palestinian state, and more agreement with the idea that Palestinian Arabs are Israel's enemy.

The roots of this project come out of ethnographic research that suggests that people see themselves as having multiple identities and that they shift the "center of gravity" with respect to identity depending on social context (Reyes Schramm 1979; Shiloah and Cohen 1985). It also comes out of work in social psychology on multiple identities (Brewer 1999; Roccas 2003). The focus here was on people's needs for differentiation and inclusion in groups, as Brewer outlines in her optimal distinctiveness theory. According to her research, people will shift the salience of their different identities in order to achieve balance between inclusion needs and distinctiveness needs. The project also draws on work in social psychology that addresses how less prototypical members of in-groups understand their identities and relate to other in-group members (Marques et al. 2001). Members of an in-group that are seen as less protypical can feel more pressure to conform with in-group norms because they are at more risk of being rejected by the in-group and thus not having their needs for inclusion met.

In this study the measures of identity gauged subjects' feelings and listening patterns toward Mizrahi music, as well as their level of contact with members of an out-group. The feelings of Mizrahi Jews toward music that is both connected to their group within broader Israeli culture and related to Arabic music offer a way of getting at the complex identity terrain in disputed territories. This study tested to see if these independent variable measures regarding Mizrahi music and contact with Arab others were related to political attitudes toward Palestinians. The closed-ended questions could be used to determine if there was a relationship, and the direction and strength of that relationship, between the cultural or identity variables and variables related to political attitudes, but the closed-ended questions do not shed much light onto how the relationship works or why we see the relationship we see between these variables.

Additionally, this study used both open- and closed-ended survey questions. The closed-ended responses were examined statistically using regression models, whereas the open-ended questions were analyzed using a more discourse analytic approach. Appendix 2 contains an English translation of the survey questionnaire.

Identity in Open-Ended Survey or Interview Methodology

While open- and closed-ended questions may often appear together on the same surveys as they do in Metskas, Horowitz, and Sylvan's (2006) report, the way in which identity is treated in open-ended questions and the purposes that open-ended questions serve in an identity research program are different enough to deserve a separate discussion. The use of open-ended survey questions, like the other methods discussed in this chapter, has both advantages and disadvantages. The primary advantage of open-ended methods is that subjects are able to talk about their identity in their own words, rather than being forced to select from alternatives that they might not feel describe them accurately. Some Mizrahi subjects, for instance, chose closed-ended choices that seemed more hawkish, while offering open-ended responses that noted their affinity with particular "Arab" individuals.

The open-ended approach also allows subjects to explain their rationale for choosing certain descriptors of their identity. These rationales may be different from what the researcher expects and may vary between subjects who put themselves in the same identity category. Access to the thought processes of the subjects filling out the survey in this way can be very helpful for generating new hypotheses, tracing the causal connections in a theory, and refining the arguments of an existing theory.

In the Metskas, Horowitz, and Sylvan (2006) project, closed-ended questions like question 1, which asks respondents to give their opinion of Mizrahi music on a seven-point scale from "don't like at all" to "especially like and admire," if used alone would rely solely on the authors conception of what is included in Mizrahi music. It creates a category known as "Mizrahi music," which may not be what the respondents are thinking of when they answer the question. From a few of the open-ended questions in the study, it was clear that there is in fact a difference in what is included in the category of Mizrahi music between people who like the music and people who claim that they do not. These differences came out especially in question 5, which asked people to classify certain singers as Mizrahi or Israeli and indicate whether they listen to them or not. Subjects who claimed not to like or listen to Mizrahi music would typically classify two of the singers, Tipex and Yehuda Poliker, as Israeli rather than Mizrahi and indicate that they listen to those singers. The differences in the preconstructed notion of Mizrahi music tapped by question 1 and the notion of it held by respondents were also evident in question 4, which asked subjects to define Mizrahi music and provided a space for them to write whatever they wanted. Similar differences emerged between preconstructed scholarly ideas coming out of the closed-ended answer to question 15, about whether Palestinian Arabs were Israel's enemies, and the open-ended responses to the same question. In the open-ended responses many respondents drew distinctions between a small group of the leadership that they considered enemies and the rest of the Palestinian people who were described by many as regular people who wanted to go about their lives.[5] These responses that differentiated a small group as the enemy came from people who circled a wide range of answer choices in the closed-ended portion of the question. That

[5] An example of this sentiment is from one respondent who circled a "2" in the closed-ended portion, indicating a low agreement with the idea that Palestinian Arabs are Israel's enemies. In the open-ended portion the person wrote: "The historical facts are speaking for themselves, beginning with the war of independence through the Khartoum conference, etc. Still, it appears to me that the 'enemies' are mostly the leadership and not the simple person in the street who wants to live his life in peace." This response is particularly interesting because it shows the contrasts in the person's own thinking about whether Palestinians are the enemy.

makes it clear that there is something in the conception many respondents have of the Palestinian out-group that is not being captured very well by the pre-constructed notion of the enemy in the closed-ended portion of the question.

The main disadvantage of open-ended questions, as compared to closed-ended, is that systematically analyzing a large number of questions or a large sample of respondents is very difficult. How does one compare the responses different subjects make to an open-ended question? In Metskas, Horowitz, and Sylvan's (2006) study, the results of the closed-ended analysis were used to create a subsample of surveys for which the authors examined the open-ended results. The authors selected subjects whose responses were prototypical of the trend that was identified in the closed-ended analysis and then looked at their open-ended answers to see the rationales they gave for their responses. For example, the trend showed that respondents who listened more to Mizrahi music were more likely to circle a response that said Palestinians are Israel's enemies. By looking systematically at the open-ended answers of respondents who fell into that category, we were able to better determine that rationales behind their responses, because they were obligated to elaborate, as opposed to simply making a "multiple choice." The open-ended responses presented different reasons that subjects give for their views. Because the respondents we looked at had closed-ended responses consistent with the correlations that emerged, we could examine the reasons being given by subjects whose views mirrored the overall trend in the results.

Like Metskas, Horowitz, and Sylvan (2006), Charlick-Paley and Sylvan (2000) also rely in part on interviews of subjects. These interviews were used as part of the data in the discourse analysis that the authors conducted, which is discussed in a later section of this chapter. When analyzed systematically, open-ended survey questions and interviews can be exceptionally useful to researchers, especially when the research task involves tracing the logic of theory, refining a theory, or generating new hypotheses.

Content Analysis and Textual Analysis for Studying Identity

Content and text analysis methods take a somewhat different approach to the study of identity than the methods that this chapter has explored so far. In all of the previous methods people are asked questions or subjected to certain conditions, and their reactions are measured. They all require either direct access to the subjects of the study themselves or a simulation using other participants. Content analysis and other textual analysis methods rely on interpreting and coding texts in order to tease out the identities that they represent. There is variation between text analysis methods in terms of how much attention is paid to the authors of the texts as subjects, as opposed to seeing the texts themselves as the object of analysis independent of their authorship. A wide range of works fits within the category of content or textual analysis. The two works discussed in this section rely on what might be termed a more quantitative form of text analysis. Discourse analysis also relies on the analysis of texts; however, the way in which texts are used in discourse analysis differs from content analysis.

Sylvan and Toronto (2004) use content analysis to create measures of media coverage on the issue of Israeli-Palestinian relations. They measure the amount of media coverage of the issue, as well as how the two sides are represented in the coverage. The authors used a sample of news transcripts from nine sources, including four newspapers and five television news networks. They then constructed two measures of the amount of media coverage given to the issue in each of the forty-seven months from January 2000 to November 2003. One measure was the daily mean number of articles on the issue, which was constructed by averaging the number of articles on the subject per day by the number of days in the month. The second measure captured the amount of time that the news outlets devoted to the issue. This measure was created by putting all of the articles for each month into a word-processing document and then deleting all of the parts of each file that did not include coverage of Israelis and Palestinians. Because the formatting was consistent across the files, the resulting number of pages could be compared from month to month to determine the amount of attention the media paid to Israeli-Palestinian relations.

Unlike the measures of the amount of coverage, which count up the number of articles or amount of text, the media representation variable used by Sylvan and Toronto (2004) is a coding of the content of the articles on a five-point scale. The article is coded as presenting Israelis as victims, presenting Palestinians as victims, or presenting a neutral view. When doing this kind of text coding, it is important to have clear replicable coding rules and, if there are multiple coders, to do testing for intercoder reliability. In the case of this study, the authors created a variable that indicated whether they felt that a text clearly fell into one of the categories and then ran tests to make sure that the articles for which the coding was clear were not statistically different from those for which the coding was less clear. Because there was no statistically significant difference between the articles that the coders determined clearly fell into one category or another and those for which the coding was less clear, they included all of the articles in the analysis. Appendix 3 contains the coding guidelines that were used to create the representation and clarity variables.

Sylvan, Grove, and Martinson (2005) also use text analysis as the method for generating the independent variables. However, unlike Sylvan and Toronto's (2004) study, in which the dependent variables of empathy and blame were more connected to identity than the independent variables of media coverage and representation, Sylvan, Grove, and Martinson (2005) use independent variables as the identity measures. The authors examine statements of leaders representing multiple actors in the Israeli-Palestinian and Northern Ireland contexts. The authors coded speeches made by Israeli, Palestinian, Northern Ireland Nationalist, and Northern Ireland Unionist leaders across the political spectrum for three different variables that are all aspects of problem representation: (1) centrality of enemy image, an ordinal scale human-coded for references to the importance of seeing the "other side" as an enemy; and (2) in-group or (3) out-group inclusivity, four scales based again on human coding of leaders' speeches and incorporating concepts from social psychology. The concepts of centrality of enemy image and in-group and out-group inclusivity are the strategies for measuring identity. The purpose of the study was to examine the effects of leaders' identity-related pronouncements on the actions of members of their community, as well as the actions of members of the opposing community.

The authors selected speeches, interviews, and press releases from leaders representing different positions on both sides of the Northern Ireland conflict and the Palestinian-Israeli conflict. For example, the leaders whose speeches were included on the Israeli side of the Israeli-Palestinian case were Shimon Peres and Ehud Barak representing the Israeli Labor Party and Benyamin Netanyahu and Ariel Sharon representing the Likud Party. In the Palestinian-Israeli case these texts came from the Foreign Broadcast Information Service (FBIS)/World News Connection (WNC). The authors also selected a time period for analysis, January 1995 to September 1999, when external structural factors remained relatively constant, so that they knew that variation from month to month in the study was not likely to be caused by structural factors. The dependent variables in this analysis were conflictual and cooperative actions taken by either side in each case toward the other side. These variables were constructed using events data from Reuters Newswire analyzed by the KEDS-TABARI program that, using computerized parsing, identifies the actor, the target of the action, and the type of action taken (Gerner et al. 1994). A composite value on each of the independent variables for each actor whose speeches were analyzed was created for each month. Those monthly values on the independent variables were then put into a regression analysis with monthly composite values of the conflictual or cooperative actions taken by either side as the dependent variables.[6]

---

[6] A separate value was generated for actions depending on who initiated them. For each month there is a score for Israeli actions toward Palestinians, and a separate score for Palestinian actions toward Israelis. The analysis was run both by looking at speeches and actions in the same month and by looking at how speeches in one month related to actions in the subsequent month.

The analysis produced some striking results. Specifically, these include the strong relationship between Israeli actions and the identity content of prior and current speeches by Palestinian leaders. In fact, this relationship was much stronger than the relationship between Israeli actions and the content of Israeli leaders' speeches. Similarly, Palestinian actions are found to have a clear relationship to the identity content of prior and current speeches by Israeli leaders, much more so than the speeches given by Palestinian leaders. Additionally, in-group and out-group inclusivity are more significant predictors of actions than the centrality of the enemy image. For Northern Ireland, the same two themes prevail, although not quite as strongly.

The central focus on coding in-group and out-group inclusivity and exclusivity as a measure of identity, which is used by Sylvan, Grove, and Martinson (2005), is consistent with Brewer's (2003) analysis, while the concept of centrality of enemy image is drawn from the work of Herrmann et al. (1997). For Brewer, in-group and out-group distinctions do not automatically lead to out-group derogation, just in-group favoring. This assumption is consistent with the operationalization of the centrality of enemy image variable and the in-group and out-group inclusivity variables. In addition, Tilly (2003) speaks to the idea that political entrepreneurs can create boundaries, but he does not discuss whether this occurs because a group is reacting to its own or the other's political elites. Tilly, therefore, can be seen as consistent with the treatment of identity in this work. These concepts are similar to what Chapter 1 of this volume would term the relational content of identity.

Because of the focus on measuring identity, it is worth explaining the variable coding in more detail. The "centrality of enemy image" variable is measured as an ordinal scale, with one being a code of low centrality of enemy image and five signifying a high centrality of enemy image. The primary concentration here is the centrality of the image of the other major actor, for example, the image that Palestinians have of Israelis and vice versa. Our empirically based assumption is that the enemy image is the most salient of the images that such scholars as Herrmann et al. (1997) discuss; however, despite its salience, the predominance of this image varies. This taps an aspect of relational identity, by looking at how focused leaders are on the conflict with the relevant outgroup.

The in-group and out-group inclusivity and exclusivity variables are based on the rationale that competing leaders often group the same people into different categories and define "similar" situations in different ways. Indeed, political competition is, at its core, a battle to delimit the kinds of groups that make up a society, the important bases of identification, and how certain peoples are similar or different. For example, the identities of the in-group depicted by nationalist leaders may be everyone in Northern Ireland, and/or Catholics, and/or nationalists, and/or republicans, and/or Irish, and/or Europeans, et cetera. Depending on the way the leaders use these labels for the in-group and the way they use these and other labels for relevant out-groups, one can get a picture of how inclusive or exclusive the leader is from the standpoint of Northern Ireland society. A leader arguing that "Nationalists" share a common "Northern Ireland" identity with Unionists would be considered more inclusive than a leader arguing that Nationalists share an "Irish" identity and that Unionists are foreign. Texts were coded on a two-point scale for how the leader describes the main in-group (in-group inclusivity) and a three-point scale for how the leader describes the principal out-group (out-group inclusivity), assigning a higher number when there are no splits in the leader's description of the groups. Getting a sense of who leaders consider as members of their group, and how permeable the boundaries are between their group and other groups is very important to understanding identity. In Sylvan, Grove, and Martinson's (2005) study, the authors expected that the more leaders described their in-groups as a unified whole, the more conflict we should see, because the in-group is a unified "us" against the other "them." On the other hand, the more leaders described their whole society as a unified whole, meaning they were inclusive of out-group members as well as in-group members, the less conflict we should see because leaders are sending the message that there is not a clear boundary between "us" and "them."

This kind of text coding can be very helpful for researchers trying to uncover how elites publicly represent their conceptions of who is a member of the group, and what is important to the group. One trade-off with this method is that you may not be getting at the actual opinions of the leaders but rather their public presentations. For many research designs this problem is not serious, because the concern of the research, as with Sylvan, Grove, and Martinson's (2005) analysis, is how other people act in response to leaders' pronouncements about identity groups. What is important in this kind of design is what the texts say about identities and how people react to those statements rather than whether the leader really believes what they are saying. For questions that try to trace the identity conceptualizations of leaders to the actions of those same leaders, this issue of public presentation versus private opinion may present more of a problem.

In the study by Sylvan, Grove, and Martinson (2005), intercoder reliability measures found 77 percent agreement among the coders on average for the Northern Ireland data. For the Israeli-Palestinian data, they report an intercoder reliability score for each of the independent variables. The intercoder reliability was 62 percent for the centrality of enemy image variable, 75 percent for the in-group inclusivity or exclusivity variable, and 81 percent for the out-group inclusivity or exclusivity variable. These measures were created by having all of the coders code a sample subset of the articles to be coded for the study and then calculating the percentage of the coding decisions on which the coders all came to the same decision. Typically if intercoder reliability scores are too low, then the coders will work to improve them by examining the cases on which they differ and making the coding rules more clear. It may be advantageous to set a percentage of agreement that must be achieved in the intercoder reliability testing and to continue to improve the coding scheme and the training of the coders until that threshold is reached. In the social sciences, 80 percent is a typical acceptable standard for intercoder reliability, with a 70 percent standard applied to research considered exploratory. In the case of the study, all of the measures except for the centrality of the enemy image measure met the 70 percent reliability standard. This means that there is more reason to question the validity of the results for the centrality of enemy image findings than the inclusivity and exclusivity findings. The findings are significant, but further study should be done to ensure that the results being generated by the centrality of enemy image codings are tapping the construct consistently.

Discourses as Measures of Identity

Discourse analysis is another method that analyzes texts, although the type of analysis conducted is more qualitative and interpretive than that used in the content analysis method discussed previously. Similar to the work reported by Sylvan, Grove, and Martinson (2005), this type of analysis also focuses on the public presentations of identities rather than the private opinions of the elites being studied. The central idea in this kind of analysis is that stories – or, in psychological terms, schemas – that people use to explain the world are a key to understanding their identities and that changes in those stories correspond with changes in the identity definitions of subjects. Charlick-Paley and Sylvan (2000) apply this method to the puzzle of how Russian and French military officers justify their new roles (related to identity) in a condition of loss of empire. This particular operationalization of "story" is rooted primarily in the psychological work of Pennington and Hastie (1986). This manner of categorizing stories decomposes the narrative structure of interviews of Russian and French military officers into the categories of initiating events relationship between actors, goals, actions, and lessons.

An example of a single story can be found in Appendix 4 of this chapter.

The measurement of identity in this piece shares a theoretical foundation with the work of Hopf (2002, and Chapter 10 in this volume) and Brubaker, Loveman, and Stamatov (2004). Hopf's attention to narrative in his analysis of

Soviet and Russian identities is consistent with Charlick-Paley and Sylvan's focus on stories, although the work examined here focuses more on elites (military officers). Charlick-Paley and Sylvan measure identity in a manner consistent with some of the arguments Rogers Brubaker highlights about how people interpret, define, and redefine their experiences. The militaries in this piece had to make sense of a new situation, the loss of empire, and one in which they risked losing their sense of purpose. Some of the officers studied in the piece created two different sets of narratives, one more optimistic and the other more pessimistic. It can be argued that the identity of these militaries were tied to the purpose of protecting the empire, and thus new stories had to be created to deal with this changing identity. Brubaker, Loveman, and Stamatov (2004) tell us about the role schemas serve in understanding identity, asserting that "they are posited to account for evidence – experimental, observational, and historical – about how people perceive and interpret the world and about how knowledge is acquired, stored, recalled, activated, and *extended to new domains.*"

One of the conclusions of Charlick-Paley and Sylvan is that a key element that changes in the postimperial stories is the nature of the relationships that officers describe between the military, the state, and society. As they perceive the world to be changing, military officers initially make modifications in their stories to try to retain the baseline relationship of unity between these three groups. In short, these stories are serving to situate the identity of military officers in the world that they see. The stories have served as a vehicle to capture the officers' expression of identity.

The discourse analysis used in this piece was conducted through a type of structured, focused comparison case study. Although the rules for selecting a set of cases are beyond the scope of this discussion,[7] the selection of sources within a case is an important consideration specifically for the discourse analysis method. In the Soviet case discussed by Charlick-Paley and Sylvan (2000), the primary source materials were a set of Soviet journals and newspapers relevant to defense policy. Within those sources, the authors limited the articles they included to those written by officers in the military at the middle level or above. The initial body of documents included all such articles that seemed to address the research question. The primary source documents were then skimmed, and those providing information that was directly relevant to the research questions were analyzed more deeply. The authors also included a sample of interviews of military officers and supplemented these primary sources with particularly relevant secondary source material.

---

[7] For a thorough and clear discussion of case selection, we recommend George and Bennett 2005.

The construction of the stories used a modified framework proposed by Pennington and Hastie (1986). This framework included events, relationships between actors, goals, actions taken, and actions advocated or lessons for the future. The stories that were constructed using these templates were composites, made up of the individual stories of many different military officers. Creating these composites allowed the authors to identify what seemed to be the dominant story or discourse, as well as any important counternarratives that might exist. The composites were created by coding each of the stories individually and then looking for those which had the main story elements in common. If two accounts differed on any one of the story elements, they were treated as distinct stories. The final analysis included only stories that had three or more influential proponents. This method allowed for the inclusion of the dominant discourse, as well as any major counterdiscourses.

One difference between this method and the survey and experimental approaches discussed in this chapter is that, although it starts with individuals, this method is focused on texts as a unit of analysis, not on uncovering the identities of individuals. Charlick-Paley and Sylvan make a point of noting in this article that they are not trying to uncover the personal beliefs of these military officers but are interested in the public arguments the officers make. In this sense this article seeks to uncover the identities of the militaries as institutions as promulgated through the words of their corps of officers rather than the individual identities of the officers themselves. This approach is thus somewhat less cognitive than the others discussed here, even though the tools that were used to create the discourse analysis draw on schema theory and other concepts in cognitive psychology.

One advantage of measuring identity through this type of coding is that it allows subjects to express their identities within a broad, narrative template. This, again, is consistent with the approach taken by Hopf. The researcher does not preordain categories of identity but allows the subject to express her own conception of identity. A disadvantage is the labor-intensive nature of the enterprise. The interview component of the research is more likely to work for elites than masses, because it is unrealistic to interview a very large group. The textual analysis component could be applied to different types of texts, including those in the popular press, government reports, or alternative sources. Selecting texts and interview subjects requires detailed theory and knowledge of the case under study. The selection criteria for the texts examined must be theoretically grounded and clearly explained in order for this method to be replicable by other researchers.

Reflecting on the Trade-offs

Which measurement strategies are best suited to particular types of puzzles? There are clear trade-offs between the approaches discussed in this chapter, perhaps the most significant being whether one seeks initially to specify categories of identity empirically or one preordains identity categories and then seeks to measure their impact or strength. From our perspective, a pure inductive approach, where one examines texts or other evidence in an effort to initially form categories of identity, is something of a fiction. Each of us has ideas in our heads from multiple sources including academic discourses and popular media that shape our initial conceptions. Therefore, it is impossible to be purely inductive. This does not mean that there are not some clear advantages to initially avoiding any specific identity categorization scheme. However, if we quickly reify the "new" categories we create in this manner, there is little difference between such an exercise and preordained categories.

Turning to a direct comparison of trade-offs between approaches to measuring identity, Table 3.2 presents a comparison of the five methodologies.

Experimental treatments are less applicable for elites but quite applicable for investigating puzzles that seek to isolate the impact of particular specifications of an identity. Discourses, on the other hand, have greater potential to be applicable to the study of elites, and their role should be more for theory development rather than for testing. Text analytic approaches that focus on such cognitive variables as centrality of enemy image and in-group and out-group inclusivity are best suited for elites (where texts are plentiful) but are likely to be confined to testing conceptions of identity that are cognitively based. Surveys that concentrate on closed-ended responses are most often applied to nonelite subjects and are best for testing prespecified identity conceptions. Finally, open-ended surveys can also be used for nonelite subjects, but probably for smaller sample sizes than can be studied in closed-ended surveys. Similar to discourse analysis, open-ended surveys have advantages in identity theory development.

For many identity puzzles, multimethod approaches are likely to be quite helpful. This preference for multimethod approaches is based in part on an aversion to quick reification and a disbelief in the existence of pure induction but, more importantly, on the view that each approach to measuring identity has clear strengths and weaknesses. In the studies used to illustrate the methods here, the researchers have relied on a combination of methods: Metskas, Horowitz, and Sylvan (2006) use open- and closed-ended survey questions; Sylvan and Nadler (2005) use experiments and supplement them with surveys of Israelis; Sylvan and Toronto (2004) use closed-ended survey questions for the dependent variables, and the coding of texts for the independent variables;

TABLE 3.2. *Trade-offs between Approaches to Measuring Identity*

Measurement Approach	Goal of Research for Which Approach Is Ideal	Focus on Elites vs. General Population	Open-Ended vs. Preformed Conceptualization of Identity	Necessity of Access to Subjects	View of Interpretation	Degree of Emphasis on Social and Psychological Bases of Identity
Experiments	Refining theory by isolating factors in a controlled environment	Could work for either: depends on level of theorizing and characteristics of subjects of experiment	Preformed categories necessary to structure experimental protocol	Not an obstacle, but external validity likely to be a concern if not used in combination with another technique	Taken by themselves, experiments can be positivist	Emphasizes psychological representations of identity
Closed-ended surveys	Testing theory that involves individuals and their attitudes; establishing relationships domain	General population	Preformed	Direct access a necessity	Positivist stances are common here	Emphasize psychological
Open-ended surveys		General population	Open-ended concept of identity more common here	Direct access a necessity	More interpretivist than closed-ended surveys	Applicable to either psychological or sociological underpinnings

Text (content) analysis	Testing preformed concepts of identity in the domain of the texts	Usually elites	Preformed	While no direct access necessary, texts must be available	Less interpretivist than narrative/story analysis	More frequently focused on psychological bases, but consistent with either
Discourse analysis	Forming initial bases for theory	As long as texts are available, either is reasonable (used with elites in example here)	Can work with either, but comparative advantage with respect to open ended	Must have texts that are relevant to chosen task	Interpretivist approach is central here	More frequently focused on sociological underpinnings, but consistent with either

Charlick-Paley and Sylvan (2000) use interviews and textual analysis to construct the discourse analysis; and Sylvan, Grove, and Martinson (2005) use text
coding for the independent variables and events data for the dependent variables. These studies put multiple methods into a dialogue in an effort to gain
insight into identity and its role. Other multimethod approaches can address
different facets of identity to gain insight into research questions. By
compensating for the weaknesses of any one method with the strengths of
another method, and using somewhat more inductive methods in the theory
development phases of research, then taking the insights from that theory to
develop appropriate preconstructed measures of identity for testing with experimental, closed-ended survey, and text analysis methods in later phases of
research, scholars can improve their measurement strategies for studying the
complex roles identity plays in political science.

APPENDIX I: EXPERIMENTAL MATERIALS FROM SYLVAN AND
NADLER (2005)

The background materials given to the subjects in each of the eight conditions
are included in this appendix. The information identifying each condition in
brackets here was not given to subjects.

Introduction

Thank you for participating in this foreign policy role-playing exercise. Please
read all material carefully and take your time in both understanding the material and answering the questions.

   In the first phase of the exercise, you will read some background information. It will tell you about who you are and some of your personal background.
You will then be asked a few questions about your impressions of the groups in
this simulation. After those questions, you will be asked to read a news story
describing a situation which involves these groups.

   After reading the news story, you will be asked to answer a series of questions about your reaction to the situation that has been described.

   Again, take your time during this exercise. For some of the questions, you
will be asked to respond in an open-ended manner. Your answers should be as
detailed as possible. Please give your best answer to each question without
conferring with other participants.

   We appreciate your participation in this exercise. We will try to tell you
more about the overall exercise later in this academic term.

[Palestinian Arab, Victim, Low Commitment]

PLEASE READ THE MATERIAL ON THIS PAGE VERY CAREFULLY. IT GIVES YOU THE BACKGROUND THAT YOU WILL NEED TO ANSWER THE QUESTIONS LATER IN THIS EXERCISE.

Since its creation in 1948, Israel has been the location of conflict between Palestinian Arabs and Israeli Jews. Early Zionist leaders argued that the return of the Jews to their ancient homeland would bring the benefits of modernization to the area. Palestinian Arabs, who also have ancestral claims to the area, saw Israel as the encroachment of foreigners supported by the major powers, including the United States and the Soviet Union. Fighting broke out almost immediately and has continued intermittently since.

Imagine that you are a Palestinian Arab living in Jerusalem. For generations your family has lived in Palestine, regarding Jerusalem as a holy city of Islam. Al Aqsa Mosque in Jerusalem, for instance, is the third holiest site in Islam. In 1947 the 650,000 Jews in Palestine owned only 7% of the land. When Israel was created the following year, they stole 77% of the land, leaving many of the 1.2 million Palestinian Arabs without homes. Many of your relatives were among the 725,000 refugees who left the area that became Israel. Arabs who remained in Palestine are denied democratic participation and kept in poverty because Israel dominates political and economic decisions. Despite a number of United Nations resolutions calling for repatriation of the refugees, Israel has refused to permit it. Additionally world public opinion is biased against Palestinian Arabs due to successful propaganda in Israel, the United States, and elsewhere portraying Arabs as religious fanatics and savage terrorists. Because of this, there is little international support for dealing with the problems that Palestinian Arabs face, and Israel receives significant political, economic, and military aid from the West.

Though you are a Palestinian Arab, you realize that you have many other roles. Your activities at work, in school, help socially define who you are at least as much as your ethnic heritage. Your political attitudes are shaped by these multiple identities and you reject extreme positions. For example, you recently saw a well-publicized television show characterizing Palestinian Arabs as terrorists. You are disappointed that both Israeli Jews and Palestinian Arabs continue to take such extreme positions.

[Palestinian Arab, Nonvictim, High Commitment]

PLEASE READ THE MATERIAL ON THIS PAGE VERY CAREFULLY. IT GIVES YOU THE BACKGROUND THAT YOU WILL NEED TO ANSWER THE QUESTIONS LATER IN THIS EXERCISE.

Since its creation in 1948, Israel has been the location of conflict between Palestinian Arabs and Israeli Jews. Early Zionist leaders argued that the return of the Jews to their ancient homeland would bring the benefits of modernization to the area. Palestinian Arabs, who also have ancestral claims to the area, saw Israel as the encroachment of foreigners supported by the major powers, including the United States and the Soviet Union. Fighting broke out almost immediately and has continued intermittently since.

Imagine that you are a Palestinian Arab living in Jerusalem. For generations, your family has lived in Palestine, regarding Jerusalem as a holy city of Islam. After all, Al Aqsa Mosque in Jerusalem is the third holiest site in Islam. In 1948, a Jewish state was created in Israel, and in 1967 its borders were expanded as a result of a war with Arab states.

You feel very proud to be a Palestinian and your role as a Palestinian Arab is extremely important to you. You participate in political and social activities with other Palestinian Arabs. You take threats made to Palestinian Arabs personally. For example, you recently saw a well-publicized television show characterizing Palestinian Arabs as heartless terrorists. You consider this as an attack against yourself as well as your friends and family. You are furious at this biased misrepresentation.

[Palestinian Arab, Nonvictim, Low Commitment]

PLEASE READ THE MATERIAL ON THIS PAGE VERY CAREFULLY. IT GIVES YOU THE BACKGROUND THAT YOU WILL NEED TO ANSWER THE QUESTIONS LATER IN THIS EXERCISE.

Since its creation in 1948, Israel has been the location of conflict between Palestinian Arabs and Israeli Jews. Early Zionist leaders argued that the return of the Jews to their ancient homeland would bring the benefits of modernization to the area. Palestinian Arabs, who also have ancestral claims to the area saw Israel as the encroachment of foreigners supported by the major powers, including the United States and the Soviet Union. Fighting broke out almost immediately and has continued intermittently since.

Imagine that you are a Palestinian Arab living in Jerusalem. For generations, your family has lived in Palestine, regarding Jerusalem as a holy city of Islam. After all, Al Aqsa Mosque in Jerusalem is the third holiest site in Islam. In 1948, a Jewish state was created in Israel, and in 1967 its borders were expanded as a result of a war with Arab states.

Though you are a Palestinian Arab, you realize that you have many other roles. Your activities at work, in school, and socially define who you are at least as much as your ethnic heritage. Your political attitudes are shaped by these multiple identities and you reject extreme positions. For example, you recently saw a well-publicized television show characterizing Palestinian Arabs as terrorists. You are disappointed that both Israeli Jews and Palestinian Arabs continue to take such extreme positions.

[Palestinian Arab, Victim, High Commitment]

PLEASE READ THE MATERIAL ON THIS PAGE VERY CAREFULLY. IT GIVES YOU THE BACKGROUND THAT YOU WILL NEED TO ANSWER THE QUESTIONS LATER IN THIS EXERCISE.

Since its creation in 1948, Israel has been the location of conflict between Palestinian Arabs and Israeli Jews. Early Zionist leaders argued that the return of the Jews to their ancient homeland would bring the benefits of modernization to the area. Palestinian Arabs, who also have ancestral claims to the area, saw Israel as the encroachment of foreigners supported by the major powers, including the United States and the Soviet Union. Fighting broke out almost immediately and has continued intermittently since.

Imagine that you are a Palestinian Arab living in Jerusalem. For generations your family has lived in Palestine, regarding Jerusalem as a holy city of Islam. Al Aqsa Mosque in Jerusalem, for instance, is the third holiest site in Islam. In 1947 the 650,000 Jews in Palestine owned only 7% of the land. When Israel was created the following year, they stole 77% of the land, leaving many of the 1.2 million Palestinian Arabs without homes. Many of your relatives were among the 725,000 refugees who left the area that became Israel. Arabs who remained in Palestine are denied democratic participation and kept in poverty because Israel dominates political and economic decisions. Despite a number of United Nations resolutions calling for repatriation of the refugees, Israel has refused to permit it. Additionally world public opinion is biased against Palestinian Arabs due to successful propaganda in Israel, the United States, and elsewhere portraying Arabs as religious fanatics and savage terrorists. Because of this, there is little international support for dealing with the problems that Palestinian Arabs face, and Israel receives significant political, economic, and military aid from the West.

You feel very proud to be a Palestinian and your role as a Palestinian Arab is extremely important to you. You participate in political and social activities with other Palestinian Arabs. You take threats made to Palestinian Arabs personally. For example, you recently saw a well-publicized television show characterizing Palestinian Arabs as heartless terrorists. You consider this as an attack against yourself as well as your friends and family. You are furious at this biased misrepresentation.

[Israeli Jew, Victim, Low Commitment]

PLEASE READ THE MATERIAL ON THIS PAGE VERY CAREFULLY. IT GIVES YOU THE BACKGROUND THAT YOU WILL NEED TO ANSWER THE QUESTIONS LATER IN THIS EXERCISE.

Since its creation in 1948, Israel has been the location of conflict between Palestinian Arabs and Israeli Jews. Early Zionist leaders argued that the return of the Jews to their ancient homeland would bring the benefits of modernization to the area. Palestinian Arabs, who also have ancestral claims to the area, saw Israel as the encroachment of foreigners supported by the major powers, including the United States and the Soviet Union. Fighting broke out almost immediately and has continued intermittently since.

Imagine that you are an Israeli Jew living in Jerusalem. Throughout their history, the Jewish people have been the victims of persecution and genocide. Your family has felt the impacts of these evils as your grandparents escaped the Holocaust in Europe by fleeing to the United States shortly before World War II and many of your relatives were murdered by the Nazis. When Israel was created the following year, your grandparents were among those who immigrated, seeking to build a Jewish homeland based on the ideals of democracy and human rights. From the beginning, this effort has been opposed by Arabs, both in Palestine and throughout the Middle East. They have fought several wars against Israel during its 52-year history, and terrorist attacks and other forms of violence and aggression continue, despite efforts of the Israeli government to compromise.

Though you are an Israeli Jew, you realize that you have many other roles. Your activities at work, in school, and socially define who you are at least as much as your ethnic heritage. Your political attitudes are shaped by these multiple identities and you reject extreme positions. For example, you recently saw a well-publicized television show characterizing Israeli Jews as the inhumane oppressors of the Palestinian people, stealing their land and driving them from their homes. You are disappointed that both Israeli Jews and Palestinian Arabs continue to take such extreme positions.

[Israeli Jew, Nonvictim, High Commitment]

PLEASE READ THE MATERIAL ON THIS PAGE VERY CAREFULLY. IT GIVES YOU THE BACKGROUND THAT YOU WILL NEED TO ANSWER THE QUESTIONS LATER IN THIS EXERCISE.

Since its creation in 1948, Israel has been the location of conflict between Palestinian Arabs and Israeli Jews. Early Zionist leaders argued that the return of the Jews to their ancient homeland would bring the benefits of modernization to the area. Palestinian Arabs, who also have ancestral claims to the area, saw Israel as the encroachment of foreigners supported by the major powers, including the United States and the Soviet Union. Fighting broke out almost immediately and has continued intermittently since.

Imagine that you are an Israeli Jew living in Jerusalem. Your grandparents escaped the Holocaust in Europe by fleeing to the United States shortly before World War II. When Israel was created the following year, they were among those who immigrated, seeking to build a Jewish homeland based on the ideals of democracy and human rights. You have lived through three wars against Israel's Arab neighbors.

You feel very proud to be Jewish and your role as an Israeli Jew is extremely important to you. You participate in political and social activities with other Israeli Jews. You take threats made to Israeli Jews personally. For example, you recently saw a well-publicized television show characterizing Israeli Jews as the inhumane oppressors of the Palestinian people, stealing their land and driving them from their homes. You consider this as an attack against yourself as well as your friends and family. You are furious at this biased misrepresentation.

[Israeli Jew, Nonvictim, Low Commitment]

PLEASE READ THE MATERIAL ON THIS PAGE VERY CAREFULLY. IT GIVES YOU THE BACKGROUND THAT YOU WILL NEED TO ANSWER THE QUESTIONS LATER IN THIS EXERCISE.

Since its creation in 1948, Israel has been the location of conflict between Palestinian Arabs and Israeli Jews. Early Zionist leaders argued that the return of the Jews to their ancient homeland would bring the benefits of modernization to the area. Palestinian Arabs, who also have ancestral claims to the area saw Israel as the encroachment of foreigners supported by the major powers, including the United States and the Soviet Union. Fighting broke out almost immediately and has continued intermittently since.

Imagine that you are an Israeli Jew living in Jerusalem. Your grandparents escaped the Holocaust in Europe by fleeing to the United States shortly before World War II. When Israel was created the following year, they were among those who immigrated, seeking to build a Jewish homeland based on the ideals of democracy and human rights. You have lived through three wars against Israel's Arab neighbors.

Though you are an Israeli Jew, you realize that you have many other roles. Your activities at work, in school, and socially define who you are at least as much as your ethnic heritage. Your political attitudes are shaped by these multiple identities and you reject extreme positions. For example, you recently saw a well-publicized television show characterizing Israeli Jews as the inhumane oppressors of the Palestinian people, stealing their land and driving them from their homes. You are disappointed that both Israeli Jews and Palestinian Arabs continue to take such extreme positions.

[Israeli Jew, Victim, High Commitment]

PLEASE READ THE MATERIAL ON THIS PAGE VERY CAREFULLY. IT GIVES YOU THE BACKGROUND THAT YOU WILL NEED TO ANSWER THE QUESTIONS LATER IN THIS EXERCISE.

Since its creation in 1948, Israel has been the location of conflict between Palestinian Arabs and Israeli Jews. Early Zionist leaders argued that the return of the Jews to their ancient homeland would bring the benefits of modernization to the area. Palestinian Arabs, who also have ancestral claims to the area, saw Israel as the encroachment of foreigners supported by the major powers, including the United States and the Soviet Union. Fighting broke out almost immediately and has continued intermittently since.

Imagine that you are an Israeli Jew living in Jerusalem. Throughout their history, the Jewish people have been the victims of persecution and genocide. Your family has felt the impacts of these evils as your grandparents escaped the Holocaust in Europe by fleeing to the United States shortly before World War II and many of your relatives were murdered by the Nazis. When Israel was created the following year, your grandparents were among those who immigrated, seeking to build a Jewish homeland based on the ideals of democracy and human rights. From the beginning, this effort has been opposed by Arabs, both in Palestine and throughout the Middle East. They have fought several wars against Israel during its 52-year history, and terrorist attacks and other forms of violence and aggression continue, despite efforts of the Israeli government to compromise.

You feel very proud to be Jewish and your role as an Israeli Jew is extremely important to you. You participate in political and social activities with other Israeli Jews. You take threats made to Israeli Jews personally. For example, you recently saw a well-publicized television show characterizing Israeli Jews as the inhumane oppressors of the Palestinian people, stealing their land and driving them from their homes. You consider this as an attack against yourself as well as your friends and family. You are furious at this biased misrepresentation.

APPENDIX 2: ENGLISH TRANSLATION OF QUESTIONNAIRE FROM
METSKAS, HOROWITZ, AND SYLVAN (2006)

Dear Sir/ Madam,

We seek your help and your participation in a survey concerning the diverse cultures in Israel. The research is an initiative of The Ohio State University, in Columbus, Ohio, U.S.A. In the survey you will be asked to consider two topics, music and politics. Your personal opinion and attitudes are important and will contribute greatly to the advancement of the research. We promise that your confidentiality will be honored. Your name will not be documented nor reported. For convenience, the questions are asked in the masculine form, but we want to emphasize that they refer equally to both genders.

1. What is your opinion and sentiment toward Mizrahi music? (Please answer according to the following scale: 1- Don't like at all, up to 7- Especially admire and like)
   Don't like at all. Especially admire and like.
   1 2 3 4 5 6 7
2. Explain why you like or do not like Mizrahi Music.
   _____
   _____
   _____

3. When do you listen to Mizrahi music?
   Never. Maybe once a month. Once a week. Approximately every day. All the time.
   How much time do you listen to Mizrahi music (in percentages 0%– 100%) from your total listening time to music in general? ___%
4. How do you define "Mizrahi music"?
   _____
   _____

5. From the list below, who are the singers you listen to? Indicate to which musical style they belong.
   Zahava Ben: Listen/ Don't listen/ Don't know/ Mizrahi/ Israeli
   Sarit Hadad: Listen/ Don't listen/ Don't know/ Mizrahi/ Israeli
   Margalit Zanhani: Listen/ Don't listen/ Don't know/ Mizrahi/ Israeli
   Tipex: Listen/ Don't listen/ Don't know/ Mizrahi/ Israeli
   Yehuda Poliker: Listen/ Don't listen/ Don't know/ Mizrahi/ Israeli
   Avihu Medina: Listen/ Don't listen/ Don't know/ Mizrahi/ Israeli
   Haim Moshe: Listen/ Don't listen/ Don't know/ Mizrahi/ Israeli
   Zohar Argov: Listen/ Don't listen/ Don't know/ Mizrahi/ Israeli

Eli Luzon: Listen/ Don't listen/ Don't know/ Mizrahi/ Israeli
Other _____
Listen/ Don't listen/ Don't know/Mizrahi/ Israeli

6. Is there any connection between Mizrahi and Arabic music?
Not at all. Definitely yes.
1 2 3 4 5 6 7
What do you think is the connection between the Mizrahi and Arabic music?

_____
_____
_____

7. To what extent do you think the Mizrahi music is representative of Arabic culture?
Doesn't represent at all. Very representative.
1 2 3 4 5 6 7

8. Do you listen to Arabic music? Yes/ no/ sometimes
If you listen to Arabic music, what is its origin?
Local
Palestinian
Egyptian
Syrian
Lebanese
Iraqi
Other _____ / Don't know

9. What is the frequency of being in touch with an Arab who is an Israeli citizen?
Never. Maybe once a month. Once a week. Approximately every day. All the time.

10. What is the frequency of being in touch with a Palestinian Arab (who is not an Israeli citizen)?
Never. Maybe once a month. Once a week. Approximately every day. All the time.

11. Is there a difference in your attitude toward an Israeli Arab citizen / Palestinian Arab?
Yes/ No
Explain why there is or there is not a difference in your attitude between Arab Israeli citizens and Palestinian Arabs.

_____
_____
_____

12. What are the situations in which you are involved with Palestinian Arabs (who are not Israeli citizens)? For example, working together, employer-employee relationship, service, friendship, passing in the street, sitting on a bus.
Specify

_____

_____

13. Do you think that the Israel government must negotiate directly with the Palestinian Authority?
Not at all. Definitely yes.
1 2 3 4 5 6 7

14. Is there any reason or any justification for establishing a Palestinian state?
Not at all. Definitely yes.
1 2 3 4 5 6 7

15. Do you consider the Palestinian Arabs as Israel's enemies?
Not at all. Definitely yes.
1 2 3 4 5 6 7
Give your answer to this question in details,

_____

_____

_____

16. Here are some personal questions. As we mentioned above, your answers are completely confidential. This survey is anonymous.
Sex F/ M
Year of Birth _____
Marital Status S/ M + ____
Country of Birth _____
Parents' Country of Birth: Father _____, Mother _____
Education _____
Profession _____
Place of residency.
Religious observance.
Range of your monthly salary, mark * in the suitable row.
___ Under the minimum salary
___ Minimum salary
___ 4,000–5,000 NIS
___ 5,000–10,000 NIS
___ 10,000–20,000 NIS

___ More than 20,000 NIS

We thank you kindly for your cooperation.

APPENDIX 3: TEXT CODING GUIDELINES FROM
SYLVAN AND TORONTO (2004)

The Victimization-Victimhood Continuum (SPSS Variable = "victim")

In general, one should ask the question, "Who is the victim here?" and then determine the extent of victimization or victimhood. It is also important to think of a balance, where weight in terms of either victimhood or victimization can tip in favor of Israelis or Palestinians. The following guidelines should be used to make the code as objective as possible. If the article or transcript makes any reference at all to Palestinian-Israeli relations, then it should be coded from "1" to "5." If mention is made of Palestinians and Israelis, but no connective relation is made, then it should be coded "n/a."

   1 = Israelis portrayed almost exclusively as victimizers. Palestinians portrayed almost exclusively as victims.

   ☐ Presents one-sided information, with little or no counter-argument (counter-arguments and justifications can be from external actors)
   ☐ Might impute vicious motives to Israelis
   ☐ Possibly asymmetric use of verbs or nouns (i.e., "move against" or "retaliation" versus "attack" or "destroy") clearly in favor of Palestinians
   ☐ Israelis might be portrayed as destroyers or attackers, and Palestinians as civilians
   ☐ Israelis could be represented as clearly more violent or unjust than Palestinians
   ☐ Human suffering can be more important to the representation of Palestinian victimhood

   2 = Israelis portrayed more as victimizers than victims. Palestinians portrayed more as victims than victimizers.

☐ The victimization-victimhood balance is "in favor" of one side over the other. If victimization remains constant throughout, an asymmetry in victimhood can tip the balance. The reverse is also true: if victimhood is portrayed equally across sides, an asymmetric representation of victimization can put a unit in this category

☐ The balance of aggression in the article can be nearly even-handed, with one or two clear references to victimhood or victimization tipping the scales from a "3"

☐ There may be facts or circumstances represented in the article or newscast that mitigate almost exclusive victimization by Israelis (counter-arguments, for instance, though not enough to justify a "3")

3 = Palestinians and Israelis portrayed relatively symmetrically on victim/victimizer continuum.

☐ An "action-reaction" framework might be present
☐ The aggression can be fairly intense, but nonetheless symmetrical on the victim/victimizer continuum
☐ The article or newscast's representation might involve negotiations, debate, or coming to the table
☐ The article or newscast may not be focused on actual incidents or attacks (though it can still be one-sided, which would preclude it from being a "3")

4 = Palestinians portrayed more as victimizers than victims. Israelis portrayed more as victims than victimizers.

☐ The victimization-victimhood balance is "in favor" of one side over the other. If victimization remains constant throughout, an asymmetry in victimhood can tip the balance. The reverse is also true: if victimhood is portrayed equally across sides, an asymmetric representation of victimization can put a unit in this category

☐ The balance of aggression in the article can be nearly even-handed, with one or two clear references to victimhood or victimization tipping the scales from a "3"

☐ There may be facts or circumstances represented in the article or newscast that mitigate almost exclusive victimization by Palestinians (counter-arguments, for instance, though not enough to justify a "3")

5 = Palestinians portrayed almost exclusively as victimizers. Israelis portrayed almost exclusively as victims.

☐ Presents one-sided information, with little or no counter-argument (counter-arguments and justifications can be from external actors)
☐ Might impute vicious motives to Palestinians
☐ Possibly asymmetric use of verbs or nouns (i.e., "move against" and "retaliation" versus "attack" or "destroy") clearly in favor of Israelis
☐ Palestinians might be portrayed as terrorists, militants, or bombers, and Israelis as civilians
☐ Palestinians could be represented as clearly more violent or unjust than Israelis
☐ Human suffering can be more important to the representation of Israeli victimhood

Clarity of the Code (SPSS Variable = "clarity")

"Clarity" here refers to the sharpness of the representations in the article or broadcast. Is the evidence in the article or broadcast clearly related to the coding you assigned to it? Is the evidence itself clear? How comfortable are you with the connection between this evidence and the victimhood code you assigned to the article or broadcast? If you are confident of this connection, then the "clarity" value for the article or broadcast should be a "1." If not, then the value should be a "0." If only a passing reference is made to Palestinian-Israeli relations, then it is usually better to lean toward a "0," whereas if the article or transcript dwells on the representations of victimhood or victimization, then it is usually better to lean toward a "1."

APPENDIX 4: SAMPLE OF STORY TEMPLATE FROM CHARLICKPALEY AND SYLVAN (2000)

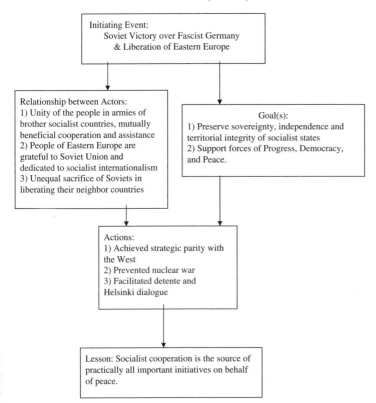

Initiating Event:
Soviet Victory over Fascist Germany
& Liberation of Eastern Europe

Relationship between Actors:
1) Unity of the people in armies of brother socialist countries, mutually beneficial cooperation and assistance
2) People of Eastern Europe are grateful to Soviet Union and dedicated to socialist internationalism
3) Unequal sacrifice of Soviets in liberating their neighbor countries

Goal(s):
1) Preserve sovereignty, independence and territorial integrity of socialist states
2) Support forces of Progress, Democracy, and Peace.

Actions:
1) Achieved strategic parity with the West
2) Prevented nuclear war
3) Facilitated detente and Helsinki dialogue

Lesson: Socialist cooperation is the source of practically all important initiatives on behalf of peace.

II

SURVEY METHODS

4

Between Social Theory and Social Science Practice

Toward a New Approach to the
Survey Measurement of "Race"

Taeku Lee

INTRODUCTION

The idea that a person's "race" is not the indelible mark of one's bloodline, phenotype, or some other biologistic notion no longer raises eyebrows, but it remains for the most part politely ignored by quantitatively oriented, survey-based social science researchers. Although we acknowledge that race, like ethnicity, is a social construct marked by fluidity, multiplicity, and contingency, we continue to measure racial and ethnic identities as fixed, categorical variables. This gap between theory and practice may be consequential if indeed it is the case that a fluid, continuous reality is measured in fixed, categorical terms. In this chapter, a new approach to measuring ethnoracial self-identification is presented, one that aims to define the parameters of this gap by explicitly taking variations in racial or ethnic self-identification as the object of inquiry.[1]

Specifically, the chapter compares the standard approach to ethnoracial self-identification in surveys against a new measurement approach in which respondents are given "identity points" to allocate across a relevant set of social

Thanks are owed to Bob Lee and Jeff Royal for their help with the instrument, to Mike Murakami, Tatishe Nteta, and Connie Hsu for their expert research assistance, and to Jake Bowers, Henry Brady, Kimberly DaCosta, Zoltan Hajnal, Yoshiko Herrera, Vincent Hutchings, David Laitin, Tom Nelson, Michael Omi, Christopher Parker, David Rousseau, Laura Stoker, Kim Williams, Nick Winter, and Cara Wong for their feedback on an earlier version of this chapter.

[1] While "race" and "ethnicity" are conceptually distinct, they are also intimately linked together as organizing principles in American society, with increasingly blurred conceptual boundaries – as in the most recent census classification system with 63 permutations of "race" and a single, dichotomous (Hispanic or non-Hispanic) measure of "ethnicity." For expository purposes, the terms "ethnoracial" and "race or ethnicity" are used to denote both the distinctiveness and the interrelatedness between "race" and "ethnicity."

identity categories. This identity point allocation scheme allows respondents, as they see fit, to identify with as many racial or ethnic groups and to weight the strength of their self-identification across these groups. This new approach not only allows us to test for the sensitivity of ethnoracial self-identification to a question format but, in doing so, also presents a visibly different portrait of racial or ethnic self-identification than is found in most social surveys. The results from a 2003 survey of adult Californians show that a strikingly greater proportion of respondents define themselves in multiracial terms under the point allocation format than do so in conventional survey formats. In addition, Californians are willing to allocate their points in a variety of hybrid combinations, leading to a substantially more continuous view of race in the aggregate. The demographic and attitudinal characteristics we infer about a given racial or ethnic category vary in meaningful and revealing ways by how we ask people to self-identify.

In working toward a new approach to the measurement of "race" in social surveys, I brook no special favor toward greater entropy in the number of ways we measure our constructs in the social sciences. The motive force behind this chapter, rather, is wholly in line with that of the editors of this volume – namely, a keen awareness of and a general frustration with the persistence of conceptual and coordination gaps in the study of identity. Accordingly, a central aim of this chapter is to encourage survey researchers to think more carefully about what it would mean, operationally, for race and ethnicity to be socially constructed. Following the framework of the volume editors, the identity point allocation approach I present here is developed in communication with, and as a complement to, existing measurement approaches. Ultimately, the choice over measurement approaches should depend on the research question at hand. One criterion that is suggested in this chapter for making this choice is whether the content and contestation of racial and ethnic identity per se is the object of inquiry or whether we need a simple and direct measure of race or ethnicity in the service of inquiry into some other topic of interest.

THE STRANGE CAREER OF ETHNORACIAL CLASSIFICATION

In *The Descent of Man*, Charles Darwin (1874: 117–118) observes that "man has been studied more carefully than any other animal, and yet there is the greatest possible diversity amongst capable judges whether he should be classed as a single species or race, or as two (Virey), as three (Jacquinot), as four (Kant), five (Pickering), fifteen (Bory St. Vincent), sixteen (Desmoulins), twenty-two (Morton), sixty (Crawford), or as sixty-three, according to Burke." This prescient reflection upon the diversity of classifications by race powerfully

TABLE 4.1. *Ethnoracial Classification in the Decennial Census, 1860–2000*

Category	1860	1890	1970	2000
Race	White	White	White	White
	Black	Black	Negro or Black	Black, African
	Mulatto	Mulatto		American, or Negro
		Quadroon		
		Octoroon		
		Indian	Indian (Amer.)	American Indian or
				Alaska Native
		Chinese	Chinese, Japanese,	Chinese, Japanese,
		Japanese	Filipino, Korean	Filipino, Korean,
				Asian Indian,
				Vietnamese, Native
				Hawaiian, Guamanian
				or Chamorro, some
				other Pacific Islander,
				some other Asian
			Other	Some other race
Ethnicity			Mexican, Puerto	Mexican,
			Rican, Cuban,	Mexican-American,
			Central or	Chicano, Puerto
			South American,	Rican, Cuban, Other
			Other Spanish	Spanish/Hispanic/Latino

illustrates the thorny, perhaps intractable, paradoxes underlying race as a concept. Even at the height of biologically based and scientifically inspired studies of this concept there is a lack of clarity and consensus on how to start – that is, how to define and categorize the concept. Thus, Darwin concludes that "this diversity of judgment does not prove that the races ought not to be ranked as species, but it shews that they graduate into each other, and that it is hardly possible to discover clear distinctive characters between them."

The mere passage of time has left us in no better stead. This is perhaps nowhere more evident than in the classification of individuals by "race" and "ethnicity" in the U.S. decennial census (M. Anderson 1988; Starr 1987; Lieberson and Waters 1993; M. Anderson and Feinberg 1999; Nobles 2000; Rodriguez 2000; Skerry 2000; Kertzer and Arel 2002; Perlmann and Waters 2003; and Snipp 2003). Table 4.1 shows a comparison of ethnoracial classification schemes used in the decennial censuses in 1860, 1890, 1970, and 2000. For the present purposes, Table 4.1 highlights two important features of these decade-to-decade changes. First, with the exception of "white," the categories that are used to define a given race have been quite variable across censuses. Second, the number of categories, in toto, has multiplied considerably over the long history of the census. This proliferation of categories has been especially notable, with the most recent "Fourth Wave" of migrants predominantly from Asia and the Americas, in the number of Asian or Pacific Islander categories and in the separation of "Hispanic" as an "ethnic" category from all other "races."

Thus, across past census enumerations, individuals of African descent have been counted in fractions (as "three-fifths" of a person) and by gradations of bloodline (as "mulatto," "quadroon," and "octoroon"); individuals of South Asian descent have been, at different times, classified as Caucasian, Native American, "Hindoo," and Asian; Mexicans in the United States have been, at different times, classified as white, Mexican, "Spanish-surname," other race, and Hispanic; and there are countless other examples.[2] This inconsistency and variation has been repeatedly and insistently described as evidence of social construction at work. The fact that bodies with, *ceteris paribus*, the same bloodline, same phenotype, and same Linnaean taxonomy could be defined in radically different ways at different points in time and by different external arbiters is indeed compelling evidence that "race" is formed out of our prevailing social norms, cultural beliefs, economic institutions, legal codes, political movements, and the like (Omi and Winant 1994; Waters 1990; Nagel 1995; Haney-Lopez 1996; Nobles 2000).

Two striking changes in how the U.S. Census Bureau goes about surveying the land and its people have been especially decisive to our present-day construction of race and ethnicity. With the 1960 census, ethnoracial classification shifted from enumerator observations to self-identification. This change from external ascription of race to self-identification marks a move from race as a concept defined by a clearly bounded set of physical traits open to observation to race as an expression of subjective personal identity. Rather than the context of census worker trained to match observed characteristics to demographic labels, we are now, individually, asked to ask ourselves, "Who am I, racially and ethnically?"

Second, with the 2000 census, self-identification shifted from choosing just one among a menu of racial groups to being able to "Mark one or more" among them. This new multiracial identifier allows individuals to check off

---

[2] Table 4.1 also shows, in the emergence of the categories "quadroon" and "octoroon" in the 1890 census, that classification systems that treat a given "race" in gradations are not novel phenomena. What has changed, however, is the basis for such gradations, from bloodline to subjective identification, and the sociopolitical context in which we care about gradations, from the hyperemic fin-de-siècle fears of race-mixing qua hypodescent in the aftermath of emancipation and Reconstruction (Du Bois 1984; Hollinger 2003) to the present-day attentiveness to the politics of respect and recognition with the more explicitly *political* construction of "Hispanic-ity," a multiracial identity, various Asian national, Alaska native, and Pacific Islander categories as "races," and the like.

as many of the standard six racial categories – white, African American, Asian, American Indian or Alaska Native, Native Hawaiian or other Pacific Islander, and some other race (almost always Latinos) – as individuals think or feel apply to them, resulting in 63 possible permutations and 126 permutations of race and ethnicity. What is more, the 2000 classification scheme further distinguished between 336 ethnoracial subtypes, 249 specific racial or ethnic groups, and 86 ancestry groups and, within panethnic groupings, 28 unique Hispanic categories, 17 Asian categories, 12 Native Hawaiian or Pacific Islander categories, 36 American Indian categories, and 5 Alaska Native tribes. Despite the fact that only 2.1 percent of the U.S. adult population chose to identify with more than one category, Kenneth Prewitt, former director of the Census Bureau, marks the 2000 census as a "turning point" for racial self-categorization in the census. Prewitt (2003: 360) further notes that "the racial measurement system is now vastly more complicated and multidimensional than anything preceding it, and there is currently no prospect of returning to something simpler."[3]

The net effect of these changes is that the census – and every social survey that follows its lead – now conflates and conjoins two potentially distinct objectives: *enumeration*, for the purposes of making public policy (or, in the case of academic surveys, political polls, and marketing research, for the purposes of better understanding our attitudes and behaviors), and *expression*, as a venue for the politics of recognition and the contestation of the identity categories themselves. For the objective of enumeration, measurement error and statistical noise are a problem. For the objective of expression, however, measurement error and statistical noise are evidence of identity politics and racial formation at work. This tension underlines the conspicuous gap that presently exists between race or ethnicity as social theorists conceptualize it – stressing its contingent, crosscutting, heterogeneous, hybrid nature – and race or ethnicity as empirical researchers study it, which is focused on a common, fixed operationalization of categories designed to measure external realities reliably and relatively free from error.

While the change in how we theorize about race and ethnicity has been breathtaking – from the late nineteenth-century accounts of social Darwinism and biological racism to later twentieth-century versions of primordialism to the current consensus in favor of constructivist accounts – the methods and measures we use to study race and ethnicity have remained, for the most part, constant (Chandra 2001; Abdelal et al. 2006). As the editor of a recent

---

[3] Because of an error in how the 2000 census forms were processed, the initial report of 2.4 percent of the population identifying with two or more races has been recently revised to 2.1 percent (see Citro, Cork, and Norwood 2004).

symposium on the comparative study of ethnic politics concludes, "it is now virtually impossible to find a social scientist who openly defends a primordialist position. . . . However, while everyone now pays lip service to constructivism, constructivist assumptions remain comprehensively unincorporated" in studies linking ethnic groups to political outcomes (Chandra 2001: 8). The social constructivist view remains substantially, if politely, ignored.

For instance, a typical opinion survey will ask respondents some version of the question, "What racial or ethnic group best describes you?" or "What is your race?" In this standard format, respondents are asked to choose from a typical menu of racial or ethnic categories – say, "black," "Asian," "Native American," "Hispanic or Latino," "white," or "other" – and the given choices are assumed to describe who a person thinks she is, racially and ethnically, in a reliable and valid manner. In contrast to constructivist theories of race or ethnicity, this measurement approach implicitly further assumes that respondents can easily self-identify with one of these given racial or ethnic categories, that the chosen category is equally salient and valid across individuals, and that the respondents' choices will be invariant across survey contexts. Even the newest refinement to this standard format – giving respondents the choice to self-identify with more than one group – fails to adequately capture the sensitivity and contingency of ethnoracial self-identification.

This gap between theory and practice is potentially crucial to our understanding of race or ethnicity because either it is the case that an everyday "snapshot" of ethnoracial self-identification measured by the census and social surveys produces valid and reliable images of "black," "white," "Native American," "Latino," "Asian," and the like because racial or ethnic boundaries are more stable and categorical than contemporary constructivist scholars would have us think; or it is the case that the seemingly fixed and categorical images of race that we obtain from the census and other social surveys are an artifact of the fixed and categorical measurement approach that quantitative practitioners adopt. In the first case, the prevailing assumption among quantitative, survey-based social scientists – that race or ethnicity can be reliably, validly measured using nominal categories – becomes more of a residual concern or a technical footnote. In the latter case, our prevailing approach would require rethinking and retooling, as a great deal of quantifiable variation would be lost if a continuous reality is measured categorically, just as valuable information would be lost if income were measured as "rich" or "poor" or the politics of America's states were measured as "red" or "blue." This potential loss of information is especially likely to matter during historical periods in which the content of race or ethnicity as an identity type – its constituent cognitions and norms, its relation to other identity types (or between racial or ethnic categories), the social purposes it serves – is shifting and becoming more contested (Abdelal et al. 2006). As suggested later in this chapter, we are likely to be the midst of just such a historical period and therefore, from the standpoint of social science knowledge, at risk of missing much critical variation in how race or ethnicity is changing by virtue of our limited methods of measuring race or ethnicity.

Ultimately, the verdict on our existing standards of measurement in social surveys and on our existing substantive knowledge about race or ethnicity hinges on getting an estimate of the quantifiable information that is lost in this gap between theory and practice. This is an empirical question, and one that warrants a unique approach to the measurement of race or ethnicity.

A NEW APPROACH TO ETHNORACIAL SELF-IDENTIFICATION

This chapter develops a new approach to measuring ethnoracial self-identification in order to test the fluidity or fixity of how race or ethnicity is expressed in social surveys. Several previous efforts exist to measure racial or ethnic identity as graded variables and social constructs. Brady and Kaplan (2000) use multiple indicators to develop factor analytic scales that yield a more graded measure of the ethnic identity of Estonians and Slavs. These factor scales only indirectly quantify one's identity, however, using items like social contact, media usage, and group evaluations that are likely to be endogenous to group consciousness and identity formation itself. Moreover, factor loadings are hard to compare against the standard, categorical ethnoracial identifiers used in social surveys. Harris and Sims (2002), by contrast, directly compare four different indicators of race in the National Longitudinal Study of Adolescent Health – self-identification by teenagers at school, at home, by their parent(s), and by interviewer observation. Their evidence for the degree to which race is socially constructed is based on the often sharp variance in the apparent racial composition of the sample across these indicators. Note, however, that the comparison is still among discrete, categorical indicators.[4] Both studies reveal some of the potential limitations of our existing measures of ethnoracial self-identifications, but we are still left wanting a more direct test of the fluidity or fixity of this self-identification.

How then do we construct such a measure? The proposal in this chapter is to give survey respondents multiple identity points to allocate as they see fit across

---

[4] Tom Smith (2001: 7) takes a similar approach by comparing three approaches to racial identification: interviewer observation, a census-based "first mention" format, and the self-identification format used in the General Social Survey, but finds "minimal impact on the GSS time-series." For instances of other such efforts, with alternative innovations, see Laitin 2000; Chandra 2004a; and Posner 2005.

a relevant set of social identity groups. This approach is somewhat analogous to Lani Guinier's (1994) proposal for "cumulative voting" in that it addresses two chief limitations common to both "one-person, one-vote" electoral systems and "one-person, one-category" ethnoracial classification systems – namely, that individual choice in these contexts is constrained to be *singular* (that just one among the candidates and racial or ethnic groups is optimal) and *equal* (that preference or identification with that choice is equally salient). Just as cumulative voting allows citizens to vote for multiple candidates and weight their votes according to their intensities of preference across candidates, the proposed "identity point allocation" scheme allows survey respondents to identify with multiple racial or ethnic groups and a quantitative means to weight the strength of their self-identification across these groups.[5]

This identity point allocation approach has a potentially wide range of applications to the study of race or ethnicity and social identity writ large. It allows us to test which identities matter and how much they matter within an identity class (e.g., between "African American," "white," "Asian American," "Latino," and "Native American"), across identity classes (e.g., between race or ethnicity, gender, class, sexual orientation, ideology, partisanship, religiosity), and across levels of an identity class (e.g., between panethnic vs. ethnic or national origin subgroups). It also allows us to compare the process of self-identification with the process of ascribing race to others. In this chapter, the focus is given to three specific research questions: First, what is the distribution of weights allocated to a given racial or ethnic category? Second, what is the frequency of self-identification with multiple racial or ethnic categories? Third, what are the implications of different types of ethnoracial self-identification for our understanding of different racial or ethnic groups?

If we gave survey respondents a means to do so, what are the different ways that identities might be weighted? To make this concrete, Figure 4.1 compares four different ways that 100 identity points might be allocated to a given racial or ethnic category in the scenario where each person in this hypothetical population is given 10 identity points to allocate. In the "invariant allocation" model, every person who self-identifies with a racial or ethnic category allocates all 10 identity points to that category. This is the model that is implicit in standard survey formats in which respondents are given a fixed menu of racial or ethnic categories to choose from and asked to choose one among them. At the other end of the spectrum is the "random allocation" model, where

---

[5] Identity point allocation is not, of course, perfectly analogous to cumulative voting, if for no other reason than that electoral design aims to generate effective decision rules for collective choice – in a winner-take-all system, where one person is chosen for each elected office.

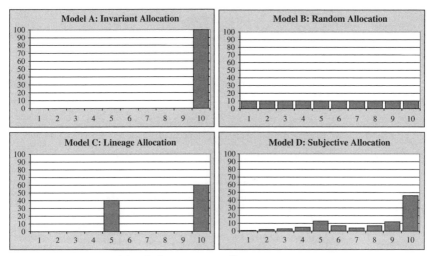

FIGURE 4.1. Four Models of Identity Point Allocation

ethnoracial boundaries are so arbitrary or contingent that, for a given group, every point allocation is equally likely.

In the "lineage allocation" model, we presume that individuals, when asked to self-identify ethnoracially, reflect on the racial or ethnic identity of their parents (or grandparents, great-grandparents, and the like) and then apply an invariant allocation of points to that racial or ethnic definition of one's parents. In the particular example of a lineage allocated distribution in Figure 4.1, individuals have defined their parents monoracially and so, for a given group, allocate either 10 points or 5 points to that group (depending on whether both parents are defined by the same race or by different races).[6] Lastly, in the "subjective allocation" model, allocation is based on multiple contexts and frames of reference – where bloodline is one among many referents, including a more variable (and perhaps faulty) recall of one's parental ethnoracial lineage and other subjective considerations like one's phenotype, geographic origin, family history, racial ascription by others, and other behavioral factors like one's friendship ties, mien, manner of dress, and cultural consumption.[7] Importantly, the term "subjective" allocation is not intended to imply that one's

[6] Figure 4.1 shows an example of a lineage allocation in which six individuals conclude that they have parents of the same racial or ethnic background and eight individuals conclude that they have parents of different backgrounds. In theory, lineage allocation would be more amenable to a base-8 scoring system.

[7] "Family history" is intended to capture the range of factors beyond the racial ascription of one's parents, such as one's marriage partner, being adopted, being raised by a single parent or non-parent relatives, and the like.

identity is purely imaginary or psychological, but it does underscore the degree to which nonlineage factors can contribute to a person's ethnoracial self-identification: a person who is, say, equally Swedish and Mexican by lineage but phenotypically "white" and educated to speak unaccented English might "pass" as fully white; another person who is ethnically Korean, but adopted by Jewish parents in America might consider herself at least partly white; and so on.[8]

The distinction between the lineage and subjective allocation models can be more formally represented by the following set of equations:

$$Self\text{-}ID|GroupA = \beta1 \times Par1\text{-}ID + \beta2 \times Par2\text{-}ID +$$
$$\beta3 \times Phenotype + \beta4 \times Geographic\ Origin + \beta5 \times Family\ History$$
$$+ \beta6 \times Ascribed\ Race + \beta7 \times Behavioral\ Factors\& + \mu$$

$$Eq(1)$$

$$Parent1\text{-}ID|GroupA = \gamma1 \times Par1\text{-}Grandp1\text{-}ID +$$
$$\gamma2 \times Par1\text{-}Grandp2\text{-}ID + \gamma3 \times Par1\text{-}Phenotype +$$
$$\gamma4 \times Par1\text{-}Geographic\ Origin + \gamma5 \times Par1\text{-}Family\ History +$$
$$\gamma6 \times Par1\text{-}Ascribed\ Race + \gamma7 \times Par1\text{-}Behavioral\ Factors\ \& + \varepsilon$$

$$Eq(2a)$$

$$Parent2\text{-}ID|GroupA = \gamma1 \times Par2\text{-}Grandp1\text{-}ID +$$
$$\gamma2 Par2\text{-}Grandp2\text{-}ID + \gamma3 \times Par2\text{-}Phenotype +$$
$$\gamma4 \times Par2\text{-}Geographic\ Origin + \gamma5 \times Par2\text{-}Family\ History +$$
$$\gamma6 \times Par2\text{-}Ascribed\ Race + \gamma7 \times Par2\text{-}Behavioral\ Factors\ \& + \gamma$$

$$Eq(2b)$$

Equation 1 defines a person's self-identification with a given race or ethnicity (Group A) as a function of the race or ethnicity they attribute to their parents, their phenotypical attributes, their geographic origin, their family history, how they are defined in racial or ethnic terms by others, and their racial or ethnic revealed preferences vis-à-vis whom they commingle with, what activities and cultural consumption they favor, inter alia. Equations 2a and 2b similarly define that person's parents' ethnoracial self-identification. Presumably, if a person's lineage were sufficiently multiethnic, multiracial, and multigenerational, we could specify her grandparents' and great-grandparents' self-identification, and so on.

---

[8] As an example of a subjective allocation of 100 identity points, Figure 4.1 shows a case where five people allocate all 10 identity points to a group, three people allocate 5 points, two people allocate 7 points, a single different person allocating 1, 2, 3, 6, and 9 points, and no one allocating 4 or 8 points.

Under the lineage model, the allocation of points is defined solely by the individual's ascription of race or ethnicity to his or her parents (Par1 – ID and Par2 – ID), with zero parameters on all other factors that might help to explain how a person self-identified ethnoracially. Importantly, the lineage parameters ($\beta 1$ and $\beta 2$) are assumed to be identical – if both parents are defined monoracially and the same racial or ethnic category is ascribed to both parents, then all 10 points are allocated to that category; if a different category is ascribed to each parent, then 5 points are allocated to each category. If the parents are not viewed monoracially, then the ascription of one's parents' race is defined by the lineage parameters in Equations 2a and 2b ($\gamma 1$, $\gamma 2$, $\zeta 1$, $\zeta 2$). The subjective allocation model differs in three key respects: the lineage parameters within a given generation may differ from one another ($\beta 1$ from $\beta 2$, $\gamma 1$ from $\gamma 2$, $\zeta 1$ from $\zeta 2$), the nonlineage parameters (phenotype, geography, culture) may be nonzero, and the parameters (lineage and nonlineage) may vary across time and context (i.e., a given individual's allocation may differ across time or in response to different formulations of the question).

Whether our standard format for asking individuals to self-identify by race or ethnicity will suffice depends critically on which of these models best approximates reality. Random allocation is more of a hypothetical distribution than something we are likely to find from our identity point allocation measure, given the omnipresence of race as a factor in our social, economic, and political worlds. How the reality of our racial-ethnic self-identification is adjudicated between the remaining three models of point allocation will depend on whether race or ethnicity as a social construction reflects a stable equilibrium state or an unstable disequilibrium state. To borrow the representation of social constructivism as the process of coming to agreement on "focal equilibria" in coordination games or what Schelling calls "convergent expectations" (Schelling 1960; Laitin 1998; Fearon 1999), in the most rigid racial orders – say, the American Deep South at the height of Jim Crow – expectations about how a person (oneself or others) is defined in racial or ethnic terms are likely to be clear, consistent, and self-sustaining. In a more fluid, shifting racial order – perhaps exemplified by the fabled versions of contemporary Hawaii, Cuba, and Brazil[9] – such expectations about racial or ethnic definition are likelier to be more ambiguous, variable, and not mutually reinforcing.

Individuals should self-identify monoracially and allocate their points in an invariant manner if it is the case that the current racial order in the United States retains enough residues of the segregationist, Jim Crow era – where

---

[9] For among those who have written about race and racial boundaries in Brazil, Cuba, and Hawaii, see Hanchard 1994; Nobles 2000; Okihiro 2001; and Sawyer 2005.

interracial intimacy was proscribed through legal and (often violent) extralegal means and racial definitions were marked by the prevailing use of "one-drop" hypodescent rules. Yet it is far more likely that in the United States today, race is a less clear and stable social construction than it was, say, fifty years ago. The most recent change to a "mark one or more" (or other multiracial) format and its concomitant mobilization of demands for the recognition of multiracial identities (K. Williams 2001; Perlmann and Waters 2003; Winters and DuBose 2003) is just the most recent capstone to a long historical transformation, from the dismantling of slavery and de jure segregation and the refutation of biologically based theories of race to the civil rights movement and the subsequent rights revolution, to the post-1965 "Fourth Wave" of immigrants from Asia and Latin America, and other fin-de-siècle social and political transformations. In this context, the distribution of identity weights should more closely approximate the subjective allocation model than either the invariant or lineage models.

In addition, there are reasons to expect the invariant, or lineage-based, or subjective allocation to vary by racial or ethnic groups. In the first instance, the simple law of numbers should make it more likely for ostensibly nonwhite individuals who are a numeric minority to marry more outside their group (and, by corollary, to be more likely to have multiracial family backgrounds than whites) than whites who are a numeric majority. In the scenario where unmarried persons met and married randomly, like atoms in Brownian motion, this would certainly be true. Of course, marriages have never been so casual or indiscriminate. There is a long history in the United States of enforcing racial boundaries and repressing interracial coupling by law, violence, segregation, and the whitewashing of memory. Yet there is an equally long history of racial intermarriage, bolstered by a growing public tolerance for such interracial unions and a steady rise in documented cases of such interracial unions (Schuman et al. 1998; Farley 1999; Morning 2003).[10]

Differences in intermarriage patterns, however, are not the sole basis for expecting racial or ethnic group differences in self-identification. If this were the case, one might demur that this hypothesis is based on a very "conventional" view of racial self-identification. Another important consideration for expecting group differences in self-identification is that there are differential psychic

---

[10] This expectation of racial or ethnic group differences and the greater multiracial identification of numeric minorities are already partly borne out by the Census 2000 "mark one or more" identifier," with only 2.5 percent of all whites identifying with a second racial or ethnic category, while 39.9 percent of "American Indian and Alaska Native" identifiers and 54.4 percent of "Native Hawaiian and Other Pacific Islander" identifiers also marking a second category.

and material costs and benefits to ethnoracial self-identification. Regardless of whether this differential cost is based on a sense of "relative group position," "realistic group conflict," "white privilege," "social dominance," "power-threat," or some other theoretical rubric (Blumer 1961; Bobo and Hutchings 1996; Lipsitz 1998; Harris 1993; Sidanius and Pratto 1999; Key 1949), the implication is that those individuals who principally self-identify with groups that fare the best within existing racial or ethnic categories – whites and, given their relatively high (vis-à-vis African Americans, Latinos, and Native Americans) socioeconomic status, maybe Asians – should be more inclined to keep all their identity points in the more privileged racial or ethnic category. In contrast, those individuals who might otherwise principally self-identify with nonwhite groups that fare less well within existing racial or ethnic boundaries should be more likely to allocate their identity points across multiple categories. This argument about psychic and material costs and benefits, importantly, falls beyond the conventional view of self-identification that is assumed in standard survey measures. These considerations, taken together, yield the first set of hypotheses:

H1.1: The "subjective" allocation model will approximate the distribution of identity points better than the "invariant" or "lineage" allocation models.

H1.2: The distribution of identity points will vary across racial or ethnic categories such that the distribution for those who self-identify as whites should look most "invariant" and the distribution for those who self-identify with less privileged and smaller nonwhite groups should look most "subjective."

A related question to the matter of how identity weights are distributed is the matter of whether a change in how we ask people to self-identify ethnoracially will result in a substantially different proportion of multiracial identifiers. The benchmarks here are the "Mark one or more" format used in the 2000 census, which resulted in 2.1 percent of the nation opting for a multiracial identity; and, among social surveys, the 2000 American National Election Studies (ANES) revised format of "What racial or ethnic group or groups best describes you?" which resulted in 2.8 percent of its respondents identifying with more than one racial or ethnic group; and the 2000 General Social Survey test of a "Indicate one or more races that you consider yourself to be" format, which resulted in 5.3 percent of its respondents indicating more than one race. In all cases, the proportion of multiracial identifiers fell below demographers' and population biologists' initial expectations (Goldstein and Morning 2000; Morning 2003), and there are several reasons to expect a target population to look significantly more multiracial under the question format proposed in this chapter.

Foremost among these is that individuals are likely to vary in how strongly one needs to identify with a particular group before choosing to acknowledge the threshold intensity of self-identification at which more than one racial group is identified. Under the "Mark one or more" format, this response function is a latent variable; the identity point allocation format, by contrast, is in a sense a measure of this threshold of self-identification. To illustrate this point, consider two types of individuals confronted with the 2000 census questionnaire, type A and type B. Type A will check off a second racial group if and only if she identifies as strongly with it as she does to the first racial group she marks. Type B will check off a second (or third) group if she in any way identifies with it – strongly or not. Now take the example of a biracial individual who identifies more strongly as "African American" than as "Asian American." If she is type A, she will mark only "African American" in census 2000; if she is type B, she will mark both. Under the identity point allocation format, both persons type A and type B will identify as biracial.

A second reason to expect a greater incidence of multiracial identification under the identity point allocation scheme is that the answers we give depend (sometimes a great deal) on the questions we ask – what words are used to ask the question, who asks it, what other questions it follows, and whether particular considerations are evoked as a result of these factors (Singer and Presser 1989; Schuman and Presser 1996; Tourangeau, Rips, and Rasinski 2000). This is, in effect, the dynamic that drives Harris and Sims's (2002) findings on the social construction of race. As we shall see, the particular question format that is used in the research presented in this chapter is worded and ordered in a way that is likely to evoke a more constructivist framing of ethnoracial self-identification and, as a result, likely to induce a greater number of individuals to allocate identity points to more than one racial or ethnic category.[11]

As with the distribution of identity weights, there are also several reasons to expect certain groups to be more likely to identify multiracially than others, especially vis-à-vis the 2000 census enumeration. As noted earlier, there are likely to be differential psychic and material costs and benefits to ethnoracial self-identification. Following the logic specified earlier, we would expect those individuals who identify with groups characterized by privilege and status to

---

[11] A third reason to expect a greater proportion of Americans who are willing to identify multiracially is that Americans are now likely to be more familiar with the idea of multiracial self-identification than they were several years ago, and this factor alone may lead to higher rates of multiracial identification in future census enumerations (Glazer 2001; Perlmann and Waters 2003).

maintain monoracial identities. By contrast, those individuals who identify with groups marked by privation and stigma should be more willing to acknowledge multiple racial or ethnic backgrounds. A second basis for expecting group differences in multiracial identification is that the organized political calculus of ethnoracial self-identification is likely to have changed since 2000. The decennial census in 2000 galvanized a vigorous effort by African American and Latino advocacy organizations like the National Association for the Advancement of Colored People (NAACP) and Mexican American Legal Defense and Educational Fund (MALDEF) to mobilize their constituencies to reject this multiple check-off format (Rodriguez 2000; K. Williams 2001; Perlmann and Waters 2003). To the extent that social surveys are fielded in the absence of such political contestation and as the public policy uses of census 2000 multiracial data have not hitherto disproportionately disadvantaged these communities, we should find a selectively greater willingness to identify multiracially among African American–only and Latino-only identifiers to the 2000 census. The second set of hypotheses is thus:

H2.1: A greater proportion of individuals will identify with multiple racial or ethnic groups under identity point allocation than do so with standard racial or ethnic self-ID measures.

H2.2: The frequency of multiracial identification of identity points will vary across racial or ethnic categories such that those who self-identify as whites should be most likely to identify monoracially and those who self-identify as African Americans, Latinos, and Native Americans should be most likely to identify multiracially.

Finally, the case against current measurement approaches would be even stronger if it were the case that what we inferred about the demographic and attitudinal characteristics of a particular racial or ethnic group varied as a function of how we asked individuals to self-identify by race or ethnicity. That is, do "standard identifiers," those individuals who identify with a given race or ethnic group under the standard question format, look different from "point allocators" – those individuals who identify with a given race or ethnic group under the proposed identity voting format, but who do not so identify under the standard format? Such demographic and attitudinal differences should be expected to the extent that the allocation of identity points accurately reflects the relative weights we give to our ethnoracial self-identification. To put a sharper point on it, these differences in identity weights are not likely to be formed arbitrarily, or merely as a function of response thresholds and survey context effects. Rather, the allocation of identity points should reflect the nature and dynamics of race and ethnicity as social structures and organizing principles in American life and, as such, should mirror observed racial or ethnic differences in material position and sociopolitical beliefs just as differences in degrees of immigrant acculturation and shades of skin color also reflect differences in material position and sociopolitical beliefs (Portes and Rumbaut 1996; Hochschild 2003). The final expectation is thus:

H3: there should be meaningful differences in the demographic and attitudinal features that we attribute to a given "race" or "ethnicity" that vary by how we ask people to self-identify ethnoracially.

THE 2003 GOLDEN BEAR OMNIBUS SURVEY

The validity of this identity point allocation scheme and the aforementioned hypotheses was tested in a module within the 2003 Golden Bear Omnibus Survey (GBO). The GBO was a California-wide, random-digit telephone survey conducted by the Survey Research Center at the University of California at Berkeley between 17 September and 22 November 2003. As an omnibus survey, the interview comprised items covering the topics of interest to several different investigators with a common pool of demographic, political, and sampling variables.[12] There were 1,050 completed interviews with an overall response rate of 32.6 percent (American Association for Public Opinion Research [AAPOR]-R1). Interviews were conducted in English or Spanish, depending on the respondents' preference. The list-assisted random-digit sampling and the limited choice of interview languages are likely to have underrepresented certain groups. Based on the GBO's version of the race question – "Which of the following best describes your race or ethnic group – Black or African-American, Native American, Hispanic or Latino, Filipino, Asian, Pacific Islander, White or Caucasian, or some other group?" – there were 62.3 percent whites or Anglos, 17.5 percent Hispanics or Latinos, 6.3 percent Asians and Pacific Islanders, 5.8 percent African Americans, 1.3 percent Native Americans, 3.7 percent "some other group," and 3.1 percent who volunteered a "multiracial" identity.

The GBO asks four different questions that use the identity point allocation format. To familiarize respondents with the task of allocating identity points, the module begins by asking respondents to define a popular celebrity, the

---

[12] Other topics surveyed in the GBO include questions about the Family and Medical Leave Act, attitudes about risk and harm prevention, perceptions of fairness in economic and labor contexts, and the relationship of information sources of political opinions. The module of questions about the point allocation format comes toward the end of the survey.

professional golfer Tiger Woods. Specifically, respondents were asked the following:

> In identifying a person's race and ethnicity, we often use just one racial or ethnic category. Sometimes, however, more than one racial or ethnic category is applicable. Suppose you could describe a person's race and ethnicity using 10 points to allocate as you wish to any group that you think accurately describes a person. For example, if you thought someone were half-white and half-Asian, you might allocate 5 points to each. Or if you thought someone were mostly black but had some Hispanic heritage, you might allocate 9 points for black and 1 point for Hispanic. Now think about the professional golfer Tiger Woods. How would you describe Tiger Woods' race using this 10 points system?

Respondents are next asked, "Now suppose you are asked to describe your own racial background in this way. How would you describe your race and ethnicity using this 10 points system?" These two questions form the core of this chapter. In addition to these, the GBO also asks its respondents to allocate identity points across the primary social identities that define them (having first chosen defining identities from the menu of race or ethnicity, gender, class, sexual identity, partisanship, ideology, and religion) and asks its Latino respondents only how strongly they identify as Latinos or with their ethnic or national origin (i.e., as Mexicans or Mexican Americans) by allocating identity points.

Note that a few seemingly arbitrary decisions are needed to operationalize this approach. First, the number of identity points given to respondents is set at 10. While arbitrary, it is a reasonable starting point that is likely to minimize the cognitive task at hand, given the ubiquity of the base-10 system and 10-point systems generally to rate a range of phenomena from the attractiveness of potential romantic partners to competitive sports to academic performance. A 100-point system is arguably equal in familiarity but would likely increase the cognitive task required of respondents (making sure the points add up to 100) and, by corollary, the interview length as well.[13] Thus a 10-point system is as familiar and expedient a scale as any that we might choose.

A second arbitrary decision is over the slate of racial or ethnic groups that individuals can choose from and allocate points to. To the extent that this is a fixed menu of identity categories, the proposed identity point allocation scheme straddles the divide between the dual aims of racial or ethnic data collection for the purposes of enumeration and the purposes of expression. The goal of this chapter is not to eliminate this divide but rather to map its geography.

---

[13] A third alternative would be a base-8 system, but this would likely prime respondents in lineage terms.

Employing the six categories of "white or Anglo," "black or African American," "Asian American," "Hispanic or Latino," "Native American or American Indian," and "other race" for residual identifications is an obvious candidate because this breakdown is commonly used and corresponds closely with everyday folk conceptions of race. It also corresponds, importantly, to the menu of identity categories used in social surveys, such as the American National Election Studies.

It is worth noting that the classification system here differs from the decennial census in that the category of "Hispanic or Latino" is not isolated as a separate marker of ethnicity and that "Alaska Native," "Native Hawaiian," and "Pacific Islander" are not offered as choice categories. Each of these differences is likely to be controversial. The inclusion of Hispanic or Latino into a joint race or ethnicity identifier makes direct comparisons to the 2000 census data tricky, because the Census Bureau categorizes "multiracial" individuals only from the racial identifier. According to the results of the 2000 ANES – which finds 2.8 percent multiracial identifiers with the same categories that are used in the GBO – this joint race or ethnicity identifier should not have a dramatic effect on our findings vis-à-vis the 2000 census.[14]

THE CONTINUITY AND MULTIPLICITY OF ETHNORACIAL SELF-IDENTIFICATION

What does this new approach to measuring race or ethnicity tell us? The most eye-catching finding is the proportion of multiracial identifiers. Defined as the allocation of at least one point to more than one racial or ethnic group, 26.3 percent of GBO respondents identify multiracially. This is several magnitudes of order greater than the proportion of multiracial identifiers we find using categorical measures. For comparison, the 2000 census found only 2.1 percent

[14] It is tricky, but we can derive an upper and lower bound by using three known facts: (1) in Census 2000, 43 percent of Hispanics or Latinos identified themselves as "other race"; (2) 97 percent of "other race" individuals were Latino; and (3) 32.4 percent of Californians in 2000 identified as Hispanic or Latino. If we assume that the first two figures, which are U.S.-based, are similar for California, the lower bound, 4.7 percent, is set by the case in which only those 13.9 percent of Hispanic or Latino identifiers who define themselves racially as "other race" are multiracial or multiethnic identifiers (i.e., the remaining 18.5 percent identify *exclusively* as Hispanic or Latino). The upper bound, 23.2 percent, is set by the case in which all 18.5 percent remaining also identifies with another race or ethnicity. A third, middle-ground estimate we can derive is the case where Latinos who do not check off "other race" identify with a second racial or ethnic category at the same rate as "other race" Latinos (i.e., 17.1 percent). In this case, the derived estimate would be an expectation of 7.9 percent multiracial or multiethnic identifiers in California if the "race" and the Hispanic identifiers were combined as it is in the GBO.

multiracial identifiers in the United States and 4.7 percent in California. In the GBO itself, 3.1 percent of respondents identified with more than one racial or ethnic category. An important precaution is that the 26.3 percent figure is based on "valid" responses (i.e., it excludes those who refused an answer or who volunteered a "don't know" response) and that roughly one in six respondents did not answer this question. This high proportion is potentially troublesome as the distribution of nonresponses, especially on matters of race, is not random and often belies substantive group differences (Reeves 1997; Berinsky 2004). If these refusals are explicitly taken into account using a standard algorithm for imputing missing data (King et al. 2001), the proportion of multiracial identifiers actually inches upward to about 28 percent of the sample.[15]

This increased likelihood of identifying with multiple racial or ethnic groups, moreover, varies across groups. There are two ways to compare the incidence of multiracial identification by racial or ethnic group – by defining racial or ethnic groups according to the GBO's standard question format and by defining groups where membership is defined by the allocation of at least one identity point to a given racial or ethnic group. Table 4.2 shows the comparison where groups are defined by the GBO's standard question. The rank ordering of groups by likelihood of identifying with more than one racial or ethnic category is consistent with our expectations: African Americans are the most likely to identify multiracially (41.7 percent), followed by Latinos (29.8 percent), Asian Americans (23.7 percent), and whites (20.4 percent).[16] These figures are especially striking relative to the proportion of each group that identified multiracially in the 2000 census, where the proportion of African Americans, Latinos, Asian Americans, and whites from California who checked off more than one category were roughly 10, 6.4, 11, and 6.2 percent, respectively.[17]

Thus, our estimates of the proportion of the multiracial population vary as a function of how we ask people to self-identify, ethnoracially. It also varies,

---

[15] Imputation is based on five simulated samples generated with AMELIA (King et al. 2001). Whites (as defined by the standard race or ethnicity question) are most likely not to respond (70 percent of noncompliant responses), followed by Latinos (10.5 percent), "others" (8 percent), Asians (5 percent), and African Americans (3 percent).

[16] When group membership is defined by point allocation, these proportions are even more elevated, with 58 percent of those respondents who allocate points to "African American" also allocating identity points to a second group; the corresponding proportions for respondents who allocate points to "Asian American," "Latino or Hispanic," and "Anglo or White" are 42.5 percent, 42 percent, and 25.8 percent, respectively. The incidence of multiracial identification among those respondents who allocate at least 1 point to "Native American" and "Other Race" is even more sizable, at 74.8 percent and 95.8 percent, respectively.

[17] Data are from the Summary File 4, from www.census.gov/census2000/states/ca.html.

TABLE 4.2. *Number of Groups Chosen, by Race or Ethnicity Group as Defined by Self-Identification in the Standard Question Format*

	Respondent Race or Ethnicity by Standard Ethnoracial Identifier						
	Asian Americans	Blacks	Latinos	Whites	Native Americans	Other Race	Total
1 group	76.3	58.3	68.2	79.6	16.7	51.6	73.7
2 groups	20.3	36.7	25.4	15.6	41.7	32.3	20.4
3 groups	3.4	5	3.5	3.4	41.7	12.9	4.4
4 groups	0	0	0.3	0.9	0	3.2	1.1
5 groups	0	0	0.6	0.6	0	0	0.5
Mean	1.27	1.47	1.42	1.27	2.25	1.68	1.34
Standard deviation	0.52	0.60	0.72	0.62	0.75	0.83	0.66
Valid responses	59	60	173	539	12	31	874

Data source: 2003 Golden Bear Omnibus Survey.

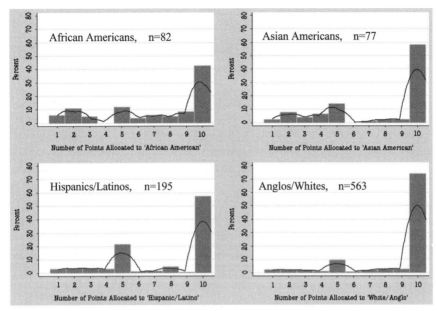

FIGURE 4.2. Identity Point Allocations, by Target Group

relatedly, as a function of how we define group membership. The point allocation approach allows us to also define group membership by the allocation of at least one identity point to a given racial or ethnic category. Defined thus, 58 percent of those respondents who allocate points to "African American" also allocate points to a second race or ethnicity. The corresponding proportions among respondents who allocate points to "Asian American," "Latino or Hispanic," and "Anglo or White" are about 42, 42, and 26 percent, respectively.[18]

The identity point allocation approach can also be used to assess whether, for a given racial or ethnic group, all individuals who self-identify with that category do so in the same, categorical way or in a diversity of graded ways. Recall that in Figure 4.1 we specified at least four distinct ways that identity points might be distributed to a given racial or ethnic category. The actual distribution of points by respondents to the GBO is shown in Figure 4.2. Respondents in Figure 4.2 are grouped into racial or ethnic categories as defined by the standard question format, and the distribution of identity points is shown in two nonparametric forms: as a histogram and as a smoothed kernel

[18] There are also a substantial enough number of respondents who allocate at least one identity point to "Native American" and "other race" to derive a reasonable estimate of the incidence of multiracial identification – a sizable 75 and 96 percent, respectively.

density. As Figure 4.2 shows, not all respondents allocate their points in obviously categorical ways (i.e., "10–0" or "5–5" point allocations). On inspection, whites, as defined by the GBO's standard race or ethnicity question, are most likely to approximate the categorical "invariant allocation" model. Roughly 74 percent of respondents who self-identify as whites in the standard question format allocate all 10 of their identity points to "White or Anglo." The distribution of identity points for Asian Americans and Latinos appears less invariant, with only 58 percent (for Asians) and 57 percent (for Latinos) of respondents who identify with these categories allocating all 10 identity points to the particular category. For African Americans, the distribution evokes the subjective allocation model, with only 43 percent of those who self-identify as African American in the standard format allocating all their identity points to "African American" and a relatively flat distribution among the remaining possible point allocations. Among the four primary racial or ethnic groups, Latinos most closely approximate the likely distribution of a "lineage" allocation, with a large proportion (22 percent) allocating exactly 5 identity points to "Hispanic or Latino."[19]

Figure 4.2 shows the gradations of identification with a particular racial or ethnic category and the group-specific differences in that tendency. On the basis of this illustration alone, it is fair to infer that quantifiable information about a person's strength of ethnoracial self-identification is indeed lost by using the standard categorical format, and this loss is especially acute for nonwhite groups. A more rigorous approach to describing the trade-offs between the standard question format and the point allocation format, however, would be to compare the group-specific distribution of identity points in the case where group boundaries are defined by self-identification in the standard question format ("standard identifiers") against the group-specific distribution in the case of respondents who do not identify with a group in the standard format – *but nonetheless allocate identity points to that race or ethnicity* ("point allocators"). This comparison is shown in Figures 4.3 and 4.4.

Figure 4.3 shows that when we look only at those respondents who ordinarily self-identify with a group in the standard racial or ethnic identifier, the allocation of points is relatively more invariant for whites and Asians. About 82 percent of those respondents who self-identify as whites in the standard format allocate all their identity points to "White or Anglo"; the corresponding proportion for respondents who self-identify as Asian Americans is just over 80 percent. Respondents who self-identify as Latinos still most closely

[19] The Epanechnikov weighting function is used to specify the kernel densities. Figures generated using Stata/SE.

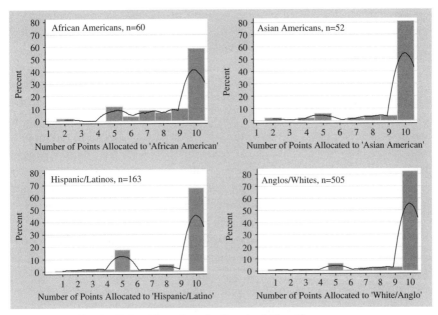

FIGURE 4.3. Identity Point Allocations, by Standard Identifier

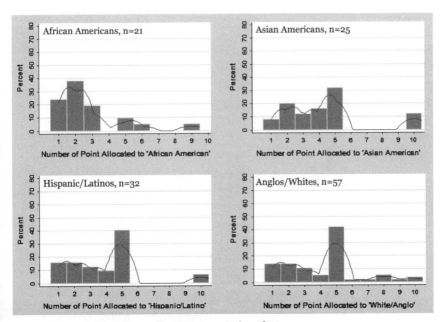

FIGURE 4.4. Identity Point Allocations, non-Identifiers

approximate the lineage allocation scheme, with 67 percent of self-identifiers allocating all 10 identity points to "Hispanic or Latino" and 18 percent allocating exactly 5 identity points to "Hispanic or Latino." African Americans, even when defined by the standard question format, demonstrate the most graded distribution of identity points, with only 58 percent of self-identifiers allocating all 10 identity points to "African American" and a relatively flat distribution of the remaining point allocations. Interestingly, when a respondent self-identifies with a racial or ethnic group in the standard question format, she almost never allocates fewer than 5 identity points to that group, a pattern that is consistent across racial or ethnic groups. Put otherwise, the "response threshold" for self-identification with one of the four primary racial or ethnic groups in the standard question format is almost always 50 percent or higher.[20]

If our standpoint for judging the racial or ethnic identifiers is the information that is lost among those individuals who identify with a racial or ethnic group in standard survey-based measures (multiracial or not), one might conclude that existing standards fare well for whites and Asian Americans and may even suffice for Latinos (especially if coupled with a question on the racial or ethnic background of the respondents' parents). As Figure 4.4 shows, however, the information loss is considerably greater if the focus is on people who would not otherwise self-identify with a racial or ethnic group under the standard format. For one thing, the number of "point allocators" is nontrivial. Fully 57 respondents who do not identify as white in response to the GBO's standard identifier will allocate identity points to "White or Anglo," and the corresponding numbers of African Americans, Asian Americans, and Latinos are 21, 25, and 32 respondents, respectively.

In addition, the distribution of identity points among these "point allocators" in Figure 4.4 is considerably flatter than the distribution of points among "standard identifiers" in Figure 4.3; it is not highly skewed with a disproportionate number of observations at the mode. Figure 4.4 also shows, rather remarkably and curiously, that there are a handful of respondents who do not self-identify in the standard format with a group who will, under the point allocation format, allocate all 10 of their identity points to that group. Finally, Figure 4.4 suggests that point allocators have quite a distinct response threshold. Recall that among standard identifiers, the allocation of fewer than 5 points to a chosen racial or ethnic category is a relatively rare occurrence, if that chosen category is black, white, Asian, or Latino. By contrast, the lion's share of self-identification among point allocators is distributed in the 1 to 5 points

---

[20] By contrast, fully 42 percent of respondents who self-identify as "other race" allocate 5 or fewer than 5 identity points to that category.

range. Among respondents who are African American, Asian American, Latino, and white by point allocation only, the proportion of identity points in the 1 to 5 points range is 90, 88, 94, and 86 percent, respectively. Thus, as anticipated in our earlier discussion, it is precisely those respondents with low identity thresholds who will escape notice under the standard categorical question formats.

These findings from the GBO make a strong case that the racial or ethnic portrait of California is substantially more multiracial and that the process of self-identification with a racial or ethnic group is substantially more subjective and contingent than we assume in our standard racial or ethnic identifiers. They also make a strong case that we stand to lose a fair bit of the potential variation in how individuals self-identify by racial and ethnic terms, especially where identification as African American or Latino is concerned. What we see, in short, depends on how we ask. But we have yet to make the case that changing the boundaries of racial or ethnic self-definition will have consequences for what we infer about a particular racial or ethnic group. Put otherwise, how do "point allocators" compare to "standard identifiers"? If point allocators are similar to standard identifiers but for the sensitivity to question format, then we should not expect to see substantial changes to our well-established and widely accepted facts about demographic and attitudinal differences between racial or ethnic groups.

As we noted earlier, however, such differences are quite likely, because the relative salience and the contingent expression of our racial or ethnic identities is likely to tell us something about one's material well-being and sociopolitical orientation. The GBO is admittedly not designed for a robust analysis of the consequences of defining racial or ethnic boundaries by identity weights rather than a standard categorical format – the number of demographic and attitudinal items we can examine are minimal, and the number of observations, once the sample is disaggregated into racial or ethnic groups and standard identifier or point allocator types, is sometimes quite small (less than twenty cases, in some cells of Table 4.3). The findings here are thus admittedly descriptive and suggestive.

In Table 4.3, standard identifiers are compared to point allocators on three demographic indicators (educational attainment and family income and two additional political indicators (party identification and support for affirmative action).[21] With the two indicators of socioeconomic status, to the extent

---

[21] The specific question wording for the affirmative action item is: "The U.S. Supreme Court recently decided that an applicant's race could be used as a factor in making college admissions decisions. Do you favor or oppose the Supreme Court's decision? [If FAVOR] Do you strongly favor or somewhat favor the decision? [If OPPOSE] Do you strongly oppose or somewhat oppose the decision?"

TABLE 4.3. *Average Point Allocations, by Race or Ethnicity (Defined by Standard Format)*

	Respondent Race or Ethnicity by Standard Ethnoracial Identifier					
	Asian Americans	Blacks	Latinos	Whites	Native Americans	Other Race
"Asian American" points	8.54	0.17	0.17	0.04	0.42	1.39
"African American" points	0.03	8.67	0.11	0.04	0.33	0.42
"Hispanic or Latino" points	0.08	0.03	8.24	0.14	0.83	1.19
"White or Anglo" points	0.56	0.40	0.68	8.60	1.83	1.55
"Native American" points	0.00	0.62	0.21	0.31	5.50	0.48
"Other Race" points	0.78	0.12	0.58	0.80	1.08	4.97
Valid responses	59	60	173	539	12	31

Data source: 2003 Golden Bear Omnibus Survey.

that there are differential material benefits and costs of how a person is defined by race or ethnicity, the differences between standard identifiers and point allocators should parallel the relative socioeconomic advantages between groups. That is, for groups that are relatively advantaged in material terms by existing group boundaries, standard identifiers look better educated and better-off (Asians and whites); for groups that are relatively disadvantaged, the point allocators look better educated and better-off (Latinos and blacks). In Table 4.3, this pattern is especially pronounced in the educational differences between standard identifiers and point allocators. For instance, roughly one in four white standard identifiers and one in three Asian American standard identifiers have some postbaccalaureate education, whereas only about one in six white point allocators and one in five Asian point allocators have a similarly high level of educational attainment. With Latinos and African Americans, the effects are opposite: Latino point allocators are more than four times as likely to have some postbaccalaureate education than Latino standard identifiers (31 to 7 percent), and African American point allocators are more than twice as likely to have some education beyond a college degree than African American standard identifiers (25 to 12 percent). Thus, the racial divide in socioeconomic status varies, in part, as a function of how intensely one self-identifies with a racial or ethnic group. Put more provocatively, loosening the prevailing racial or ethnic boundaries to include point allocators will have the effect of seemingly narrowing the vast income and educational gaps between blacks and Latinos on one side and Asians and whites on the other.

With our political variables, we see hints of a different organization to race (i.e., different from the antipodes of black or Latino and white or Asian). For party identification, the only discernible difference between standard identifiers and point allocators is for African Americans, and it is a big effect. While standard identifiers are disproportionately Democratic in their partisanship (72 percent identifying as Democrats and 26 percent as Independents), the party identification of point allocators is significantly more dispersed (with only 42 percent Democrats, 37 percent Independents, and 21 percent Republicans). This result echoes previous research on the strong, perhaps uniquely so, linkage of racial group identification with Democratic Party identification for African Americans (Tate 1993; Dawson 1994). In Table 4.3, we see that, if the group definition for "African American" is loosened to include point allocators, African American party politics no longer looks as monolithically Democratic.

Finally, with affirmative action, Table 4.3 shows sensitivity of the black-white divide in public opinion to the way we define group membership as "white" or "African American." When membership is defined by the standard question format, there is a sizable gap between whites and blacks: 36 percent of African Americans and only 13 percent of whites strongly support the Supreme Court's decision in the University of Michigan cases; 46 percent of whites and only 28 percent of blacks strongly oppose the decision. When we compare point allocators, this black-white divide virtually vanishes. If anything, white point allocators appear somewhat likelier to strongly support affirmative action than African American point allocators, albeit with a number of observations that is too small for any strong inferences to be drawn. As with income and education differences and partisanship, these differences in support for affirmative action should not be surprising, but they confirm the meaningful effects that moving from our existing standard, categorical ethnoracial identification formats to something more flexible and graded, like identity point allocation, are likely to have.

LIMITATIONS AND FUTURE RESEARCH

In reflecting back on the 2000 census, Ken Prewitt (2003: 357) observes that our current measurement of race and ethnicity is "less well grounded in science than any other population characteristic measured by the nation's statistical agencies." Not coincidentally, no other population characteristic generates as much political fire as how we count Americans by race and ethnicity. The most recent changes to our ethnoracial classification system have galvanized a concerted and mounting challenge from Nathan Glazer, George F. Will, and others against the very notion of collecting data by race or ethnicity. As Glazer (2002: 22, 31) articulates this challenge, "The census contains a message to the

American people, and like any message it educates them to some end: It tells them that the government thinks the most important thing about them is their race and ethnicity." Glazer wistfully imagines a future "when the present questions on race and Hispanicity will seem as outlandish as the attempt to count quadroons and octoroons in 1890."

In this chapter, I have suggested that a measure of the political controversy results from the Census Bureau's attempts to navigate between two potentially antagonistic and analytically separable currents: the Scylla of enumeration (for the instrumental purpose of implementing public policy or understanding public opinion) and the Charybdis of expression (for the intrinsic purpose of recognizing and respecting individuals). This tension is further exacerbated by the gap between race or ethnicity as social theorists describe it (as a fluid and contingent social construction) and race or ethnicity as social scientists measure it (as a fixed and categorical observable reality). This chapter investigates one promising means of separating out these potentially distinct aims by designing a new ethnoracial identifier that gives individuals substantial latitude over how to define themselves in racial or ethnic terms.[22]

According to data from a study of adult Californians, the proposed "identity point allocation" scheme appears to be a valid and potentially useful new approach to studying how we define ourselves in ethnic and racial terms. The findings show a markedly more multiracial and ethnoracially diverse California than we find from census data or from social surveys. Furthermore, the findings in this chapter show some conspicuous group differences in self-identification. From the standpoint of survey research methodology, the implications of this chapter are potentially far-reaching. By asking individuals to define their race or ethnicity only in categorical terms, as social surveys almost always do, we are not simply reflecting the reality of a target population that views its race or ethnicity in such categorical terms. Rather, we are missing potentially critical variation in this reality by simplifying the choice set for our respondents.

As powerful and provocative as these results are, they beg as many questions as they answer. One obvious potential limitation of the GBO study is that

---

[22] It is a somewhat open question as to which of the two alternatives examined in this chapter – point allocation or the standard categorical measure – is a more "constructivist" approach On one view, identity point allocation is more constructivist in that it more faithfully captures the multiplicity and intensity of ways that people identify with a given menu of identity categories (e.g., the five racial or ethnic categories used here). On another view, the standard approach is more "constructivist" in that it forces individuals into choices they might not otherwise opt for and do so on the basis of prevailing social conventions and durable habits. The difference here is, in the main, semantic.

California may be a unique case, as it often is on matters of race relations and ethnic politics. If social construction is a coordination game with a tipping point between societies with fixed, rigid racial orders and societies with more fluid, flexible ethnoracial boundaries (Laitin 1998), California may yet still be the exception to the rule in the United States today – especially by comparison to a region like the Deep South, where racial boundaries may remain commonly understood and well defined.[23]

A second limitation stems from potential bias in the way that the identity point allocation measure was asked in the GBO. Most obviously, the question wording is rather cumbersome, especially in relation to the decidedly more economical "Mark one or more races to indicate what this person considers himself/herself to be" wording of the census, or commonly used variants found in the National Election Studies (NES), General Social Survey (GSS), and other social surveys. Occam's razor cuts unwieldy survey questions just as sharply as it does convoluted social theories. A second concern with the question format of the GBO is that respondents are primed to consider Tiger Woods's race before self-identifying themselves. Conjuring up Woods – who is celebrated for his racial polysemy and his self-monikered "Cablanasian" background – as a relevant consideration may invite a more fluid view of one's ethnoracial identity. More generally, allocating identity points in a nonpolitical context (vis-à-vis a professional golfer) may invite a more symbolic, cultural view of identity than the more instrumental, political context of Census 2000 – in which one's ethnoracial self-identification is asked by the federal government for the purposes of counting the body politic, distributing federal resources, and apportioning electoral offices.

These limitations caution against any strong conclusions from our study. They also chart a road map for future work. One obvious path to take is to compare the results from California against a random national sample of adults. For that matter, the potential for what we infer about racial or ethnic composition and its empirical correlates – inequality, violence, democratization, contentious politics, and the like – to vary as a function of question format is not a cause for concern isolated to the study of American politics. As academic fora like the Laboratory in Comparative Ethnic Processes, the Harvard Identity Project, and the symposium in the 2001 American Political Science Association comparative politics newsletter indicate, there is ample interest and need for new research into social constructivism in comparative contexts as well.

---

[23] Some of the most striking increases in the foreign-born and ethnic minority population in the 2000 census, however, have been in the historically Deep South states.

Beyond the generalizability of the findings in this chapter, another venue for
further work is to continue to refine and develop alternative measurement
approaches. The most immediate in this regard is to continue to test the validity
of the identity point allocation item in the GBO through embedded survey
experiments that vary the wording and order of the identity point allocation
measure. Another possibility would be to experiment with a broader menu of
racial or ethnic choices – for instance, disaggregating the category of "Whites
or Anglos" (to see if "whiteness" can be made less "invariant") or preceding
the point allocation question with an open-ended item where respondents name
the racial or ethnic categories that they will be allocating identity points to.
Respondents could, for instance, be randomly assigned to one of three conditions: a control group that is asked the 10-point question without any prior
framing; a treatment group that is asked to describe Tiger Woods before self-
identifying (replicating the GBO format); and a second treatment group that is
asked to self-identify but with question wording that primes them to think of
the census questionnaire. A third possible path for future research would be to
compare identity point allocation not just to our standard racial or ethnic
identifier but also to other commonly used measurement approaches to group
identity such as the psychometric use of a battery of items or the use of single-
item and or multiple-item scales that measure concepts like "linked fate,"
"feeling thermometers," "group consciousness," "relative group position,"
"social dominance," "conjoint measurement," and "implicit association."

Substantively, two venues for future work are to examine the other dimensions of social identification (beyond ethnoracial self-identification) using the
point allocation approach and to test for the consequences of shifting away
from the standard format of mutually exclusive racial or ethnic categories on
various social, economic, and political phenomena of interest. On the first of
these, the identity point allocation approach can be used in other contexts that
allow us to examine heterogeneity (by comparing superordinate to subordinate
identification – that is, between "panethnic" identification as Asian American,
Latino, Native American, and white to "ethnic" identification as Chinese,
Cuban, Cherokee, and Czech), intersubjectivity and hybridity (by comparing
self-identification to external ascription), and multiplicity and intersectionality
(by comparing racial or ethnic identification to self-definition by gender, sexual
orientation, religion, partisanship, ideology, class, inter alia) of social identification. Pursuing these questions, importantly, will require the coupling of
survey-based methods with more qualitative in-depth interviews and focus
group discussion. On the second venue, the results shown in Table 4.4, while
suggestive, are highly descriptive and based on a very small number of observations. Using a larger sample, a more complete stock of indicators, and more

TABLE 4.4. *Demographic and Attitudinal Characteristics of Standard Identifiers and Point Allocators*

	Bk(pt)	Bk(std)	APA(pt)	APA(std)	LAT(pt)	LAT(std)	Wh(pt)	Wh(std)
Education								
High school or less	20.0	23.7	25.0	7.7	28.1	58.4	19.6	18.0
Some college	40.0	50.9	50.0	28.9	28.1	28.6	42.9	34.1
College degree	15.0	13.6	4.2	30.8	12.5	6.2	21.4	23.4
Postcollege	25.0	11.9	20.8	32.7	31.3	6.8	16.1	24.6
Observations	20	59	24	52	32	161	56	505
Pearson's chi-square (sig.)	2.18 (0.54)		11.80 (0.01)		20.66 (0.00)		2.80 (0.42)	
Family income								
< $25K	17.7	22.0	8.7	8.9	11.1	42.9	12.2	10.7
$25–50K	23.5	18.0	26.1	13.3	18.5	17.9	24.5	20.1
$50–100K	47.1	40.0	47.8	48.9	37.0	31.4	44.9	36.0
> $100K	11.8	20.0	17.4	28.9	33.3	7.9	18.4	33.3
Observations	17	50	23	45	27	140	49	439
Pearson's chi-square (sig.)	0.95 (0.81)		2.22 (0.53)		18.54 (0.00)		4.55 (2.08)	
Party identification								
Republican	21.1	1.9	27.3	21.4	23.1	18.3	26.5	33.6
Independent	36.9	25.9	36.4	42.8	26.9	30.0	32.7	27.0
Democrat	42.1	72.2	36.4	35.7	50.0	51.7	40.8	39.4
Observations	19	54	22	42	26	120	49	452
Pearson's chi-square (sig.)	10.13 (0.01)		0.36 (0.83)		0.33 (0.85)		1.21 (0.55)	
Affirmative action								
Strongly support	15.8	36.2	12.0	14.6	19.4	27.1	23.6	13.2
Somewhat support	42.1	17.2	24.0	25.0	16.1	23.9	30.9	21.2
Somewhat oppose	15.8	19.0	32.0	16.7	29.0	18.1	18.2	19.6
Strongly oppose	26.3	27.6	32.0	43.8	35.5	31.0	27.3	46.0
Observations	19	58	25	48	31	155	55	485
Pearson's chi-square (sig.)	5.79 (0.12)		2.42 (0.49)		3.01 (0.39)		9.83 (0.20)	

exacting statistical methods, we might examine whether moving to a more fluid and flexible measure like the point allocation approach induces individuals to think differently about policy debates around education, employment, immigration, and voting rights; about partisanship, core political values, and active citizenship; or about group stereotypes and attitudes about interracial marriages, residential integration, and the like.

Finally, the fact that a substantially greater proportion of individuals chooses a multiracial category under the identity point allocation format than does so under the standard identifier does not necessarily imply that people are dissembling in their responses to the census or that identity point allocation somehow taps into people's "true" identities. For that matter, neither does it imply that the claims by multiracial movement advocates of a pervasively multiracial America are more valid nor does it imply that the mobilized opposition to the multiracial identifier is somehow alarmist and mired in a "special interests" political spoils system. This chapter is agnostic on these matters and aims to hew as closely as possible to the principal goal of insisting on certain empirical standards for theoretical accounts of race as a social construction. In doing so, a corollary goal has been to develop the identity point allocation scheme as a context-specific *complement to,* and not a *substitute for,* the standard ethnoracial self-identifier.

The need for greater precision and specificity in our measurement approaches is critical to understanding how race and ethnicity work as organizing principles in our social, economic, and political life, especially so amid dynamic contemporaneous changes like the rise of the rights revolution and the politics of recognition, the post-1965 wave of immigration, the rise of the multiracial identity movement, the backlash of racial conservatism and white nativism, and the resurgence of patriotism and national identity in the aftermath of 9/11. Greater precision and specificity is also critical, as I hope this chapter has shown, to better understanding the content of and contestation over "what the group means to its members" (Abdelal et al. 2006). Ultimately, greater conceptual clarity and empirical specificity are our best hope for addressing and adjudicating between the growing chorus of advocates and skeptics of the existing scholarship on identity and politics (Hacking 1999; Junn 1999; Brubaker and Cooper 2000; Omi 2000; Brady 2004a; Granato and Scioli 2004; R. Smith 2002; and Abdelal et al. 2006).

5

Balancing National and Ethnic Identities

The Psychology of E Pluribus Unum

Jack Citrin and David O. Sears

INTRODUCTION

In a challenge to the ongoing American experiment of reconciling unity and diversity, Ernest Gellner (1983) called a multiethnic nation-state an oxymoron, arguing that minority groups ultimately would have to assimilate or secede. Using history to assess the validity of Gellner's claim that cultural unity is necessary for sustaining a sense of common national identity is difficult, however, given the slipperiness of key terms such as "culture" and "nation." Does culture refer just to a common language or to a thicker layer of common understandings and, if so, just how thick? And does a sense of national identity mean an emotional attachment to one's homeland and everyone living there or a more bounded sense of solidarity with only those who share one's physical characteristics or cultural norms?

Despite the problems with testing Gellner's proposition, its contemporary relevance is obvious. Indeed, globalization and migration-driven multiculturalism are twin threats to Gellnerian nationalism and its institutional expression, the sovereign state. In the United States, ethnic identities have become more salient because of immigration, religious sectarianism, the development of linguistic enclaves, and the ideology of multiculturalism. At the same time, as the aftermath of September 11 shows, patriotic feelings continue to run very high (Huntington 2004).

One policy for achieving unity in the face of cultural diversity is forced assimilation, as with the aggressive "Americanization" program aimed at the immigrants of the early twentieth century. Another is to enshrine publicly a

The authors thank Amy Lerman, Michael Murakami, and Kathryn Pearson for their contributions to this chapter.

dominant national culture but leave minority groups alone; France has tended to follow this approach. A third solution, followed by the United States for at least part of its recent history (Walzer 1997), is to proclaim no single ethnic or religious preference as the nation's defining identity but simply to demand as a price of nationhood that everyone endorses democratic political principles and tolerates everyone else's customs. A final approach is to elevate the value of difference, going beyond simply accepting diversity to strengthening it through government policies. In multicultural nationalism, there is virtually nothing on the *unum* side of the scale of identities.

In a democracy, the choice among these policies – the meaning of one's national identity – depends in part on the attitudes of citizens who must also balance the claims of unity and diversity. At the individual level, this dilemma entails the accommodation of multiple identities, or, more specifically, the negotiation of identity claims deriving from membership in both an overarching national group and a more restricted ethnic group. This chapter uses survey data to describe how Americans order their national and ethnic identities, to investigate the factors giving rise to different modes of structuring, and to track the influence of strong national and ethnic identifications, respectively, on several public policies. The substantive goal is to investigate when national and ethnic identities should be viewed as competing or complementary. The methodological goal is to improve the conceptualization and measurement of American national identity.

DEFINING IDENTITY

As the introductory chapter to this volume shows, the voluminous academic literature on "identity" resembles a quagmire rather than a tunnel ending in conceptual clarity. Because the term is used to mean both sameness and difference, both commonality and individuality, this should not be surprising. Still, the drawing power of "identity" makes it unlikely that the suggestion to consign it to the dustbin of scientific history will take hold (Brubaker and Cooper 2000), so the best one can do is to stipulate a definition that helps address the dominant theoretical and empirical issues concerning "identity politics." And although definitions of "identity" abound, there is a surprising consensus about the nature of these questions. We outline seven main points of agreement.

1. National and ethnic identities are *social* identities. They have *relational content* in the sense spelled out in the introductory chapter of this volume. Identities refer to dimensions of one's self-concept defined by perceptions of similarity with some and difference from others. Social identities develop because people perceive themselves as belonging to groups and pursue their

goals through membership in these groups. Social identities arise from a process of social comparison and their formation inevitably requires drawing boundaries between "us" and "them." Visible markers may define the relational content of identity, the aspect of one's self shared with a specified set of others. But group boundaries also may be socially constructed. Sometimes "we" draw the boundaries, sometimes "they." In Sartre's famous comment: anti-Semitism assures that Jews (and a Jewish identity) will endure. So one important question with implications for group conflict is whether there is agreement about the boundaries of group membership. The assimilated German Jews thought of themselves in national rather than ethnic terms; the Nazis viewed things differently.

2. Politics can be critical in the "social construction" of group identities. That is, the *relational* content of a group's identity is *purposive* (see Abdelal et al., Chapter 1 in this volume). Members of the group are connected by common goals such as attaining political independence, securing representation, or obtaining symbolic recognition for prior achievements. Nation building is a process of inclusion and exclusion, and political decisions reflect the balance of power among contending groups' boundaries and determine their permeability. The answer to the question, Who is an American? has changed over the country's history. Lind (1995) refers to the first American nation as Anglo-Protestant, the second as European and Christian, and the third in the post–World War II era as cosmopolitan and multiracial. Rogers Smith (1997) has documented how immigration and naturalization laws have embodied these competing definitions of nationhood and established a racial hierarchy. By linking demographic classifications to political purposes, the U.S. Census has also played a part in demarcating group identities. In the nineteenth century, the "one drop of blood" rule was used to limit the mobility and power of blacks. More recently, however, some black activists have sought to use that rule to increase the official size of their ethnic group as part of the competition for government benefits allocated on ethnic grounds. More generally, politics constrains identity choice and provides incentives for the maintenance and intensification of particular group identifications.

3. In defining social identities, it is critical to distinguish among the cognitive and affective dimensions of their relational content (Citrin, Wong, and Duff 2001; Brubaker and Cooper 2000). The act of self-categorization answers the cognitive, Who am I? question, but the *strength* of one's identification with a particular membership group – the emotional significance of a social identity – varies. One can call oneself an American without feeling strongly patriotic or believing that nationality is fundamental to one's self-concept. Identifying *as* is not the same as identifying *with*. The motivational basis for strongly

identifying with a group is the individual's need for a positive sense of self-esteem, which seemingly derives in part from the worth accorded to one's group.

4. The content of a social identity gives concrete meaning to membership in a particular group. Identities may be defined by their purposes, but typically there are constitutive norms that define full membership in a group. The normative content of an idea spells out the physical features, values, and conduct represented by the prototypical member of the group. A standard expectation is that strong psychological identification with the group will engender conformity to the group's constitutive norms. The bases on which collective judgments of sameness or difference rest can vary across time and space (Horowitz 1985). In other words, the content of national identity can be contested as well as constructed. Content and contestation are the two dimensions of collective identity isolated in the introductory chapter, and contestation focuses on the content of a collective identity rather than on the fact that particular group boundaries are important. One can agree that there are Americans and non-Americans, yet debate whether popular attitudes and public policy have conceived of the nation in inclusionary, cosmopolitan terms or in ethnocultural terms that privilege members of particular racial and cultural groups. Assessing the competing claims on this point presents formidable methodological problems, but at bottom the task is to specify the content of the constitutive norms defining American national identity.

5. Social identities have political relevance because they channel feelings of mutuality, obligation, and antagonism, delineating the contours of one's willingness to help other people and the boundaries of support for policies allocating resources based on group membership. Indeed, the intimate connection between the personal and the social bases of self-regard becomes clear when one recalls how quickly an insult to the dignity of one's group can trigger ethnic violence (Horowitz 1985). Identities can be a matter of life and death. In the name of the nation, ethnic group, or religion, people are willing both to die for "our people" and to commit unspeakable crimes against the dehumanized "others." More generally, identity politics refers to the mobilization of group pride to advance perceived collective group interests, calling upon people to judge events, policies, and candidates primarily in terms of how they would affect the standing and heritage of one's group. In the study of group conflict, the *politicization* of identities is an important research question.

6. The connection between group identity and political cohesion is a major focus of inquiry. One leading hypothesis is that social identities are more likely to influence behavior as they acquire emotional significance (Tajfel

1981a). A strong sense of identity is hypothesized to engender a willingness to conform to and defend group norms.

7. In modern society, individuals belong to several, usually overlapping groups, including national, regional, ethnic, and professional groups – hence, the familiar assertion that individuals have multiple identities based on contrasting themselves with varied sets of "others" (Sen 2000; Brewer and Roccas 2001). The number, nature, and relative significance of these varied social identities change with life circumstances and political events. The existence of multiple identities raises the problem of prioritization. That is, when confronting a political choice, which of one's several memberships and identifications ultimately governs one's actions? The particular relationship examined in this chapter is the subjective balance between nationality and ethnicity in the United States.

IDENTITY CHOICE: NATION OR ETHNIC GROUP?

Nationalists insist on the priority of identity with the nation over all other foci of affiliation. Along these lines, the British politician Norman Tebbitt proposed the "cricket test" for national identity. He proclaimed that the failure of British citizens of South Asian or West Indian origin to cheer for the English team when it played India, Pakistan, or Jamaica meant that their strongest identification was with their country of origin and not their physical and political home. Linda Chavez echoed this sentiment when Latino fans rooted for Mexico and booed the American national anthem at an international soccer match in Los Angeles. More recently, Samuel Huntington (2004) predicts that the ongoing pattern of Mexican immigration into the United States will fragment the nation by eroding the cultural unity underlying its sense of common identity and purpose.

In rebuttal, Amartya Sen (2000) argued that the "fan's test," does not prove that nationality and ethnicity were competing identities; one could root for the Pakistani cricket team and still fulfill all the responsibilities of citizenship. The same holds true for the African-American tennis fan supporting Serena Williams when she plays fellow American Jennifer Capriati. If Sen is correct, then nationality and ethnicity do not always compete. Put another way, context helps determine the salience of group identities and their relevance for behavior. Yet there are occasions when these loyalties do tug in opposite directions. After Pearl Harbor, Japanese-Americans faced a choice between loyalty to their new country and support for their country of origin. Overwhelmingly, and despite internment by their own government, they demonstrated the primacy of their American national identity.

In a multiethnic society like the United States, the individual's national and ethnic identities do not completely overlap; Americans share membership in the overarching national group with people from ethnic "out-groups." Brewer and Roccas (2001: 5–10) introduce the concept of "social identity complexity" to represent the coexistence of these multiple group memberships and outline four alternative ways for an individual to reconcile the tensions that may emanate from this circumstance. Of particular significance is what each mode of ordering one's multiple identities implies for the inclusion or exclusion of others from what David Hollinger (1995) evocatively calls the "Circle of We."

Dominance is the strategy of subordinating all potential group identities to one primary attachment. Nationalists insist that one's American identity take precedence; indeed, we shall see that most whites define themselves as "just" Americans and eschew ethnic labels even when pressed. From the perspective of immigrants, assimilating to the host country at the expense of their original ethnic heritage is one variant of the dominance model. Exclusive identification with one's ethnic origins combined with separation from the mainstream culture is another.

Compartmentalization is a solution in which the particular identity activated depends on the situation. Another way of characterizing this approach is that the individual's primary identity is domain-specific. According to Horowitz (1975: 118), all ascriptive identities are "heavily contextual." In Europe, the authors of this chapter are Americans; in Boston, we are Californians. Sometimes only one social identity is evoked by a situation; for example, local elections and environmental policies rarely activate nationalist sentiments. Yet there are contexts in which more than one kind of self-categorization is relevant and when choice is inevitable.

Intersection is a third mode of reconciling multiple identities. In a multiethnic society, this involves the formation of a "blended bicultural identity." The definition of one's in-group thus becomes those who share both ethnic heritage and residence in the host country (Brewer and Roccas 2001: 13). The preferred self-representation is the "hyphenated" identity of *African*-American, *Mexican*-American, or *Italian*-American These terms imply more than the mere addition or concomitance of two group memberships; rather, this mode of identification intimates the existence of a unique configuration of interests derived from the specific experiences of particular ethnic groups in the American context (Brewer and Roccas 2001: 13).

Merger, the final model for managing multiple group identities, widens the boundaries of the in-group to include people who share any of one's important memberships. This merged social identity is highly inclusive and diverse as when both national and ethnic identities are subordinated to the norms and values of a cosmopolitan, humanitarian ideology held by individuals who see themselves as "world citizens."

It is, of course, misleading to conceive of identity choices in purely individualistic terms. As noted, how to integrate national and ethnic identities is a collective problem for which there are competing ideological solutions. Hence, social norms and official policies toward multiculturalism are likely to influence the distribution of identity choices. Here we ask whether Americans do in fact experience a tension between their national and ethnic identifications. If so, which takes precedence, loyalty to nation or pride in ethnic group? And does this ordering of identities vary across the country's main ethnic groups? More specifically, does a strong sense of ethnic identity among America's minority groups and immigrants undermine their sense of national identity or are national and ethnic loyalties compatible?

Two images of ethnic relations in America frame this analysis. One emphasizes a process of assimilation through which immigrants gradually become more similar to native-born Americans in their self-identification and patriotism. The second emphasizes the exceptional status of "people of color," both as targets of discrimination and prejudice and as a group estranged from the national political community as a result of its history of oppression. In conceptual terms, these images combine the relational, normative, and purposive dimensions of group identities in different ways. The assimilation model regards the relational boundary of membership in the American national community as permeable: newcomers may belong once they acquire the cultural norms that constitute this group identity. The "people of color" model of black exceptionalism rests on the persistence of a racial divide between "ins" and "outs," whether black, Asian, or Latino, and implicitly links that divide to divergent political preferences and behaviors.

PREDICTING IDENTITY CHOICE

Ethnicity is a likely correlate of identity choice in a multicultural society. Because people tend to live and interact with others like themselves, the majority group is likely to perceive most other citizens as sharing their physical characteristics and values. So there is a simple perceptual or cognitive basis for members of the majority ethnic group to define themselves as "just Americans," particularly when the structural integration of white immigrants is virtually complete (Alba 1990; Glazer 1997). In addition, the majority group has an interest in the dominance of its own cultural norms and thus is less likely to favor identities based on other cultural heritages. On the other hand, members of groups that differ markedly from the majority are likely both to perceive themselves as different and to be treated as such. Particularly when the boundaries between ethnic groups are sharp and impermeable, minority groups should be more likely to identify in ethnic terms. *Ceteris paribus,* it is expected that whites will define themselves exclusively in terms of their national identity more often than blacks, Latinos, or Asians.

Similarly, immigrants should be more likely than the native-born to adopt the ethnic-dominant or hyphenated self-definition. However, if it is true that assimilation proceeds in a straight line over time, this gap should diminish with each succeeding generation of immigrants. The outcome here has obvious relevance for the current debate over whether immigrants from Asia and Latin America will follow the assimilationist path of their European predecessors (Barone 2001; Brimelow 1995; Huntington 2004).

Political socialization is another source of identity choice. As already noted, people are exposed to different norms regarding the relative merits of assimilating or maintaining one's original ethnic culture. Multiculturalism, which posits the preeminence of ethnicity in defining one's identity and inter-ests, is a relatively new ideology most widely diffused in the nation's colleges and universities. Exposure to these ideas therefore may foster political outlooks that devalue nationalism in favor of subgroup identifications. So a reasonable expectation is that the relatively young and better-educated segments of the population are more likely to adopt or approve hyphenated and ethnic self-definitions.

The political relevance of social identities rests partly on how they influence attitudes and behavior toward one's own and other groups. If the assimilation model of American ethnic group relations remains accurate, then over time today's immigrants and their offspring should come to identify themselves as Americans first and as members of a particular ethnic group second. Ethnic differences in patriotism should be relatively small and primarily reflect a group's length of tenure in the United States.

Expectations about how national and ethnic attachments should be associated over time depend on what one means by the melting pot. If melting means cleansing, then successful assimilation would mean that a strong sense of national attachment should have washed away the residues of an earlier, primary loyalty to the ethnic group (Sidanius et al. 1997). By contrast, if melting means blending, strong identifications with both nation and ethnic group are not merely compatible but may even be mutually reinforcing. The contrast between these two images of the melting pot centers on how minority groups prioritize their national and ethnic identities.

DATA AND MEASURES

The analysis in this chapter derives from a larger project on American identity conducted by the authors. The data come from the 1992 and 2002 American National Election Studies (ANES), the 1994 and 1996 General Social Surveys (GSS), and the series of Los Angeles County Social Surveys (LACSS) conducted between 1994 and 2000. The ANES and GSS report the results of face-to-face interviews administered to nationally representative samples of adults. The GSS surveys employ a split-sample design, and the data presented here come principally from the multiculturalism modules administered to half the sample in both 1994 and 1996. The national scope of the ANES and GSS is a great advantage, but this is offset by the paucity of minority respondents. As a result, one must be cautious in interpreting the results reported for the relatively small numbers of blacks and Hispanics in these national surveys.

The LACSS is a random-digit-dialed, computer-assisted telephone survey of a representative sample of adults living in Los Angeles County. By pooling these surveys it is possible to obtain a sufficient number of respondents from minority groups for multivariate analysis. It is also possible to subdivide Hispanic respondents according to their nativity and citizenship status. The continuing salience of ethnicity in Los Angeles, an extraordinarily diverse community, makes it a particularly useful case for studying the interplay between national and ethnic identities. And the nature of the items included in the LACSS enables us to implement a straightforward classification of respondents into the categories of identity choice proposed by Brewer and Roccas.

Before discussing the measures of identity employed here, it is worth commenting on the advantages and pitfalls of relying on the survey method. Designing the appropriate sample is one major problem when identities may be multiple and contested. If there is an interest in the general public, a national sample, even if a representative cross section, is unlikely to yield a sufficient number of respondents from minority groups, either because they are too few and scattered or because they are concentrated in just a few localities. In the present instance, for example, national samples of the U.S. population customarily include too few black, Hispanic, or Asian respondents to allow for systematic analysis of these groups. This often dictates a strategy of over-sampling followed by complicated weighting processes, but this may still fail to allow for comparisons of identity formation in a range of demographic contexts. For this reason, the analysis reported here relies on a pooled set of Los Angeles County Surveys. This strategy provides enough cases to compare beliefs across ethnic groups and immigrant generations but can make no claim to representativeness across locales.

In a multiethnic society, the language and race of interviewers also are factors that may condition responses about political identities. For example, English-speaking ability among Hispanic and Asian-Americans depends substantially on whether they and their parents were born in the United States. Again, findings about the distribution and strength of ethnic identification in these groups may be influenced by the ability to conduct interviews in languages other than English.

Additional issues arise when it comes to operationalizing the tripartite conceptualization of identity that distinguishes among cognitive, affective, and normative dimensions. Self-categorization is relatively straightforward, as people can be asked directly what ethnic category they perceive themselves as a member of. Assessing the strength of identification arguably is more complex, but there is a range of available measures, including the "feeling thermometers" pioneered by the American National Election Studies and a readily exported measure of collective self-esteem developed by Luhtanen and Crocker (1992). Among the constituent items in this scale when adapted to tap a sense of national identity are "I often think of myself as American," "Being an American is very important to who I am," and "I am proud of being an American" (Citrin, Wong, and Duff 2001; Sniderman, Hagendoorn, and Prior 2004).

Measuring the *content* of national identities through surveys is a complex task that implies designating a prototypical member of the nation when the meaning of being American, British, Dutch and so forth may be contested. One distinction that pervades the literature on nationalism is between "civic" and "ethnic" or "cultural" conceptions of nation. The former category includes as a member of "the Circle of We" any legal member of the polity prepared to assume the obligations of citizenship. The latter perceives the boundaries of the national group as including only those who share a common ancestry and cultural heritage with the historically ethnic core or majority.

But how to determine what concept of national identity prevails? One method is to distill the statements of political leaders, founding documents, laws, literature, and the impressions of commentators such as de Tocqueville and Bryce (in the American case). This is the tack taken by Huntington (2004) in his depiction of American national identity as defined by the fusion of a civic political creed and "Anglo-Protestant culture." In a related approach, Reicher and Hopkins (2001) explore the content of Scottish national identity by recording the ideas of political activists across the political spectrum about what makes that people distinctive. Whether one accepts this formula or not, it is quite another matter whether ordinary citizens imagine the national community in the same way or adhere to these norms.

In previous research (Citrin, Reingold, and Green 1990; Citrin et al. 1994), we integrated expert judgments about American national identity with popular beliefs assessed by both open-ended and closed-ended questions. Respondents first were asked whether "there are unique American qualities that make us different from citizens from other countries." The answer was overwhelmingly affirmative; 80 percent agreed that there are uniquely American qualities. When asked to name the distinctive American qualities, the most common response referred to individual freedoms, and the second most common response mentioned the quality of independence or individual effort and opportunity (Citrin et al. 1994: 11).

To get at subjective conceptions of the prototype of American identity more directly, we developed a question that asked respondents to rate the importance of various qualities in making someone a "true American." This methodology recently has been applied to measure the content of British national identity (Rothì, Lyons, and Chryssochoou 2005). In the American case, the attributes listed were drawn from scholarly descriptions of both civic and ethnic or cultural conceptions and included universal qualities such as social equality, self-reliance, civic engagement, and "feeling American" as well as more particularistic characteristics such as believing in God, speaking English, and being born in America. It should be emphasized that this is a measure of normative beliefs rather than the respondent's personal conduct. As with all survey-based measures, one might question whether the range of relevant attributes was adequately represented and whether response effects, including social desirability or order effects, resulting in nonrandom measurement error engender serious validity problems. Clearly, there is more work to be done in the measurement of the content of national identities. Nevertheless, it appears that many Americans simultaneously endorse important tenets of the inclusionary political creed and more exclusionary definitions of American identity based on nativity and religion (Citrin, Reingold, and Green 1990).

In the present analysis, the starting point for measurement is the distinction between identifying *as* and identifying *with*. Whether the identity choices of ordinary citizens reflect a dominance or intersection strategy is assessed by a single question regarding self-categorization. Respondents in the LACSS were asked, "When it comes to political and social matters, do you think of yourself mainly as just an American, mainly as a member of an ethnic group, or both?" The answer resulted in classification in a "national," "ethnic," or "hyphenated" American category.

A variety of indicators measured the affective component of national identity or the strength of one's national attachment. The 1992 and 2002 ANES surveys and the GSS asked about love of country and feelings about the

American flag. The same indicators of patriotism were included in the LACSS, along with a question about pride in America. These items were combined to create a Patriotism Index, with scores ranging from 0 to 6. The 1996 GSS asked three questions about the psychological significance of being an American and also contained ten items assessing pride in specific aspects of American history and society ranging from achievements in science to the quality of group relations. These ten items were combined to form a Pride in America scale, another indicator of patriotism.

Finally, the LACSS included three questions that tapped the importance of ethnicity to respondents. One question asked how strongly people identified with their own (named) ethnic group, another asked how often people thought of themselves as a white (black, Latino, Asian), and a third asked about the importance of ethnicity to one's "overall sense of identity." These questions also were combined to create an Ethnic Identity Index with scores ranging from 0 to 3.

RESULTS

Self-Categorization

The indicator of identity choice used here is the question "When you think of social and political issues, do you think of yourself mainly as a member of a particular ethnic, racial, or nationality group, or do you think of yourself as just an American?" As reported by Sears et al. (1999: 54) in the 1994 GSS national sample, the most important result is that 90 percent chose the "just an American" response. Only 7 percent opted to categorize themselves as mainly a member of a particular ethnic or racial group. And while one might think people would squirm at the bald choice, only 2 percent gave "both" or "it depends" as an answer. A follow-up question asked whether they thought of themselves that way on "all issues, most issues, some issues, or just a few issues." Of the total sample, more than half (54 percent) stated that they thought of themselves as "just an American" on "all issues," and 28 percent said they felt this way on "most issues." Less than 2 percent said they thought of themselves as being in some subgroup on "all" or "most" issues.

The LACSS surveys have larger numbers of minority respondents and Table 5.1 reports the answers of the Los Angeles samples to the basic identity choice item. It shows that the LACSS data largely parallel the national results: 80 percent of respondents in the pooled 1994, 1995, and 1997 surveys chose the "just an American" identity over the "mainly ethnic" response. In the public as a whole, then, American national identity rather than membership in an ethnic subgroup is the dominant choice for self-categorization.

TABLE 5.1. *Identity Choice by Race and Ethnicity, %*

	Trichotomous Choice				Dichotomous Choice		
	Just an American	Both	Ethnic Group	Total N	Just an American	Ethnic Group	Total N
White	75	20	5	702	95	5	791
Black	28	55	17	270	72	28	359
Hispanic	11	57	32	631	67	33	613
Born in United States	25	65	11	188	83	17	187
Naturalized citizen	10	74	16	118	72	28	110
Noncitizen	3	47	50	322	56	44	311
Asian	6	71	23	121	77	23	149
TOTAL	40	18	43	1,724	80	20	1,912

Note: Question text: When it comes to political and social matters, how do you primarily think of yourself: just as an American, both as an American and (ethnicity), or only as (ethnicity)? Columns present the percentage of each racial group with the indicated response. Rows may not total 100% because of rounding error.
Source: LACSS cumulative file.

In a national sample, of course, whites are by far the largest group of respondents. And whites were the most likely to select the "just an American" identity. In the 1994 GSS, 95 percent of the whites did so, as did 95 percent of the whites in the LACSS. However, in both cases most of the ethnic minorities selected an American identity as well. In the GSS, 79 percent of the Hispanics and 66 percent of the blacks opted for this "just an American" category when asked in the forced-choice format. More than two-thirds of each minority group also preferred the superordinate national identity to thinking of themselves primarily as a member of a specific ethnic group. In the supposed ethnic cauldron of Los Angeles, the "just an American" appellation prevails in all four ethnic groups. Even among minority groups, then, nationality generally trumped ethnicity; in addition, among both blacks and Hispanics, a majority said they thought of themselves as "just Americans" on all or most, rather than just some, issues.

The dichotomous self-categorization question does not offer people the choice of what Brewer and Roccas call the intersection strategy of calling oneself a hyphenated American. The 1995, 1999, and 2000 LACSS surveys permitted this by asking people who first said they thought of themselves as "just American" this follow-up: "Which of the following is most true for you: just an American or both American and (ethnicity)?" Thus, respondents could reveal either an intersection strategy, by selecting both American and ethnicity, or a dominance strategy, by selecting either "just American" or "just ethnicity." Given this opportunity to use the intersection strategy, most whites do not take it: 75 percent continued to call themselves "just an American" and only 20 percent, most of whom are immigrants, shifted to the "both" category. Among the three minority groups, however, the dual or hyphenated identity is the majority choice. In this follow-up question, this is especially true for Asians (71 percent), but also for blacks and Latinos (55 and 57 percent each).

However, there is some divergence among the minority groups. A substantial minority of blacks (28 percent) did not budge from the "just an American" identity. And given that 55 percent chose a hyphenated identity and only 17 percent in the initial question made ethnicity their dominant choice, it is clear that relatively few blacks are denying a sense of identification with the nation as a whole. Indeed, given other evidence that African-Americans have a stronger sense of ethnic solidarity than other groups (see Table 5.4; also Sears and Savalei 2006), the "just American" response is surprisingly common. What Du Bois called the double consciousness of being American and black is the modal identity choice.

Among Hispanics in the LACSS surveys, there is a reversal of the pattern of identity choice observed among blacks. Here, one-third opted for the solely ethnic identity and only 11 percent say they feel themselves to be "just an American." Similarly, Asians prefer a purely ethnic label to the "just an American" identity by a margin of four to one.

This contrast between blacks and these new immigrant groups begins to make more sense when we compare native-born and foreign-born Hispanics. Among the native-born, an American identity (25 percent) far outstrips a purely ethnic identity (11 percent). The opposite holds for those who are foreign-born: a purely ethnic identity is far more common (44 percent) than an American identity (5 percent), and this difference is accentuated when one looks only at the foreign-born noncitizens. Moreover, when we compare Hispanic respondents subdivided by their place of birth and citizenship, it is clear that ethnicity is far more likely to be the dominant choice among immigrants, particularly those who are not yet citizens. Indeed, native-born Hispanics are less likely to prioritize their ethnic identity than blacks, suggesting that the traditional process of assimilation continues to hold sway, with successive immigrant generations identifying themselves simply as Americans. This is another indication that the immigrant status of Hispanics and Asians is far more important in contributing to how they balance their national and ethnic identities than is their position in a supposedly rigid American racial and ethnic hierarchy. And given that the process of change occurring among groups largely comprised of recent immigrants does not apply to blacks, this outcome seems likely to endure.

The Pilot National Asian American Political Survey, a multiethnic, multi-lingual, and multicity study of 1,218 adults eighteen years or older residing in five major population hubs,[1] asked respondents whether they identified themselves, *in general*, as either American, Asian-American, Asian, ethnic-American (e.g., Chinese- or Korean-American), or just one's national origin. The authors of this study, Pei-te Lien, Margaret Conway, and Janelle Wong (2004) report that 61 percent of the sample chose some form of American identity: 34 percent preferred a hyphenated national-origin American self-designation, 15 percent opted for the panethnic Asian-American, and 12 percent of this sample chose the American identity. Only 30 percent chose the purely ethnic identity.

What, then, should we conclude about how Americans are balancing their national and ethnic identities? First, a clear majority in all ethnic groups tend to choose "just an American" if forced to choose between that and a purely ethnic label. Even among ethnic minorities, most prefer an American identity if given such a stark choice. Among whites, this preference remains intact even when they are offered the option of a dual, hyphenated self-categorization. For them, the ethnic label has little salience or resonance; it is an optional identity (Alba 1990) that few whites choose, either because ethnic ties have lost emotional significance and practical relevance for many whites or because, as some scholars allege (Devos and Banaji 2005), they do not make a cognitive distinction between their national and racial identities. However, majorities in all three ethnic minority groups tend to shift to a hyphenated label, or even prefer one from the outset, if they are given the opportunity. Finally, the only group in which a majority prefers a purely ethnic identity consists of the foreign-born immigrants to the United States. Native-born ethnics tend to prefer to be thought of as hyphenated Americans, with an emphasis on the "American." But that seems to be a kind of halfway house in terms of social identity, much as the hyphenated-American identities tended to be in the early and mid-twentieth century for many European immigrant families. Given the large proportions of immigrants in this Los Angeles sample of Hispanics and Asians, it seems probable that the data reported here record an early stage in a process of assimilation.

A Multivariate Model of Identity Choice

A multinominal logit model of responses to the trichotomous indicator that allowed for a "both" or hyphenated self-categorization provides a more comprehensive analysis of the antecedents of identity choice. The predictors in the

---

[1] These were New York, Los Angeles, San Francisco, Honolulu, and Seattle.

model included race and ethnicity, with whites the baseline or excluded category. To index immigration status, we combined nativity, citizenship status, and length of residence in the United States. Respondents were classified into five categories: "recent immigrants" (noncitizens having lived in the United States less than ten years); "long-term noncitizens" (noncitizens who have lived in the United States for ten or more years); "naturalized citizens"; the "second generation" (native-born citizens with foreign-born parents); and "natives" (native-born citizens with parents born in the United States as well). Finally, we included controls for age, income, and education.

The three columns in Table 5.2 report the results of this analysis. Responses are coded so that the "just an American" answer has the highest score, meaning that positive coefficients indicate an increase in the likelihood of prioritizing one's national identity. The first column compares those who identify as "just Americans" with those preferring a purely ethnic identity. As Table 5.1 showed, identifying as "just an American" is less likely among all three ethnic minorities than among whites. However, each category of immigration status has a significant effect: the more integrated into American society by virtue of birth, citizenship, and experience, the more likely one is to identify oneself as "just an American." These effects of ethnicity and immigration status hold with controls on age, sex, education, and income. The probability of choosing a purely national identity as one's primary self-identification increases with age. These effects of age do not have a simple interpretation, however. They could reflect aging effects, such that one becomes more attached to one's nation as one ages. Or they could reflect cohort effects, suggesting a possible waning of American identity in the future due to the replacement of older cohorts more attached to the nation by younger, more ethnic cohorts. In any case, the main story is that American identity is somewhat weaker among ethnic minorities than among whites, while American identity strengthens as the immigration experience recedes into minorities' pasts. These data should alleviate Huntington's concerns that recent Mexican immigrants may not assimilate over time.

Modeling the comparison of those who identify as just American as opposed to those who select a hyphenated identity (both American and ethnic group) also yields findings similar to the earlier bivariate effects (see column 2 in Table 5.2). Blacks, Hispanics, and Asians are again more likely than whites to claim hyphenated identities. But the effects of immigration status continue to be strongly significant, though their coefficients shrink in magnitude relative to the previous model, suggesting that the "distance" between a solely ethnic identity and a hyphenated identity is less than that between an ethnic and an American identity. Again, the effects of ethnicity and immigration status remain with other demographics controlled. Age continues to be associated

TABLE 5.2. *Multinomial Logit Analysis of Antecedents of Identity Choice*

	Comparisons		
	Just American vs. Just Ethnic	Just American vs. Both	Both vs. Just Ethnic
Ethnicity			
Hispanic	−1.72*** (.32)	−2.29*** (.22)	.57# (.29)
Black	−2.83*** (.34)	−2.13*** (.20)	−.70* (.33)
Asian	−2.50*** (.58)	−3.34*** (.50)	.84* (.36)
Immigrant status			
Second generation	−.89* (.36)	−.14 (.21)	−.92** (.34)
Naturalized citizen	−2.14*** (.37)	−1.26*** (.22)	−1.25*** (.34)
Long-term noncitizen	−3.79*** (.43)	−1.82*** (.34)	−2.27*** (.33)
Recent immigrant	−5.18*** (.79)	−2.78*** (.75)	−2.61*** (.36)
Demographic controls			
Sex	−.44* (.20)	−.24 (.14)	−.20 (.17)
Education	.04 (.08)	−.15 (.06)	.08 (.07)
Income	.10* (.04)	.06* (.03)	.04 (.04)
Constant	1.41***	1.16**	1.72**
−2*Log-likelihood	1779.11		
c^2	867.46***		
Pseudo-R^2	.51		
N	1,458		

Note: Table entries are multinomial logit coefficients with estimated standard errors in parentheses. Excluded dummy variables: race (white), age (18–29), and tenure (natives).
*** $p < .001$; ** $p < .01$; * $p < .05$; # $p < .10$.
Source: Pooled LACSS surveys 1995, 1999, 2000.

with stronger American identity, for uncertain reasons. Again, the increasing attraction of American identity as immigration recedes into the past seems to contradict Huntington's notion of unassimilable waves of Mexican immigrants (Citrin et al. 2007).

Finally, when hyphenated identifiers and ethnic identifiers are compared (column 3 in Table 5.2), the observed effects of race and ethnicity weaken considerably. Blacks are more likely to identify as ethnics, while Asians and Hispanics are more likely to adopt the hyphenated identity as both ethnic and American. In all cases, however, the magnitude and statistical significance of these ethnicity effects decrease relative to the previous models. Children of immigrants, new citizens, long-term noncitizens, and recent immigrants are all more likely to identify in primarily ethnic terms, and these effects are again monotonic. Again, age is associated with a lesser likelihood of a purely ethnic identification, for uncertain reasons. In short, consistent with Huntington's concern, ethnic minorities are more likely than whites to identify as ethnics, whether in pure terms or as hyphenated Americans. But that is offset by the fact that the longer they live in American society, and the more deeply embedded they are in the society, the more they surrender those ethnic identities in favor of American national identity.[2]

Patriotism

The core meaning of patriotism is simply the love of one's country. To measure this emotional attachment to the nation, we employ questions about love for and pride in America and a leading national symbol, the flag. Table 5.3 reports the results from the ANES, GSS, and LACSS surveys.

The evidence of pervasive patriotism and emotional attachment to symbols of nationhood is overwhelming. In the 2002 American National Election Study, 91 percent of the sample said their love for the United States was either "extremely" or "very" strong, and a slightly lower proportion, 85 percent, said they felt extremely or very proud when they saw the American flag. These very high levels of national attachment are not mere artifacts of the patriotic fervor that followed the terrorist attacks of 9/11. The same two items had yielded estimates of national attachment almost as high ten years earlier, in 1992: 89 percent and 79 percent, respectively.

Moreover, the great majority within all ethnic groups voice high levels of patriotism, as also shown in Table 5.3. True, love of country and pride in its flag are lower among blacks than among whites. But, again contrary to Huntington, Latinos show just as much patriotism as whites. This replicates the finding of the National Latino Election Study conducted in 1989 that, adjusting for background factors and ability to speak English, patriotism among Hispanics, including the foreign-born, is as high as among white Americans.

The LACSS surveys asked identical questions about love of country, pride in America, and feelings about the flag. Pooling responses from these surveys provides evidence about ethnic differences and the political assimilation of recent immigrants lacking in the national data. As in the nation as a whole, patriotism is the predominant outlook in Los Angeles: 94 percent of the survey

---

[2] Estimating the same logit models separately for each of the main ethnic subgroups – excepting Asians, who are excluded because of the small number of Asian respondents – confirms that citizenship status and immigrant generation (i.e., "tenure") significantly affect the likelihood of defining oneself as "just an American." Age has a relatively stronger influence on the preference for an exclusively American identification among whites and blacks than among the largely immigrant Hispanic respondents. These data are not included here because of space limitations but will be made available on request.

TABLE 5.3. *Patriotism by Race and Ethnicity, % (N)*

	How Strongly Do You Love America?			How Much Pride in the American Flag?			How Proud to Be American?		Pride in America Index
	NES 2002	NES 1992	LACSS 1997–99	NES 2002	NES 1992	LACSS 1997–2000, 2002	GSS 1994	LACSS 1994, 1997	GSS 1996
White	94[a] (1,064)	92 (1,747)	94[b] (846)	87[c] (1,058)	83 (1,739)	82[d] (1,241)	88[e] (994)	80 (548)	8.2[f] (823)
Black	71 (112)	69 (284)	89 (197)	56 (110)	53 (280)	73 (491)	75 (143)	75 (288)	7.5 (111)
Hispanic	94 (77)	92 (72)	92 (693)	92 (760)	84 (148)	81 (1,083)	89 (50)	53 (462)	7.6 (40)
Native citizen	–	–	93 (216)	–	–	86 (329)	–	79 (129)	–
Nonnative citizen	–	–	90.3 (134)	–	–	82 (228)	–	64 (91)	–
Noncitizen	–	–	91 (342)	–	–	78 (519)	–	35 (241)	–
Asian	–	–	91 (159)	–	–	78 (207)	–	59 (102)	–
TOTAL	91 (1,253)	89 (2,103)	92 (1,895)	85 (1,244)	79 (2,167)	80 (3,022)	86 (1,187)	69 (1,400)	8.1 (974)

[a] Percentage is proportion of the sample who gave an "extremely" or "very" response to the question "How strong is your love for your country: extremely strong, very strong, somewhat strong, or not very strong?" Question wording and response categories are identical in the 1992 NES.

[b] Percentage is proportion of the sample who gave a "strongly agree" or "somewhat agree" in regards to the statement "I have great love for America."

[c] Percentage is proportion of the sample who gave an "extremely" or "very" response to the statement "When you see the American flag flying does it make you feel: extremely good, very good, somewhat good, or not very good?" Question wording and response categories are identical in the 1992 NES.

[d] Percentage is proportion of the sample who gave a "strongly agree" or "somewhat agree" in regards to the statement "I find the sight of the American flag moving."

[e] Percentage is proportion of the sample who gave an "extremely" or "very" response to the question "How proud are you to be an American: extremely proud, very proud, somewhat proud, or not very proud?" Question wording and response categories are identical in the LACSS.

[f] The Pride in America Index is a count of "very proud" or "somewhat proud" responses to questions about American arts or literature, democracy, economy, fair and equal treatment of groups, history, armed forces, political influence, science and technology, sports and social security. The index ranges from 0 to 10.

respondents there either agreed or strongly agreed that they "loved" the United States, and 79 percent said they found "the sight of the American flag moving." In the pooled 1994 and 1997 LACSS samples, 69 percent of the respondents said they felt extremely or very proud to "be an American," substantially lower than the 86 percent figure for the 1994 national GSS sample.

Our theme of the gradual assimilation of immigrant populations to American national attachment seems to explain this difference between the Los Angeles and national samples, given the many recent Hispanic and Asian immigrants in the Los Angeles samples. Native-born Hispanics in Los Angeles express the same level of attachment to the United States as whites. The patriotic outlook of even naturalized Hispanics is similar to that of those born in the United States. In contrast, only 35 percent of Hispanic noncitizens expressed pride in "being an American," compared to 79 percent of native-born Hispanics. It is clear that the psychological incorporation of immigrants is ongoing.

Patriotism too gradually strengthens as the immigration experience recedes into the past, according to multiple regression analyses of scores on the Patriotism Index constructed from answers to the LACSS questions about finding the American flag moving and love for America (full results not presented here). True, blacks expressed less patriotism than whites, consistent with social-structural theories. But when we turn to Latinos, the foci of Huntington's concerns about nonassimilable immigrants, native-born Hispanics had significantly *higher* scores on this measure of patriotism than did whites, after adjusting for differences in age and years of formal education. Among Hispanics, more formal education seems to strengthen such sentiments, another sign of the political incorporation of the largest category of recent immigrants to the United States. Again, age is positively associated with patriotism among all ethnic groups.

Finally, the general feeling of attachment translates into highly favorable assessments of specific aspects of American society in the population as a whole. The 1996 GSS asked respondents how proud they felt about ten specific features of American life and history ranging from achievements in sports and sciences to how democracy works and the treatment of social groups. As an example, 83 percent of the 1996 GSS sample said they were proud of the way democracy works in America, and 80 percent were proud of America's influence in the world. Among all ethnic groups patriotic responses dominated. This is reflected in scores on the ten-item Pride in America Index constructed by summing the number of "very proud" and "proud" responses. The mean score for whites was a high 8.2. To be sure, the figures for blacks (7.5) and Hispanics (7.6) were lower but still recorded a high level of patriotism. And while we do not report the figures here for reasons of brevity, these group differences reflect mainly divergences of opinion on the items dealing with political life, such as the nation's record for achieving full equality, rather than on items dealing with society-wide cultural and scientific achievements.

Strength of Ethnic Attachment

Ethnic identity is the other side of the potential conflict between attachment to the nation and loyalty to one's own in-groups. The primary measures of the strength of ethnic identity are the following three items: "How strongly do you identify with other (ethnicity) people?"; "How important is being (ethnicity) to your sense of identity?"; and "How often do you think of yourself as an (ethnicity) person?" Each item provided four response alternatives, and the frequencies with which respondents of each ethnic group gave the most extreme ethnic response are shown in Table 5.4.

First, and least surprisingly, the members of all three ethnic and racial minority groups express a far stronger sense of ethnic identity than do whites. All those differences are highly statistically significant (p < .001), except that Asians only marginally (p < .10) more strongly identified with their ethnicity than did whites. In fact, the data shown in Table 5.4 actually understate the gulf between whites and the ethnic minorities. Whites show very high levels of indifference to their own ethnicity. For example, on the "how often think of yourself as an (ethnicity)?" item, 72 percent of the whites said "almost never" or "not very often," while only 10 percent of the Latinos and 29 percent of the blacks were comparably indifferent to their ethnic groups. This is not remarkable from one perspective: whites have been by far the most numerous ethnic group in America from the beginning and so are less likely to have experienced race as a salient dimension of identity. But the finding illustrates the striking persistence of that view even in a region where they are no longer in the majority. Hispanics express the strongest sense of identification with their ethnic group even though they now are the largest ethnic group in Los Angeles County.

Second, recent Hispanic immigrants show the strongest ethnic identity, as well as the weakest sense of American identity and patriotism, as shown earlier. For example, 72 percent of the foreign-born Hispanics felt that their ethnicity is "very important," whereas only 58 percent of the U.S.-born Hispanics did so.

Third, from the "black exceptionalism" hypothesis (Sears and Savalei 2006), we would have expected blacks to have the strongest racial consciousness of all the major ethnic groups. Rather, Latinos actually had somewhat stronger senses of ethnic identity than did blacks (though the difference was

TABLE 5.4. *Strength of Subjective Ethnic Identity, by Race and Ethnicity, %*

	Identify "Very Strongly" with Ethnic Group[a]	Ethnicity Is "Very Important"[b]	Think of Self as Ethnic "Very Often"[c]	Composite Index[d]
White	25	14	11	1.38
Black	59	61	53	2.27
Hispanic	55	68	71	2.48
Born in United States	44	58	56	2.25
Naturalized citizen	59	72	73	2.57
Noncitizen	60	72	76	2.57
Asian	38	41	43	2.12
TOTAL	41	46	42	1.93

Note: Columns present the percentage of each racial group with the indicated response. Rows may not total 100% because of rounding error.
[a] "How strongly do you identify with other (ethnicity) people? Would you say very strongly, somewhat strongly, not very strongly, or not at all strongly?"
[b] "How important is being (ethnicity) to your sense of identity? Very important, somewhat important, not very important, or not at all important?"
[c] "How often do you think of yourself as a (ethnicity) person? Very often, somewhat often, not very often, or almost never?"
[d] Column indicates each racial group's mean score on a composite index, which ranges from 0 to 3 and was constructed as the mean of the three ethnic identity questions listed immediately above.
Source: Pooled 1997, 1998, and 1999 LACSS.

highly significant [$p < .001$] only on the "how often do you think of yourself as an (ethnicity)?" item). Applying the assimilationist model to Hispanics, however, yields the expectation that their sense of ethnic consciousness would decline over time. That apparently has been the trajectory of most of the turn-of-the-century European immigrants, as they have become integrated into the mainstream of American society (Alba 1990; Alba and Nee 2003). Ultimately, we would expect weaker ethnic identity among Hispanics when they have become several generations removed from immigration. Blacks, for the most part far distant in time from their African origins, have historically had a more difficult time crossing the color line and assimilating into the broader society.

To provide a crude preliminary test of this idea, we divided the Hispanics into those born in the United States and those born elsewhere. As can be seen, only the immigrant Hispanics have a stronger sense of ethnic identity than do blacks. The immigrant Latinos have a far stronger sense of ethnic identity: 75 percent say they think of themselves as Hispanic "very often," compared to 53 percent of the black respondents. By comparison, the native-born Hispanics are not sharply different from the blacks; only 56 percent think of themselves as Hispanic "very often."

For purposes of further analysis, we developed a composite "strength of ethnic identity" scale by averaging responses to these three items. The mean scores on this scale (which has a range of 0 to 3) are also shown for each ethnic group in Table 5.4. All three ethnic minority groups show a stronger sense of ethnic identity than do whites. Beyond that, the U.S.-born Hispanics have a sharply reduced sense of ethnic identity compared to recent immigrants. New immigrants may feel alien in America and their sense of ethnic consciousness could be reinforced by residential and economic segregation. However, the sense of ethnic attachment is diminished among native-born Hispanics, as the assimilation model would predict. As a result, only the foreign-born Hispanics have a stronger subjective sense of ethnic identity than do blacks.

Do Strong National and Ethnic Identities Collide?

Our other main question is whether strong ethnic identities compromise attachment to the nation, and so national unity. First, in the limiting case of ethnically homogeneous societies, nationality and ethnicity completely overlap, and the possibility that national and ethnic identities clash is moot. They are one and the same, so patriotism and feeling close to your own ethnic group are bound to go together. Japan is Japanese, and so the idea of a loyal but hyphenated Japanese identity has no meaning there.

In multicultural societies like that in the United States, however, the matter of reconciling one's national and ethnic identities is more complex. In these countries, one racial, linguistic, or religious group typically constitutes the nation's ethnic core because of its historical role in creating the state, its numerical preponderance, or its political and cultural dominance. In the United States, of course, whites of European ancestry have traditionally represented that ethnic core. For this group, nation and ethnic group may be perceptually fused, and, again, attachments to the two entities should be positively associated. For the minority groups, though, national and ethnic attachments potentially compete. Their intersection should reflect both how the nation defines its own identity and whether they view a strong ethnic identification as compatible with loyalty to the values of the more inclusive national community. So a second possible solution is the civic nation, which envisions a common identity founded on political ideals as the best guarantor of national unity. Accordingly, France today is insisting on imposing the republican values of egalitarianism and secularism on an increasingly diverse society by banning religious symbols such as the Islamic veil, Jewish yarmulke, or Christian cross from being worn in public schools.

A third possibility, however, is that most Americans, whatever their ethnic background, endorse the motto of *e pluribus unum* and the idea of sharing a common culture that evolves as newcomers add elements of their cultural heritage to the American way of life. Even if their own immigrant roots are in the distant past and attachment to their cultural heritage has faded away, Americans might still acknowledge that an egalitarian "festival multiculturalism" – the acceptance of growing diversity in song, food, dance, and cultural heroes – helps define America's identity as a nation of immigrants. In this pluralistic version of the melting pot, ethnic allegiances and patriotism are complementary rather than competing identities.

But in cases of oppressed minorities, perhaps ethnic identities need to be privileged rather than treated as entertaining sideshows. Perhaps an ethnic solidarity based on a strong sense of ethnic identity and common fate is critical to mobilizing the group's interests when greatly outnumbered and outgunned. Indeed, strong multiculturalists similarly envisage a negative association between national and ethnic identities among minorities, but they welcome the outcome, arguing that cultural assimilation, culminating with the offspring of immigrants identifying with mainstream Americans, is a form of subordination that must be resisted.

There is a potential danger in that, though. Demands for a "muscular version" of cultural differences might lead to an erosion of patriotism and feelings of national solidarity among minority groups. Indeed, the French mock the American multiculturalism for pandering to ethnic diversity in a way that undermines the meanings of nationality and citizenship. American writers like Arthur Schlesinger Jr., Michael Barone, and Samuel Huntington share the French anxieties about the risks of giving in to identity politics and institutionalizing diversity. They predict and fear that strong ethnic identifications and attachment to the nation will clash rather than reinforce one another. An important piece of Huntington's argument is that the strong ethnic identities of immigrants are likely to persist rather than weaken with time, and will compete with and ultimately compromise American identity and national unity.

In evaluating these alternative images of American opinion, determining the empirical connections between ethnic and national attachments within each of the main ethnic groups is crucial. The approach adopted here is to examine the relationships between patriotism, ethnic identification, and identity choice or self-categorization, relying on the LACSS data and omitting the Asian respondents because of the paucity of cases. Table 5.5 presents a simple cross-tabulation between the trichotomized self-categorization item and mean scores on the

TABLE 5.5. *The Relationship between Identity Choice and Patriotism and Ethnic Identity, by Race*

Race (N) and Identity Choice	Mean Score on Ethnic Identity Index[a]	Mean Score on Patriotism Index[b]
White (445)		
Just American	1.2	4.5
Both	1.8	4.4
Just ethnic group	1.5	3.2
Black (200)		
Just American	1.9	4.4
Both	2.4	4.3
Just ethnic group	2.6	3.5
Hispanic (456)		
Just American	2.0	4.5
Both	2.6	4.3
Just ethnic group	2.7	3.8

[a] The ethnic identity index ranges from 0 to 3 and was constructed as the mean of the three ethnic identity questions listed at the bottom of Table 5.4.

[b] The patriotism index ranges from 0 to 5 and was constructed as the mean of the responses from the following two items: (1) Do you strongly agree, somewhat agree, somewhat disagree, or strongly disagree with the following statement: "I find the sight of the American flag moving," and (2) "How proud are you to be an American: extremely proud, very proud, somewhat proud, or not very proud?"

Source: Pooled 1999 and 2000 LACSS.

Patriotism and Ethnic Identity indices, respectively among whites, blacks, and Hispanics.

In all three ethnic groups, those identifying themselves as Americans have the highest patriotism scores. However, the differences between the "just American" and "both" groups are very small, and the main gap in the level of patriotism is between these groups and respondents who define themselves in purely ethnic terms. When it comes to feelings of ethnic consciousness, however, the pattern is reversed. Those choosing a purely national identity are least likely to express a strong sense of ethnic identity, as one would expect. But here those in the hyphenated group are consistently closer to their co-ethnics who categorize themselves without reference to the nation; the Ethnic Identity scores of the "both" and "ethnic" groups are very close.

Prioritizing one's national identity is *positively* related to patriotism and negatively related to a strong sense of ethnic identification, then. This may seem to be a confirmation of the criticisms leveled against identity politics as harbingers of fragmentation. However, it is worth repeating that, for a recent immigrant, describing oneself as "ethnic" rather than "American" may be closer to a census report than a political statement. And among blacks, where the opposite may be true, the "mainly ethnic" self-designation remains the choice of a small minority. Moreover, the more compelling result in Table 5.5 is that minority group members choosing the "ethnic-American" self-categorizations do not have significantly less patriotic sentiment than do those who choose "just American." National allegiances seem not to be diminished by retaining a hyphenated ethnic-American self-categorization.

A second approach to this question looks at whether affectively strong ethnic identification, as opposed to ethnic self-categorization, compromises national attachment. To assess this in a more systematic way, we performed a more rigorous statistical test that takes account of the full range of scores on both the Patriotism and Ethnic Identity measures. Sidanius and his colleagues (1997) hypothesized that ethnic and national identities would be positively related among whites and negatively associated among minority groups and blacks in particular. Following their lead, we examined the bivariate unstandardized regression coefficients to estimate the degree to which patriotism is a function of ethnic identification.[3] In fact, Ethnic Identity and Patriotism are not significantly related for any group. The same null results also held when we explored whether the magnitude and direction of the relationship between ethnic and national attachments might be conditioned by the respondent's age or education. Among whites, blacks, Hispanics, and Asians alike, patriotism and a strong sense of ethnic identification were unrelated in each of the age and educational groups.[4] By this test, a positive sense of ethnic identity among minority groups does not undermine their patriotism.

The nature of the interface between national and ethnic attachment has implications for the feasibility of *e pluribus unum*. For this reason, the puzzling differences in the effects of self-categorization and ethnic identification on patriotism need to be explained. To repeat, ethnic self-categorization is associated with reduced patriotism (Table 5.5), but the strength of ethnic identification is not, as just indicated. One possible explanation is that the self-categorization question asks explicitly about people's self-concept "when they think about political and social matters." This suggests that the item taps a *politicized* collective identity. On the other hand, questions about the importance of one's own ethnicity and how often one thinks about one's ethnic identity may reflect patterns of social interaction and consumption habits as much as political

---

[3] The reasons for using this estimator is that, unlike the more intuitively grasped correlation coefficient, it is essentially unaffected by between-group differences in variances.

[4] We do not present these null results to save space, but these data are available on request.

views. In any event, future analysis should probe the antecedents of these distinct measures of identity to see whether they have different ideological or social foundations.

A more complete analysis of the effects of ethnic self-categorization and ethnic identification on national attachment comes from a multiple regression analysis reported in Table 5.6. For the 1997, 1999, and 2000 LACSS samples self-categorization, ethnic identity, liberalism-conservatism, age, education, income, and gender were included in an equation estimating scores on the Patriotism Index, both for the sample as a whole and for subsets of white, Hispanic, and black respondents. The first, in the left-hand column, uses the sample as a whole. The main finding is that, *ceteris paribus,* blacks are less patriotic than whites. However, contrary to Huntington's concerns about the long-term effects of heavy Mexican immigration to the Southwest, native-born Hispanics have even higher patriotism scores than whites. In the sample as a whole we see the same contradictory effects of ethnic self-categorization, which reduces patriotism, and ethnic identification, which here actually increases it.

The best tests of the effects of ethnic identities on national attachment, however, come in the analyses within separate ethnic groups. A purely ethnic self-categorization consistently has a strong negative effect on patriotism. However, minorities with a hyphenated identity choice do not have signifi- cantly less patriotism than do those who choose "just American." Moreover, even strong ethnic identification fails to reduce patriotism among the ethnic minority groups, as in the bivariate results just reviewed. A conservative political self-identification and age also are consistently associated with stron- ger feelings of patriotism, suggesting that cohort replacement and changes in political socialization are more likely than immigration to contribute to the waning of American national identity.

In short, in both the bivariate analyses and the regression analyses, only those ethnic minorities who categorize themselves solely in ethnic terms show diminished patriotism. Neither hyphenated ethnicity nor strong ethnic identification reduces attachment to the nation. As seen earlier, the only substantial numbers who categorize themselves in purely ethnic terms are new immigrant Latinos. Overall, ethnic identity appears to compromise patriotism toward America only at the extremes.

CONCLUSION

The survey evidence presented here confirms that a positive sense of national identity is pervasive in the United States. In both national and Los Angeles County polls, an overarching American identity is the preferred political

TABLE 5.6. *Multivariate Models of Patriotism*

Variables	Coefficient (Standard Error)			
	All Respondents	Whites	Blacks	Hispanics
Identifies hyphenated American	−.234**	−.194*	−.195	−.258#
	(.069)	(.085)	(.167)	(.149)
Identifies only as member of ethnic group	−.820***	−.256***	−.994***	−.731***
	(.094)	(.167)	(.267)	(.169)
Ethnic Identification Index[a]	.112**	.075	.184#	.118
	(.037)	(.046)	(.099)	(.074)
Liberal-conservative	.042**	.080***	.086*	−.000
	(.013)	(.018)	(.038)	(.022)
Race and ethnicity dummies				
Black	−.207*	−	−	−
	(.082)			
Foreign-born Hispanic	−.066	−	−	−
	(.091)			
Native-born Hispanic	.196*	−	−	−
	(.096)			
Asian	.006	−	−	−
	(.115)			
Demographic controls				
Age	.147***	.116***	.250***	.097**
	(.019)	(.025)	(.053)	(.037)
Education	−.022	−.009	−.085	.013
	(.022)	(.032)	(.060)	(.038)
Income	.000	.016	−.009	.014
	(.010)	(.012)	(.031)	(.024)
Female dummy	.026	.040	.191	.045
	(.051)	(.067)	(.154)	(.089)
Constant	3.860***	3.755***	3.200***	3.940***
	(.140)	(.183)	(.396)	(.281)
R^2	.177	.269	.226	.097
N	1,020	388	172	391

Note: The dependent variable for each model is the patriotism index described in Table 5.5. Table entries are unstandardized OLS coefficients and estimated standard errors. *** $p < .001$; ** $p < .01$; * $p < .05$; # $p < .10$.

[a] The ethnic identity index ranges from 0 to 3 and was constructed as the mean of the three ethnic identity questions listed in Table 5.4.

Source: Pooled 1999 and 2000 LACSS.

self-definition for a large majority of residents. To say that nationality dominates ethnicity, however, tells only part of the story. The varied approaches to measuring political identity employed here demonstrate that Americans recognize the existence of plural identities and do not regard their Americanness as incompatible with positive attachment to their specific ethnic group. If forced to choose, most members of minority ethnic groups will place their national identity first; however, the largest segment of the blacks, Hispanics, and Asians in the LACSS samples selected a hyphenated ethnic-American self-designation when they could. One implication of these results is methodological and concerns the importance of developing multiple measures of identity. Researchers must be able to capture the dimensions of the individual's self-concept, the emotional significance and value of each, and the nature of the subjective boundaries for these several in-groups.

The results reported here conform to the scholarly literature suggesting that the dominant group in society generally does not think of itself in ethnic terms. Minority groups, by contrast, are more inclined to emphasize their ethnic identity, and one can speculate this is both because of exclusionary behavior by the majority and because ethnic solidarity can boost collective self-esteem and political power. One could speculate that national and ethnic identities may often be merged among whites, whereas they may intersect for many members of minority groups.

A central concern is the degree of ethnic conflict and consensus in identity choice and national attachment. Three main conclusions emerge from these data. First, while the strength of national identity is pervasive, it is strongest among white Americans. In addition to ethnicity, age and immigrant status are the leading social antecedents of identity choice. The younger cohorts are *less* likely to define themselves as "just American" and to express patriotic feelings. It does appear that generational differences in political socialization may exist, with those born in the late 1960s and 1970s more likely to have been raised in a political climate hostile to overt expressions of nationalism. Nevertheless, assimilation to a dominant "just American" self-identification prevails, which should dampen fears about the effects of immigration on national cohesion. As Hispanic and Asian immigrants acquire citizenship, they and their children become less likely to opt for either an ethnic or hyphenated identity. On the other hand, the anticipated association with structural integration, as measured by educational and economic attainment, does not appear, possibly because of the socialization experiences linked to attending college.

As expected, identification *as* an American and identification *with* America go together. Self-categorization engenders in-group pride. People who think of themselves mainly as members of a particular ethnic group are less likely to express pride in America. From a political perspective, however, it is significant that this tendency does not generally apply to those who opt for a hyphenated identity, which appears to function as a stepping-stone, or halfway house, for immigrants undergoing the process of assimilation. More pointedly, the strong sense of national attachment among ethnic minorities should calm anxieties about America's increasing cultural diversity. There is reason to believe that today's immigrants, like their predecessors, become *desocialized* from their native customs over time (Glazer and Moynihan 1975: 8).

This chapter has not explored beliefs about the content of national and ethnic identities. The introductory chapter explains that *cognitive models* of one's group identity can provide a mental framework that helps people interpret the world in a particular way and thus guides action. A cognitive model of an identity can be connected to a group's constitutive norms by communicating how someone should think and act. Cultural stereotypes, stories of peoplehood, and official rituals and ceremonies provide evidence about these cognitive models for both group members and scholarly observers.

These worldviews and the degree to which they are consensual seem to matter. For example, there is evidence that how national identity is conceived has consequences for policy preferences. For example, Wong (2002) created a National Community Index by summing the responses of the 1996 GSS sample to the seven items regarding what makes someone a "true American." She found that the more exclusive an individual's sense of American national identity, even controlling for education, immigrant status, and ideological orientation, the more likely he or she is to want to limit immigration, oppose the presence of political refugees in the United States, and favor protectionist measures. Here it is the normative content of national identity, the subjective sense of what it means to be an American, rather than the strength of patriotism that matters. Wong found that simply feeling close to and having pride in the United States had no significant effects on preferences about immigration, refugees, and isolationism. Still, improved measurement of the content of national identity is a major task for future research. Multiple methods including qualitative and experimental research are critical here, with survey work coming at the end of the process.

The substantive question motivating this analysis of how to study national and ethnic identities is whether *e pluribus unum* is possible? The results reported here provide no reason for alarm about the impact of new immigrants on the strength of American national identity. Strong ethnic allegiances do not automatically compete with patriotism or putting one's country first. So Gellner (1983) goes too far in assuming that demographic diversity guarantees cultural disunity. On the other hand, the politicization of ethnic identity in a way that gives it priority does conflict with the nationalist vision. To the extent that one believes that a strong national identity has value, the tendency of politicians and interest groups to elevate the politics of difference by legitimizing the allocation of benefits on ethnic lines poses a danger because the likely consequence of this kind of identity politics is to foster the kind of identity choice that chips away at the solidarity of the national political community.

6

Black and Blue

Black Identity and Black Solidarity in an Era of Conservative Triumph

Michael Dawson

> We believe it is the duty of the Americans of Negro descent, as a body, to maintain their race identity until this mission of the Negro people is accomplished, and the ideal of human brotherhood has become a practical possibility.
> — W. E. B. Du Bois. "The Conservation of the Races," 1897

> Say it loud, I'm Black and I'm proud!
> — The Temptations, "Message from a Black Man," circa 1970

The concept of racial identity – and, particularly in the United States, black racial identity – is ubiquitous in scholarly work on race in the social sciences and the humanities as well as in everyday political discourse. Several social scientists, however, have generally questioned the utility of the concept of "identity," racial or otherwise, for social analysis. Scholars such as Rogers Brubaker and Frederick Cooper argue that the concept is used to capture a variety of confusing and sometimes contradictory clusters of meanings. They would have social scientists abandon the term for a range of more precise terms. Some philosophers have also questioned the analytical, moral, and political utility of both the general concept of identity and the more specific concept of black identity. Scholars such as Tommie Shelby, for example, call for the abandonment of the notion of a "collective black identity" in order to place the project of building philosophically liberal and politically progressive black solidarity on stronger philosophical, political, and moral grounds.

In this chapter, I examine the empirical and theoretical utility of the conceptualization of black racial identity that has most deeply taken root among students of empirical black politics. Much of the work on black political identity, and increasingly work focused on Latino/a and Asian American political identity as well, has focused on one particular construction of racial identity – that of "linked fate."[1] Empirically, I test the degree to which racial identity, operationalized by the concept of "linked fate," is still able to shape African Americans' political beliefs. I then address theoretically the question of whether the concept of black racial identity is salvageable as both a tool for empirical analysis and a basis for reconstructing black solidarity in an era of black political weakness.[2]

OBJECTIONS

The question of whether identity is a concept that is even worth salvaging has generated significant discussion among social theorists and other interested parties. Perhaps the most influential critique is "Beyond 'Identity'" by Brubaker and Cooper (2000). The authors vigorously argue for abandoning the use of the term "identity" in favor of a series of narrower concepts that they claim better capture the often-contradictory aspects of "identity" that are of interest to empirical researchers and theoreticians alike. The list of narrower conceptions that they recommend includes identification and categorization; self-understanding and social location; and commonality, connectedness, and groupness.

Brubaker and Cooper (2000: 27) argue that the types of questions that empirical researchers want to address are served better by exploring these concepts than by focusing on "identity":

The extent to which official categorizations shape self-understandings, the extent to which the population-categories constituted by states or political entrepreneurs approximate real "groups" – these are open questions that can only be addressed empirically. The language of "identity" is more likely to hinder than to help the posing of such questions, for it blurs what needs to be kept distinct: external categorization and self-understanding, objective commonality and subjective groupness.

While Brubaker and Cooper are correct to identify the type of confusions that often plague theorizing and research about "identity," other researchers argue that they go too far in arguing for its elimination (see Abdelal et al., Chapter 1 in this volume). More problematic than "going too far" for our

---

[1] While I discuss the concept in much more detail later, "linked fate" for now can be defined as individuals' belief that their fate is linked to that of their racial group (Dawson 1994).

[2] See Dawson (forthcoming) for an extended discussion of the political weakness found in black politics in the early twenty-first century.

purposes here, is their treatment in the same essay of what they label identi-tarian political movements. Their approach is particularly problematic if we want to consider the nature of racial identity and identifications in the United States.

Brubaker and Cooper (2000: 7) claim without supporting evidence that the type of identitarian theorizing that they criticize fails to correctly make the distinction between universal social structures and "particularistic" categorical attributes:

Many (though not all) strands of identitarian theorizing see social and political action as powerfully shaped by position in social space. In this they agree with many (though not all) strands of universalist, instrumentalist, theorizing. But "social location" means something quite different in the two cases. For identitarian theorizing, it means positions in a multidimensional space defined by *particularistic categorical attributes* (race, ethnicity, gender, sexual orientation). For instrumentalist theorizing, it means position in a *universalistically conceived social structure* (for example, position in the market, occupational structure, or mode of production). (emphasis in original)

Part of the problem is that the authors fail to see that the racial order in the United States is a social structure in the same way that a labor market is. As William H. Sewell Jr. (1992) makes clear in his seminal article, structures have both an instrumental and an ideational component. The latter in-corporates, among other things, phenomena such as schema, norms, and "identities." As I demonstrate when applying Sewell's work to the analysis of African American social position, the racial structure in the United States distributes both material resources (including likely positions in and out of labor markets) and ideational components, such as racial identities, roles, and norms (Dawson 2001).

For example, both racial orders and labor markets assign all individuals in society to categories in an institutionalized hierarchy. The racial order gen-erates sets of interests tied to racial categories just as labor markets generate sets of interests tied to categories that constitute that hierarchy. These inter-ests reflect the (contested) power dynamics that infuse the racial order just as the interests that characterize labor markets reflect the power dynamics of that social structure. Racial orders also generate identities that are associated with categories such as "black," "white," and "Asian American" no more or no less than labor markets generate identities by categories such as worker, manager, technician, or owner. Brubaker and Cooper combine nostalgia for a politics of class (which to the degree that it exists at all in the United States does not follow traditional European paths), a confused critique of "identity politics," and a belittling of movements such as the black power movement in such a manner as to undermine their intellectual, research, and political agendas.[3]

Their approach leads to a massive distortion of the history of the black liberation movement and, for that matter, a distortion of the history of the American left, as well as massive intellectual confusion about how to think about the role of "identity" in relationship to black movements:

> With the rise of the Black Power movement, and subsequently other ethnic movements for which it served as a template, concerns with and assertion of individual identity, already linked by Erickson to "communal culture," were readily, if facilely, transposed to the group level. The proliferation of identitarian claim-making was facilitated by the comparative institutional weakness of leftist politics in the United States and by the concomitant weakness of class-based idioms of social and political analysis. (Brubaker and Cooper 2000: 3)

What Brubaker and Cooper either are ignorant of or ignore are the following key points. The black power movement was primarily focused on demands that centered on power, the redistribution of economic resources, self-determination of what was perceived as an oppressed nation by both black nationalists and black Marxists, and the gaining of political and economic power in both communities (the community control movement) and the larger state. These instrumentalist, power-based demands had relatively little in common with "identitarian claim-making" that Brubaker and Cooper so bemoan. Further, as even a cursory examination of the history of the modern left in the United States would highlight, the black power movement, the Chicano movement, and other allied movements from the 1920s through the 1970s were at the center of class-based political, economic, and social movements.[4] Finally, the spread of the black power and similar movements had less to do with the weakness of particularly white-dominated leftist institutions and more to do with a white supremacist racial order that had suffered some severe body blows because of the success of the civil rights movement in toppling Jim Crow, but

---

[3] See Dawson 2001 for a more detailed discussion of the relationship between black liberation movements and movements based on class and gender. Horton 2005 provides an important perspective on the historic role that racism played in undermining various efforts at working-class mobilization. The divergence of class politics in the United States from European paths is due largely to racism and the myopia of the American left. That is to say, the politics of class in the United States has often been entangled in various forms of racial politics as well. See also the work of Michael Rogin; essays in both *Ronald Reagan, the Movie* (1997) and *Blackface, White Noise* (1998) analyze these themes.

[4] For a detailed recounting of this history for the black liberation movement, see my book *Black Visions* (2001). Robin Kelley has provided the most detailed and varied history of the intersection of the black and various left movements within the United States. Two more recent examples are *Race Rebels* (1994) and *Freedom Dreams* (2002).

which was still capable of sustaining systematic black disadvantage, particularly in the economic arena. The contestation around black racial identity that
did occur in black communities during the black power era was firmly tied to
social movements aimed at a fundamental rearrangement of power and resources within the United States.

Jennifer Lee and Frank Bean (2004) illustrate the importance of understanding that the foundation for analysis of racial and ethnic identities within
the United States is an understanding of the nation's racial order.[5] They emphasize several points, which they consider necessary for understanding the status
of black identity in the United States – especially in its relationship to other
racial and ethnic identities. First, they argue that the earlier period of European
immigration and the current period of immigration from the Americas and Asia
are characterized by the immigrants' struggle to be defined as being "not
black." The ability, Lee and Bean (2004: 233) argue, to avoid "black" identification has led to fairly mutable categorizations and identities for all but
African Americans: "Although boundary crossing may be more common for
all groups, it appears that the legacy of institutional racism in the country . . .
more forcibly constrains the identity options for blacks compared to other
nonwhite groups."

Lee and Bean are not optimistic about the future, They fear that America's
racial order, which was initially inscribed in a black-white paradigm, is now
being reinscribed in a black-nonwhite paradigm: "Hence, America's changing
color lines could involve a new racial/ethnic divide that may consign many
blacks to disadvantaged positions qualitatively similar to those perpetuated by
the traditional black/white divide" (Lee and Bean 2004: 237). Under the conditions Lee and Bean describe, oppression would continue to, I argue, facilitate
the formation of black collective identity across a wide range of the African
American population.

As Iris Marion Young (1990) argues, the concept of "oppression" is one
not normally found in mainstream social science research in this country.[6]
Yet, it is a term that helps us theoretically situate black racial identity in its
proper historical context. There are a number of reasons that any particular

---

[5] I explain my rationale for characterizing the racial social structure in the United States as a racial
order in *Black Visions* (Dawson 2001). See also Kim (2000) for a somewhat different, but
excellent theorization of the racial order in the United States.

[6] On the basis of Iris Marion Young's (1990: 38) definition of oppression and domination, it is
clear that through much of U.S. history blacks were both dominated and oppressed. Since the
partial victories of the civil rights and black liberation movements, black status is perhaps better
characterized by the concept of oppression because the actions of both of those movements were
aimed squarely at systems of domination against blacks (white supremacy). It should be noted,
however, that I believe that blacks still endure elements of both domination and oppression.

group identity should be historically situated – one reason examined later in the chapter concerns the effects of whites' and blacks' beliefs that individuals' fates are linked to their racial groups' fortune. Specifically for this discussion, the reason is that within any society the nature of social identity is shaped by the power relations within which any group is embedded. Lee and Bean's analysis of the historical nature of the racial order in the United States allows them to understand the power dynamics that constrain African Americans in ways that do not affect other groups. These constraints are systemic and institutional and have led to political mobilization throughout the nineteenth, twentieth, and twenty-first centuries that have produced "instrumental" and "identity" claims. Brubaker and Cooper were wrong to counterpoise identity and instrumental claims in their discussion of racial and ethnic mobilizations within the United States. The social structure or racial order within which racial identities are generated also produces the widespread systematic and systemic set of racial disadvantages that Young (1990) calls oppression. Laissez-faire racism is the label that Bobo (2004: 17) attaches to the current era of the American racial order and is defined in part by "... persistent negative stereotyping of African Americans, a tendency to blame blacks themselves for the black-white gap in socioeconomic status, and resistance to meaningful policy efforts to ameliorate U.S. racist social conditions and institutions."[7]

This system of racial disadvantage that Bobo describes provides the milieu within which modern black racial identity flourishes, evolves, and reproduces itself. Some philosophers, however, do not critique the project of black racial identity from the perspective of a misplaced nostalgia for a class politics that largely never existed and which the structure of racial disadvantage within the United States has largely foreclosed but instead offer their critiques in order to build stronger and more moral antiracist movements.

Moral and Ethical Considerations

> It is clear to the most reductionist intellect that black people think differently from one another; it is also clear that the time for undiscriminating racial unity has passed.
>
> – Toni Morrison, 1992

---

[7] Bobo, like Dawson (2001) and Kim (2000), views racial orders as historically situated. Drawing on the work of Holt (2000), Bobo argues that the racial order in the United States has distinct historical configurations. He labels the current historical configuration by the label "laissez-faire" racism.

Is the loss of a national black identity a bad thing? I think it is, unless we believe that this country as a whole currently embodies those values and goals we seek to be identified with. If it does not, then we must seek to present alternative values and goals as forcefully as possible. This struggle is not new.

– Charles P. Henry, 1992

A more rigorous and historically grounded critique of the politics of racial identity than that of Brubaker and Cooper comes from the philosopher Tommie Shelby. Shelby has a clear understanding of American history and of the effects that white supremacy has had on African American identity formation. Brubaker and Cooper's concerns come from an anxiety that the politics of race in the United States not only results from "weak" leftist institutions but also undermines the possibility for a more traditional politics of class.[8] Unlike Brubaker and Cooper, however, Shelby's criticism of the identity projects of various black social movements over the years is rooted not in the concern about the suppression of a politics of class but in the argument that a politics centered on collective black identity may suppress the politics of difference *within* black communities.

Specifically, Shelby objects to black "collective identity theory." In a thoughtful extended philosophical critique, Shelby (2002: 234) argues that despite its advantages, "cultivating a collective black identity is unnecessary for forging effective bonds among blacks, [and] would create (or exacerbate an already) undue constraint on individual freedom, and is likely, in any case, to be self-defeating." Shelby makes three points in support of his claim that collective black identity is likely to be self-defeating. First, he argues that any reliance on collective black identity "inevitably" leads to debilitating conflicts over what it means to be "authentically" black.

Second, emphasis on a common black identity would surely, Shelby argues, exacerbate class tensions among African Americans. Perhaps surprisingly, unlike some (Dawson 1994; Reed 1999), Shelby emphasizes the cultural differences of class as opposed to potential differences in interests that have emerged since the victories of the civil rights and black liberation movements.[9] For Shelby, "cultural" (culture for him signifying bundles of behaviors, tastes,

---

[8] I thank Lisa Wedeen for helping to sort out the underlying concern motivating Brubaker and Cooper's critique of identitarian politics.

[9] I tend to use the phrase "black liberation" rather than "black power" movement for several reasons. First, it was more often the term used by activists themselves in the late 1960s and early to mid-1970s. Second, "black power" in the end was a vague phrase that was embraced by a very wide range of activists from black nationalists of various persuasions, some black liberals, and black capitalists. "Black liberation," on the other hand, was a narrower term that implied a more radical and redistributive agenda.

and values) conflict between affluent and less affluent blacks is a straightforward outgrowth of an emphasis on collective identity. As many scholars have
noted, conflict along these lines between urban middle-class and poor blacks
throughout the twentieth century has been a prominent feature of black social
and political urban life (Gaines 1996). Because, for Shelby, maintaining a
common black identity is tied to maintaining a common ethnic and/or cultural
identity, the cultural conflicts likely to emerge from emphasizing a common
black identity would undermine black solidarity.

Relatedly and third, requiring a common black identity is likely to "aggra-
vate" what Shelby (2002: 250) sees as the conflict "between black men and
black women over gender issues."[10] Because of the strength of patriarchal
dominance in black communities both historically and in the current period,
calls for a common black identity lead to the dominance of male preferences
and less freedom for black women.

Shelby recognizes the advantages that black collective identity can provide.
He notes that proponents of black collective identity argue that it is necessary
for at least two reasons. First, it provides a partial solution to the free-rider
problem; the invocation of collective identity makes it easier to mobilize blacks
across various divisions (some would argue, and Shelby implies, particularly
across class lines). Second, one might support abstract principles without
necessarily moving to action. Black collective identity makes these principles
"real." But, as suggested, Shelby finds the unity imposed by collective racial
identity to be at least in part to be imposed coercively and to come at the cost of
suppressing real political, social, and cultural difference. Shelby finds even
"thin" racial identities (those imposed from outside) problematic.

Shelby is careful to argue that abandoning collective black identity does not
mean that African Americans should also abandon black solidarity. To the
contrary, Shelby is quite firm in his belief that building and maintaining black
solidarity is important to the construction of a strong progressive movement for
racial justice. But black solidarity, Shelby asserts, has provided a sounder
foundation by understanding common oppression rather than by a notion of
collective social identity. As Shelby (2002) argues, "the goal of this program is
to simply free blacks from anti-black racism."

For our purposes there are two interrelated problems with Shelby's analyses.
First, there are now two decades of work showing that, as indicated by a variety
of measures, a large majority of African Americans share a collective racial

---

[10] I would probably characterize it more as a struggle among African Americans over gender and
(sexuality) issues. As the firestorms of the 1990s that ensued around the Million Man March
and the Hill-Thomas Hearings suggest, black women *and* men could be found on both sides of
the gender conflicts.

identity (Dawson 1994; Gurin, Hatchett, and Jackson 1989; Tate 1993). Even if one agreed with the moral and ethical objections that Shelby raises to the collective identity project, one could not just flip a switch and turn off collective identity among African Americans, particularly under conditions of, if not oppression (and I do think that is an accurate descriptor for the conditions under which most blacks live), systematic disadvantage. Shelby makes several valid points in his analysis of the potential moral pitfalls of embracing black collective identity, but his project is not one confined to just analytical philosophy. Shelby, to his credit, is also concerned with building real-world antiracist movements on a foundation of black solidarity. For this aspect of his project, the ubiquity and deep-rootedness of black collective identity provides a pragmatic as well as an analytical problem. Given the reality that a sense of collective identity remains embedded within the African American population, analytical tools, both theoretical and empirical, need to be developed to both analyze and theorize the current ebbs and flows in collective black identity, its causes, and how it affects black politics and life.

Second and even more fundamental, Shelby needs to address the analytical problem that the black solidarity that he wants to generate will, as it has in the past, in and of itself engender the strengthening of black collective identity. Similarly, structural disadvantage is still pervasive enough to facilitate the joint formation of collective identity and black solidarity. There is also the pragmatic reality that political entrepreneurs will encourage black collective identity as a way to build and maintain political movements that will not only achieve a set of collective goals but also yield payoffs to the entrepreneurs who promote collective identity.

Further, forging a collective project based on opposition to racism is more problematic than Shelby acknowledges. The content of such shared projects is contested, and indeed a "common" political program almost automatically is accompanied by debate around whom and what is included within the project and what and whom is excluded. One's political program (e.g., support for affirmative action or the civil rights movement, or position on gender questions) can come to be viewed as being "outside" the (contested) boundaries of an antiracist movement, just as Shelby worried that a movement based on collective black identity could exclude some on the basis of "different" cultural values. Examples of strong norms of excluding the politically scorned from black communities are abundant in black history – one example is the exclusion of black democrats during the era of Reconstruction at the end of the Civil War (Dawson 2001).

Philosophers such as Anthony Appiah argue that it is difficult to avoid tensions owing to one's ethical obligations that are generated by one's identities (i.e., one's just partiality toward one's comrades in a social movement) and to moral concerns that are generated by concerns about social justice (i.e., guarding against unjust exclusions from social movements), because, as Appiah (2005: xiv) argues, "Identities make ethical claims because – and this is just a fact about the world we human beings have created – we make our lives *as* men and *as* women, *as* gay and *as* straight people, *as* Ghanaians and *as* Americans, *as* blacks and *as* whites" (emphasis in the original). Solidarity, according to Appiah, gives rise to moral concerns (i.e., concerns about social justice) because it carries with it a positive ethical obligation to be partial toward those with whom one has thick ties, whether those ties be in the domain of the family, the race, or one's comrades in a progressive social movement (although Appiah notes that not all such ties are equally "thick" – kinship ties, for example, are for Appiah "thicker" than those produced by the nation). Appiah (2005: 229) goes on to argue that such thick ties need not necessarily lead to exclusion:

Solidarity worries us because we take its obverse face to be exclusion; but should we? The difference between treating others better than you must because you like them and treating others worse than you might because you dislike them is one that only an economist could fail to see. Racism, for example, typically involves giving people less than they are owed, failing to acknowledge their due as fellow human beings; to succumb to racism is to fall short of our obligation to "take seriously and weigh appropriately the fact that they are persons in deliberating about what to do" (as Darwall glosses "recognition respect"). Yet I can give you your due and still treat my friend better.

It is beyond the scope of this chapter to sort through the moral and ethical entanglements with which Appiah and Shelby wrestle. But from Shelby we can take away a just concern with the type of exclusions, which occur all too frequently as a result of collective identity projects, including that of black racial identity. From Appiah we should take away the caution, one that he did not perhaps mean for us to apprehend, that projects that seek to build solidarity on political rather than identity-based considerations are still subject to the same sort of risks that worry Shelby.

Be that as it may, black social identity is a phenomenon that will be an integral part of the social and political landscape for the foreseeable future. The racial order in the United States is still alive and well and produces the type of systematic disadvantage conducive to the robust reproduction of black social identity. I return to the moral and ethical concerns raised by the existence of black social identity in the conclusion of this chapter. But now I consider the empirical task at hand – evaluating approaches to measuring the antecedents, distribution, and effects of one measure of black social identity. We start with an assessment of the applicability of one approach to studying black collective identity – an assessment of the concept of linked fate.

LINKED FATE

More than ten years have passed since the publication of *Behind the Mule: Race and Class in African-American Politics*, and it is time to assess whether the concept of linked fate is still useful for understanding black collective identities and their effect on black politics.[11] It is also a useful point to examine, as suggested earlier, the concept's utility to the range of applications to which linked fate has been applied. Several dozen articles, books, dissertations, conference papers, and unpublished papers have either used or examined "linked fate" over the past several years[12] – for example, to evaluate the probability of blacks and Latinos forming coalitions, to study both ethnic and panethnic identifications among Asian Americans, to study political mobilization and vote choice among both Latino/as and Asian Americans, and to study respondents' selection of Spanish when participating in social surveys (Weaver 2005). The overwhelming domain within which we find the concept of linked fate used, however, is in research on African American beliefs, ideology, and politics. I argue that this is proper, not because I believe that blacks are cognitively different from other Americans; I decidedly reject that belief. But I do believe that "black" linked fate is relevant in the context of an institutional framework specific to black communities. It is not clear, as a comparison of the antecedents and effects of linked fate among blacks and whites will show, that either the survey question that indexes "linked fate" or the concept itself has the same meaning to citizens of different racial and ethnic groups. Minimally, it seems, an argument needs to be made in each case about how one's attachment to one's racial or ethnic group is shaped by the power dynamics of both intergroup conflict and cooperation within a given historical era.

The first published use of the term "linked fate" is found in my first book *Behind the Mule* (1994). The argument I made at the time was straightforward, if often subsequently misunderstood. Linked fate was defined simply as the perception on the part of individual African Americans that their own fate was "linked to the fate of the race." It was a conceptual component of the "black utility heuristic," which was defined as follows:

It is quite clear that, until the mid-1960s, race was the decisive factor in determining the opportunities and life chances available to virtually all African Americans, regardless of their own or their family's social and economic status. Consequently, it was much more

---

[11] It is actually sixteen to twenty years in terms of the data. *Behind the Mule* used data from surveys conducted in 1984 and 1988.

[12] I am grateful to Vesla Weaver for compiling the bibliography on linked fate and related concepts that is the basis for this discussion. Copies of this bibliography are available from the author by request.

efficient for African Americans to determine what was good for the racial group than to determine what was good for themselves individually, and more efficient for them to use the status of the group, both relative and absolute, as a proxy for individual utility. (Dawson 1994: 10)

I went on to explain:

As long as race remains dominant in determining the lives of individual blacks, it is "rational" for black Americans to follow group cues in interpreting and acting in the political world. This tendency of African Americans to follow racial cues has been reinforced historically by institutions developed during the forced separation of blacks from whites during the post-Reconstruction period. These institutions, particularly the black church, tended to transmit the lesson of how to respond to the shifts in race relations, economic climate, and political environment across generations. (Dawson 1994: 57–58)

Several points should be noted in these passages. First, my conceptualization of linked fate entails that black collective identity gets produced and reproduced through the institutions of the black community, such as families, the church, social movement organizations, barber and beauty shops, and the associational networks of the black communities. I would now add that black collective identity also gets produced and reproduced through the shared practices engaged in by members of these institutions, movements, and communities.

I make the further argument in *Behind the Mule* (1994), which is elaborated in *Black Visions* (2001), that exposure to the information networks of black communities (including songs, novels, and movies, as well as black-oriented print and broadcast news) also served to reinforce a sense of linked fate. More generally, combining both of these arguments, I now argue that linked fate – and, more generally, black collective identity – is generated and reproduced in the black public sphere (more properly the black counterpublic) of black civil society (Dawson 2001). Black civil society shifts with changes in American society and the American political economy (Holt 2000).

It is also through the black public sphere, within black civil society, that the development of linked fate is associated with the development of shared social identities. According to the argument I make in *Behind the Mule*, from precolonial times through slavery, through Jim Crow, and through the massive civil rights and black liberation struggles from midcentury through the early 1970s, black collective identity had at its core the shared purpose of achieving racial justice. Black collective identity was at first centered on ending slavery and then, a generation later, dismantling Jim Crow. One of the greatest controversies among activists, scholars, pundits, and grass-roots African Americans is whether such purposive content is still an integral part of black identity, and if it is or is not, *should* it be? In the absence of slavery and Jim Crow is there a common goal (or set of goals) that is embedded in African American identity, or do suppressed class, gender, sexuality, and now generational differences make the attainment of a set of "common" goals a potentially dangerous fantasy?

Studying linked fate, therefore, necessitates situating research within the relevant historical context. Contestation over black collective identities during Jim Crow, for example, is very different from contestation over black identities today. For example, the debate and conflict over whether a black feminist identity can or should be encompassed within a broader black collective identity, while never fully suppressed, was much more muted during the Jim Crow era than during the current period. Finally, the specific idea of linked fate is rooted in the traditions of social psychology pioneered by Henri Tajfel as extended by later researchers such as John Turner.[13] As such, linked fate in general and specifically the black utility heuristic were conceptualized as cognitive constructs that operated at a subconscious rather than conscious level.

Scholars such as Cathy Cohen (1999) and Adolph Reed Jr. (1999) have criticized research on black identity generally, and the concept of linked fate specifically, arguing that it and similar concepts serve to over-homogenize black communities, with the effect that difference and conflict along the dimensions of gender, class, and sexuality in particular are minimized and indeed suppressed. This critique results from a misapprehension of the concept of linked fate. While the treatment of gender in *Behind the Mule* was clearly poorly developed, the concept of linked fate was explicitly developed and argued to facilitate the theoretical inclusion of contestation as part of the identity formation process. In an era when central, mammoth targets of oppression such as slavery and Jim Crow had been formally dismantled, large numbers of African Americans could (and do) agree that their fate is linked to that of the race *without agreeing on either the ends that black struggles for racial justice should pursue or the strategy and tactics with which these ends should be pursued.* Indeed, the prediction that was made in *Behind the Mule* was that there would be increased political conflict regardless of the level of linked fate in the black community as disagreement over goals emerged, and the level of linked fate itself would decline if in particular the

---

[13] See *Behind the Mule* (1994), chap. 3, for an extended discussion of how the concept of linked fate was characterized as being derived from social psychological understandings of group consciousness.

institutional and informational infrastructure that was necessary for the reproduction of linked fate eroded.[14]

In the next section, I present preliminary analyses of the utility of linked fate for research on contemporary black collective identity. I then present results from parallel analyses of linked fate among white Americans. I conclude the section with suggestions for analytical extensions of the research agenda on linked fate.

DATA AND ANALYSIS

The data used in the analyses are from the "2004 Racial Attitudes Study" (principal investigator, Michael C. Dawson). The study was conducted between October 1 and October 18, 2004. The total number of respondents was 1,079 – 530 whites and 549 blacks. The completion rate for the study was 67 percent. The data were collected by Knowledge Networks using an on-line computer methodology. Knowledge Networks' panel is drawn from a random sample of the population of American households. Computers and Internet connections are installed in sample households that do not already have Internet access. The 2004 study is a component of a multiyear survey research project being conducted by Dawson and Lawrence Bobo that aims to examine racial attitudes during the first George W. Bush administration.[15]

Table 6.1 displays the distribution of linked fate among black and white Americans. African Americans' belief that their fate is linked to that of the race has remained about the same for the past two decades. Seventy-five percent of blacks believe that their fate is linked to that of the race, with more than 70 percent believing that the linkage is at least somewhat strong.[16] The distribution is more evenly divided among whites than it is for blacks. While nearly 60 percent of whites agree that their fate is linked to that of other whites, "only" 50 percent believe that linkage to be relatively strong. Nevertheless, it is clear from Table 6.1 that a substantial proportion of both

---

[14] Michael Fortner (2009) is the rare scholar who argues that linked fate developed and was reproduced not because of the institutions and their successors that developed indigenously in black communities during the Reconstruction era after the Civil War but as a result of political institutions and processes during the postsegregation era.

[15] There are two reasons that this analysis makes the compromise of confining the analyses to blacks and whites. First, cost constraints made it impossible to do a more desirable study that would have better represented the full scope of the American racial and ethnic terrain. Second, given our cost constraints, we chose blacks and whites for analyses because numerous studies show that, on a very wide array of items and policies, blacks and whites still occupy the polar ends of both the American attitudinal spectrum and the polar ends of the American racial order.

[16] The total includes the responses "a lot," "some," and "not much."

TABLE 6.1. *Distribution of Linked Fate among Blacks and Whites in the United States,* %

Linked Fate	Blacks	Whites
No	25.0	41.4
Not much	3.3	8.3
Some	26.0	33.4
A lot	45.7	16.9
N	525	480

Note: The table reports the weighted frequency distribution of responses to: "Do you think that what happens generally to black people in this country will have something to do with what happens in your life?" If yes, "Will it affect you a lot, some, or not very much?" (for blacks). Do you think that what happens generally to white people in this country will have something to do with what happens in your life?" If yes, "Will it affect you a lot, some, or not very much?" (for whites).

TABLE 6.2. *The Antecedents of Linked Fate for Blacks and Whites*

Variable	Black Linked Fate	White Linked Fate
Gender	−.005 (.114)	−.056 (.115)
Age	−.002 (.039)	−.027 (.034)
Education	.295 (.193)	**.535**** (.207)
Income	−.001 (.014)	.004 (.017)
South	−.013 (.113)	.136 (.123)
Black/white comparison	**.619**** (.201)	.402 (.214)
Group Belonging Scale	.034 (.061)	.042 (.046)
Church	−.104 (.121)	
Black Information Networks Index	.080 (.038)	
Member of black improvement organization	**.370*** (.156)	
N	432	393
R-squared	.033	.023

Note: Regression results: Determinants of linked fate. The reported coefficients were generated using ordered probit. Standard errors are in parentheses below the estimate. * p < .05; ** p < .01; *** p < .001. Coefficients that are significant at the p < .08 level appear in boldface.

black and white citizens believe that their own prospects are tied to those of their respective races.

Tables 6.2 and 6.3 display the antecedents for both black and white linked fate. The antecedents of an African American's belief that one's fate is linked to that of other African Americans are the degree to which one believes that African Americans fare more poorly in the economy than whites, the frequency of exposure to black information networks, and whether one belongs to an

TABLE 6.3. *The Increased Probability of Believing One's Fate Is Linked to the Race*

Variable	Black Linked Fate (a lot)	White Linked Fate (a lot)
Education		12.2
Black/white comparison	24.1	9.5
Black Information Networks Index	15.6	
Member of black improvement organization	14.5	

organization dedicated to improving the status of African Americans. These three factors highlight how a sense of linked fate, and therefore black collective identity, is rooted in perceptions of the structural disadvantages that still afflict African Americans, on the one hand, and both the associational and public sphere components of black civil society, on the other.[17] Black perceptions of the relative economic status of blacks and whites are rooted in their objective economic well-being and reflect a racial order that still provides significant economic benefits to whites (Dawson 1994). This measure of perceptions is an accurate indicator of black economic reality. This factor has by far the largest effect on the probability of seeing one's fate linked to that of the race. Those who believe that whites are doing much better than blacks are almost 25 percent more likely to believe their fate is linked to that of the race than those who believe the reverse. Those who are exposed the most to black information networks, a key component of the black public sphere, were substantially more likely, more than 15 percent, to believe their fate is linked to the race a lot than those who lacked exposure to black media and artistic production. An institutional component of black civil society, membership in an organization that advances the welfare of blacks, also significantly raised one's likelihood of perceiving a strong linkage. Overall, we see in this modest estimation of the antecedents of linked fate how black collective identity is produced and reproduced through the structural workings of the racial order as well as within the various components of black civil society.

The pattern for white linked fate is somewhat different, and where the estimation produces similar results, one strongly suspects that the interpretation of the results is different from that for blacks. There are two factors that lead to beliefs in stronger linkages between one's own fate and that of other

[17] See I. Young 2000 for a useful discussion about the relationship between the public sphere and associational components of civil society.

whites. More educated whites are likely to exhibit belief in higher levels of linked fate more than less educated whites. Some may find this result counter-intuitive, but as far as I know there are not strong theoretical grounds for making a prediction about the relationship between white linked fate and education. Conflicting evidence can be found in the literature about the relationship between education and white racial attitudes, although most studies make the argument that greater education tends to be associated with white racial liberalism. The second result has an intuitive if chilling interpretation. Whites who strongly believe that whites are faring better in the economy than blacks feel more strongly linked to the fate of other whites. While one could make a case that whites who resent blacks doing better than they do in the economy would feel stronger ties to other whites, it is those who see whites prospering who have the strongest sense of white collective identity.

But again I would argue that the interpretation of these results, particularly in conjunction with the results for whites that I report in the next section, should not be trusted, despite one's ability to construct a plausible post hoc explanation for the pattern of results. Black collective identity theory was constructed to explain the racial identities of a group that had been historically oppressed in the United States and had been at the bottom of the racial order for an extraordinarily long time. The power dynamics that this group experienced in American history are very different from what members of the racial group that were the prime beneficiaries of the American racial order experienced. It seems reasonable that until we do further theoretical and empirical research on white collective identity we should assume for now that we have a poor understanding of how the measure will work in white public opinion; and, even when we think we may understand the underlying logic of the relationships we estimate in this area, we should not expect that logic to correspond closely to that of African Americans.

Table 6.4 shows selected effects of black linked fate on a variety of attitudinal variables. Across a wide range of phenomena, black linked fate has an impact on black political attitudes. Linked fate has a particularly strong effect on questions that embody the intersection of race and politics in the United States. Questions not affected by the degree that one perceives strong linked fate include questions on nonracialized issues and personages such as evaluations of Ralph Nader, Powell and Rice, Colin Powell, and Condoleezza Rice and one's stance toward Gulf War II. As previously explained in *Black Visions* (Dawson 2001), I show that with the exception of black conservative activists, black activists from a variety of ideological persuasions (liberal, in the philosophical sense, and nonliberal alike) are perceived in a racialized manner within the African American public sphere. Therefore, it is predictable that the

TABLE 6.4. *The Effect of Linked Fate on a Variety of Black Political Beliefs*

Dependent Variable	Coefficient	z	p > |z|	First Difference (increase in support/ agreement/favorability)
Blacks much worse off than whites	.25	.84	.40	1.9
Protest against war is unpatriotic	−.12	−.61	.54	−2.6
Vote for Bush	**−.56**	**−2.12**	**.03**	**−7.9**
Black political party	.27	1.22	.22	8.4
Apology for slavery	.30	1.41	.16	8.5
Reparations for slavery	**.40**	**1.75**	**.08**	**12.9**
Apology for Jim Crow	.21	.86	.39	3.8
Reparations for Jim Crow	.24	1.03	.30	6.9
Reparations for Tulsa and Rosewood	.34	1.34	.18	7.5
Going to war with Iraq	−.04	−.26	.79	−1.3
Disenfranchisement was important problem in Florida in 2000	.59	2.79	.01	11.3
Disenfranchisement will be important problem in 2004	.48	2.76	.01	14.6
Blacks should control politics in black communities	.50	3.29	.00	14.9
Economic system is unfair to poor	.42	2.33	.02	13.5
Blacks will never achieve racial equality	.18	1.17	.24	5.6
Identify as a Democrat	.18	1.12	.26	7.2
Bush opposes the interests of people like you	.48	3.40	.00	10.1
Bush feeling thermometer	**−8.60**	**−2.50**	**.01**	**−8.6**
Anan thermometer	**7.75**	**2.38**	**.02**	**7.4**
Jackson thermometer	**6.23**	**1.98**	**.05**	**6.3**
Nader thermometer	.96	.31	.76	1.06
Powell thermometer	2.85	.80	.42	3.0
Rice thermometer	3.33	.88	.38	3.1
Cheney thermometer	−1.21	−.36	.72	−1.2
Edwards thermometer	**5.49**	**1.78**	**.08**	**5.36**
Kerry thermometer	3.70	1.23	.22	3.7
Obama thermometer	**8.13**	**2.33**	**.02**	**8.11**

Note: Regression results: Black linked fate. The reported coefficients were generated using probit, ordered probit, and OLS regression. The following controls were included, but are not reported here: gender, age, education, income, South dummy, Black Information Networks Index, member of organization to improve status of blacks, Group Belonging Scale, member of church, blacks worse off than whites (when it was not a dependent variable), and party identification (for expressly political outcomes). The quantities of interest in the final column were estimated using the CLARIFY program (King, Tomz, and Wittenberg 2003). To explain the size of the effect of linked fate on a given dependent variable, CLARIFY was used to simulate the change in the probability of support, increasing linked fate from its minimum (none) to its maximum (a lot), while holding all other variables at their mean. First differences that are statistically significant at the p < .05 level appear in boldface, if significant at the p < .1 level then in italics.

evaluation of public figures from these ideological tendencies is shaped by one's racial identity.[18] Another reason that linked fate fails to predict some survey items is the lack of variation among African Americans on some key political questions. For example, there is substantial variation among blacks on whether there should be reparations for slavery (an approximately 2–1 split in favor; see Dawson and Popoff 2004); thus, the level of linked fate in an individual provides useful leverage in estimating the level of support for reparations for slavery. On the other hand, there is no variation to speak of among African Americans on the question of whether the U.S. government should apologize to blacks for slavery. African Americans overwhelmingly believe that there should be an apology. Thus, linked fate has no role to play in estimating who is more likely to support an apology because African Americans are virtually equally likely to support an apology regardless of how strong a linkage individuals perceive. A similar item on which there is little variation and which therefore linked fate does not predict well is that of party identification. Such a large percentage of blacks identify with the Democratic Party that there is virtually nothing to predict. Be that as it may, linked fate, the results demonstrate, consistently influences African American political attitudes, and in some domains strongly so. Further, as an inspection of Table 6.3 indicates, linked fate, even when not statistically significant, predicts black attitudes in the direction that theory would suggest. As a measure of black collective identity, linked fate still, as other researchers have also found (Weaver 2005), serves as an effective construct – one that suggests that, more generally, black collective identity still remains a powerful, coherent, force in shaping the beliefs, politics, and, by extension, the actions of African Americans in the early twenty-first century.

The pattern among white Americans is very different from that found among blacks (Table 6.5). It is difficult, if not impossible, to construct a credible, coherent interpretation of the results.[19] As with African Americans, linked fate has the strongest effect on items and personages that are perceived as racialized. The stronger the perception that one's fate is linked to that of other whites, the more likely that one supports an apology for slavery, reparations, the belief that disenfranchisement of black voters in Florida during the 2000 election was an important problem, and increased support for Senators Edwards, Kerry, and Obama. One could argue that increased awareness of one's whiteness and one's place in the racial order leads to a more racially

---

[18] See Dawson 2001 and 2004 on how black conservatives become deracialized in the eyes of the American electorate.

[19] These results are *so* counterintuitive that we went back to the raw data to make sure there were no coding mistakes.

TABLE 6.5. *The Effect of Linked Fate on a Variety of White Political Beliefs*

Dependent Variable	Coefficient	t	p > |z|	First Difference (increase in support/ agreement/ favorability)
Blacks much worse off than whites	.003	.02	.99	−.06
Protest against war is unpatriotic	−.19	−.96	.34	−2.1
Vote for Bush	−.10	−.39	.69	−4.1
Apology for slavery	**.57**	**2.59**	**.01**	**14.8**
Reparations for slavery	**.63**	**1.89**	**.06**	**5.5**
Apology for Jim Crow	**.42**	**2.01**	**.05**	**14.0**
Reparations for Jim Crow	.05	.12	.91	.26
Reparations for Tulsa and Rosewood	−.01	−.02	.98	.18
Going to war with Iraq	.21	1.33	.18	-7.7
Disenfranchisement was important problem in Florida in 2000	.29	1.70	.09	11.1
Disenfranchisement will be important problem in 2004	.18	1.15	.25	6.8
Economic system is unfair to poor	.11	.68	.49	.04
Blacks will never achieve racial equality	.04	.22	.83	.10
Identify as a Democrat	.15	.98	.33	5.1
Bush opposes the interests of people like you	−.14	−.87	.39	.94
Bush feeling thermometer	−1.07	−.29	.77	−.99
Anan thermometer	4.43	1.38	.17	4.3
Jackson thermometer	4.21	1.28	.20	4.4
Nader thermometer	−.85	−.25	.80	−.94
Powell thermometer	−.34	−.10	.92	−.37
Rice thermometer	−.41	.11	.91	−.32
Cheney thermometer	−2.36	−.69	.49	−2.3
Edwards thermometer	**7.60**	**2.32**	**.02**	**7.6**
Kerry thermometer	**10.01**	**2.81**	**.01**	**10.0**
Obama thermometer	**5.00**	**1.51**	**.13**	**5.0**

Note: Regression results: white linked fate. The reported coefficients were generated using probit, ordered probit, and OLS regression. The following controls were included, but are not reported here: gender, age, education, income, South dummy, group belonging scale, blacks worse off than whites (when it was not a dependent variable), and party identification (for expressly political outcomes). The quantities of interest in the final column were estimated using the CLARIFY program (King, Tomz, and Wittenberg 2003). To explain the size of the effect of linked fate on a given dependent variable, CLARIFY was used to simulate the change in the probability of support, increasing linked fate from its minimum (none) to its maximum (a lot), while holding all other variables at their mean. First differences that are statistically significant at the p < .05 level appear in boldface, if significant at the p < .1 level then in italics.

progressive outlook on American politics. This is consistent with one interpretation of the finding that those with higher levels of education are more likely to feel that the fate of other whites affects their own. While the reader may or may not believe that this is a credible account of the results found in Table 6.4, it is clearly the case that there is a dynamic that is different from the one that produced the pattern of African American responses.[20] While the case of the difference between the *pattern* of white and black responses may be extreme, it does highlight the dangers of trying to transport measures of collective identity across different historical, political, and social contexts. The basic point of the exercise is to suggest that particularly for whites, but perhaps for other non–African American racial and ethnic groups as well, our understanding of the role that "linked fate" plays in racial identity is not well enough understood to justify usage in models of (at least white) racial opinion.

CONCLUSION AND DISCUSSION

To what degree in the current political context can we reconcile the theoretical task of constructing a measure of racial "identity" that satisfies the social theorists, while simultaneously meeting the philosophical and pragmatic goals of those such as Shelby? How does the concept of linked fate fulfill either set of demands? Given recent data, what can we say about the empirical grounding of linked fate among African Americans, the nature of black political solidarity in the era of conservative triumph, and the relationship between the two? Finally, to what degree should the concept of linked fate be used as a measure of collective identity for other racial and ethnic groups? Two clear patterns emerged from the analysis.

First, it is clear that African Americans continue to retain a strong collective identity, are unified and pessimistic in their assessment of the prospects for gaining racial equality within the United States, and remain on the leftward edge of a vast political gulf between blacks and whites on a range of political issues that include evaluation of President Bush, support for protest activities, assessment of Gulf War II, and the desirability of either reparations or an apology for slavery, Jim Crow, and twentieth-century antiblack pogroms

---

[20] I asked two white friends, who are a couple, the linked fate question. Both are openly and unabashedly left in their political orientations and antiracist in their outlooks. One responded yes and the other no to the white linked fate question. One responded that she was aware everyday of her white "privilege" and how that benefited whites as a group. The other responded that he did not think of his identity racially but more in terms of class. This provides more evidence that this question has more ambiguity even for whites who share similar political outlooks than it does for African Americans.

(Dawson 2004; Dawson and Popoff 2004). Even in the most conservative era in decades, blacks still on all but some social issues remain the left-wing of the American polity, and it is on this set of issues, the ones that involve war and peace, economic redistribution, and racial issues, that primarily drives the political practices of the great majority of African Americans. The combination of strong consensus around many key political questions, the political isolation of African Americans from much of the rest of American citizenry, and the continued strong effect of a collective black identity provides a firm foundation for the maintenance, strengthening, and mobilization of black political solidarity. It remains to be seen if the weaknesses in black political leadership and organizational capacities represent too great an obstacle to fully take advantage of the political potential of black solidarity.

While linked fate for African Americans remains correlated with a wide range of racialized political issues (as the historical record suggests), and black collective identity remains imbued with shared social purposes (as well as constitutive norms and practices) (Dawson 1994, 2001; Dawson and Popoff 2004), the empirical and historical record also shows, and Shelby worries, that black collective identity both is the site of and engenders significant contestation. This dimension of contestation has generated much less quantitative research than the analyses of the content of black social identity. But the content of black collective identity, like all collective identities, is contested in every historical epoch. Abdelal and his colleagues (Chapter 1 in this volume) argue that contestation is a key component for understanding "the most theoretically significant and empirically useful conceptualization of social identity" – "what the group means to its members." One area of both consensus and contestation associated with debates over African American identity is that over what constitute the "social facts" that come bundled with some representations of black identities. Specifically, this post–civil rights and black liberation struggles era is *not* for African Americans a "[period] where intersubjective understandings of . . . social facts are stable enough that they can be treated as if fixed," but I do not think this bars us from going ahead and analyzing this ground "with social scientific procedures" (Cox 1986: 246), particularly because "scientific procedures" should be used to study conflict as well as consensus. There are some social "facts" that are constitutive of black collective identity – while not "fixed," they are relatively stable in this period. These include a belief that racial equality is a distant if at all achievable goal; that the government owes African Americans apologies for slavery, the system of American apartheid known as Jim Crow, and twentieth-century antiblack pogroms that occurred in Tulsa and Rosewood; and that one political party's positions are more advantageous than that of the other major party's. These "social facts," despite some (for this particular set in this period) limited contestation, enjoy over-whelming support among African Americans. This overwhelming support is in contrast to their status among white Americans, where the group means indi-cate a sharply divided white public or a strong consensus in the opposite direction than that embraced by blacks. But contestation is fierce *among* African Americans about such issues as whether one can embrace simultane-ously black collective identity and black feminist identity; the degree to which black identity necessitates support for some black nationalists such as Minister Farrakhan of the Nation of Islam; or whether one can have gay or lesbian identities and still be said to embrace black identity. Scholars such as Cathy Cohen (1999) and Robin Kelley (1994) show that both historically and in the current period an overemphasis on black collective identity as a social force can serve to mask the substantial degree of contestation that occurs among class lines (Kelley) or along the lines of the politics of gender and sexuality (Cohen).

Black collective identity is richly complex in both its content and the degree to which it has been contested over the decades. Certainly well into the post-segregationist era researchers have found that black collective identity played a powerful role in shaping African Americans' political and social opinion and behavior. Empirically within political science a solid vein of research has devel-oped around one particular take on how to conceptualize, measure, and ana-lytically use black collective identity. In the two decades since the emergence of this one approach, we have witnessed profound shifts in the racial, political, and social terrain as a result of high levels of immigration not only from Asia and the Western Hemisphere but from the African diaspora as well; the extreme rightward shift in American politics; and an increasing remove from the struggles that dismantled the formal system of Jim Crow. These develop-ments represent a shift of such magnitude that a reevaluation of the utility of the conceptual and empirical framework for analyses of black collective iden-tity is warranted, as well as discussion of whether such a concept is even needed in this era. At the same time as this massive shift has occurred in the American racial landscape, another related, development warrants examination.

While researchers such as Cohen (1999) have made significant progress in assessing the nature of contestation around black collective identities, quanti-tative researchers have been slow to follow. Although most quantitative researchers emphasize the study of means in their research, quantitative polit-ical methodologists, particularly over the past decade, have made it clear that this need not be the case. Let's return to the logic of the black utility heuristic and the rationale for the measure of linked fate. I argued that blacks make political and social decisions at a cognitive level as if they were assessing what was "good for the race" as a proxy for what was good for them and/or their family. This is a fairly thin conceptualization of social identity. Uncertainty or conflict about what's good for the race as applied to a specific person, policy, or opinion should be mirrored in greater variance around that item. So one way to measure contestation, it would seem, would be to model the variance. One source of variation reduction should clearly be exposure to black information networks; another would be membership in black organizations. Shared practices among members of communities, institutions, and movements should also be a source of variance reduction, though perhaps difficult to measure quantitatively. Another source may be partisan cues and education as a proxy for various levels of information. One benefit of this approach, in addition to its potential for allowing us to get a handle on contestation, is that it would allow us to inductively develop theoretical insights on what type of phenomena linked fate was a good predictor of and what type of items displayed significant variation and what the sources of the variation were.

Another area ripe for future research is that of trying to better understand the meaning of linked fate for different ethnic and racial groups particularly in relation to each other. Researchers of the collective identities of nonnative populations of African descent, Asian Americans, Latino/as, and even white Americans have begun to examine the usefulness of the concept of "linked fate" for their analyses. One possibility that Abdelal and his colleagues (Chapter 1 in this volume) propose is the method of semantic differential protocols. This approach offers a mechanism implemented through survey research that can be used to explore the relational content of identities. It requires that the survey researchers cooperate with ethnographers. Perhaps the most important theoretical task that remains for researchers who want to apply the concept of linked fate to other domains is for them to specify how the concept makes sense in the political, social, and historical context within which it is applied.

The need for this research is demonstrated by the direct evidence we have for white Americans and the secondary literature on Asian Americans and Latino/as, which suggest that the combination of concepts and measures embodied in "linked fate" may be difficult to transport across racial and ethnic boundaries. Minimally, researchers who use the measure for other racial and ethnic groups should specify how the measure indexes both the historical and contemporary experience of those groups. The researchers further need to specify not only how those experiences translate into theoretical predictions about the antecedents and effects of linked fate but also whether there are alternative theoretical concepts and measures that make more sense for the specific application.

As for the moral quandaries that worry Shelby, there are two answers I think. Black collective identity remains a foundation for both the black political belief systems and black political practices. The analysis I present here and elsewhere suggests that black collective identity is going to be a central feature of black politics for quite awhile. Part of our pragmatic task then is to work with its strengths while trying to struggle to ensure that it does not lead to the type of homogenization and suppression of difference about which Shelby, Morrison, Cohen, and others justifiably worry. Lisa Lowe's view of Asian American identity (quoted in Laitin 1998: 19) provides a useful template for thinking about and working with black identity:

It is possible to utilize specific signifiers of ethnic identity, such as Asian-American, for the purpose of contesting and disrupting the discourses that exclude Asian-Americans, while simultaneously revealing the internal contradictions and slippages of Asian-Americans so as to insure that such essentialisms will not be reproduced and proliferated by the very apparatuses we seek to disempower. On the one hand, identities such as African or Asian-American can mobilize thousands of adherents; on the other hand, these identities, when careful archaeological work is done, are revealed as fabrications.

This is a useful lesson to take with us as we explore the contours and consequences of black collective identity in the early twenty-first century.

III

CONTENT ANALYSIS AND COGNITIVE MAPPING

7

Quantitative Content Analysis and the Measurement of Collective Identity

Kimberly A. Neuendorf and Paul D. Skalski

CONTENT ANALYSIS INTRODUCED

Content analysis, simply put, is the quantitative investigation of message characteristics. Most definitions are a bit more specific than this, often delineated by the degree to which a scientific method is assumed.[1] The following definition is employed here:

Content analysis is a summarizing, quantitative analysis of messages that relies on the scientific method (including attention to objectivity-intersubjectivity, *a priori* design, reliability, validity, generalizability, replicability, and hypothesis testing) and is not limited as to the types of variables that may be measured or the context in which the messages are created or presented. (Neuendorf 2002: 10)

In content analysis, as in all quantitative investigations, the quality of a measure is dependent on several factors. First, there must be a clear conceptualization of the construct of interest, for it is the congruence between conceptualization and operationalization (measurement) that constitutes basic internal validity (Babbie 1998).[2]

First, We Conceptualize

With the construct of collective identity, conceptualization can be problematic, in that theoretic approaches abound. Abdelal et al. (2006: 695) refer to the

---

[1] Some definitions allow for direct inferences from message characteristics to source or receiver characteristics, but this is a point of debate (Berelson 1952; Neuendorf 2002; Riffe, Lacy, and Fico 2005; R. Weber 1990).

[2] Other key criteria must be met – external validity (the generalizability of the measure), and reliability (something that, when human coders are engaged, is essential to the content analytic measure). Additionally, the measures ought to be as precise and accurate, and at as high a level of measurement as possible.

"definitional anarchy" of identity research and, as Bruland and Horowitz (2003: 1) note, "the existence of identity as a universal but largely implicit concept makes it difficult to isolate and understand its use." It is not the purpose of this chapter to exhaustively cover all theoretic or conceptual approaches to the study of collective identity,[3] as this has been addressed elsewhere in this volume, most clearly in the four types of identity delineated by Abdelal et al. In this chapter, various conceptual definitions have been utilized as the bases for quantitative content analyses, and a specific definitional assumption is presented for each example given in this chapter. Thus, we present a variety of content analysis measurement techniques, based on portions of the wide array of possible conceptualizations for collective identity.

Previous Research

In the past, content analysis has rarely been used explicitly to measure identity of any type. But content analysis has been used to measure an incredible range of message characteristics. Scholars have charted the violent content of television (Wilson et al. 1997), the gender role portrayals of film characters (A. M. Smith 1999), the structure of news Web sites (Scharl 2004), and even categories of restroom graffiti (Schreer and Strichartz 1997). Other analyses have used the content analysis of naturally occurring speech to pinpoint patterns indicative of psychological pathologies (Gottschalk 1995). And contrary to some authors' opinions, content analysis is *not* limited to simple counting of messages. Some analyses have been layered and complicated, some have charted complex changes over time, and some have identified significant statistical relationships between

---

[3] For reviews of the use of identity in the social scientific literature, see Ashmore, Deaux, and McLaughlin-Volpe 2004 and Gleason 1983. Here, a brief summary of how identity has been conceptualized might be useful. On a basic level, Horowitz (2002), in his study of the use of a multitude of identity constructs in the academic literature on international relations, has delineated between definitions that are "essentialist" (i.e., preestablished or primordial), socially "constructed," or a blend of the two. Additionally, a review of the relevant literature finds four nonmutually exclusive types: (1) self-identification (i.e., the individual decides), as demonstrated in work on cultural identity (Brass 1991), perceptions of self (Bem 1972; Berger and Luckmann 1966; Fiske and Taylor 1991), and self-concept (Burke and Tully 1977; D. M. Taylor 2002; J. Turner 1985); (2) attribution by others, as exemplified by work by John Turner (1985); (3) identity as defined by the roles one plays, pioneered by Mead (1934) and further explored in political and other contexts (Brewer and Gardner 1996; Monroe, Hankin, and van Vechten 2000), and referred to as "identity theory" by some scholars (Stryker 1987); (4) one's identity as defined by one's position in a larger aggregate, variously referred to as collective identity (Ashmore, Deaux, and McLaughlin-Volpe 2004), group affiliation (Brubaker and Cooper 2000; J. Turner 1985), social identity (Abrams and Hogg 1990, 1999; Reykowski 1994; Tajfel and Turner 1986), and acculturation (Berry 1980; Chun, Organista, and Marin 2003; Padilla 1980). These four ways of viewing identity, derived from a review of the literature, are compatible with those presented by Abdelal et al. (2006).

message content and social movements – for example, as in work indicating that news coverage precedes, rather than follows, public opinion on critical topics (Hertog and Fan 1995; Willnat and Zhu 1996; also see Neuendorf 2002 for examples of the complexities to which content analysis may be applied).

The application of content analysis to political science arenas has been rather limited, although the methodology seems to be growing in popularity, particularly when used in concert with other, more qualitative methods.[4] For example, Yoshiko Herrera's (2005) book on contemporary Russian regionalism freely integrates original content analyses with more traditional historical, economic, and discourse analyses of the context in which regionalism has developed. In one of her two quantitative content analyses, she examined Sverdlovsk local newspaper articles whose content was relevant to the sovereignty movement for a Urals Republic, finding evidence that the movement was characterized in the press by "negative interpretations of economic conditions, and, in particular, concerns over constitutional inequality and economic autonomy" (Herrera 2005: 10). She also found key differences in whether the articles contained arguments favoring or opposing the Urals Republic, with local communicators more favorable than those in Moscow.

National identity was the subject of a content analysis by Laitin (1998), who examined the frequency of identity term use in Russian-language newspapers. Laitin compared articles from Kazakhstan, Estonia, Latvia, and Ukraine to get a sense of how identities had been formed within the post–Soviet Union republics. To do this, he developed a number of analysis categories specifically tailored to Russian populations (e.g., references to Russian-speakingness) that could be used to classify and discriminate along identity lines. Though it has a strong focus on Russian identity, Laitin's research suggests several possibilities for using content analysis to study national identity in general. Importantly, his content analysis is one part of a well-integrated track of study that includes survey and experimental work, as well as more qualitative ethnographic and discourse analyses.

In one of the best examples of content analysis by political scientists, Richard Merritt examined markers of common identity in colonial newspapers as part of his book *Symbols of American Community, 1735–1775* (1966). Building on the pioneering work of his adviser Karl Deutsch (1953), who used materials such as first-class letters and phone calls as indicators of emerging national identity in his

---

[4] Discourse analysis, a more qualitative and "inductive" method of analyzing messages (Hardy, Harley, and Phillips 2004), has enjoyed greater popularity in the political science literature. The pros and cons of discourse analysis and content analysis were explored in a special symposium in *Qualitative Methods: Newsletter of the American Political Science Association Organized Section on Qualitative Methods* in 2004 (see Hardy, Harley, and Phillips 2004; Hopf 2004; Lowe 2004a; Neuendorf 2004a).

seminal work on national identity, Merritt developed a richly complex and carefully delineated coding scheme for his newspaper analysis. In what he called "symbol analysis research," Merritt's focus was on place-name words that were not solely geographic, such as colony names (e.g., Virginia, Pennsylvania), British symbols (e.g., British Isles, Irish), and symbols of common identity (e.g., Americans, British Americans). He was able to chart the growing trend for newspapers to refer to Americans as a single group, and an increasing use of terms identifying the colonists as Americans rather than as members of a British political community (Merritt 1966: 180). Merritt, ahead of his time, executed a basic intercoder reliability assessment and explicated his entire coding scheme as an appendix (resulting in high replicability).

In a rare example of work that looks at individual identity measured via content analysis, Stone (1997) reports on proprietary research that identified four ways that individuals talk about a topic: goals and gratifications, rules and responsibilities, feelings and emotions, and unique outlook and ways of understanding. Typically applied to consumers' reactions to products and services, this typology of identity, Stone notes, could be applied in nonconsumer contexts, such as one's own national identity as an American.

And in a unique application of basic content analysis methods to nation-level analyses, George Barnett and Han Woo Park (2004) have collected and analyzed data on international hyperlinks. Barnett (2004: 2) suggests that, because of increased communicative contact via the Internet, differences among national cultures will diminish, resulting in the formation of a single "transnational identity." In earlier work, Barnett (2002) tracked international telephone calls over the period 1978 to 1999, concluding that during the latter part of the period, a trend toward decentralization was exhibited, with East Asian nodes becoming less integrated with North American and Western European nodes. These studies show how the sheer *volume* of communication might be studied to draw conclusions about the connectedness of different nations and therefore their unique or increasingly interdependent "identities."

CONTENT ANALYSIS OPTIONS

There are several ways in which content analysis methodologies appropriate to the task of identity research might be considered. First, there are basic choices for execution of a content analysis.

Human Preset Coding

The historically standard method of executing content analysis is via "human" coding, the application of a set of written rules for measurement to a set of messages by trained individuals. This a priori development of a coding scheme is the norm in classical content analysis – a researcher devises measures based on theory, past research, and, often, pilot work that includes immersion in the message pool under investigation. The coding scheme is made up of a code book (instructions to the trained coders) and a coding form (a form or questionnaire-type sheet or spreadsheet into which coders write or enter their assessments). It should be noted that such human coding is not limited to the analysis of text; images, emblems, and symbols may all serve as the messages one might analyze for the measurement of collective identity. With all human-coded projects, intercoder *reliability* is vital, and variables for which it is not achieved should be dropped from the analysis.[5] In content analysis, the emphasis is on the coding scheme as the critical instrument, rather than on the observer's or coder's expertise.

Computer (CATA) Preset Coding

In recent decades, there have been numerous advances in the development of automated "machine" coding of text messages – that is, computer-assisted text analysis (CATA). Usually, CATA coding involves the use of preset dictionaries, that is, lists of words and/or word combinations that are counted via a computer application. These dictionaries may be provided in the software or created by the researcher. In the case of programs such as the General Inquirer and Diction 5.0, numerous measures are already built into the program, some with mathematical algorithms that go beyond simple word counts. Other programs, such as VBPro and Yoshikoder, require that the researcher establish dictionaries. Some, such as Diction 5.0 and WordStat, allow for both built-in and researcher-devised dictionaries.[6]

Devising one's own dictionary is typically a long and painstaking process. First, words consistent with the conceptual definition of that construct must be

---

[5] Reliability criteria vary, but all content analysis methodology sources agree – for human coding, intercoder reliability should be measured by an appropriate statistic and reported for each measured variable separately (Krippendorff 2004; Lombard, Snyder-Duch, and Bracken 2002; Neuendorf 2002). Appropriate reliability coefficients include Cohen's kappa, Krippendorff's alpha, and Lin's concordance coefficient, but not simple percent agreement, which fails to remove the effect of chance agreement. Reliability assessment requires that a representative subset of the messages under study be coded independently by two or more trained coders.

[6] Nearly a score of other CATA packages are available. See Neuendorf 2002; Skalski 2002 and the corresponding Content Analysis Guidebook Online (http://academic.csuohio.edu/kneuendorf/content); Alexa and Zuell 2000; Popping 2000; Lowe 2004b or the Text Analysis Info Web site (http://www.textanalysis.info) for more options and comparisons. There are CATA programs that attempt higher-order functioning such as grammatical parsing; however, these are uniformly weak in their summative powers – that is, they tend to act more simply as aids to human perusal than as true content analysis engines. The bottom line is that none of the CATA programs have been specifically designed or adapted for the measurement of identity.

exhaustively identified. Then, variations on those root terms need to be added (e.g., if "pleasure" is a root word, then "pleasurable," "pleasure-seeking," "pleasured" and others might be added). Checks for inappropriate variations and for words too ambiguous to be validly included need to be made (e.g., "pleasant" may be deemed to be too far from the conceptual origins of the root word). Some CATA programs and related adjunct softwares include dictionary-building facilities. For example, WordStat is programmed to allow the addition to a base dictionary of antonyms, synonyms, similar terms, hypernyms, hyponyms, holonyms, and several other classes of words. And, WordStat and other programs allow for "wild card" specifications of root words (e.g., including "pleasur*" would capture all words beginning with "pleasur"). But, the researcher needs to be intimately involved in the decision to include or exclude each term; there is nothing automatic about dictionary construction.

Computer (CATA) Emergent Coding

This type of coding is less universally accepted among content analysts, because of its apparent deviation from the accepted positivist, a priori assumptions of the method. In "emergent coding," dimensions or patterns of text are derived from the data at hand (i.e., the texts under investigation), without any preset dictionaries.[7] Such programs as CATPAC, TextSmart, and TextAnalyst are well designed to allow a visual representation of the frequency of occurrence, co-occurrence, and/or correspondence of words and text segments through cluster analysis, multidimensional scaling, and neural networking. We present this non-traditional option for two reasons: advances in computer text content analysis have made some emergent techniques more objective and replicable; and, increasingly, we and others have found emergent techniques to be useful tools in the early stages of a content analysis project. That is, dimensions derived from emergent coding may be used in a second-stage, ordinary preset coding process.

THE SELECTION OF DATA RELEVANT TO THE MEASUREMENT OF
COLLECTIVE IDENTITY

The Pragmatics of Content Analysis

In all content analyses, one must decide what "data" will be collected – messages, to be sure. But, what types of messages? And is the goal to simply describe the messages, or make inferences to the sources of those messages?

---

[7] Note that we do not address the possible option of "emergent human coding" as we view this as simply pilot work, an essential part of the process of developing a preset coding scheme.

Early content analysis scholars (e.g., Berelson 1952) argued that content analysis was a gateway to inferences that would illuminate the intentions of speakers. Even some contemporary authors (e.g., Krippendorff 2004; R. Weber 1990) allow for ready inferences from message to source intentionalities or receiver impacts. But elsewhere (Neuendorf 2002) we argue against the inferential approach to the conduct of content analysis,[8] presenting instead what is called an "integrative model of content analysis," which calls for the collation of message-centric (i.e., content analysis) data with other available empirical information regarding source, receiver, channel, or other contextual state, whenever possible.

An alternative to trying to draw logical or statistical inferences from message characteristics is to focus on the messages themselves. This follows nicely from the seminal work of Watzlawick, Bavelas, and Jackson (1967), who introduced the framing of the "pragmatics of human communication," wherein the focus is on the behavioral effects of communication for both receiver and source. Following Gregory Bateson's (1958: 175–176) definition of social psychology as "the study of the reactions of individuals to the reactions of other individuals," Watzlawick, Bavelas, and Jackson (1967) focus on the message content rather than the traits and states of source or receiver. However, they extend their pragmatic approach to *all* aspects of message exchange, including nonverbals and paralinguistic cues of all types, making the complete study of communication rather challenging.

Here, we adopt an essentially pragmatic approach to content analysis with regard to collective identity. When conceptual definitions of identity include message attributes, then direct measurement via content analysis is appropriate. When conceptual definitions of identity are focused more on internal states (e.g., cognitive structure) or motivations, then content analysis might not be appropriate as a central measurement technique.

Individual versus Aggregate Messages

The messages to be analyzed via content analysis may be either at the individual or the aggregate level – that is, generated by an individual or forwarded by

---

[8] The only case in which a type of inference from message data alone becomes a viable option is when the linkages between message data and source or receiver data have become well established through replication via numerous research investigations over time. For example, the works of Gottschalk (1995) and certain thematic content analysis coding schemes (e.g., Veroff's power motivation scheme; 1992) have established well-worn paths between psychological traits and states and message characteristics indicative of their status. These researchers have validated their schemes with multiple datasets over time. Such validation between message characteristics and source attitudes, cognitions, and/or behaviors takes the form of construct validity (testing the measure's relationship to other constructs that theory would predict would relate) or criterion validity (testing the measure's relationship with a relevant behavior or action that is external to the measure) (Carmines and Zeller 1979).

an institution representing a collective entity.[9] The collection and analysis
of individual-level messages are somewhat straightforward. Original speech
or text may be collected either as it occurs naturally (e.g., transcripts of group
discussions; chat room postings; letters to the editor) or in response to prompts
(i.e., using content analysis as applied to essays or open-ended responses to a
questionnaire or interview protocol). When attempting to access aggregate
(e.g., nation-level) messages, the task provides many options. Cultural products
providing the grist for content analysis at the cultural or national level are
varied.[10] They might include[11] official codifications (e.g., constitutions, laws;
see, e.g., Stratigaki 2004), official news releases, news stories about a nation
(either internal or external, if one adopts an attributional perspective to identity; see, e.g., Chang 1998), official Web sites, or other cultural products such
as folk ballads, the visual arts, television programming, commercial film
releases, and architecture (Carley 1994; Chon, Barnett, and Choi 2004; Corn
1999; Custen 1992; Sirgy et al. 1998; A. D. Smith 1993). They might also

---

[9] It should be noted that comparisons are possible – for example, we may compare individual-
level messages about the self with those representing the collective in order to assess the "fit" of
the individual into the larger collective identity. This may match a conceptual definition of
collective identity that focuses particularly on the individual's position within a larger social
construction.

[10] National identity seems uniquely suited to measurement via content analysis of cultural
products. As noted by Ringrose and Lerner (1993: 1), "the concept of the nation is one of
the most powerful and ubiquitous organizing principles of modern times." National identity
(Hooson 1994) may be viewed as a particular application of identity, discrete from the
construct of nationalism (most commonly referring to political movements; see Goldmann,
Hannerz, and Westin 2000; Lazarus 1999; Oshiba, Rhodes, and Kitagawa Otsuru 2002). In
the social scientific literature, national identity has been mainly studied ad hoc, with anec-
dotal evidence for a particular nation at a particular point in history. Specific examples of
evidence include the use of language in border territories, French wine, Argentinean sports,
and Brazilian cinema. However, national identity also may be conceptualized in the range
of manners explored here for identity in general – as a psychological construct, as attributions, as role structures, and as collectivities. Clearly, identity is a multifaceted construct
and may be measured via a wide variety of variables. In the study of national identity,
numerous scholars have acknowledged a probable weakening of national identities in the
wake of cultural imperialism (Lazarus 1999), media imperialism (Nordenstreng and Schiller
1993), and Internet penetration (Chinn and Fairlie 2004). Others have examined specifically
the growth of world consumer culture (Costa and Bamossy 1995; Neuendorf, Blake, and
Valdiserri 2003), the transnational nature of ethnicity or cultural identity (Featherstone
1990; Goldmann, Hannerz, and Westin 2000; A. D. Smith 1990), the "globalization" of
political, economic, and social spheres (Yamada 2002), the growth of a "global identity"
(Crawford 2004), and the growing cultural hegemony of American mass media (Gitlin 1979;
Kellner 1990). Importantly, these trends might readily be tested via content analysis of
representative cultural products.

[11] Please note that none of these studies of cultural products have included explicit measures of
identity.

be official political communications such as party platforms (Budge and Hofferbert 1996), speeches and debates (Satterfield 1998), governmental annual reports (Andersson et al. 2003), national leaders' vision statements (Oliver 2004), and other political documents (Anheier, Neidhardt, and Vortkamp 1998; Beriker and Druckman 1996).[12] Other representations might include such quasi-official sources as history textbooks (Gordy and Pritchard 1995; Holt 1995).

Schwartz (1994) has taken on the challenge of measuring constructs (in his case, cultural values) at both the individual and aggregate levels, attempting an exhaustive coverage of essential cross-cultural values. He concludes that at the aggregate level, one must rely on cultural products, making this task ideal for the method of content analysis. Similarly, Inglehart and Baker (2000: 19) contest that from cross-cultural differences derive national cultures, which are then transmitted by educational and mass-media institutions. Anthony Smith (1993) sees the nation as an "imagined community," whose members will never know most of their fellow members, a construction made possible by the technologies of communication (e.g., the newspaper).

A MODEL OF CONTENT ANALYSIS OPTIONS FOR THE MEASUREMENT OF COLLECTIVE IDENTITY

If we consider both the type of execution of the content analysis and the type of "data" collected for the measurement of collective identity, we may develop a useful typology of options for such measurement. We note a three-type breakdown of the nature of the messages to which one might apply measures of collective identity:

1. Response-based messages (not naturally occurring; individuals generate messages in response to assigned identity-related tasks or prompts)
2. Naturally occurring messages that one might *assume* to constitute identity messages (e.g., individual-level messages such as personal ads or speeches, or aggregate-level cultural products such as films, news stories, or literature that might represent a culture or society)
3. Naturally occurring messages from which identity messages might be *extracted* (i.e., the messages are not wholly identity-related and must be inspected and partitioned, and then the identity messages may be

---

[12] It should be noted that nearly all extant content analyses of official national or political messages have examined European communications.

analyzed; this is a two-step process, involving inspection or extraction according to stated rules, followed by coding).

An intersection of the three types of execution and the three types of data produces the following typology (see Table 7.1). We hold that the intersection of emergent coding and "extracted" identity messages is logically inconsistent. Thus, there are eight possible options for content analysis coding of identity measures. In the sections that follow, we present a brief example of each – some are original small analyses, and others are examples of previously conducted research.

Option 1: Human Preset Coding, Response-Based Messages

A small, original exemplar dataset served as the raw material for several examples, including this one. The data were open-ended responses to prompts that asked respondents to describe themselves "as an American" and to describe the "typical American." Twenty individuals associated with the communication program at Cleveland State University (i.e., graduate and undergraduate students, staff) completed unrestricted written responses to these national identity prompts.

An example coding scheme for human-coding measurement was constructed. The "National Identity Pilot Coding Scheme" was devised to demonstrate key options for human coding and is shown in the Appendix. The scheme was applied to the responses to the "self as American" prompt by two coders. The analysis focused on each sentence in the verbal descriptions collected, counting the number of sentences that contained mention of each of the series of content dimensions. The measures were derived from several sources. Some of these measures were established from a simple review of the various ways in which collective identity has been conceptualized and measured in

TABLE 7.1. *A Model of Content Analysis Options for the Measurement of Collective Identity*

	Human Preset Coding	Computer (CATA) Preset Coding	Computer (CATA) Emergent Coding
Response-based messages	Option 1	Option 2	Option 3
"Assumed" identity messages (naturally occurring)	Option 4	Option 5	Option 6
"Extracted" identity messages (naturally occurring)	Option 7	Option 8	Not applicable

survey, experimental, and qualitative work – the "macro" variables of self-identification, role identification, and collective identification. Four measures were based directly on Stone's (1997) conceptualization of identity as manifested in four distinct ways: goals and gratifications, rules and responsibilities, feelings and emotions, and a unique outlook and way of understanding. Other measures were derived from elements of Ashmore, Deaux, and McLaughlin-Volpe's (2004) model for collective identity. Their model includes a compilation from several earlier theoretic treatments,[13] plus their own additions. Finally, from pilot work that examined the respondent essays with regard to both self as American and typical American, using simple visual inspection and a word-frequency analysis via CATPAC, several measures were added: physical characteristics, ascriptive social categories, rights, freedom, power, opportunity, patriotism, and worldview. Across the sets of measures, those for which a logical negative was possible had the added option of negation (e.g., "The typical American is *not* very religious"). These various measures represent common choices for coding scheme development – basing measures on existing conceptualizations and models, adapting measures from other contexts, and developing measures from a pilot inspection of the "raw" data.

As with every human coding scheme, revisions were made after coder training and trial coding. A "wide net" was cast with regard to attempted measures, with the anticipation that some measures would "fail" because of infrequency of occurrence or poor intercoder reliability. Typically, some measures were indeed found wanting – that is, in order to explore the viability of applying Abdelal et al.'s (2006) delineation of content versus contestation, the dimension of contestation was adapted for some measures.[14] This dimension was dropped when it was found that it was rarely invoked in the content under examination and when intercoder reliability was found to be unsatisfactory.[15]

---

[13] Ashmore, Deaux, and McLaughlin-Volpe (2004) combine elements from Tajfel and Turner's (1986) social identity theory, J. Turner et al.'s (1987) self-categorization theory, Stryker's (1987, 2000) identity theory, and Cross's (1991; as cited by Ashmore, Deaux, and McLaughlin-Volpe 2004) nigrescence model in a comprehensive model of social identity.

[14] The following language was included in the code book: "Additionally, when the number of sentences in (a) is greater than 0, then in (c) record whether there is contestation reported for the sentences referred to in (a). Contestation refers to language that contests, or debates, the particular target topic; this contestation may be first person (e.g., 'I'm not certain that this is typical for Americans . . .') or third person (e.g., 'Most people would not view the typical American as very isolationist, but I . . .')."

[15] Additionally, a fair number of other measures did not exhibit sufficient range in the small pilot dataset for meaningful, statistical reliability assessment (Neuendorf 2002). Thus, the coding scheme should be considered "under construction," presenting a range of possibilities for researchers but not a final coding scheme.

The human coding measures summarized in Table 7.2 show that the majority of the descriptive content (76.3 percent of sentences, on average) used a self-identification mode, with about 10 percent of sentences including reference to some type of social role. References to collective identification were less frequent, at 6.2 percent. With regard to Stone's (1997) template of identity, the most common framing for one's national identity seems to be via feelings and emotions, with an average of 21.7 percent of statements containing such a reference. This is followed by 13.9 percent of statements with reference to goals and gratifications, 5.6 percent containing reference to rules and responsibilities, and 4.7 percent having some reference to a unique outlook or ways of understanding. The measures derived from Ashmore et al. (2004) showed 20.9 percent of a respondent's statements to be positive in tone and 17.4 percent negative, with, on average, 6.9 percent of a respondent's sentences containing reference to behavioral involvement and 5.3 percent to ideology. Finally, with regard to "novel" measures devised particularly for this analysis, ascriptive social categories were the most prevalent mode of description, contained in 13.1 percent of a respondent's sentences. Other framings were less prevalent –

TABLE 7.2. *Option 1: Findings for Human Coding of "Self as American" Essays (average percent of sentences)*

Number of Sentences	Mean = 10.5 per Essay
Self-identification	76.3
Role identification	9.9
Collective identification	6.2
Goals and gratifications	13.9
Rules and responsibilities	5.6
Feelings and emotions	21.7 (2% negated)
Unique outlook or ways of understanding	4.7
Positive	20.9 (5% negated)
Negative	17.4 (3% negated)
Ideology	5.3 (13% negated)
Behavioral involvement	6.9
Physical characteristics	0.0
Ascriptive social categories	13.1
Rights	8.0 (8% negated)
Freedom	8.6
Power	0.9 (50% negated)
Opportunity	2.8
Patriotism	8.2 (46% negated)
Worldview	8.5 (26% negated)

8.6 percent of sentences contain reference to freedom, 8.5 percent to world-view, 8.2 percent to patriotism, 8.0 percent to rights, 2.8 percent to opportunity, and only 0.9 percent to power.

Some of the advantages and disadvantages of human coding are apparent. More nuanced measures are possible than with computer coding, including disambiguation and the recognition of negation.[16] However, human coding is labor-intensive and completely dependent on the ability of the researcher to create a coding scheme and training procedure that will result in reliable measures.

Option 2: Computer (CATA) Preset Coding of Response-Based Messages

For this example of CATA preset coding, the same national identity exemplar dataset was used. At present, no standard CATA dictionaries have been developed for the express purpose of measuring identity. Two computer applications with preset built-in dictionaries were selected as most relevant to the measurement of identity: the General Inquirer (used in this example) and Diction (to be used in example 5).

The venerable General Inquirer (Buvac and Stone 2001) includes more than 180 dictionaries and subdictionaries measuring a wide variety of attributes, with the goal of what is called "thematic content analysis" – the attempted measurement of psychological constructs via the analysis of messages. Composed principally of constructs from the Harvard IV-4 dictionary and the Lasswell value dictionary, it was developed in the 1960s as a human-coded scheme. A number of constructs measured by the General Inquirer might meet the needs of a researcher whose conceptual definition of national identity includes expressions of affective states (e.g., positive tone, negative tone, emotionality), role identifications (e.g., religion, political, work, family, academic), or expressions of attachment to larger social units (e.g., race).

The General Inquirer system demands that each message to be analyzed be contained in a separate text file. Thus, the sample dataset of twenty responses to the two prompts resulted in forty separate files, submitted "batch" to the PC version of the program. The dataset that was generated included both basic dictionary counts and percentage of words figures.

---

[16] A pilot analysis reported by Neuendorf (2004b) compared CATA measures with comparable human-coded versions for both Diction and the General Inquirer computer applications. Importantly, human coding found far more "political" references than did General Inquirer; human coding identified fewer than half as many references to "centrality" as did Diction, and 15 percent of the human-coded references were instances of negation, a central concern for the use of CATA.

Sample results for this analysis are presented in Table 7.3. Here we see a comparison between texts generated by male and female respondents for selected General Inquirer measures. Differences are not major, although we see a tendency for the male respondents to use criteria related to strength (i.e., the dictionaries for "strong" and "weak") when describing their own national identity more often than do females, and for males to use language referring to things "academic" less frequently than do females.

We see some of the typical advantages and disadvantages of preset CATA coding – a large amount of text is analyzed very quickly; however, CATA is insensitive to (i.e., cannot measure) nuances such as negation and colloquial speech, which can be tapped by trained human coders, and generally cannot disambiguate (e.g., note the difference among a "fine" for a traffic violation, "fine" linens, and feeling "fine"). Additionally, although the ready-made measures provided by the General Inquirer are attractive for their ease, the researcher's needs may not be met precisely by the particular dictionaries available.[17]

Option 3: Computer (CATA) Emergent Coding of Response-Based Messages

Once again, the exemplar open-ended text data were used for this sample analysis, focusing on descriptions of the "typical American." Several CATA programs allow for some type of emergent coding. CATPAC is a particularly intriguing option for discovering dimensions of discourse and concept differentiation as emergent from text. For our purposes, it might allow us to discover the most common terminology used by individuals to describe national identity, and to see the patterns of word co-occurrence that could reveal clusters of concepts and/or dimensions of concept differentiation. Here, the implicit conceptualization of identity is, quite simply, the manner in which one verbally identifies the "typical American."

---

[17] Ready-made dictionaries included with CATA programs should be scrutinized before being used, to assure their quality and appropriateness for a particular project. And some CATA dictionaries are simply not intended to be used for anything other than demonstration purposes, such as the "seeking" dictionary packaged with WordStat. This dictionary includes several dubious coding categories – a "sports" category, for example, includes only the terms aerobics, baseball, boxing, bowling, skating, skiing, soccer, sport, and swimming. In other words, it is missing key sports such as basketball, football, hockey, and many others. Clearly, this dictionary would miss important sports references in messages, making it virtually worthless for serious scientific inquiry. In fairness to the author of WordStat, an otherwise stellar program, this dictionary was created merely to demonstrate the features of the program. But other dictionaries may suffer from similar deficiencies, so users should exert caution before jumping on the premade dictionary bandwagon.

TABLE 7.3. *Option 2: Findings for CATA Preset Coding of "Self as American" Essays – Male-Female Comparisons for Selected General Inquirer Measures*

Dictionary	Males		Females		Total	
	Mean	Std. Dev.	Mean	Std. Dev.	Mean	Std. Dev.
Academics	0.66	0.78	1.39	1.69	1.07	1.38
Politics	7.72	2.68	7.67	3.33	7.69	2.97
Religion	0.12	0.23	0.06	0.20	0.09	0.21
Work	1.71	0.87	1.43	1.33	1.55	1.12
Collectivities	2.75	1.79	2.71	1.59	2.73	1.63
Strong	9.82	3.57	8.03	2.73	8.83	3.17
Weak	1.95	1.51	0.50	0.54	1.14	1.28
Emotional	0.52	1.69	0.96	0.53	0.77	0.70

Note: All means are average percentages of words fitting the General Inquirer dictionary. For example, on average, 9.82% of a male respondent essay's words fit the "strong" dictionary. On average, 8.03% of a female respondent essay's words were "strong."

The texts for "typical American" were submitted in a case-delimited fashion to the CATPAC program. A typical "negotiated" process of examining the most frequently occurring words and adding nonmeaningful words to the default "exclusion" list (i.e., those words not included in the analysis) in several passes through the program resulted in a twenty-five-word analysis.[18] Using a seven-word moving window, CATPAC assessed the co-occurrence of these words and provided a dendogram (cluster analysis output, not shown) and multidimensional space coordinates (where proximity in space indicates frequent co-occurrence).

Figures 7.1 and 7.2 show the latter, an example of the type of "emergent" coding possible with CATPAC. The output for the "typical American" text descriptions has been graphed via SPSS's Interactive Graph function. Figure 7.1 displays the typical three-dimensional output; Figure 7.2 presents the first two dimensions only and is given to assist in discriminating among closely placed concepts. We see a clear clustering of the practical considerations of money, time, things, goals, and better, which seems to indicate a coalescence of concepts related to practical and secular aspects of life. On the other side of the space, we find such concepts as religion, culture, good, trying, children, and work. This may indicate a divergence of discourse about the typical American, with practical-oriented concepts as quite separate from other modes of description. Thus, in the future, we may wish to add a measure or two to the human

---

[18] Forty-seven words were added to the exclusion list, including such words as seen, will, seem, however, down, along, and anything.

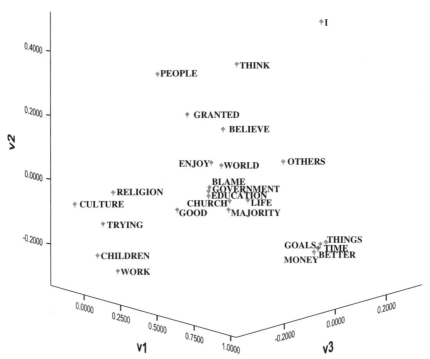

FIGURE 7.1. Option 3: Findings for CATA Emergent Coding of "Typical American" Essays – CATPAC Output in Three Dimensions

coding scheme, or develop appropriate dictionaries for CATA analyses, that look at monetary-based definitions of national identity.

To date, only qualitative comparisons among CATPAC solutions are possible. However, the current work of Hsieh (2004) is aimed at providing a quantitative method of convergence of two or more CATPAC solutions, allowing an empirical basis for pinpointing concepts that differ significantly from one solution to another. Thus, one might assess whether the constellation of discussion about the "self as American" differs from the constellation for the "typical American," for example.[19]

The advantages of emergent coding include the "fresh" look provided by the unrestricted analysis. However, it is not standard procedure to consider emergent coding results as the final outcome in a content analysis but rather as a guide to subsequent, more concerted a priori analyses.

---

[19] Such discrepancy-congruence analysis might serve as an appropriate measure for those forwarding a conceptual definition of national identity as the degree to which one "fits" with the standard or aggregate national profile.

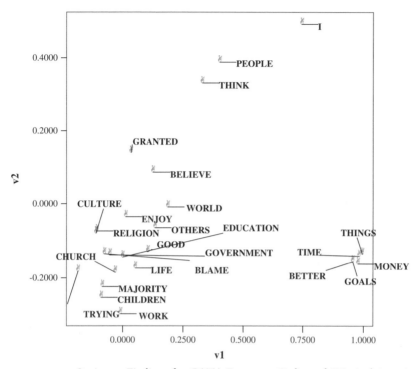

FIGURE 7.2. Option 3: Findings for CATA Emergent Coding of "Typical American" Essays – CATPAC Output in Two Dimensions

Option 4: Human Preset Coding of "Assumed" Identity Messages

The research of Jacques Hymans (2006) into the national identity conceptions (NICs) of world leaders provides a useful example of the application of human coding to "assumed" identity messages, in this case the speeches of selected prime ministers from four nations – France, Australia, Argentina, and India – over a sixty-year period. The work is concerned with leaders' nuclear policy decisions and how NICs might relate to them. Hymans (2006: 2) has conceptualized each leader's NIC as "how the leader understands the natural positioning of the nation with respect to its key comparison other(s) . . . along two basic dimensions . . . of 'solidarity' and 'status.'" He then *assumes* that their major public speeches contain representations of these dimensions.

Hymans first identified the frequently occurring "comparison others" (i.e., any human community not primarily based inside the speaker's national boundaries) for each prime minister.[20] Then, he coded these references in one

---

[20] Any "other" that was referenced twenty or more times was retained for further analysis.

particular way – whether the comparison other included the speaker's nation (inclusive references – e.g., the United Nations, Europe [for France only], the free world) or not (exclusive references – e.g., Germany, the Palestinians). From this simple content analysis measure, Hymans created two new indicators: (1) a measure of solidarity that was the ratio of the number of exclusive references to the number of inclusive references, ranging from 0 (entirely sportsmanlike) to 1 (entirely oppositional), and (2) a measure of status that was the ratio of paragraphs containing exclusive references only to the number of paragraphs containing exclusive references (with or without inclusive references in the same paragraph), ranging from 0 (entirely subaltern) to 1 (entirely nationalist).

Fruitfully, Hymans then used the prime ministers' ratings on these two dimensions to develop country-by-country typologies that categorized prime ministers as follows:

Sportsmanlike Nationalist	Oppositional Nationalist
Sportsmanlike Subaltern	Oppositional Subaltern

This typology, created from quantitative analyses, was then compared with qualitative, in-depth analyses of the political contexts in which the various prime ministers operated. This analysis is what Neuendorf (2002) would call a "second-order" integrative model of content analysis, combining source data and message data across selected time points.

Hymans (2006) provides an excellent example of how content analysis might be integrated into an overall investigation that also includes a strong qualitative component. This linking of qualitative and quantitative information is to be applauded; as Budge and Hofferbert (1996: 83) point out, "the information we can get is often richest and most revealing when we can put both together." In Hymans's case, the quantitative and qualitative analyses prove to be mutually supportive, each aiding in the interpretation of the other.

Option 5: Computer (CATA) Preset Coding of "Assumed" Identity Messages

Rod Hart's development of the Diction 5.0 program followed a process similar to that of the General Inquirer. As a political communication scholar, he became interested in the objective and reliable tracking of political speech – in the form of debates, speeches, and the like. He first devised a coding scheme for human coders, then later the computer program, measuring forty variables with standardized dictionaries. Over the years, he has expanded the constructs measured by Diction and has added a variety of "comparative" indicators for other types of communication (thirty-six types, in fact, including such normed categories as campaign speeches, emails and telephone conversations, student essays, poetry, and newspaper editorials). However, the system's forte remains political speech.

For this example, Diction was used to analyze the first State of the Union Address by each of nine recent U.S. presidents, from Dwight D. Eisenhower to William J. Clinton, along with the second State of the Union Address by George W. Bush, which took place shortly after the 9/11 terrorist attacks. These texts were considered examples of assumed, naturally occurring identity messages because of the strong emphasis State of the Union Addresses typically place on establishing a national identity. The second George W. Bush speech was chosen to compare past presidential addresses and other political policy speeches to the first State of the Union Address in the current "Age of Terror." The addresses were obtained online from Kenneth Janda's PoliTxt Digital Archive (http://janda.org/politxts/index.html), which includes a complete collection of State of the Union texts. Once the addresses were obtained, analyzing them in Diction was fast and easy, with the program's included dictionaries providing an instant array of results.

Some of the preset Diction dictionaries purport to measure the constructs of accomplishment, communication, (group) centrality, cooperation, and (social) exclusion, all of which relate to conceptualizations of national identity that include interaction, role behaviors, and a collective orientation. In our case, we see in Tables 7.4 and 7.5 results from the analysis of George W. Bush's 2002 State of the Union Address compared to other political public policy speeches. Table 7.4 illustrates the standard dictionary measures and analyses in Diction, while Table 7.5 shows those for the master variables. As Table 7.4 shows, Bush's address was above the normal range on the constructs of satisfaction, inspiration, and cooperation, indicating greater emphasis on these than in typical political speeches, which makes sense following 9/11. The cooperation score is particularly interesting from an identity standpoint and could be indicative of a desire to shift U.S. national identity toward greater internal and external cooperation in an effort to more effectively fight terrorism.

The Diction 5.0 CATA program provides five "master variable" indexes that sum multiple dictionaries. The numerical values of these master variables are meaningful only in comparison to the Diction-provided "normal ranges" for various text sets that have been previously analyzed by Hart (2000). Table 7.5 shows the scores for this speech on the five master variables. Only one master variable, optimism, is out of range. This score of 57.22 indicates greater emphasis on optimism than in most political speeches, which again makes sense given the post 9/11 desire to reassure the American people.

TABLE 7.4. *Option 5: Sample CATA Preset Coding via Diction of George W. Bush's 2002 State of the Union Address – Standard Dictionary Totals*

Variable	Frequency	Percentage of Words Analyzed	Normal Range		Standard Score
			Low	High	
Numerical terms	6.42	1.28	0.3	15.04	−0.17
Ambivalence	7.57	1.51	6.49	19.21	−0.83
Self-reference	7.8	1.56	0	15.1	0.1
Tenacity	23.69	4.74	23.32	39.76	−0.95
Leveling terms	7.69	1.54	5.02	12.76	−0.31
Collectives	13.57	2.71	4.04	14.46	0.83
Praise	8.99	1.8	2.77	9.59	0.83
Satisfaction	16.67	3.33	0.47	6.09	4.77
Inspiration	12.01	2.4	1.56	11.1	1.19
Blame	1.59	0.32	0.06	4.16	−0.25
Hardship	9	1.8	1.26	10.48	0.68
Aggression	8.59	1.72	1.07	9.79	0.73
Accomplishment	18.04	3.61	4.96	23.78	0.39
Communication	5.79	1.16	2.21	11.79	−0.25
Cognition	7.01	1.4	4.43	14.27	−0.48
Passivity	6.78	1.36	2.1	8.08	0.56
Spatial terms	14.49	2.9	4.17	19.85	0.32
Familiarity	111.34	22.27	117.87	147.19	−1.45
Temporal terms	18.45	3.69	8.36	21.82	0.5
Present concern	9.33	1.87	7.02	16.6	−0.52
Human interest	31.3	6.26	18.13	45.49	−0.04
Concreteness	27.52	5.5	10.7	28.5	0.89
Past concern	1.8	0.36	0.97	6.19	−0.68
Centrality	3.17	0.63	1.19	7.54	−0.37
Rapport	2.84	0.57	0.42	4.26	0.26
Cooperation	8.73	1.75	0.36	8.44	1.07
Diversity	1.69	0.34	0.07	3.81	−0.14
Exclusion	0.72	0.14	0	4.31	−0.65
Liberation	3.62	0.72	0	4.72	0.57
Denial	3.09	0.62	2.57	10.35	−0.87
Motion	2.27	0.45	0.17	4.35	0

The State of the Union Addresses were also scanned for interesting overall trends. Diction can analyze multiple texts at once and allows for quick interactive switching of results from one text to another. This exploratory technique revealed an interesting and perhaps counterintuitive difference in the use of "collectives" in State of the Union Addresses by Republican and Democratic presidents. Republican presidents (Nixon, Ford, Reagan, Bush I, and Bush II) all used collective language above the normal range, while Democrat presidents

TABLE 7.5. *Option 5: Sample CATA Preset Coding via Diction of George W. Bush's 2002 State of the Union Address – Master Variables*

Master Variable	Score	Normal Range		Out of Range
		Low	High	
Activity	50.1	46.74	55.48	
Optimism	57.22	46.37	52.25	*
Certainty	49.96	46.9	51.96	
Realism	49.75	46.1	52.62	
Commonality	51.18	46.86	52.28	

(Kennedy, Johnson, Carter, and Clinton) all used collectives within the normal range. It should be noted that these analyses were done using the default Diction setting of analyzing only the first 500 words of a text. The program can also be set to analyze longer texts by averaging 500 word "chunks," which is what was done for the analysis of George W. Bush's address reported here. Finally, it should be noted that the data from multiple text Diction analyses, such as a collection of State of the Union speeches, could be imported into statistical programs such as SPSS for further analysis.

The preset coding technique offered by programs such as Diction can be very useful to identity scholars when the program's coded constructs tap relevant identity constructs. Though there are some limitations to preset coding, as mentioned elsewhere in this chapter, this CATA technique benefits from its ability to quickly and reliably elucidate interesting features of texts.

Option 6: Computer (CATA) Emergent Coding of "Assumed" Identity Messages

Some scholars have assumed that news media descriptions of issues constitute important "images" or "identities" of these issues (e.g., Chang 1998); this conceptualization of "collective identity" is one of simple attribution by widely available institutional information sources. For this example, we developed a small original analysis of recent U.S. newspaper coverage of the Northern Ireland political party Sinn Fein, using TextAnalyst software. Recent events have brought renewed attention to Sinn Fein, and the changing color of the discourse about the political entity makes it uniquely suited for emergent content analysis.

For the collection of news stories, we used the LexisNexis database, perhaps the largest single information database in the world. The search was of major U.S. newspapers as defined by LexisNexis (of which there are fifty-three), for all articles with the term "Sinn Fein" in the headline, appearing between January 1

and March 15, 2005. A total of twenty-five articles met the search criteria, and
the body of these articles served as the raw material for an exploratory analysis
via TextAnalyst. The articles had to be individually stripped of extraneous
information (e.g., dateline, name of publication) and saved as an aggregated
text file for ready presentation to the CATA application.

TextAnalyst is designed primarily for managing texts, rather than true content analysis, but its neural networking application can provide an interactive
look at how news articles discuss or "identify" our targeted topic, Sinn Fein.
While not divulging the algorithms used to do so, the program documentation
claims that TextAnalyst determines "what concepts – word and word combinations – are most important in the context of the investigated text" (Froelich
2000: 2).

Figure 7.3 provides a screen shot of TextAnalyst results for the Sinn Fein
articles. The tree-branching structure we see at the left indicates the strength of

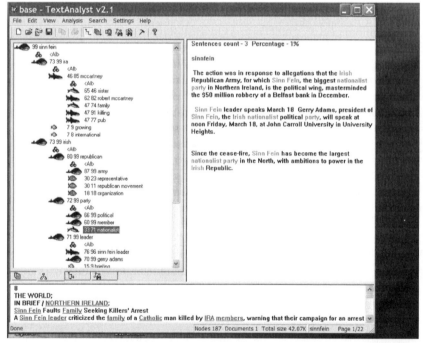

FIGURE 7.3. Option 6: Findings for CATA Emergent Coding of News Stories about
Sinn Fein, TextAnalyst Output. *Note:* The TextAnalyst output is presented in three
windows: (1) the View Pane (*at left*) provides the branching "topic structure" that is the
main focus of our example; (2) the Results Pane (*at right*) displays all sentences in which
the selected concept (here, "nationalist," as selected and highlighted in the View Pane)
occurs; and (3) the Text Pane (*at bottom*) provides the original text in full length.

co-occurrence of terms. The program has identified "Sinn Fein" as the most central substantive term in the collection of texts – it appears at the top of the outline. It is linked most strongly with the terms "IRA" and "Irish." Each of these terms is shown to be linked with other terms – for example, "IRA" is most strongly linked with "McCartney," and "McCartney" with "sister," "Robert McCartney," "family," "killing," and "pub."[21] The numbers indicate relative "semantic weights" for each concept, ranging from 0 to 100.[22] The first number reflects the strength of the semantic relationship of the concept to the parent concept above (e.g., "McCartney" is related to "IRA" with a strength of 46); the second, the semantic weight of the concept in the entire text (e.g., "McCartney" is related to the text as a whole with a strength of 85). While the numbers do not have an objective meaning beyond their 0–100 range, a number of researchers have developed cutoff values after inspection of their semantic network solutions. For example, Bourret et al. (2006) used a criterion for co-occurrence semantic weights of 50 or 75, depending on the number of nodes in the analysis. Also, J. Adams and Roscigno (2005) have established a cutoff score of 30 in their study of identity, interpretational framing of cause and effect, and political efficacy in the text of white supremacist Web sites.

TextAnalyst has a very interactive interface, and it is difficult to do it justice in this static presentation. For example, if we were able to click on "killing," more terms linked to that word would appear.

This "snapshot" of contemporary communication about Sinn Fein in major U.S. newspapers can provide us with ways of thinking about how the discourse is being shaped in the popular media. Although not truly a content analysis in the traditional sense, it may help us devise a suitable coding scheme or begin to construct an appropriate set of dictionaries.

Option 7: Human Preset Coding of "Extracted" Identity Messages

A study by Eilders and Luter (2000) examined the ways in which media assessed Germany's first participation in military action since World War II – the Kosovo war of 1999. They studied editorials in the top five German newspapers over a three-month period, utilizing a qualitative framing identification

---

[21] This section of the semantic analysis is clearly referencing a cluster of news coverage of the January 2005 murder of activist Robert McCartney outside a Belfast pub, purportedly by members of the IRA.

[22] These figures may be interpreted as indicators of the probability that the concept is important in the studied text and are determined by the concept's frequency of occurrence, and by its co-occurrence with other concepts. The TextAnalyst Web site indicates that the program, using internal (proprietary) algorithms, determines the semantic weights via a neural networking procedure (www.megaputer.com/textanalyst.php).

process (Goffman 1974) to locate frames within editorials, finding 364 distinct frames in 190 editorials. A total of 25.8 percent of these framings were deemed to constitute "identity frames" (another 29.1 percent were decided to be "diagnostic framing" and 45.1 percent to be "prognostic framing"). Their conceptualization of an "identity frame" was communication that addresses the national self-image, particularly in this case of German involvement in the Kosovo war; they looked for a motivational framing that provides an answer to "Why should *we* become involved?" Their assumption was that war approval was likely to be based on a "convincing construction of collective identity" (Eilders and Luter 2000: 417). This process is one example of what we might call the "extraction" of identity messages from a larger pool of messages – that is, many messages were screened, and only a subset was deemed to be identity-related and was retained for further analyses regarding identity. Eilders and Luter (2000) then content-analyzed the 94 identity framings as to type, finding 30 percent to fit a category of "Germany in a moral dilemma," 16 percent as "Germany as a loyal NATO member," 15 percent "Germany as part of Europe," 10 percent "Nazi experience calls for defence of human rights," and 29 percent "other." Although the piece did not report reliability figures for the extraction process or the coding of type, the research presents a clear option in the straightforward content analysis of public communications that may contain relevant "identity" messages.

Option 8: Computer (CATA) Preset Coding of "Extracted" Identity Messages

A CATA program that combines elements of preset coding and emergent coding is WordStat, a companion to the statistical package SimStat (www.simstat.com). WordStat allows for the ready creation of researcher-established dictionaries, with some basic example dictionaries provided[23] and synonyms suggested via the program's dictionary builder. And finally, WordStat provides cluster analysis and multidimensional scaling options for the dictionary results. Thus, although the dictionaries are preset by the researcher, their configuration and dimensions of discrimination emerge from the analysis.

For this example, the Schwartz (1992, 1994) cultural values dimensions were used as the basis for the development of a WordStat set of dictionaries that could be applied to autobiographical texts from Project Gutenberg Online.

---

[23] WordStat's example dictionaries are Appearance, Arts, Communication, Education, Family, Finance, Humor, Nightlife, Outdoor, Sexuality, Spirituality, Sports, and Work. They were designed for research on personal ads. Each includes only a small number of words, ostensibly as "seeds" for further development via the dictionary builder by the researcher.

These autobiographies were specially selected for this section from the vast Project Gutenberg collection based on a scan of each for their relevance to the study of identity, making this an example of "extracted" identity messages. The texts selected were considered to contain insight into the identity of each subject, in part by revealing their cultural values as an important component in their cultural identity. In sum, six complete autobiographical texts were selected for this section, three by famous Caucasian Americans (Benjamin Franklin, Theodore Roosevelt, and "Buffalo Bill" Cody) and three by famous African Americans (Booker T. Washington, Sojourner Truth, and Frederick Douglass). Texts were chosen in this manner so that Caucasian American and African American identities could be compared.

The dictionary development began by taking the ten key Schwartz cultural values and their subdimensions and coming up with synonyms that seemed to appropriately tap each value dimension of interest. To validate these choices, the dictionaries were checked and further refined using the WordStat Dictionary Builder (discussed earlier). Once the nine dictionaries were settled on,[24] the texts were analyzed in WordStat separately for Caucasian and African Americans.

WordStat output includes a full array of analyses of interest to the content analyst, including basic word counts, cross tabulations ("crosstabs") of dictionary categories with other variables of interest (e.g., gender, race), key-words-in-context (KWIC), and the more advanced analyses mentioned at the start of this section.

Table 7.6 shows an example of a crosstab analysis from the Schwartz values–biography text analysis, with each row representing a cultural value and the columns comparing the Caucasian biography texts with those by African

---

[24] Dictionaries routinely include dozens, possibly hundreds, of search terms, depending on the construct being measured. In our case, we tried to stay close to Schwartz's original measures, limiting the number of terms. For example, Schwartz's dimension of "STIMULATION" includes three questionnaire items to which respondents are instructed to respond using an eight-point scale of how important the cultural value is to them: "An Exciting Life (stimulating experiences)," "A Varied Life (filled with challenge, novelty, and change)," and "Daring (seeking adventure, risk)." Our measure includes the root terms and synonyms, many of which are included as wild cards (e.g., "excit*"), expanding the number significantly (i.e., 12 terms, 9 of which are wild cards). The other Schwartz dimensions resulted in dictionaries of the following sizes:

STIMULATION: 17 terms, 12 of which are wild cards
HEDONISM: 12 terms, 6 of which are wild cards
ACHIEVEMENT: 14 terms, 10 of which are wild cards
POWER: 16 terms, 7 of which are wild cards
SECURITY: 10 terms, 6 of which are wild cards
CONFORMITY: 13 terms, 11 of which are wild cards
SPIRITUALITY: 10 terms, 7 of which are wild cards
BENEVOLENCE: 13 terms, 11 of which are wild cards
UNIVERSALISM: 14 terms, 11 of which are wild cards

TABLE 7.6. *Option 8: Findings for CATA Preset Coding of Autobiographical Texts Using Researcher-Created Dictionaries of Schwartz's Cultural Values, Applied with WordStat*

	Caucasian Americans	African Americans	Chi-Square	p (2-tailed)
Achievement	8.60%	8.10%	2.63	0.27
Benevolence	24.10%	19.40%	0.72	0.70
Conformity	1.40%	2.00%	8.80	0.01
Hedonism	5.60%	6.90%	16.89	< 0.01
Power	9.40%	12.70%	45.12	< 0.01
Security	11.20%	9.90%	1.17	0.56
Self-direction	8.80%	11.90%	42.30	< 0.01
Spirituality	4.30%	14.90%	315.90	< 0.01
Stimulation	6.20%	3.90%	5.39	0.07
Universalism	20.50%	10.20%	50.63	< 0.01
TOTAL	100.00%	100.00%		

Note: A total of 517,974 words were processed in these analyses, 6,923 of which were dictionary terms. Broken down by race, the Caucasian American texts, which had 364,771 total words, contained 4,598 terms identified as fitting one of the Schwartz dictionaries, and the African American texts, which had 153,203 total words, contained 2,325 dictionary terms.

Americans. The percentages represent the percent of total value mentions in each category (Caucasian or African American) accounted for by each individual value. So, for example, in the African American–generated texts, 19.4 percent of value word occurrences tapped the "benevolence" dimension. This type of analysis can reveal how often different values or other identity terms appear in relation to one another, and how frequently they appear in one set of messages compared to another set.

As an example of the latter, consider the "spirituality" row of Table 7.6. This suggests that the African American authors studied here were more likely to have spirituality as an expressed cultural value, relative to other values, than the Caucasian Americans were, with a percentage difference of 14.9 percent versus 4.3 percent. WordStat also allows statistical testing of differences and the results for this comparison (as assessed though a chi-square test) are indeed significant. Other significant differences shown in Table 7.6 include greater reference to conformity, hedonism, power, and self-direction in the African American–generated texts, and more references to stimulation and universalism in the Caucasian-generated texts. WordStat also presents such findings in graphical form (see Figure 7.4).

As discussed throughout this chapter, the overall merit of these types of analyses to identity researchers stems from an assumption that the developed dictionary terms tap into identity conceptualizations of interest. In the present

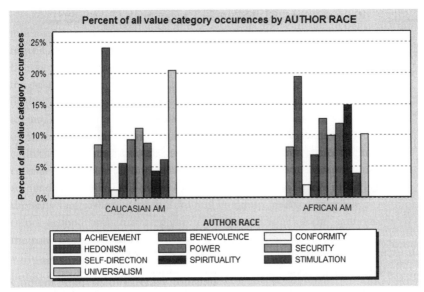

FIGURE 7.4. Option 8: Findings for CATA Preset Coding of Autobiographical Texts Using Researcher-Created Dictionaries of Schwartz's Cultural Values, Applied with WordStat

example, one might view the Schwartz dictionary categories as indicators of different types of collective (cultural) identity, and the biography texts as messages containing information about collective identity.

DEVELOPING CONTENT ANALYSIS MEASURES FROM EXISTING SURVEY OR OTHER MEASURES OF COLLECTIVE IDENTITY

Our examples thus far have focused on national and cultural identities, as most relevant to political discourse. However, other collective identities might certainly be assessed via content analysis. No standard coding schemes have been devised to date. One tack that can prove fruitful is to adapt standard measures of collective identity for content analysis purposes, as shown earlier in option 8 (using an adaptation of Schwartz's survey instrument for cultural values) and as exemplified by many of the General Inquirer indexes.

Other existing models and measures of identity might serve as the base for content analysis measures. For example:

1. Stephan and Stephan's (2000) roster of self-identification measures for racial and ethnic identity could serve as the basis for dimensions of content analysis indicators.

2. In Chapter 2 of this volume, Brady and Kaplan provide a wealth of conceptualizations *and* possible measures for ethnic identity.

3. Phinney's 14-item MEIM (Multigroup Ethnic Identity Measure) has three dimensions that might be informative – ethnic identity achievement, affirmation and belonging, and ethnic behaviors (Richard M. Lee and Yoo 2004) – as well as individual survey items that might be adaptable to content analysis applications (e.g., "pride in ethnic groups," "participation in cultural practices").

4. In addition to the work on cultural values by Schwartz (1992, 1994), the substantial body of work on cultural and national values by Triandis (1994), Inglehart and Baker (2000), and Kabanoff and Nesbit (1997) would be useful starting points (see also the World Values Survey 2004).

5. Hoffman's (2001) summary of the history of the measurement of masculinity and femininity gives us many ideas as to how gender identity might be measured, from the early Bem Sex-Role Inventory to the recently developed Hoffman Gender Scale; we might also examine the Worthington et al. (2002) model of heterosexual identity development at the individual and social levels.

6. Puddifoot's (1995) dimensions of community identity are concrete enough to provide easy guidance for the construction of content analysis measures – for example, residents' perceptions of community boundaries; evaluations of quality of community life including friendliness, sense of mutuality, and cooperativeness; and evaluations of community functioning including leisure services, health services, and material quality of life.

7. Postmes's (2003) approach to measuring social identity in organizations provides many clues to original measures, including nonverbal indicators such as clothing and the public expression of group goals.

8. Marcia's (1993) handbook for the study of ego identity provides a raft of open-ended interview measures related to understanding of self and various social roles one plays.

9. In Chapter 12 of this volume, McDermott reviews the conceptualization and measurement of identity from a psychological perspective.

LIMITATIONS AND POTENTIALITIES OF CONTENT ANALYSIS AS A TOOL TO MEASURE IDENTITY

Content analysis is dependent on a clear conceptualization of the construct(s) under examination. The examples presented here cover a wide range of implicit conceptual definitions – from national identity as a collection of ascriptive characteristics (e.g., social categories) to expressed emotional or affective orientations (e.g., patriotism, ethics, worldview) to general life outlooks (e.g., goals and gratifications, opportunity) to structural states (e.g., rights, freedoms). The utilization of content analysis for measuring identity makes the assumption that we take a pragmatic approach to the study of communication and identity – that is, that we are willing to conceptualize identity as something that is constituted from communication behavior.

For the sample results presented for options 1–3, it must be recalled that the dataset – that is, the set of verbal identity descriptions – is small and from a nonprobability sample. Therefore, firm conclusions should not be reached from the findings. Rather, the results are presented as options for the types of analyses that might be done with content analysis. There may be additional debate concerning the assumption or conceptualization that "identity" may be reflected in responses to prompts. However, open-ended interviewing and surveying are commonly used to tap ethnic identity, cultural identity, and acculturation (Arends-Tóth and van de Vijver 2004; Berry 1980; Chun, Organista, and Marin 2003; Stephan and Stephan 2000).

Other novel analyses presented as examples here are also limited in their generalizability and statistical power. However, we believe that these examples present a full range of options for the identity researcher, and we have placed them in a model that encourages comparisons among options for content analysis execution (i.e., CATA vs. human coding, preset vs. emergent coding) and for types of communications to analyze (i.e., responses to prompts, naturally occurring communication).

CATA procedures offer easy reliability and standardization. However, CATA techniques are what we might call "knee-jerk"– they blindly count dictionaried words, regardless of context, negation, or, in general, ambiguation.[25] Most important, a program-provided dictionary may not match a definition of the construct it purports to measure. The development of identity-focused dictionaries is certainly possible but will require a long and careful process.

When compared with CATA, human coding is amenable to much more in-depth, nuanced measures, and is more flexible. With human coding, our measures will be sensitive to various grammatical operations (e.g., negation, as in "I do not feel an affinity for flag-waving Americans"). And we may attempt measures of content and contestation. But it is held to the high

---

[25] Diction 5.0 does attempt disambiguation, assigning fractional words to dictionaries on the basis of common usage. For example, the word "well" might be divided among positive mentions (e.g., "I don't feel well"), physical objects (e.g., "He drew water from the well"), and non-fluencies (e.g., "Well . . ."), among other usages.

standard of intercoder reliability. If we fail to develop a coding scheme and a training procedure that can be reliably applied by nonexpert coders, all is for naught. The human-coded examples presented here do not emphasize inter-coder reliability to the extent that we would like because of the pilot nature of some examples and the limited reporting by other researchers for other exam-ples. Any full reportage of a human-coded content analysis must include variable-by-variable reporting of appropriate reliability coefficients (see note 5).

Abdelal et al. (2006) introduce the notion of identity as content and contest-ation. The various human and CATA coding examples in this chapter present a wide array of content types, and the frequency of occurrence of each type has been assessed in various ways.

Contestation proved to be problematic as a dimension for human coding in option 1, occurring very rarely and thus revealing that the sample respondents tended not to *discuss* identity in terms of its contested nature. However, con-testation may perhaps be more directly assessed by the *variances* of the mea-sures. For example, the General Inquirer measure "strong" showed moderate variance across respondent essays for the description of the typical American (with a standard deviation/mean ratio of .51). But, the General Inquirer mea-sure "economic" showed greater variance across respondents (with a ratio of 1.14). We might interpret this difference to indicate greater contestation with regard to whether the typical American is defined in economic terms rather than whether the typical American is defined by strength.

The procedures outlined here have focused on the analysis of verbal (i.e., word-based) communication. It should be remembered that content analysis may also include an analysis of nonverbal and pictorial variables. Indeed, Watzlawick, Bavelas, and Jackson's (1967) pragmatic approach to communi-cation would demand such inclusion. Once again, the conceptualization of the construct of collective identity must set the stage. If one were to subscribe to a conceptual definition of identity as including nonverbal behaviors such as (lit-erally) flag waving or choice of clothing (Oshiba 2002), then measures of such behaviors would be quite properly executed via content analysis.

The example procedures presented here are intended to initiate a dialog among researchers about the viability of using standard and novel content analysis techniques for the measurement of collective identity. The conceptual definition is the vital origin for every content analysis, and the arena of collec-tive identity seems marked by significant definitional contestation that must be further explored if standardized measurement techniques are to be developed for the study of collective identity via content analysis. Abdelal et al. (2006) have begun the process of definitional clarification. In the meantime, the palette of options provided by human and computer content analysis procedures offers much to the identity researcher.

APPENDIX: NATIONAL IDENTITY PILOT CODING SCHEME FOR HUMAN CODING

National Identity Pilot Coding Scheme

Codebook (Coding Instructions)

Unit of data collection: Each essay/open response will serve as the unit of data collection. For each essay/response, fill out one coding form.

I. General Information

1. Coder#: Record the coder ID #
    1 K.N.
    2 R.O.
2. Essay #: Record the essay # found above each essay, which refers to the *referent* for that essay, as follows:
    1 Self as American
    2 Typical American
3. ID#: Record the respondent ID # found at the top of the essay set
4. Number of sentences: Count and record the number of sentences contained in the essay, as delimited by standard punctuation (i.e., period, question mark), and whether or not the sentence is grammatically complete.

II. Macro Variables

For variables 5–7, record the number of sentences that contain at least some reference to each of the following.

5. Self-identification: This type of statement provides some identifying information about the referent (see #2 above), phrased in the first person (e.g., "I am a religious person," "I believe that America is headed in the wrong direction").
6. Role identification: This type of statement provides some identifying information about the referent relevant to social roles that the referent performs (e.g., "America is the protector of Third World countries," "I'm close to my two sisters").

7. Collective identification: This type of statement provides some identifying information about the referent relevant to an in-group, or outgroup, status (e.g., "I'm typical of most Americans in that I enjoy sports," "Americans are much ruder than other nationalities").

NOTE: Items 5–7 are *not* mutually exclusive; that is, a sentence may be counted as more than one type.

III. Constructs from Stone (1997)

For variables 8–11, (a) record the number of sentences that contain at least some reference to each of the following. Then, (b) record the number of those sentences that contain an explicit verbal negation for the target topic after the "N" (e.g., "I do not feel a responsibility . . .").
NOTE: For each measure, the number for (b) is a subset of the number recorded for (a).

8. Goals and gratifications – references to hopes, intentions, objectives or motives for acting, and/or recompense, reward, or type of satisfaction sought by the actor
9. Rules and responsibilities – references to rules, guidelines, laws, norms of behavior, and/or the acknowledgment of responsibility, answerability, duty, or obligation toward other individuals or toward a collective
10. Feelings and emotions – references to internal and subjective affective states (e.g., anger, joy, sorrow, pity, passion, love, grief, etc.)
11. Unique outlook/ways of understanding – references to any cognitive activities (beliefs, knowledge, etc.) and/or perspectives that are unique, one-of-a-kind, and/or distinctive

IV. Additional Constructs from Ashmore, Deaux, and McLaughlin (2004)

NOTE: Other Ashmore et al. aspects are covered by dimensions above (e.g., Self Identification, Collective Identification). Once again, the same coding procedure as for 8–11 is to be used.

12. Positive evaluation – contains reference to a positive outlook or favorable judgment
13. Negative evaluation – contains reference to a negative outlook or unfavorable judgment

14. Ideology – contains reference to beliefs about a group's experience, history, and position in society
15. Behavioral involvement – contains reference to *actions* that directly implicate the collective identity category in question

V. Additional Constructs Derived from the Data

Again, the same coding procedure should be used; variables 16–17 are exceptional, not allowing for a negation tally.

16. Physical characteristics – contains reference to observable human physical characteristics, including hair color and type, and skin tone (but NOT race/ethnicity)
17. Ascriptive social categories – contains reference to such demographic and social categories information as race, ethnicity, and gender.
18. Rights – contains reference to rights of the individual or group
19. Freedom – contains reference to freedoms of the individual or group
20. Power – contains reference to power status or relationship of the individual or group
21. Opportunity – contains reference to positive opportunities available to the individual or group
22. Patriotism – contains reference to an aspect of pride in country as expressed at the individual or group level
23. Worldview – contains reference to a recognition of or comparison to groups/nations/individuals outside of the referent nation (i.e., America)

National Identity Pilot Coding Scheme
Coding Form

1. Coder#:_____
2. Essay#: _____
3. ID#:_____
4. Number of sentences: _____

Macro variables: Number of sentences that include:

5. Self-identification _____
6. Role identification _____

    7. Collective identification _____

Stone (1997):

      8. Goals and gratifications _____ (N_____)
      9. Rules and responsibilities _____ (N_____)
     10. Feelings and emotions _____ (N_____)
     11. Unique outlook/ways of understanding _____ (N_____)

Ashmore et al. (2004):

     12. Positive _____ (N_____)
     13. Negative _____ (N_____)
     14. Ideology _____ (N_____)
     15. Behavioral involvement _____ (N_____)

From the data:

     16. Physical characteristics _____
     17. Ascriptive social categories _____
     18. Rights _____ (N_____)
     19. Freedom _____ (N_____)
     20. Power _____ (N_____)
     21. Opportunity _____ (N_____)
     22. Patriotism _____ (N_____)
     23. Worldview _____ (N_____)

8

The Content and Intersection of Identity in Iraq

Robalyn Stone and Michael Young

INTRODUCTION

We apply our cognitive mapping methodology to the question of identity using the analytical framework of Abdelal et al. (Chapter 1 in this volume) as our starting point. In their contribution, Abdelal et al. begin by establishing their view of a collective identity as a social category that varies along two dimensions, content and contestation. They further suggest that the content of a collective identity can be of four types: constitutive norms, social purposes, relational comparisons with other social categories, and cognitive models.

Constitutive norms refer to the formal and informal rules that define group membership. Social purposes refer to the goals that are shared by members of a group. Relational comparisons refer to the views of other groups or identities that are implied or defined by having a particular identity. Finally, cognitive models refer to the worldviews or understandings of political and material conditions and interests that are shaped by a particular identity (Abdelal et al. Chapter 1 in this volume).

Of these four types of content, cognitive mapping can be applied to the latter three (most directly to cognitive models and relational content, and perhaps least directly to social purposes) on the assumption that all of these types of content are contained in the belief systems of individuals and may be expressed to varying degrees in their speech and writings. However, the first form of content, constitutive norms, may never be expressed in speech or writings but rather is observed and followed in ways that do not show up in texts.

Our approach to measuring identity focuses on the cognitive model aspect of Abdelal et al.'s conceptualization of content and is based on four assumptions:

1. An identity is composed of some set of beliefs. To the extent that a social or collective identity exists, it exists because one or more individuals believe themselves to be members of a group.

2. The set of beliefs that constitute an identity will make reference to a core identity concept such as "Kurd," "nerd," "Scot," or "feminist." Identification with a group suggests knowledge of a presumably shared name for the group and a set of beliefs connected to the group name that consists of attributes of the group, membership rules, goals, purposes, and the like. In other words, all four forms of content should be associated with the group name within the individual's belief system.

3. To the extent that two individuals share an identity, their beliefs that refer to the core identity concept will be similar. If two individuals believe they belong to the same group, "Foobars," then one should not believe that the group consists only of women and the other that the group consists only of men. In other words, a shared identity requires more than a feeling of affiliation with a named group.

4. The best data available on an individual's beliefs are contained in the records of his or her discourse. Despite tremendous advances in neuroscience, we do not yet have any technology capable of extracting beliefs or memories directly from the brain. The most common and easily accessible records of an individual's beliefs are his or her words and actions. Though both can be ambiguous, we find words to be less ambiguous than actions. Even though people are capable of lying and often do not express all of their beliefs in their spoken or written communication, either by deliberately omitting beliefs or by relying on unspoken agreement with their correspondents, words are subject to less interpretation than actions because many diverse and potentially contradictory beliefs can lead to identical actions.

Of these four assumptions, the second is the most easily violated, as we could extend our concept of identity to encompass an individual's entire belief system. However, this would eliminate the possibility of an individual possessing multiple identities that are salient in different contexts. This seems to be an aspect of identity (and, more generally, of belief systems) that is important to preserve. This definition is also compatible with cognitive mapping. However, we recognize that the methodology can be used to represent a distributed collective identity if documents from some class of people are grouped together and a composite cognitive map created.

The cognitive map measure that is best suited to assessing identity is Incongruence, which measures the difference between two sets of beliefs that both include a specified concept. In this case, the concepts of interest are the core identity concepts "Islam," "Arab," and "Kurd."

METHODOLOGY

Our methodology follows quite directly from our assumptions and has five steps: collect documents from subjects of interest; extract expressed beliefs from the documents; collate the beliefs expressed in those documents into cognitive map representation of the underlying belief system; extract from the cognitive map of each individual a subset of beliefs that refer to the core identity concept(s) and are within a specified distance from the identity concept; and measure the similarity between those subsets. How this actually unfolds is somewhat more complicated, and we deal with each step in the process in turn before illustrating the methodology with data from four Iraqi leaders: Ahmed Chalabi, Ibraham al-Jaffari, Jalal Talabani, and Massoud Barzani.

Document Collection

We typically collect documents containing both prepared comments and interviews from LexisNexis, the World News Connection, official Web sites, and media Web sites. The documents are then marked up to exclude all but the subject's verbatim text from the analysis. Although we recommend that as many documents as possible are used, document selection strategy can have a dramatic effect on the outcome of cognitive mapping studies, and other scholars may find it appropriate to include or exclude classes of documents by level of spontaneity, audience, or apparent purpose. We considered none of these issues in this project. Regardless of the documentation strategy, in order to achieve meaningful results, at least one of the documents selected for each individual must contain the identity concept of interest.

Belief Extraction

We used our general purpose text coding engine, Profiler Plus to extract beliefs from the texts. When texts are coded with Profiler Plus, the software tokenizes, builds sentence data structures, assigns a part of speech and lemma to each token, manipulates the tokens and generates output.

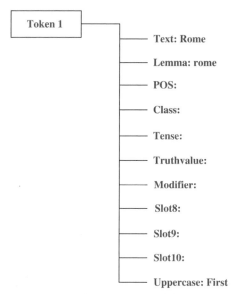

FIGURE 8.1. The token created for the word Rome in "Rome was destroyed by the Huns"

Tokenizing

The tokenizing process breaks the text into sentences and limits the scope of token matching to a single sentence and separates punctuation from words so that we do not have to concern ourselves with trailing periods, commas, semicolons, and the like when writing rules.

Sentence Data Structure

During the tokenizing process, Profiler Plus creates a list of the tokens in the sentence, adds beginning and end of sentence tokens, and creates a data structure for each token that contains eleven memory addresses (slots) that can contain values. At this stage, the slots that hold values are text, which contains the original word or punctuation; lemma, which contains the root form of the token; and uppercase, which contains a value indicating whether the first, all, or none of the letters in the token in the original text were uppercase.

After this stage in processing, the token created for the word "Rome" in the sentence "Rome was destroyed by the Huns" would have the values shown in Figure 8.1.

TABLE 8.1. *A Simple Passive-Voice Transformation Rule*

Anchor	Pattern	Reduction
Verb	< variable > < token: −3 item = a class = actor >	< swap a b >
	< token: 0 class = verb >	< delete 1 >
	< token: 1 lemma = by >	
	< token: 4 item = b class = actor >	

TABLE 8.2. *Data Summary*

Leader	Sunni/Shia	Arab/Kurd	Document Count	Time Frame
Chalabi	Shia	Arab	43	20000125 to 20030725
al-Jaffari	Shia	Arab	55	20030713 to 20040824
Barzani	Sunni	Kurd	70	19910412 to 20041012
Talabani	Sunni	Kurd	68	19980917 to 20040710

Part of Speech

The next step in processing is the assignment of potential part-of-speech values data from WordNet (http://wordnet.princeton.edu/). These values are used later by our part-of-speech tagging coding scheme to finalize the part-of-speech assignment and record it in the part-of-speech slot.

Manipulation of Tokens

Once these preliminary processes are complete, Profiler Plus applies to the sentence any rules specified in the coding scheme. These rules can contain operators that create, move, or delete tokens; compare and change values of the slots in the tokens; or generate output. Each rule has an Anchor that must match a slot value in a token for the rule to be applied. Additional conditions can be specified in the Pattern section of the rule, and the Reduction section lists the changes to be made or the output to be generated. An example of a simple passive voice transformation rule is shown in Table 8.1.

Application of the rule in Table 8.2 (along with some others) to the sentence "Rome has been destroyed *by* the Huns" would produce the sentence "Huns destroyed Rome." Using these capabilities of Profiler Plus, Stone developed a cognitive mapping coding scheme that transforms the text into a series of data statements in the form: subject-concept relationship truth-value[1] tense[2] modi-fier[3] object-concept. In these statements both the subject and object concepts can themselves be propositions. The recursion of embedded propositions is limited only by the length of a single sentence.

For example, consider the simple sentences "I was a British citizen. I am an American citizen. I am a father." Applying the coding scheme transforms them into:

> (i be past true na a-british-citizen)
> (i be present true na an-american-citizen)
> (i be present true na a-father)

Representation of Beliefs

Because our intention is to represent expressed beliefs in as accurate a manner as possible, we have adopted the associative network model of memory (Estes 1991). The structure of an associative network is a node and link structure. There are three important features of this model of memory, the first being that links between nodes are associative. This model stipulates that links between nodes refer to associations between concepts and that links can be established and strengthened by the occurrence of these associations in experience – for example, when the links are activated by perception. Second, these links are directional, that is, any particular association is one way between nodes, although a link in the opposite direction may exist. Third, there are different types of relational links between concepts (class membership, etc.). This characterization of cognitive architecture leads to a "shoe box" model of a belief system, in which the connectedness of individual concepts varies. The belief system is therefore clumpy, with structures of different complexity that may or may not be connected to other structures. For example, your beliefs about chocolate sundaes may have no connections to your beliefs about politicians. Figure 8.2 illustrates this idea by showing some of the fragments in Talabani's cognitive map. Note that we do not believe Talabani's belief system is quite this fragmented; Figure 8.2 also illus-trates the limits of the current coding scheme and effect of the small volume of material used. In general, the more material used, the fewer fragments we expect in the cognitive map, as concepts used in conjunction with one concept in one document are used with different concepts in other documents.

---

[1] Typical values are true, false, possible, or impossible.
[2] Typical values are past, present, or future.
[3] Typical values are goal, hypothetical, or imperative.

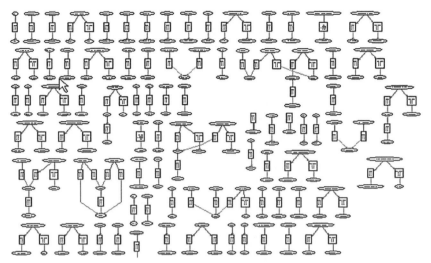

FIGURE 8.2. A sample of the disconnected fragments in Talabani's cognitive map

We use WorldView (M. Young 1996), our cognitive mapping tool, to collate the data statements produced using Profiler Plus and the cognitive mapping coding scheme to generate a network representation of the beliefs extracted from the source documents. We refer to this representation as a cognitive map. WorldView creates a unique node for each unique concept, conjunction, and relationship in the data statements produced using Profiler Plus. Each node has associated with it both a list of the relationships of which it is the subject and a list of the relationships of which it is an object. In addition, conjunction and relationship nodes have associated lists of their subjects and objects. Lastly, relationship nodes have tense, truth-value, modifier, and salience values (salience is a count of how often a unique relationship occurs in the dataset).

WorldView can combine the beliefs extracted from many documents to provide a composite and complex structure that is not readily amenable to manual analysis. From our simple example about citizenship and fatherhood, WorldView generates the cognitive map shown in Figure 8.3. Figure 8.4 shows a more complex cognitive map created by extracting all the propositions that contain the concept "Kurd" in Massoud Barzani's cognitive map.

Extract and Measure Identity

In addition to tools for representing and manipulating beliefs, WorldView incorporates several measures. We use one of these, *Incongruence*, to measure

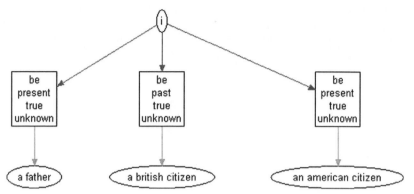

FIGURE 8.3. A small cognitive map generated from: "I am a father. I was a British citizen. I am an American citizen."

the similarity of identities. Incongruence measures the difference between two submaps that both include a specified concept. Incongruence is similar to a Levenshtein measure of difference (Kruskal 1983) and is based on the number of additions and deletions required to transform one sequence into another. For example, the difference score for "Michael" and "Michelle" is 5. That is, it takes five equally weighted steps to transform one into the other:

Michael (1) Delete *a*
Mich_el (2) Delete *e*
Mich__l (3) Add *e*
Miche_l (4) Add *l*
Michell (5) Add *e*
Michelle

Incongruence is calculated by dividing the number of discrete changes required to make the second submap a duplicate of the first by the maximum possible number of changes for two submaps of the same size and structure as those selected. Each of five types of discrete change is assigned a weight of 1:

1. *Relationship-addition*: the creation of a relational link between two concepts
2. *Relationship-deletion*: the removal of a relational link between two concepts
3. *Relationship salience increase or decrease*: a unit change in the strength of a relationship between two concepts
4. *Concept-deletion*: the removal of a concept (Conception-deletion requires that all connecting relationships be deleted.)

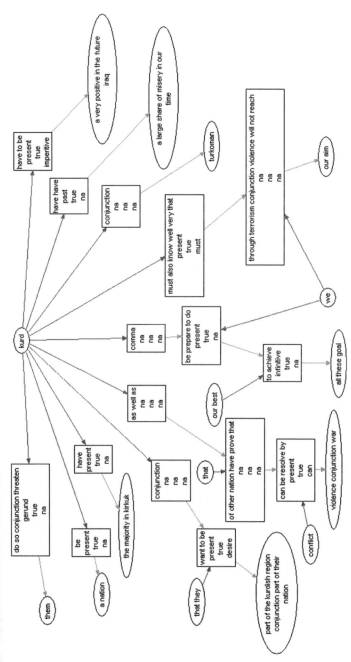

FIGURE 8.4. A small portion of Barzani's cognitive map centered on the concept "Kurd" with a depth of 1

245

5. *Concept-addition*: the creation of a new node that reflects the addition of new information into the cognitive map (Concept additions
   are normally accompanied by one or more relationship additions
   linking the new concept to at least one other concept.)

To measure the similarity between identities, we limit the scope of the
cognitive map to some area around the identity concept (depth 4), load the
cognitive maps of two subjects into WorldView, and select the incongruence
option. WorldView then offers a list of all concepts common to both cognitive
maps. Once a concept is selected, WorldView calculates an incongruence score.
The higher the incongruence score, the greater the difference between the two
cognitive maps.

DATA AND EXPECTATIONS

We selected Iraq to illustrate the use of cognitive mapping and incongruence for
three reasons. First, Iraq provided a contemporary example (circa 2005) of a
state with multiple and potentially competing identities, including Kurd versus
Arab ethnic identity and Sunni versus Shia religious identity, each of which
could be the subject of contestation in Iraq.

Second, we had data for two Arab-Shia leaders (Ahmed Chalabi and
Ibraham al-Jaffari) and one Kurdish Sunni leader (Jalal Talabani) available
from a previous study (Lazarevska, Sholl, and Young 2006) and were able to
easily obtain documents for Massoud Barzani, a second Kurdish Sunni leader.
Our collection goal in the previous study was to collect at least fifty English-
language documents (original or high quality translation) for each individual,
containing at least fifty codable words for an overall minimum of 10,000 words
and punctuation. No other collection criteria were used. We searched for documents using LexisNexis, the World News Connection, BBC Monitoring, official
Web sites, and Web sites of news organizations. We achieved the minimum
number of words and punctuation for all four individuals but located only
forty-three documents for Chalabi (see Table 8.2). A complete listing of the
documents used is available by request from info@socialscience.net.

Third, the time period for which we had source documents (1998–2004)
includes U.S. and international challenges to Saddam Husayn's Sunni regime,
including the U.S. invasion, as well as increasing autonomy for the Kurds in the
protected areas of northern Iraq – all of which made Arab, Kurd, Sunni, and
Shia identities highly salient.

Given the opposition of both Kurds and Shia to the Arab Sunni regime in
Iraq, we expected greater similarity within the Kurd-Shia pair of leaders and the

TABLE 8.3. *Incongruence Scores for "Arab"*

	Chalabi	al-Jaffari	Barzani
al-Jaffari	0.396		
Barzani	0.665	0.647	
Talabani	0.701	0.658	0.306

TABLE 8.4. *Incongruence Scores for "Kurd"*

	Chalabi	al-Jaffari	Barzani
al-Jaffari	0.934		
Barzani	0.575	0.970	
Talabani	0.458	0.959	0.334

TABLE 8.5. *Incongruence Scores for "Islam/Muslim"*

	Chalabi	al-Jaffari	Barzani
al-Jaffari	0.905		
Barzani	0.961	0.647	
Talabani	0.701	0.658	0.306

Arab-Sunni pair of leaders than between them for comparisons around the identity concepts of "Islam," "Arab," and "Kurd."

RESULTS

The results presented in Tables 8.3–8.5 support our expectation and, to that extent, lend some face validity to the methodology. The two Kurds, Talabani and Barzani, are more similar to each other (incongruence scores are smaller) for the concept "Arab" (Table 8.3) than they are to either of the Arabs. And the two Arabs, al-Jaffari and Chalabi, are also more similar to each other than they are to the Kurds.

This pattern becomes more complicated for the concept "Kurd," however. Again, the two Kurds are more similar to each other than to the two Arabs, but Chalabi is more similar to either Kurd than he is to his fellow Arab al-Jaffari. In fact, on this identity concept al-Jaffari is not similar to any of the others.

When we measure incongruence around the concept "Islam" (composed of both Islam and Muslim; see Table 8.5), the two Sunnis, Barzani and Talabani, are again most similar to each other. However, for this identity

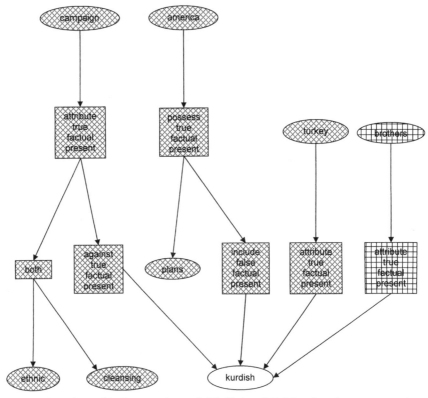

FIGURE 8.5. A graphical comparison of al-Jaffari and Talabani's submaps centered on "Kurd" with a depth of 1. Nodes unique to al-Jaffari's submap are diagonally checked; nodes unique to Talabani's are vertically checked.

concept, al-Jaffari (Shia) is more similar to the two Sunnis than to Chalabi (Shia) and is less similar to Chalabi than Talabani.

Although these results are included only for illustration and are not conclusive by any means, the results are encouraging enough for us to continue to pursue this methodology. We believe that we can improve the usefulness and validity of the measure by incorporating planned improvements to the still unfinished cognitive mapping coding scheme and exploring in more detail the overlapping content of belief systems using graphical comparisons like the one shown in Figure 8.5 comparing al-Jaffari and Talabani's cognitive maps centered on "Kurd" with a depth of 1.

Our results may also have been more distinctive if we had selected only documents that we considered to contain identity relevant discourse. However, we are resistant to limiting collection on any basis because the cognitive maps from disparate documents may link together or overlap in unexpected ways. Limited document collection thus may eliminate the possibility of the surprises that are so useful in the scientific process.

CONCLUSION

In this study we have shown how cognitive mapping may be used to compare the identities of different individuals using incongruence. In a similar manner, we could also study the evolution of an identity by producing cognitive maps from consecutive time spans and generating incongruence scores for each pair of identity-focused submaps. The expectation is that consecutive maps will be more similar to each other than the first and last maps are to each other. In addition, we could use "connectedness," a measure of the density of relationships to concepts in a cognitive map, to explore the formation of an identity. As an identity is first being formed, we expect the identity concept to be poorly integrated into the belief system (low local connectedness) and to be more and more integrated and connected to a larger number of concepts over time, resulting in increased local connectedness. In a similar manner, cognitive mapping could easily be extended to studies that focus on the evolution of an identity in a group over time and by comparing the incongruence scores between group members over time.

We see some danger in using cognitive mapping to suggest that a particular behavior option or way of thinking is unimaginable for an individual with a particular identity because it does not appear in the cognitive map. Although this may be the correct interpretation of the absence of the belief from the cognitive map, it may also be true that the belief is held by the subject but is, possibly deliberately, unexpressed. However, to the extent that some people voice an option that others do not, it suggests that the option is less salient to those who do not express the opinion.

In the immediate future, we are going to work on improving the cognitive mapping coding scheme and revisit the results from the four Iraqis studied here. Once we are comfortable with the performance of the coding scheme, we will explore other uses of cognitive mapping for the study of identity.

9

A Constructivist Dataset on Ethnicity and Institutions

Kanchan Chandra

Constructivism – the principal theoretical revolution in the study of ethnic identities over the past thirty years – has established that individuals have multiple ethnic options with a choice of which one to activate in any given context, and that the ethnic identities they activate can change over time, often endogenously to political and economic outcomes.[1] The implication for our data collection efforts is that they must make a distinction between ethnic "structure" (the set of potential ethnic identities that characterizes a population) and ethnic "practice" (the set of identities actually activated by that population), must accommodate the possibility of the multiplicity of identities in both structure and practice, and must be sensitive to context and time in collecting these data. But our cross-national datasets on ethnic groups, and the measures constructed on the basis of these datasets, are resolutely primordialist – they do not distinguish between structure and practice, do not accommodate the possibility of multiplicity, and are not sensitive to time and context. The lack of theoretically justified data hampers the production of high-quality research on the origin and effect of ethnic diversity and on related concepts. Although there is now a steadily increasing number of studies on the role of ethnicity in determining economic growth, the consolidation of democracy, the

---

[1] There is little agreement among those who describe themselves as, or are described as, being constructivist beyond these minimal propositions. "Instrumentalist" approaches suggest that ethnic identities change as a result of instrumental calculations at the individual level, while "structuralist" approaches emphasize the importance of large-scale processes larger than the individual. "Behavioralist" approaches, similarly, track changes in ethnic identity based on changes in behavior rather than changes in the underlying self-understandings that inform such behavior. But as long as these approaches share in the belief that ethnic identities can be fluid and endogenous, they can all be called "constructivist."

distribution of public goods, the study of large-scale violence, and the shape of party systems, the poor quality of the data on which these studies are based means that we cannot be confident of their results.

This chapter describes a new, constructivist dataset on several concepts related to ethnic identity and institutions – referred to as Constructivist Dataset on Ethnicity and Institutions, or CDEI – which I have been building in collaboration with MIT graduate students. CDEI, which currently covers 100 countries for the year 1996, generates a range of variables related to ethnicity and institutions constructed explicitly on constructivist insights. These cross-national data are a complement to and not a substitute for within-country comparisons, ethnographic and quantitative. I focus here on one key variable – EVOTE, or the percentage of the vote captured by ethnic parties in each country for the year 1996. EVOTE is based on a content analysis of party rhetoric – that is, what parties actually say to voters rather than what they write in their manifestos – in the election campaign closest to but before 1996. My own interest in collecting data on EVOTE is to account for variation in the performance of ethnic parties across political systems and to test for the relationship between the emergence of ethnic parties and democratic consolidation. But EVOTE, as well as the archives that support it, has the potential to illuminate a very diverse set of research agendas related to the origins or effects of politically activated ethnic identities, especially when expanded over time.

In this chapter, I describe first the variables contained in CDEI and their relation to the umbrella concept of "ethnicity" and then consider EVOTE specifically and the procedure for coding EVOTE. I contrast CDEI and EVOTE with the primordialist bases of previous cross-national datasets on ethnic groups and with the Index of Ethnolinguistic Fractionalization (ELF), the main measure constructed using these data. Next I describe how CDEI can be used to answer questions about the rise of ethnic parties and democratic stability and identify some of the broader questions that CDEI and EVOTE can be used to answer in social science research as well as their biases and limitations. I conclude by locating CDEI and EVOTE within a broader family of efforts by comparative political scientists to collect data on different aspects of "ethnicity" from a constructivist perspective.

CONSTRUCTIVIST DATASET ON ETHNICITY AND INSTITUTIONS (CDEI)

CDEI starts with an obvious point, worth stating only because it has so often been ignored: "Ethnicity" is a big concept, much like "politics." Big phenomena are best captured not by big concepts and measures but by the proliferation and conjunction of several small ones. For instance, if we wanted to study how "politics" matters in explaining some outcome of interest, we would not construct datasets on and measures of "politics" in general. Rather, we would (and do) identify narrow concepts that name some specific aspect of political structure (e.g., democratic vs. dictatorial regimes, presidential vs. parliamentary regimes, the effective number of parties in a political system) or political practice (e.g., the content of campaign rhetoric, the allocation of budgets, the degree of politically motivated violence) and collect data and design measures that operationalized these concepts. By the same logic, concepts, measures, and data designed to explore the role of "ethnicity" must be narrow, tailored to specific questions and contexts.

Accordingly, CDEI collects data on more than forty variables related to ethnicity, each of which captures only one aspect of the large number of ways in which ethnic identity might manifest itself in structure or practice, and all of which, taken together, do not exhaust the ways in which we can measure the role of ethnicity. In particular, it focuses on collecting data and designing measures for the explicit and implicit ways in which ethnic identity is activated by political parties in election campaigns. The relation of the variables generated by CDEI to the broader concept of ethnicity is summarized in Figure 9.1

At the broadest level, we can imagine the term "ethnicity" to encompass two families of concepts – the "structure" of ethnic identities, and the "practice" of ethnic identification. Ethnic "structure" refers to that set of identities that are considered commonsensically real by a population, whether or not individuals actually identify with them. Ethnic "practice" refers to the act of actually using one or more identities embedded in this structure to guide behavior. Ethnic "practice" in other words refers to the set of "activated" identities that individuals actually employ in any given context. The set of "activated" ethnic identities for any given country is typically a subset of the identities contained in the ethnic "structure." For instance, the identities "Czech American" and "African American" are both embedded in the ethnic structure of the United States to the extent that both are among the set of commonsensical identities that people would acknowledge as real in the United States. But the identity "African American" belongs in the subset of activated identities, while the identity "Czech American," arguably, does not.

The ethnic identities activated in practice differ according to whether they are activated in private life or political life. By private life, I mean that aspect of life which concerns individuals alone, or their immediate family and friends. By political life, I mean that aspect of life which concerns collective action by individuals who are not bound by immediate personal ties. Caste identity in Sri Lanka (e.g., Goyigama) is an example of an identity that informs private

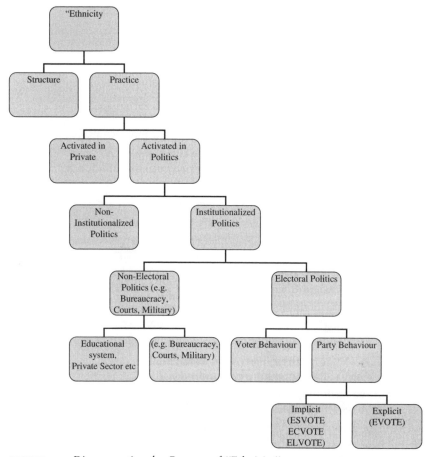

FIGURE 9.1. Disaggregating the Concept of "Ethnicity"

actions such as the choice of a marriage partner. But religious and linguistic identities (e.g., Buddhist or Sinhala) rather than caste are the principal identities invoked in collective action (Rajasingham-Senanayake 1999; Tambiah 1986; Chandra 2005a).

Among the set of identities that are politically activated, we can distinguish again between identities that are activated in institutionalized politics, parliament, party politics, the legal system, and so on and identities that are activated in noninstitutionalized contexts, such as civil war, riots, and social movements. In many countries, the set of identities activated in both contexts may be identical. But in others, especially in states that outlaw certain types of political participation, they can diverge. In Indonesia, for instance, institutionalized participation by political parties activates religious identities (Muslim and Christian), whereas regional identities are more likely to be found in the arena of noninstitutionalized politics (CDEI data).

Among identities that are activated in institutionalized politics, we can distinguish further between identities mobilized in electoral contexts (party politics and voting behavior) and in nonelectoral contexts (in the corridors of parliament, the military, the judiciary, and the bureaucracy). In Uganda, for instance, the identity of "Nubian" was an identity mobilized principally in the military and the corridors of the bureaucracy of Idi Amin's regime, while the identities Baganda or Catholic have frequently been mobilized in the course of electoral politics (Kasfir 1976, 1979).

Among the identities mobilized in electoral politics, we can distinguish between identities that drive voter behavior and those that drive party strategy. In principle, we should expect there to be some connection between the identities that parties activate and identities that condition voter behavior. But the two concepts are analytically distinct and may sometimes diverge. In South Africa, for instance, the African National Congress mobilizes voters by making multiethnic appeals targeted to all South Africans and, in some contexts, appeals based on the racial category "Black." But voters often vote for it, not as "South Africans" or "Blacks" but on the basis of their particular tribal identities (Xhosa, Zulu, etc.).

Finally, among the identities mobilized by political parties, we can distinguish between identities mobilized implicitly and identities mobilized explicitly. The Willie Horton advertisements used by the Republican Party in its 1988 presidential campaign in the United States are an example of an implicit appeal to race (Mendelberg 2001). By contrast, the election campaign run by Slobodan Milosevic in 1992, in the immediate aftermath of Communist rule, made an explicit appeal to Serbian identity (CDEI data).

The set of identities mobilized by political parties currently forms the principal domain of CDEI. The forty-eight variables currently included in CDEI can be divided into three families.

Seventeen Variables on the Explicit Mobilization of Ethnic Identities by Political Parties

These variables are all derived from a classification of all political parties in the dataset into "ethnic," "multiethnic," and "nonethnic" parties. The most important of these is EVOTE – the aggregate percentage of the vote captured by ethnic parties in each country. Others in this family include variables coding the aggregate vote captured by nonethnic and multiethnic parties, the names and sizes of the ethnic groups explicitly mobilized by political parties, the types of identities explicitly mobilized by political parties, the number of identity types mobilized in each country, the proportion of an explicitly mobilized ethnic group that votes for its "own" party and so on.

Seventeen Variables on the Implicit Mobilization of Ethnic Identities by Political Parties

These variables are informed by the insight that political parties may often activate ethnic identities without explicitly naming any ethnic category. Such implicit mobilization may be based on "coded" appeals. In the 2002 race for the position of mayor in Newark, for instance, the incumbent's campaign slogan was "The Real Deal." In a context in which race mattered, and both candidates were black, the slogan was an implicit attempt by the incumbent to cast doubt on the authenticity of his competitor as a representative of "black" interests. Implicit mobilization may also be based on the identity of the candidates and leaders of a political party. In India, for instance, it is routine to distribute party tickets according to complicated formulas of ethnic balancing – but the official manifestos of parties engaged in such detailed ethnic balancing often do not say a word about ethnicity explicitly. Finally, implicit mobilization can also be based on the arena of contestation parties can convey which ethnic groups they are for simply by confining their message to voters from this ethnic group rather than explicitly championing the cause of the group. The nature of implicit appeals makes it difficult to code them on the basis of party rhetoric – they either are designed to be open to multiple interpretations or are invisible in speech, relying on the context to reveal them. However, we try to get at them by including three other variables in CDEI. ESVOTE measures the aggregate percentage of vote obtained by political parties that have an ethnically identified support base. The logic behind ESVOTE is that if a party is making an implicit ethnic appeal, it should show up in the nature of its support base even if we cannot code it in its message. ELVOTE measures the aggregate percentage of vote obtained by political parties that have an ethnically identified leadership. ELVOTE tries to capture the surreptitious signals sent by political parties that court ethnic groups by giving their representatives positions of power. And ECVOTE – the aggregate percentage of vote obtained by political parties that have an ethnically identified arena of contestation whether or not they make an explicit ethnic appeal – tries to capture the implicit signal sent by parties that court ethnic groups by choosing their audience rather than choosing their words. CDEI also includes variables measuring the name, size, type, and number of types of ethnic identity category that are implicitly mobilized in each country.

Fourteen "General" Variables on Each Country or Party

These include the year of the election, the year of founding of the political party, whether there are laws preventing parties from making explicit appeals, whether the election is boycotted by any significant party, whether the election in question is a "founding" election, the percentage of votes obtained by each party, the percentage of seats obtained by the party, and so on. These variables are useful in their own right and in the interpretation of the variables on explicit and implicit mobilization.

We currently expect to expand CDEI in three directions. First, we expect to collect data on variables located on other branches in the conceptual tree drawn here for the cross-national dataset. In particular, we have begun to collect data on ethnic structure (STRUCTURE), by summarizing all mentions of ethnic identities in our source materials as commonsensically describing a country's population, whether or not these identities are actually mobilized by political parties. But the coding of this variable is in its very early stages. Second, we expect to expand the dataset over time to include the years 1956, 1966, 1976, 1986, and 2006, so that we will obtain a time-series coding for six decades. Finally, we expect to expand the country coverage to include all countries in each year for which we are able to obtain vote share data.

EVOTE: THE AGGREGATE PERCENTAGE OF VOTES WON BY ETHNIC PARTIES

EVOTE is constructed as follows: first, we classify each political party in each country for which we can obtain data as "ethnic," "multiethnic," or "nonethnic" on the basis of its campaign in the legislative election closest to but before 1996. Then, we add up the total percentage of votes obtained by all ethnic parties in a given country. Thus, EVOTE for Country A is constructed as follows: EVOTE96 (Country A) = Vote for Ethnic Party 1 (Country A) + Vote for Ethnic Party 2 (Country A) + Vote for Ethnic Party 3 (Country A) + . . . Vote for Ethnic Party N (Country A). In principle, the value of EVOTE could range between 0 (for countries with no ethnic parties) to 100 percent (for countries in which all votes are captured by ethnic parties). In reality, EVOTE for the year 1996 ranges from 0 percent (e.g., in Greece) to 85.63 percent (in Yugoslavia), with a mean value of 12.95 percent.

Table 9.1 summarizes the regional distribution of parties and countries on which we have data on EVOTE. Chandra et al. (2005) provide a full description of the patterns revealed in EVOTE.

TABLE 9.1. *Regional Distribution of Parties and Countries in CDEI for Which We Have Data on EVOTE, no. (%)*

	Countries	Parties
Latin America	17 (17)	143 (10.62)
Europe	31 (31)	554 (41.16)
Asia	16 (16)	183 (13.6)
Post-Soviet	10 (10)	202 (15.01)
Africa	22 (22)	215 (15.97)
Middle East	2 (2)	33 (2.45)
North America	2 (2)	16 (1.19)
TOTAL	100 (100)	1,346 (100)

Note: The large number of ethnic parties in Europe relative to other regions does not necessarily reflect the greater political salience of ethnic identity in Europe compared to parties in other regions. CDEI may well have captured more parties, ethnic and otherwise, in Europe because data on Europe were available at a more disaggregated level than data on other continents.

The classification of parties that is the foundation of EVOTE is based on the definitions proposed by Chandra (2004a: 3), according to which an ethnic political party is "a party that represents itself to voters as the champion of the interests of one ethnic category or set of categories to the exclusion of another or others, and makes such a representation central to its strategy of mobilizing voters." The key aspects of this definition are exclusion (an ethnic party must make an appeal on behalf of some ethnic group[s] that excludes others), explicitness (the appeal must be open), and centrality (the appeal must be central to its mobilizing strategy). A multiethnic party also makes an open appeal related to ethnicity central to its mobilizing strategy but assumes a position of neutrality or equidistance toward all relevant groups. In other words, it differs from an ethnic party only in its inclusiveness. A nonethnic party is one that does not make an ethnic appeal central to its mobilizing strategy. Note that these definitions classify parties according to their message. And because messages can change across elections, they are time-sensitive: a party classified as an ethnic party in one election need not be classified the same way in subsequent elections.

An ethnic group, in turn, is defined as an impersonal social category in which membership is determined by inherited attributes and which comprises a subgroup of a country's population (Chandra 2004b). This typically includes most (but not all) groups defined by caste, tribe, nationality, race, religion, region, and language. Note that there is nothing in this definition that requires individuals in the same ethnic group to share a common sense of group identity or even a consciousness of the existence of other group members. I use the terms ethnic "category" and ethnic "group" interchangeably to emphasize this point. Considered in relation to the definition of identity laid out by Abdelal et al. in the Introduction to this volume, this is a minimalist definition of ethnic identity, which distinguishes between ethnic identity categories based purely on their "constitutive norms" (i.e., rules of membership) and not on their shared goals, frames of comparison, and cognitive content, or the degree of contestation over any of these things.

The coding of the parties is based on a content analysis of the election campaign of the party in question using four sources: the *Europa World Yearbook,* the *Political Handbook of the World,* news sources from FBIS (Foreign Broadcast Information Service), and LexisNexis searches. For each party, we obtain a sample of campaign materials (speeches at election rallies, policy pronouncements, and so on) as reported in FBIS and LexisNexis for a period up to three months before the election date. These include reports from the international media and translations of local news reports from newspapers, radio, and television. These samples have three advantages: (1) They are primary sources that report what parties are actually saying to voters rather than what they print in their manifestos. (2) Many of these sources are translations of what parties say to voters in local languages. (3) They are time-sensitive sources that report party statements for the year of election. Where the samples are too small to permit reliable codings, we turn to local newspapers and secondary sources as a last resort. These sources give us a sample of articles for the election platform of each party individually. We archive the materials for each party for each country after completing the coding. This archive, composed of a uniform set of source materials for each observation (country or party), makes it possible both to double check old variables as we proceed and to construct new variables as they become important.

The coding is based on a protocol that establishes rules for the identification of an appeal as ethnic, explicit, and central. In contrast to the analyses described by Abdelal et al. (in the Introduction) and in other chapters in this volume, the content analysis is qualitative rather than quantitative. Thus, rather than establishing centrality simply by counting the number of times an issue is mentioned, the protocol identifies rules of interpretation for centrality – an ethnic appeal can be considered central not only on the frequency of an issue but also on the way in which an ethnic appeal is used. For instance, suppose a party makes a statement that associates an ethnic group with ownership of the state, such as "This is a government of the Meskitos." We would code this party as an ethnic party even if statements to this effect were not frequent, by reasoning that once such a statement is made, it colors the interpretation of other statements. If, on the basis of the content analysis, we find that a political party makes an open and exclusive appeal to some ethnic category or set of categories and that such an appeal is central to its campaign, we code it as an ethnic party. If we find that a political party makes an open and inclusive appeal to all ethnic categories that define a population and makes such an appeal central to its election campaign, we code it as a multiethnic party. And if we find that a political party does not make an open or a central appeal to an ethnic category, whether exclusive or inclusive, we code it as a nonethnic party. We document each coding for each party on each country, compare it with codings in other datasets where available, check for consistency across coders, and assign a reliability score to the coding (1 = high certainty, 2 = moderate certainty, 3 = low certainty) based on the quality of information in the sample. Because countries can sometimes have more than a hundred parties, each with a separate sample, this level of documentation adds considerably to the time that constructing this dataset requires. But it is important that other researchers can replicate our efforts and estimate the bias and error in the data.

Consider the case of India as an example of our coding procedures. Hundreds of parties competed in India in the 1991 parliamentary elections (the elections closest to but before 1996) but most of them obtained a minuscule percentage of the vote. We obtained disaggregated data on all parties that obtained at least .01 percent of the vote, thus including sixty-six parties in our dataset. We then coded each of these sixty-six parties on the basis of a content analysis of its party platform. Of the sixty-six parties, we coded thirteen parties, accounting for 51.81 percent of the vote as nonethnic, and eighteen parties, accounting for 38.95 percent of the vote as ethnic, but were not able to find sufficient articles on election platform to code the remaining thirty-five parties, accounting for 10.24 percent of the vote (these were very small parties, with a mean vote of .14 percent).

Once we have coded EVOTE, we can also obtain data on other variables from the same source materials in relatively short order. We can immediately record the names and population of all explicitly mobilized categories. In India, for instance, ethnic parties, taken together, explicitly mobilized the following ethnic categories: Hindus (82 percent), Muslims (12.12 percent); Sikhs (1.94 percent); Other Backward Castes (OBCs) (52 percent), Scheduled Castes (16.48 percent), Jharkhandis (3.18 percent), Assamese (2.64 percent), and Tamils (6.6 percent). We can also use the archive of materials on each country (which typically includes background information on the country from *Europa* and *Political Handbook of the World*, third-party assessments of the main parties, and specific information on the rules governing the elections from the local news sources) to code the variables on the implicit mobilization of ethnic identities, on laws governing ethnic appeals, on party registration procedures, and so on.

WHAT MAKES CDEI AND EVOTE CONSTRUCTIVIST?

In order to highlight the constructivist features of CDEI and EVOTE, we must first relate them to previous datasets that also collect data on and construct measures for some aspect of "ethnicity."

There are currently three cross-national datasets on ethnic groups (1) the *Atlas Narodov Mira*, published by Soviet Ethnographers in 1964; (2) a dataset on ethnic groups in 190 countries published by Alesina et al. in 2003; and (3) a comparable count of ethnic groups in 160 countries published by James Fearon in the same year (2003). The principal measure constructed on the basis of these data is the Index of Ethnolinguistic Fractionalization (ELF), which measures the degree of ethnic diversity in a population. The ELF Index is calculated according to the formula

$$1 - \sum s_i^2,$$

where s_i is the proportion of the ith activated ethnic category, $i = \{1, 2, \ldots n\}$, where the ethnic groups are mutually exclusive (i.e., if you are in ethnic group 1, you are not in ethnic groups $2 - n$) and exhaustive (every member of the population is in some ethnic group). It measures the probability that two randomly chosen individuals from a country's population belong to different groups. Thus, a society with two groups, a majority of 80 percent and a minority of 20 percent, would have an ELF score of $1 - (.64 + .04) = .32$. A society with several small groups of 25 percent each would have a higher ELF score of $1 - (.0625 + .0625 + .0625 + .0625) = .75$.

Below, I raise at least four questions suggested by a constructivist perspective about what these data and measures refer to: (1) Do they measure ethnic "structure" or ethnic "practice"? (2) If "structure," then why do the datasets ignore the problem of multidimensionality, and what does the ELF Index mean, given such multidimensionality? (3) If "practice," then why do these datasets ignore the problems of overlap and incompleteness? And how can the ELF Index, which requires the assumptions of mutual exclusiveness and exhaustiveness, be meaningful? (4) Whether structure or practice, what time period and context do these data refer to? None of these questions would be worth raising in a primordialist world, in which there is no distinction between structure and practice, individuals have unidimensional ethnic identities that are mutually exclusive and exhaustive, and they retain these identities in all times and contexts. But these questions are critical from a constructivist point of view. Although the authors of the more recent datasets acknowledge that some of these questions can create problems for a data collection exercise in theory, they do not provide answers about how they actually solve these problems in their coding criteria. Without answers to these questions, these data cannot be satisfactorily interpreted, replicated, and extended. This section elaborates on these problems and shows how CDEI and EVOTE address them.

Do the Data and ELF Measure Refer to Ethnic "Structure" or "Practice"?

Do the three previous datasets count the ethnic groups that are commonsensically real or the ethnic groups that are activated? And does the ELF Index measure the degree of ethnic heterogeneity given the set of commonsensically real identities, or the degree of ethnic heterogeneity given the set of activated ones?

The approach taken by *Atlas Narodov Mira* is not spelled out. Alesina et al. (2003: 161) refer to ethnic groups as the product of "persistent identification," thus conflating structure and practice. Fearon (2003: 203), by contrast, makes an explicit distinction between the two and aims to code for ethnic structure by trying to capture commonsensically real identities – "how people in the country mentally divide the social terrain in ethnic terms" – and not ethnic practice, at least in the political realm. But the criteria for operationalizing this distinction in the coding procedures are not laid out, and if we look at the data, we find that all three datasets veer inconsistently between collecting data on ethnic structure and ethnic practice.

Consider the example of Albania. Each of the three datasets code ethnic groups in Albania as "Albanian," "Greek," and "Macedonian." But why not include ethnic groups on the basis of religion (Catholic, Orthodox, and Muslim) or dialect (Gheg-speakers, concentrated in the north, and Tosk speakers, concentrated in the south) in their count? These other identities appear also to be commonsensically real. The principal distinction between the excluded and included groups seems to be that the groups Albanian, Greek, and Macedonian have more political resonance in the present than the others. Inadvertently, then, in the case of Albania the datasets appear to be coding practice rather than structure.

But in Italy, the pattern is reversed. The *Atlas Narodov Mira* codes Italy as 98 percent Italian, with a range of smaller groups including Austrians, French, Slovenians, and Albanians making up the remaining 2 percent. Fearon codes Italy as an almost entirely homogeneous country, with a 98 percent majority of "Italians." Alesina et al. code Italy in a comparable way, as 94 percent Italian, 2.7 percent Sardinian, 1.3 percent "Rhaetian," and 1.9 percent "other." But if we look at politically mobilized identities in Italy, at least in electoral politics, we see several other identities mobilized by political parties, including regional identities ("North" and "South"), subregional identities (Milan and Lombardy), and racial identities ("native" versus immigrant Italians). Germany, similarly, is consistently coded by all three datasets as having an overwhelming German majority (ranging from 91 percent in Alesina to 98.8 percent in *Narodov Mira*), with several tiny minorities. But why count only groups identified by nationality or race in Germany and not groups classified by region – East Germans, for instance, or Bavarians – which CDEI reveals are identities activated by political parties? By excluding these identities, the datasets all appear to be attempting to capture some undefined notion of structure rather than practice.

CDEI corrects for this problem by coding variables based on ethnic practice, consistently separating this from ethnic "structure," which we are now beginning to code.

If "Structure," Then How Do We Address the Multidimensionality and Level of Aggregation in Datasets and Measures?

The structure of ethnic identities in most countries is multidimensional, although the number and type of dimensions can vary. The set of identities that are commonsensically real in the United States, for instance, includes identities based at least on the dimensions of race, nationality, region, religion, and tribe. In India, it includes identities based on the dimensions of caste, language, tribe, region, and religion. In Zambia, it includes identities based on the dimensions of tribe and language. In South Africa, it includes identities based on the dimensions of race and tribe. In Malaysia, it includes identities based on the dimensions of race, language, region, religion, and tribe.

Further, categories on each dimension are arrayed at multiple levels – which level should we count on (Laitin and Posner 2001)? When faced with the dimension of tribe in India, should we count categories at the highest level of aggregation (e.g., Scheduled Tribe) or at the lowest level (Santhal, Munda, Bhil, and so on) or somewhere in between? When faced with the dimension of religion in the United States, should we count according to metacategories (Christian, Muslim, Jewish) or microcategories (Methodist, Baptist, Presbyterian, Shia, Sunni, Ismaili, Hasidic, Orthodox, and so on)?

Alesina et al. (2003) and Fearon (2003) acknowledge these problems and discuss them at some length. But they do not furnish the decision rule that they employ to solve them, and we cannot infer the rule from actually looking at the data. To illustrate, consider the coding for India across the three datasets and CDEI presented in Table 9.2.

TABLE 9.2. *Coding of Groups in India by Four Datasets*

	Groups Included in Count	ELF	Size of Largest Group
Atlas Narodov Mira	Hindi-speaking peoples of North India (.25), Bihars, Maraths, Bengals, Gujarats, Rajastans, Oriya, Panjabs, Assams, Kumaoni, Kashmirs, Bhils, Gujars, Sindhi, Gurkhi, Pars, Jhats, Shina, Kho, Kohians, English, Jews, Pushtuns, Portuguese, Telugs, Tamils, Kannara, Malayali, Gondi, Tulu, Oraoni, Kandhi, Kodagu, Badaga, Irula, Urali, Maler, Mannans, Malavedans, Kurumba, Kadari, Paniabs, Toda, Kota, Chenchu, Santals, Munda, Ho, Savara, Korku, Bhumidji, Kharia, Gadaba, Djuangs, Minipuri, Naga, Garo, Balti, Lushei, Kachars, Tipera, Mikiri, Kirats, Kuki, Tamangs, Ladahs, Bhoti, Thado, Miri, Abor, Mishmi, Dafla, Limbu, Lepcha, Kanauri,Lahauli, Gurungs, Nevars, Magars, Sherps, Sunvars, Burmese, Kachins, Chinese, Khamti, Khasi, Nikobars, Burishs, Andamanese.	.89	.25
Alesina et al.	Indo-Aryan (.72), Dravidian (.25), Other (3)	.42	.72
Fearon	Speakers of Hindi (.39), Bengali (.08), Telugu (.08), Marathi (.07), Tamil (.06), Gujarati (.05), Malayalam (.05), Kannada (.04), Oriya (.03), Punjabi (.03), Sikhs (.02), Assamese (.01)	.81	.39
CDEI	Hindus (.82), Muslims (.12), Sikhs (.019), OBCs (.52), Scheduled Castes (.16), Jharkhandis .031), Assamese (.26), Tamils (.066).	NA(EVOTE = .3895)	.82

The *Atlas Narodov Mira* counts a cluster of groups based on several dimensions – language (e.g., Hindi speakers and Tamils), nationality (Portuguese, English), Tribe (Santals, Munda), Religion (Jews), Caste (Gujars, Jats). But the choice of groups included from each dimension is arbitrary, and I cannot discern the logic to the level of aggregation chosen.

Alesina et al. (2003) include two groups from the highest level of aggregation on the dimension of language (Indo-Aryan and Dravidian). But, given that they are concerned with a count of "ethnic" groups, it is not clear why they chose the dimension of language rather than the dimensions of caste, religion, region, and tribe, or why they chose the highest level of aggregation in this case, in express contradiction of their intention to collect data at as disaggregated a level as possible (Alesina et al. 2003: 160). (In the same dataset, Alesina et al. [2003] collect data separately on the dimensions of religion and language but never make clear how these dimensions are separate from rather than contained within the concept of "ethnic" identities.)

Fearon (2003) reports the ethnic structure as made up of several groups defined on the dimension of language – speakers of Hindi (.39), Bengali (.08), Telugu (.08), Marathi (.07), Tamil (.06), Gujarati (.05), Malayalam (.05), Kannada (.04), Oriya (.03), Punjabi (.03), and Assamese (.01), and one group on the dimension of religion, Sikhs (.02). But why not include other groups on the dimensions of religion (Hindus and Muslims, for instance) or tribe (Scheduled Tribes and others) or caste (at the highest level of aggregation, this would include Upper Castes, Backward Castes, and Scheduled Castes)? And on the dimension of language, why not include groups at a higher level of aggregation – for example, Indo-Aryan languages (including Hindi, Bengali, Gujarati, Punjabi) and Dravidian languages (including Telugu, Tamil, Kannada, and Malayalam)?

In an improvement over the other two datasets, Fearon (2003: 201) does provide a conceptual justification for his count. He attempts to include in his count groups that fulfill as many of the following prototypical criteria as possible: (1) Membership is reckoned primarily by descent; (2) members are conscious of group membership; (3) members share distinguishing cultural features; (4) these cultural features are valued by a majority of members; (5) the group has or remembers a homeland; (6) the group has a shared history as a group that is "not wholly manufactured but has some basis in fact"; and (7) the group "is potentially stand alone in a conceptual sense – that is, it is not a caste or caste-like group" (Fearon 2003:201).

But I cannot tell how these conceptual criteria are operationalized in the coding process. Determining whether the members of a group have a factual rather than a fictitious history, whether they value distinguishing cultural features, or whether they are conscious of group membership is no easy task, even for those who specialize in a particular country or a particular group. How might a coder make these decisions, and how might others replicate them? Nor is it clear how many prototypical criteria a group must satisfy in order to be included, or how a coder should decide between multiple candidate groups on multiple dimensions that fit the prototypical criteria. Why, for instance, was the category "Jat" (included in *Atlas Narodov Mira* but not in Fearon), which appears to meet criteria 1–6 but not 7, not chosen over the category "Punjabi," which appears to meet criteria 1, 3, 4, and 5 but not 2 and 6, and arguably 7? Some of the groups included in Fearon's count do not seem to meet several of the conditions. "Hindi-speakers," for instance, is not a "group" in which members are conscious of group membership, share distinguishing cultural features that are valued by a majority of members, and have or remember a homeland. Further, several groups excluded from this count also appear to meet several of the prototypical criteria, such as Indo-Aryans and Dravidians, Hindus and Muslims, and Scheduled Tribes.

These differences are consequential: the ELF Index jumps from .42 to .89 depending upon the data chosen. And the size of the largest ethnic group, also a common measure constructed on the basis of these datasets, ranges from .25 to .72.

The multidimensionality of ethnic identities also poses a problem for the ELF Index as a measure of ethnic diversity. The ELF Index can give us only a measure of ethnic diversity based on a set of mutually exclusive groups chosen from within or across dimensions. But it cannot be used to capture the ethnic diversity of a country if we take the multiple dimensions together, along with the relationship between them, into account. To illustrate the problem this poses, compare India and Zambia. I noted that at least five dimensions of ethnic identity are commonsensically real in India (Chandra 2004a), with approximately two to seven categories arrayed on each, if we confine ourselves to the highest level of aggregation. In Zambia, only two dimensions of identity are salient: tribe and language (Posner 2005). The dimension of language currently has four groups arrayed on it at the highest level of aggregation: Bemba speakers, Nyanja speakers, Tonga speakers, Lozi speakers. The dimension of tribe has roughly seventy: Chewa, Tembuka, Bemba, and so on. Which country is more diverse, given variation in the number of dimensions and categories in each? We cannot use the ELF Index to tell us.

The CDEI variable on ethnic "structure," aims to collect separate data on all dimensions of ethnic identity that are commonsensically real in a given country, at all levels of aggregation. We also propose a new measure, a

Multidimensional ELF (MELF) Index that allows comparison in the degree of ethnic diversity across countries taking these multiple dimensions into account and allows for differences in the number of dimensions and the number of categories on each dimension, across countries (Chandra 2005b). But in the realm of ethnic "practice," currently our main concern, the categories and dimensions counted in CDEI are those that are named by the parties in question. Thus, the CDEI count of explicitly activated ethnic categories in India is based on all the categories explicitly mobilized by political parties in the 1991 parliamentary election campaign (the national legislative election closest to but before 1996). (We could in principle also construct a list of all categories activated in an election campaign, explicitly or implicitly.) These data cannot be used to calculate an ELF Index, because they are neither mutually exclusive nor exhaustive. But they can be used to calculate EVOTE (.3895) and to measure the size of the largest activated ethnic category (.82).

If Practice, Then How Do We Account for the Overlap and Incompleteness in Our Datasets and Measures?

What if we take the datasets to report data not on the groups embedded in an ethnic structure but on ethnic groups as they are activated in practice, whether they are mobilized in politics or otherwise? In this case, we run into the problems of overlap and incompleteness. Take, first, examples of overlap. We have no reason to expect that the ethnic categories that individuals activate in practice should be mutually exclusive. Indeed, in many of the cases I have looked at in CDEI, the mobilized categories are overlapping. In CDEI's count of politically activated ethnic categories in India, summarized in Table 9.2, the categories Hindu, Muslim, and Sikh are mutually exclusive in relation to each other but overlap with the categories OBCs, Scheduled Castes, Jharkhandis, Assamese, and Tamils. Sometimes, there are cases of total overlap, so that one category is entirely nested within another. In Belgium, for instance, among the categories mobilized by political parties are native Belgians (vs. immigrants), who constitute 91 percent of the population, and French speakers, who constitute 42 percent of the population, who are largely contained within the native-Belgian category.

Take, next, examples of incompleteness. There is no rule that individuals in a population should all activate their ethnic identities exclusively. Indeed, it is only a few very polarized countries at particular points in time, such as Yugoslavia in 1992, where almost the entire population lines up behind an ethnic identity – but even in such countries, the ethnic identification may not be complete. CDEI shows that 86 percent of the population in Yugoslavia voted for ethnic parties in 1992, leaving a minority of voters who voted for other types of parties. In other countries, we typically see several types of identities activated in practice. In the recent U.S. presidential elections, for instance, some voters activated their class identities (e.g., middle-class), others their party identities (Republican or Democrat), others identities based on age (e.g., retirees) and still others their racial identities (e.g., black).

Given the problems of overlap and incompleteness, it is not clear, how the three datasets produce a count of groups in all countries that is conveniently mutually exclusive and exhaustive. Further, it is not clear what the ELF Index, which requires mutual exclusiveness and exhaustiveness, means.

CDEI addresses these problems by constructing a variable – EVOTE – that does not impose any assumptions about mutual exclusiveness and exhaustiveness. For instance, in the Indian case, the value of EVOTE is .3895. This proportion is unaffected by whether the ethnic parties in question mobilize mutually exclusive or overlapping categories. In India, it so happens that the parties activate overlapping categories. But the value of EVOTE would be the same even if the parties in question activated mutually exclusive categories: we might get the same value of EVOTE if a party mobilizing Hindus obtained 30 percent of the vote and a party mobilizing Muslims obtained 8.95 percent of the vote. Similarly, EVOTE also does not impose the requirement that the categories activated by political parties be complete, because it is the votes won by the parties that mobilize each category that are added, not the proportion of the population made up by the categories themselves. Rather, it allows us to observe such completeness in the data. In countries in which all individuals activate ethnic identities in their voting behavior, the value of EVOTE would be 100 percent. In countries in which only some individuals activate ethnic identities in their voting behavior, the value of EVOTE would be less than 100 percent.

Whether Structure or Practice, What Time Period and Context Do the Data Refer To?

Finally, a key constructivist insight is that both the structure of ethnic identities and the set of politically mobilized identities can change over time and by context. Ideally, this insight suggests that we should collect time-series data on ethnic identities, just as we collect time-series data on regime type, per capita income, and other variables that are dynamic in nature. Cross-sectional datasets should at a minimum explicitly identify the time and context in which they are collected.

But the three previous datasets do not date their sources and locate them in a particular context. This creates a problem in using the data: how can we use them for an analysis of democratic stability in 2000 if we do not know whether the ethnic groups in question were counted in 2000, 1950, or 1900, and we do not know whether this count reflects the groups relevant in electoral politics, or anticolonial mobilization, or violence? The lack of information on the time and context in which the data are collected also makes it difficult to expand any of these datasets – if we do not know which time period and context these data refer to, how can we know which time periods and contexts to add?

CDEI and EVOTE have yet to be expanded over time. But the data are restricted to a single context and to a specific time period – electoral politics at the national level and the legislative election closest to but before 1996. We do not incorporate data on political parties, which do not apply to the election campaign for the election under study. A party might well have been an ethnic party in some previous election, but if we do not find evidence of an explicit ethnic appeal in that particular election campaign, we do not code it as ethnic regardless of its political history. This means that the data can be located at a particular point in time and that we can expand the dataset to include other points in time in a meaningful way.

These criticisms of previous datasets highlight not that these previous datasets are "wrong" but that we do not know whether they are wrong or right. When the counts in the three datasets disagree, as in the case of India, we do not know why and have no criteria by which to determine which dataset to trust. And when they agree, as in the cases of Italy and Germany, we do not know if they are right and what they are right about, given that all three datasets inexplicably exclude the same identities. The ELF indices based on the three datasets are moderately well correlated (Fearon 2003: 214), but we cannot tell whether the correlation is an indication that the data are correct or an indication of systematic bias. At least among the Alesina and Fearon datasets, agreement when it occurs may simply be a consequence of the fact that both rely on some of the same data sources (the *CIA World Factbook* and the *Encyclopedia Britannica*). In comparison, the advantage of CDEI in an analysis of democracy (and in other analyses described in the concluding section) is not that the variables it generates are "correct" or suitable for all purposes. CDEI has both bias and measurement error, which I discuss in the conclusion. But the coding criteria are sufficiently transparent for other researchers to make judgments about what these biases and errors might be and how to compensate for them.

USING THESE DATA TO INVESTIGATE THE RELATIONSHIP
BETWEEN ETHNIC PARTIES AND DEMOCRATIC STABILITY

My purpose in building and expanding CDEI is to test competing propositions on the relationship between the rise of ethnic parties and democratic stability. According to a classic proposition in empirical democratic theory, ethnically divided societies invariably give rise to ethnic political parties, and ethnic political parties destabilize a democratic system (Horowitz 1985; Rabushka and Shepsle 1972). The logic of this proposition goes as follows: (1) the rise of even a single ethnic party infects the rest of the party system; (2) ethnic political parties engage in outbidding behavior, with each side seeking to exclude the supporters of the other from electoral competition; and (3) sooner or later democracy is subverted, either because the winning party tampers with the rules of free and fair competition or because the losing side engages in preemptive violence to prevent exclusion. This proposition has gained wide currency, not only among democratic theorists but also among governing elites in multiethnic democracies, who try hard to prevent the emergence of such parties, sometimes by outlawing them altogether.

Multiethnic democracies are also believed to be under threat for reasons not explicitly linked to political party behavior: they do not possess the minimal sense of political community necessary for democracy to function (Mill [1861] 1991); the demands made by ethnic groups are more intractable than demands made by nonethnic groups (Rustow 1970; Horowitz 1985); and multiethnic democracies are more likely to produce incipient nations than societies divided on class lines (Geertz 1973a). Although these additional propositions all suggest that the emergence of ethnic parties is not *necessary* to destabilize democracy in multiethnic societies, they imply that ethnic parties are *sufficient* to destabilize democracy, because an ethnic party system should surely activate one or more of these mechanisms by activating ethnic differences.

But other work, including my own, suggests a different hypothesis about the effect of ethnic parties. On the basis of a study of the anomalous behavior of ethnic parties in India, I argue that political systems that encourage the proliferation of ethnic parties can safeguard democratic stability by making it more profitable for losing political entrepreneurs to play within the rules of the game and manufacture new electoral majorities than to subvert the system through violence (Chandra 2005a, 2004a).[2] A new manuscript by Johanna Birnir

[2] Chandra 2004a also argues that successful ethnic parties are not invariably produced by ethnic divisions but result from a conjunction of demographic, electoral, and organizational variables. I use CDEI data to test this hypothesis in other research (Chandra et al. 2005). Here, I am concerned principally with the effect rather than the origin of ethnic parties.

(2004) makes the argument that institutionalized access – a concept that includes representation in political parties – reduces the tendency of ethnic groups to engage in conflict. Earlier work by Arend Lijphart (1977) implies that ethnic parties that enjoy the support of their followers can play a benign role in democratic politics by negotiating and guaranteeing consociational bargains. These works all suggest a positive correlation between successful ethnic parties and democratic stability, although each isolates a different mechanism explaining this correlation.

Neither hypothesis has been subjected to empirical tests for the reason that we have not yet had cross-national data on ethnic political parties. The studies that we do have test for the relationship between "ethnic diversity," measured using the ELF Index, constructed on the basis of cross-national data on ethnic groups. In principle, these data could have served as a partial test of the hypotheses outlined previously, by establishing at least whether there is a negative relationship between ethnic diversity and democratic breakdown. But these data, and the ELF Index, are unreliable for reasons that I detail at some length in the subsequent section. Partly because of the poor quality of these data, studies of the relationship between ethnic diversity and democratic stability are inconclusive. In the principal work on the determinants of democratic consolidation, Przeworski et al. (2000: 125) find that ethnic diversity destabilizes all types of regimes, democracies, or dictatorships. However, they note that, given the quality of the data, they are not confident of these results, and note that these results are not robust to model specifications. Studies of the onset of civil war, a subject related to democratic destabilization, are similarly inconclusive. They find that different measures of ethnic diversity are negatively related, positively related, and not significantly related to the probability of civil war onset (Collier n.d.; Collier and Hoeffler 2001; Fearon and Laitin 2003; Sambanis 2001).

I expect to test the two hypotheses outlined here by replicating the test for democratic consolidation conducted by Przeworski et al. (2000: 124, table 2.17), with some important modifications in both model specification and data. Using a time-series cross-sectional dataset with annual observations on 141 countries, Przeworski et al. used a dynamic probit model to estimate the effect of the level of economic development on democratic stability, controlling for ethnic diversity, culture, political history, and the influence of the international environment. The variables they used to measure the effect of ethnic diversity are ELF or RELDIF (religious fractionalization, calculated on the basis of the proportion of Catholics, Protestants, and Muslims in a country's population). Once the time-series version of CDEI is complete, I expect to replicate their analysis by replacing the ELF and RELDIF variable with

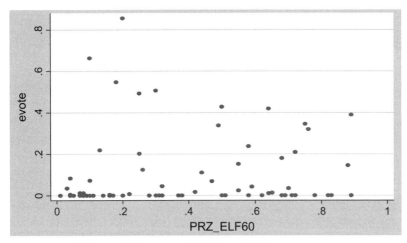

FIGURE 9.2. Relationship between EVOTE and ELF

EVOTE (and also to experiment with supplementing or replacing EVOTE with the several CDEI variables measuring the strength of political parties that mobilize ethnic identities implicitly). At least on the basis of the cross-sectional data collected so far, there appears to be no significant relationship between EVOTE and the ELF measure used by Przeworski et al. The correlation between EVOTE and ELF is only .07 (the correlation between EVOTE and ELF based on the Fearon (2003) and Alesina et al. (2003) datasets described in the preceding section is similarly weak).[3] The relationship between the two measures is summarized in Figure 9.2.

Apart from replacing the ELF Index with EVOTE, I expect to modify the analysis in two other ways: by introducing variables on institutional structure drawn from existing datasets (Golder 2005; Rodden 2004; Rodden and Wibbels 2002; Keefer 2002) – these include variables on electoral rules, district magnitudes, federal systems, and presidential and parliamentary regimes, which I expect to consider separately, and in combination, in a four-point scale of "consociationalism" (Chandra 2005b) – and by employing several different specifications of the dependent variable, using at least the following sources of data: the Polity IV scale of democracy, the Fearon-Laitin data on the onset of civil war, and the Banks and MAR data on civil violence. These two modifications are important to do, respectively, because we have a theoretical literature that indicates that the effect of ethnic divisions and ethnic parties on democratic stability may be mediated to some extent by institutional designs

[3] The correlation between EVOTE and ELF squared is even weaker: .04.

and because we can see if the results are robust across different specifications of the dependent variable.

Once the correlation between the rise of ethnic parties and democratic stability has been established, I expect to conduct further tests for the mechanism explaining this correlation, using the time-series data on EVOTE and other variables to examine whether ethnic parties "infect" a party system (this can be investigated by seeing whether ethnic parties at any one point in time are positively correlated with the vote for ethnic parties at a later point), whether particular types of ethnic identity (e.g., religion) are more likely to be associated with democratic breakdown than others (this can be tested by considering the effect of the politicization of individual identity types on democratic stability), whether exclusion from participation in government for ethnic parties is especially destabilizing (this can be tested by coding a new variable for the number of times an ethnic party has been included in government), and so on.

USING THE DATA TO ASK OTHER SOCIAL SCIENCE QUESTIONS

Although my own interest in constructing EVOTE and CDEI is to investigate the relationship between the rise of ethnic parties and democratic stability, these data are of value to social scientists interested in exploring the effect of the politicization of ethnic identities, at least as measured through the party system, on a wide range of outcomes. Other social scientists can use the data in three ways: to take one or more of the forty-eight off-the-shelf variables contained in CDEI for use in their own analyses, combining them with data already collected from other sources; to modify and recode one or more of these forty-eight variables for their own use; and to use the archive of materials that informs CDEI to generate additional variables. In each case, the dataset can be organized by country or party or group.

One important question that can be answered using the off-the-shelf variables in CDEI includes, What is the effect of the explicit politicization of ethnic divisions (measured using EVOTE) or the politicization of ethnic divisions generally (measured by combining the vote share for parties that engage in the implicit or explicit mobilization of ethnic identity) on some outcome of interest, including war, riots, economic growth, public policy, welfare spending, and so on? There is already a voluminous body of work in political science and economics that examines the effect of the ELF Index on these outcomes. But, as I argued earlier, we do not know what ELF measures. Replacing ELF with EVOTE in this body of work would be a meaningful test of whether one specific concept – the degree to which ethnic identities are explicitly politicized in the party system at a particular point in time – matters in explaining any of these outcomes, while leaving open the possibility that "ethnicity" might matter in ways not captured by EVOTE.

Other questions that can be immediately answered using CDEI data include the following: Is the politicization of particular types of ethnic divisions (e.g., region or religion or language or tribe) associated with particular types of outcomes? This would entail using the percentage of votes won by regional or religious or linguistic or tribal parties across countries as measures of the political salience of these particular types of divisions across countries. What determines the size of the coalition that an ethnic party is likely to mobilize? This would entail using the party as the unit of analysis and taking the proportion of the ethnic party's target category as the dependent variable. Are we more likely to see the ethnification of politics in new democracies? This would entail treating EVOTE (or one of its substitutes) as the dependent variable and using the age of the democracy (measured in the Przeworski dataset) or the presence of founding elections (measured by CDEI) as an independent variable. Is there a link between colonial history and the degree of ethnic politicization? This would entail regressing EVOTE (or its substitutes) on the range of variables on colonial history being collected by Wilkinson (2008) and others. In these cases, the researcher simply needs to combine CDEI variables with other variables already collected in other datasets.

Questions that can be addressed through a minor modification of existing variables include the following: How rapidly do politically activated ethnic identities change over time and what explains such change? This would entail constructing a "volatility" index comparing changes in mobilized identities across election periods. When might political parties activate complex categories rather than simple ones? This would entail constructing a variable measuring the degree of complexity in an ethnic coalition. Do ethnic parties mobilize minimum winning coalitions? This would entail creating a new variable subtracting the size of the coalition that a party mobilized from the winning threshold imposed by an electoral system. Is there a link between ethnic "majoritarianism" and conflict? This would entail coding a dummy variable based on whether the size of the ethnic group mobilized by a political party was a majority or minority. These variables could be constructed by using the recode commands in Stata or another statistical package.

Finally, the archives supporting the dataset can also serve as the basis for constructing "spin-off" variables, which allow researchers to ask a broader range of questions. The archives can be used, for instance, to produce a more fine-tuned classification of parties, based on the particular issues they emphasize, rather than the blunt typology of ethnic, multiethnic, and nonethnic parties that CDEI has used so far. Rachel Gisselquist, one of the graduate students working on the data, for instance, has created a new variable on economic parties using our source materials. This is an important variable that disaggregates the residual category of "nonethnic" party according to the issues and groups that nonethnic parties activate. Gisselquist uses this variable, combined with the dataset as a whole, in a dissertation that asks, Under what conditions do economic rather than ethnic cleavages become salient? Another student, who wrote a paper investigating the theories linking economic inequality and democratic transitions and consolidation, has explored the possibility of using the source materials on election campaigns to operationalize and test one of the basic assumptions of these theories – that elections are about the redistribution of economic resources. She developed a coding protocol for coding redistributive versus nonredistributive election campaigns that can be used to test theories of the relationship between economic inequality and democratic breakdown (Acemoglu and Robinson 2005; Boix 2003). CDEI could also be used to test predictions about whether the nature of political rhetoric (e.g., promising public rather than private goods) has an effect on the nature of political governance. These data may be more useful for this purpose than existing party data on party programs, which rely on the written manifestos of political parties rather than an analysis of their actual rhetoric. These variables can be constructed fairly efficiently, because construction requires only that the researcher can use the archives that support CDEI rather than having to construct them from scratch.

CONCLUSION: OTHER ROUTES TO "CONSTRUCTIVIST" DATA COLLECTION

Although EVOTE and other variables generated by CDEI can be put to broad use, CDEI is not the only way in which a constructivist approach to ethnic identity might be employed in data collection. As I have tried to emphasize in this chapter, it is a very specific route, focused on the behavior of political parties in a cross-national perspective, which produces several very precisely defined variables that measure some aspect of ethnicity. But progress in the field of ethnic politics depends upon diversified attempts by several scholars to collect data on these and other variables.

Several other datasets informed by a constructivist perspective collect data on variables located elsewhere on the conceptual tree breaking down the many concepts related to "ethnicity." Posner (2004) and Scarritt and Mozaffar (1999) have independently compiled data on politically significant ethnic categories in Africa. The Scarritt and Mozaffar dataset is unique among cross-national datasets in coding categories at multiple levels. The MAR (Minorities at Risk Dataset), initially time-insensitive, now updates its data periodically, tracking changes in the composition of ethnic groups included in the dataset. Wittenberg (2004) uses Gary King's Ecological Inference (EI) method to track voting patterns among ethnic groups in Eastern Europe. EI is especially useful from a constructivist perspective because it allows the researcher to impose different ethnic categories on a population and to investigate which category predicts voter behavior rather than imposing ethnic categories on the analysis ex ante. Taeku Lee (2008) is exploring variation in the self-identification of voters in the United States using an innovative survey design that allows voters to distribute "identity points" across a range of ethnic identity categories. Steven Wilkinson (2008) is opening up avenues for collecting constructivist inspired data on the activation of identities in noninstitutionalized contexts, by constructing a time-series dataset on all instances of noninstitutionalized collective action in postcolonial India, including riots, strikes, and demonstrations and coding each event according to all the identities that are relevant to describing it. Each of these datasets measures some distinct aspect of ethnicity in some context not included in CDEI. Further, while CDEI is cross-national in its coverage, each of these datasets, with the exception of MAR, is focused on a single country (United States, India) or region (Eastern Europe, Africa). Studies based on data in CDEI would be complemented and deepened by further analyses based on these data. In particular, the data on voting patterns in individual countries should allow us to test the implications of the patterns of party behavior revealed through CDEI.

Constructivist approaches to data collection are currently in their infancy and can only improve and increase over time. Ultimately, we will know when we have made progress when the all-purpose concepts, variables, and datasets that currently dominate the field have been replaced by several narrow concepts, variables, and datasets that compete with and complement each other.

IV

DISCOURSE ANALYSIS AND ETHNOGRAPHY

10

Identity Relations and the Sino-Soviet Split

Ted Hopf

Theory should determine method. How one theorizes about some outcome should drive which methods one chooses to assess the relative validity of competing claims about that outcome. In this chapter, how I theorize identity drives my methodological choice of discourse analysis. Had I chosen some variable other than identity, say objective military power, or had I chosen to theorize identity differently, say as the subjective perceptions of decision makers, then the method chosen would have been different. Because I theorize identity as an intersubjective social structure, the method I choose must somehow recover this intersubjective reality as experienced by its subjects. Intersubjectivity is the reality generated within a community, society, or group, of shared understandings of the world out there. It cannot be reduced to either objective reality – that is, the reality that is out there independent of our perceptions of it, or subjective reality, the reality each one of us perceives as individuals. If it were the latter, then one need only look into the heads of individual decision makers to find out what they believed. If it were the former, one need only catalog the objective indicators presumed to be causal for any particular theory.

In what follows, I present a constructivist theory of identity that is at once social, structural, and cognitive. I explore three logics of social order – consequentialism, appropriateness, and habit – and relate them to the theory of identity I apply to the study of a state's foreign policy choices. I then elaborate the methodology in relationship to the theory as presented, and the case of the Sino-Soviet split, and assess the empirical validity of a constructivist

The author would like to acknowledge the very useful comments of the editors of this volume, two anonymous reviewers, as well as Jason Lyall, Ulrich Krotz, Jacques Hymans, Srdjan Vucetic, Henry Brady, Roger Petersen, Cynthia Kaplan, Amanda Metskas, and Keith Darden.

account for the Sino-Soviet move from amity to enmity. I conclude with some thoughts about the possibility of a fruitful marriage between an interpretivist epistemology and ontology and positivist methods.

THE SOCIAL CONSTRUCTION OF IDENTITY AND THE LOGIC OF HABIT

The constructivist account of identity I develop here is social, cognitive, and structural. It assumes that identities are products of social interaction, are cognitively necessary to make one's way in the world, and are embedded in social structures of everyday life. The latter point foregrounds the logic of habit, or the way in which people rely upon taken-for-granted knowledge to go on in the world.

Identities are relational.[1] At the individual level, this implies one cannot understand oneself as male absent a comparison to female, homosexual without heterosexual, black without white, and so on. For a state, this means a Soviet understanding of itself as European cannot happen without some non-European Others against which to define itself.

Identities operate cognitively, helping to ensure a predictable social environment.[2] Given cognitive limitations on our information-processing capacities, it is hard to imagine going on in the world if one had to treat each interaction as sui generis, rather than responding in one of a limited number of ways to situations we understand to be similar to a type of situation we have previously encountered and placed in a categorical scheme. Already in infancy, humans formulate categories to go on in the world.[3] The human need to understand and to be understood, combined with limited cognitive resources, results in identities emerging as shortcuts to bounding probable ideas, reactions, and practices toward categorized others.[4] These are the human needs for "ontological security," or the certainty that you and others are meaningfully the same from one day, or year, to the next (J. Turner 1988: 51, 164; Giddens 1991: 35–63).

Identities are social products of interactions with others. What it means to be female is not concocted by an individual mind out of the material available at

---

[1] This is conventional wisdom among constructivists and rests on decades of research in experimental social psychology (Neumann 1996; M. Barnett 2002). Rationalist accounts of states assume fixed identities and preferences, independent of context and interaction with particular other states. In so doing, they are challenging an extraordinarily robust collection of empirical findings in making one of their foundational assumptions.

[2] Institutions are frequently ascribed the same effects: uncertainty reduction (North 1990: 6; Powell and DiMaggio 1991: 13–27). The relationship between institutions and identity is ripe for future multidisciplinary theorization and research.

[3] For a review of this literature, see Barr, Dowden, and Hayne 1996: 79–120.

[4] For an early account of the cognitive role of "typifications," see Schutz 1973a: 237.

birth. Instead, a female identity is constructed not only by the obvious means of parental and familial instruction, or primary socialization, as Berger and Luckmann put it some forty years ago, but thereafter, through the mundane social practices that constitute everyday life (Berger and Luckmann 1966).

How do mundane taken-for-granted daily practices re/produce identity? When a white woman walking down the street shifts her handbag away from an oncoming pair of African American men, she is both agent and object. She is an agent in two ways. First, she has chosen to move her purse. But second, she has inadvertently reproduced a particular discourse on racial identity: African American men are potential dangers. Meanwhile, she is an object to the extent that her actions are partly the product of the predominant discourse on race in America. Her almost automatic response to approaching black men is not only her choice but also the output of a social structure that writes her as white and, so, a potential target.[5]

Identities are social structures that both enable and discourage particular understandings of the external world.[6] Social structures of identity operate in three interrelated ways. First, they punish deviation from and reward adherence to the prevailing intersubjective understanding of a social identity. For example, a young boy called out to play by his pals is likely to grab the bulldozer rather than the Barbie on the way out the door, having made a quick cost-benefit calculation. Second, these structures also tell the young boy how he should act, if he wants to maintain his masculine identity in front of his peers: structures have normative bite. Finally, the prevailing discourses of gender identity may ensure that the young boy just grabs his bulldozer without thinking. His masculine identity is so deeply internalized that he neither consciously chooses between rewards and punishments nor thinks about what he should do. Instead, he just does. Any other choice would be nearly unimaginable and unthinkable. These three logics, of consequences, appropriateness, and habit, are discussed in more detail later in the chapter.

These elements add up to a social theory of identity because one's identity is relevant only in relationship to other individuals and groups, and is re/produced only in interaction with them. It is a cognitive theory of identity because the presocial need for identity is psychological, arising from the insuperable obstacles posed by our limited information-processing capacities as humans. It is a structural theory of identity because the identities an individual has are not meaningfully enacted by the individual on her own, but rather their effectiveness, utility, availability, and – still more – possibility are enabled and discouraged by the prevailing social identities of the community in which the individual lives.

---

[5] On the connection between identity and discourse, see Hall 1996.
[6] Jeffrey Alexander calls this approach "structural hermeneutics" (Alexander and Smith 2003).

Social constructivism is a theory of social order.[7] How do we explain the remarkable everyday predictability of an average individual's conduct in society while at the same time granting that this individual possesses the agency to disrupt that order any time she wishes? This does not mean that constructivism cannot also account for change, but rather points out the fact that its origins and evolution over the past century have been concerned with explaining why more change has not occurred than one might feasibly expect given the brute material world and stark inequities. Three answers to this question have been offered over the past 150 years of social theory: cost-benefit calculation, norms, and habit. These yield three logics: consequentialism, appropriateness, and habit.[8]

Both Weber and Durkheim foreshadowed these three logics in their work on social order and concluded that habits, custom, and tradition account for the preponderance of behavior most of the time (M. Weber 1968: 24–43, 212–216, and 319–325; Durkheim 1982: 51–55).[9] Habits predominate, in part, because they are the behavioral manifestations of the cognitive need for simplification.[10] Habit, custom, and tradition, neither conscious cost-benefit calculations nor considerations of oughts and shoulds, enforce social order most of the time. As Raymond Williams put it, "if our social and political and cultural ideas and assumptions and habits were merely the result of specific manipulation, a kind of overt training . . . then society would be very much easier to move and to change than in practice it has ever been or is."[11] Pierre

---

[7] For a contrary view, see Adler 2002: 95–10. It is the researcher's own normative choice, whether to concentrate on "what makes the world hang together," as Ruggie (1998b) put it, or, instead, to use that information to discern how to pull it apart. What we must keep in mind, however, is that constructivism itself points in neither direction to the exclusion of the other. To claim that it is a theory only of social change justifies those critics, like John Mearsheimer, who assert that constructivsts are biased toward seeing a world characterized by change, rather than constancy (Mearsheimer 1994–1995: 37–47). As Robert Cox (1981: 135), a critical theorist of international relations of note, observed, "A proper study of human affairs should be able to reveal *both* [my emphasis] the coherence of minds and institutions characteristic of different ages and the process whereby one such coherent pattern succeeds another."

[8] For the introduction of the logics of consequences and appropriateness into international relations theory, see March and Olsen 1998: 951–954. For a critical discussion of the logic of appropriateness, see Sending 2002 and Hurd 1999: 380–381.

[9] Douglass North (1990: 22) suggests the percentage of nonreflective actions in a day is 90 percent.

[10] On habit's utility as a cognitive economizing mechanism, see Simon 1947: 88. For earlier intuitions along these lines, see also Dewey 1957: 57–59; James 1981: 125–126; Tuomela 2002: 58; S. Turner 2002: 1–12. Habit, or "automaticity," has also been demonstrated experimentally by neurocognitive psychologists (Bargh and Chartrand 1999). Neuropsychology demonstrates that people really do "act before they think."

[11] Williams quoted in Higgins 2001: 168.

Bourdieu (1990: 54) has observed that habits "tend to guarantee the 'correctness' of practices, and their consistency over time, more reliably than all formal rules and explicit norms" (emphasis added).

William James (1981: 126) put it bluntly 100 years ago: "There is no more miserable human being than one in whom nothing is habitual but indecision, and for whom the lighting of every cigar, the drinking of every cup, the time of rising and going to bed every day, and the beginning of every bit of work, are subjects of express volitional deliberation."

Foregrounding the third logic implies theorizing domestic sources of identity in a particular way. What we want to empirically recover from any state's identity relations with its society is the collection of identities that are experienced habitually in mass society. These everyday naturalizing practices have been a major focus of many of the most important social and political theorists for the past century and a half, each of whom has elaborated the idea of a collective social structure that constrains and enables individual choices. Beyond Durkheim's collective conscience, we have Ludwig Wittgenstein's form of life, Alfred Schutz's lifeworld, Pierre Bourdieu's habitus, Clifford Geertz's web of meaning, Walter Benjamin's imaginary, Michel Foucault's discursive formation, Peter Berger and Thomas Luckmann's symbolic universe, John Searle's Background, Antonio Gramsci's common sense, and Jean Baudrillard's simulacrum.[12]

What each of these has in common is the insight that intersubjective social reality is a primary cause of observable regular patterns of social conduct and that mundane daily practices are a most powerful reproducer of those patterns.[13] We want to find the natural, unquestioned, mundane daily practices that constitute everyday life and commonsense lived reality, what March and Olsen (1995: 30) refer to as "the sets of shared meanings and practices that come to be taken as given."[14]

Schutz (1973a: 14) claimed that "everyday language is the typifying medium par excellence. . . . It can be interpreted as a treasure house of ready made preconstituted types and characters, all socially derived." We want to gain

---

[12] Durkheim 1982: 1–13, 97–124; M. Weber 1968: 24–26, 29–38, 40–43, 212–216, 319–325; Wittgenstein 1958; Schutz 1973a: 116–132; Bourdieu 1990; Geertz 1973b: chap. 1; Benjamin 1969; Foucault 1971; Berger and Luckmann 1966; Searle 1995; Gramsci 1971; and Baudrillard 1994.

[13] George Steinmetz (1999: 2) also sees fit to group these scholars together. See Cederman and Daase's inclusion of Georg Simmel's theorization of "sociation" in this group (Cederman and Daase 2003: 11–18; Guzzini 2000: 164–169).

[14] My conceptualization is consonant with Lisa Wedeen's (2002) "semiotic practices." Kratochwil (2000: 88) suggests the need to bring in what he calls the "hidden faces of power" theorized by Foucault and Bourdieu, among others. For experimental work that differentiates the "taken for granted" from the instrumental, see Zucker 1991.

access to this "treasure house" through an ethnography or anthropology of the everyday, a collection of overheard conversations, the assortment of identities that predominates when individuals are not thinking in particular about identities at all. "This is the real point of social and cultural analysis of any developed kind: to attend to the manifest ideas and activities, but also to the positions and ideas that are implicit, or even taken for granted."[15] The societal constructivist hypothesis is that these everyday discourses of identity will obtain as well among elites making foreign policy choices for their states, to the extent that these leaders have been socialized by the prevailing social structure with its collection of taken-for-granted knowledge about the world.[16] These discourses are the "societies in tow" that Wendt alluded to as a necessary component of any constructivist account of identity and world politics. When a Soviet leader looks at China, he will read China through the identity terrain prevailing in the Soviet Union at that time.

The deepest stability a social structure can attain is when no questions of disruption arise, not when ideas of disrupting it are periodically entertained, but then rejected after calculating relative costs and benefits, or after deciding one had better not. If order in the world really works as I suggest, and how the many scholars cited previously have theorized the problem of social order, that is, according to logics of unthinkability and unimaginability, relationships are far more stable, institutions are far more durable, and enmities and amities are far more long-lived.[17] Certainty, not uncertainty, predominates, even under anarchy.[18] And this certainty is about both one's friends and one's enemies.[19]

DISCOURSE ANALYSIS: A NOVEL APPROACH TO THE TAKEN FOR GRANTED

The best method for investigating the naturalized daily practices of identity construction in the Soviet Union in the 1950s and 1960s would probably

---

[15] Williams quoted in Higgins 2001: 231.

[16] Societal constructivism is distinguished from systemic constructivism that assumes the identities of states are constructed by interaction among them, and norm-centric constructivism, which concentrates on how a state's identity affects its readiness or unwillingness to adopt some norm of conduct.

[17] On the power of unimaginability, see Reus-Smit 1997: 569–570). Hedley Bull (1977: 46) wrote of the social order secured by habit or inertia. Deutsch (1954: 40) wrote of the "habits of compliance." Tannenwald (1999: 460) describes the nuclear taboo as making nuclear use "unthinkable." On discursive intelligibility and the land-mine ban, see Price 1998: 628–629. On discursive im/possibilities and imaginability, see Doty 1993: 297–320; Weldes 1999: 16; M. Barnett 2002: 61–65; Hurd 1999: 387; and Kier 1997: 26–27.

[18] For a contrary view, see Copeland 2000.

[19] This is why scholarly attention to the security dilemma, and its resolution, is most probably a lot higher than its actual existence in international politics (Hopf 1998).

have been an ethnographic study of that society at the time. Therefore, the method used here, textual analysis of discourse of the time, is a second best technique.[20] If we are looking for the unintentional taken-for-granted common sense of a society, then we should not be looking at texts on identity but rather at a wide variety of texts that are about everything but identity.[21] Given that we are interested in the identities that are revealed and expressed unintentionally and unreflectively, using texts or articles written about identity per se would not be an appropriate source of evidence, that is, consistent with the theory as specified.[22] What we want to do is find out which identities predominate numerically across a number of genres of texts. Then we wish to contextualize those identities, that is, assess what they mean in the texts in which they are found. The next step is intertextualization, a term in discourse analysis that means the recovery of the meaning of an identity across the genres. The final step is to synthesize these intertextualized identities into discourses of the actor in question, in this case, the Soviet Union itself.

Sampling Texts

To find the prevailing discourses of identity in a society, we first have to select a sample of texts in which to look. This means developing a list of texts sufficiently numerous and diverse so as to approximate a representative sample of the discourses of identity in any society, a collection of texts that are most read by the mass public. This cannot be done absent basic knowledge or research about the society in question. Best sellers, textbooks, newspapers of record, weekly and monthly magazines, and professional journals are certainly a good place to start. But if one's society instead has oral traditions of storytelling, watches traveling madrigals, or has abandoned reading for watching television, then relying on the materials listed previously would be mistaken. Circulation, ticket, subscription, book sales, viewership, and listenership figures should be gathered. Relevant sources about the daily information consumption habits of one's population should be read.

---

[20] For an interpretivist analysis of texts in lieu of ethnography, see Kier 1997: 30–31. For an ethnographic recovery of identity combined with other more indirect methods, see Laitin 1998.

[21] Texts here refer to media more generally: newspapers, journals, television shows, poetry, theater performances, and popular music.

[22] Of course, as a way of validating one's own interpretation of texts, it would be very useful, if rare, to find other scholars' work on the discourses of identity in the society of interest, recovered ethnographically, or through a discourse analysis of a variety of texts, especially if those texts were sampling genres different from one's own sample, in my case, for example, poetry or popular songs.

Quantity must be matched by diversity. This means sampling across genres. Novels and high school textbooks, academic journals and mass-circulation newspapers, poetry and pulp fiction, opera and folk music are all examples of possible genres. The more of these one is able to sample the better. In this particular instance, texts published or circulating in 1955 were oversampled, and subsequent years were sampled in order to see if the original predominant discourse of Soviet identity and its primary challengers remained consistent, or changed, over the decade until 1966. Particular attention was paid to the archives of the Central Committee's Culture, Ideology, and Propaganda Departments, because these keepers of the predominant orthodox Soviet identity responded directly and often to all emergent counterhegemonic discourses. The complete list of texts appears in the Appendix.

But why novels read by the mass public, rather than private memoranda of the relevant state decision makers, or, perhaps, the very books that leader has read herself?[23] There are several reasons. I have specified an intersubjective theory of identity, not a subjective one; a structural, not an individualistic one; a social, not a personal one. The theory expects these identities to operate independently of whoever occupies the position of head of state. If, instead, we find that individual decision-making schema determine outcomes, rather than the prevailing discourses of identity, then the theory I have offered is disconfirmed.[24] Despite the theory's more onerous evidentiary demands, it promises to be more parsimonious than a subjectivist theory. Instead of finding a particular belief to account for every perception of some other state, we generate a predominant discourse of state identity that accounts for many relationships.

Instead of developing an account that hinges on a particular leader with autocratic powers in foreign policy choices, we expect that the social structure will imply a limited menu of identity relationships regardless of how autocratic or pluralist the political system. Finally, a subjectivist account explains outcomes only so long as the particular leader is in office, a very inefficient theory for states with robust democratic turnover, many coalition governments, or serial coup making. The social structural theory offered here, however, predicts continuity in identity relations across governments. In this particular case, for example, Khrushchev's removal in 1964 is predicted

---

[23] I use the word novel here to refer to many other forms of popular mass culture, say prime-time television shows, rock and roll and folk songs, jokes, etc.

[24] If we find that the decision maker's understanding of the world is instead constructed within a different intersubjective community, say the foreign ministry or an elite school, then societal constructivism's hypothesis is also disconfirmed. This issue comes up again in the discussion of norm-centric constructivism in the next section.

not to change identity relations with China, Soviet interests in China, or actual policy toward China, expectations borne out by the empirical evidence presented later in this chapter.

Two additional methodological advantages accrue from the intersubjectivist approach. The first is that we, in principle, generate many more falsifiable implications for the theory than we would if it were a decision-making approach concentrating on the belief system or cognitive heuristics of an individual decision maker. This is so because the predominant discourse of identity implies identity relations with more than a single other state, and so all these can be empirically evaluated as well. Moreover, these identity relations extend to within the state, to ethnic or religious minorities, for instance. Falsifiable predictions may be made about these identity relations, as well.

Another methodological advantage is the distance between the independent and dependent variables afforded by a social structural theory. Averting tautology demands keeping the independent variable, in this case, Soviet identity, separate from understandings of other states, or policies toward those states, the dependent variables (Zehfuss 2001: 326–327). We wish to "avoid describing the explanatory variable [discourses of Soviet identity] on the basis of the outcome [understandings of China]" (Kier 1997: 34). We accomplish this by finding Soviet identities in a sample of texts that are then not used to generate the value of the dependent variable, or understandings of China.[25]

The theory determines the method. The sample of texts must be many and variegated because the theory's implications cannot be operationalized or assessed without such a sample.

Finding the Taken for Granted

One way to find what is taken for granted in society is to take advantage of the sampling strategy. By casting one's net broadly, one is likely to find counter-hegemonic discourses, versions of Soviet identity that are contrary to the predominant one advanced by the state. In these alternative versions of the Soviet self, we will find challenges to what the predominant discourse takes for granted, treats as given, or assumes by default as normal. These contrary visions of what it means to be Soviet are the imaginable identities available to Soviet decision makers once the death of Stalin permits greater agency for society in determining what becomes the official predominant discourse propagated by the state.

---

[25] This violates a strict definition of both an intersubjectivist ontology and an interpretivist epistemology, but is necessary for analytical purposes.

We also can use yet another advantage afforded by mass popular texts, such as novels. "The novelist offers to show people and their relationships in essentially knowable and communicable ways."[26] Therefore, authors deliberately select words the average reader will immediately recognize as communicating enough information about the character. These are rich sources for predominant discourses of identity. Because "the aspects of things that are most important for us are hidden because of their simplicity and familiarity," they are not manifestly observable (Wittgenstein 1958: 50). Novelists make those things that are hidden from us obvious for a living. Anthony Giddens (1984: 285), in making methodological recommendations for how a social scientist might go about studying the daily practices that constitute going on in the world, should "draw on the same sources of description as novelists or others who write fictional accounts of social life."

Novelists, because of their desire to be understood, are unintentional ethnographers for the societies about which they write. Much of a novel is spent setting the scene, describing the background, limning the essential features of each character, and, very importantly, dwelling on deviations from normal everyday life. The small, peripheral, bit roles may be especially revealing, as the author often uses only a sentence or two to describe who they are.

Otherwise, the author would need to spend a great deal of space explaining idiosyncratic aspects of the character. If this occurs, then the novelist is telling us what is not commonplace in the society, what is not part of the predominant discourse, perhaps. Novelists describe these mundane realities as a matter of course in their texts. For example, if a novelist spends a page or two explaining why John cooks for his wife when she comes home from work, elaborating about how exceptional John is, or how exceptional his wife is for working at such a demanding job or not expecting to cook when she gets home, this is a discourse on a particular kind of gender identity that reflects a particular intersubjective reality that prevails in this society. Here the novelist relates what is "normal" by highlighting a deviation from it. But another way of relating the same information is to remark in a single sentence or two, as if in passing, that Mary came home from work and cooked dinner for John. The author, through her relative silence, tells the reader what is the norm in that society.

Finding Identities

Phenomenology and induction are two fundamental implications of an interpretivist epistemology that privileges intersubjective reality. Together, they

---

[26] R. Williams 1970 quoted in Higgins 2001: 123.

demand that the subjects' points of view are the reality of interest and that the empirical recovery of these views should be as unalloyed by prior theorization as possible. While pure induction is a fantasy, there is a continuum of intrusiveness. Testing of a priori theorizations of identities is one extreme violation. For example, one could oppose national identity to communist identity and then survey a sample of texts to see which was most prevalent in Soviet discourse. This simply imposes one's own precategorizations onto the Soviet case. Moreover, it increases the probability that the researcher will miss identities that do matter. Another method that applies the researcher's categories is survey research. Even a long list of identities with which the respondent can express her relative agreement and disagreement still forces respondents to use the prearranged list of the researcher.[27]

Open-ended survey questions would be an improvement, but are mostly eschewed by mainstream social scientists, as they produce too many noncomparable responses, reducing the usable "n" to levels beneath which statistical techniques can be reliably applied. Better still would be the use of focus groups with semistructured conversations on themes designed to evoke unintentional discussions of identity. As I have already acknowledged, discourse analysis is only a second-best method to a genuine contemporaneous ethnography, but even the latter still suffers from the unavoidable interaction effects of observer and subject.[28]

The fundamental question in finding identities is to figure out who is the "we" in the texts and who are the "others" with or against whom we identify. In the case at hand, I am interested in the Soviet "we." I am trying to figure out as well who its significant others might be. The first step is to simply enumerate the identities one finds in texts. But almost simultaneously, these "raw" identities must be contextualized.

Contextualizing Identities

The contextualization of an identity involves discerning what that identity means within the context in which it was found, in this case in the text of origin. The initial stages of this process entail a seemingly verbatim transcription of the first text with which we choose to start. This is so because it is impossible, at this stage of research, to know whether an identity one has found

---

[27] As I remarked in note 22, this does not mean one should not use others' work on identity as a means of assessing one's own findings, keeping in mind the methodological implications of abandoning an interepretivist recovery of subjects' own intersubjectivity, for one's own a priori theoretical expectations.

[28] On that insuperable problem, see Clifford and Marcus 1986.

is one that will appear in other texts, or whether it is idiosyncratic to this particular text. This means that a 200-page novel may produce 100 pages of notes.

Each subsequent text, however, yields fewer and fewer notes, as the researcher comes to see what the predominant discourses of identity are across the genres. It is critical, however, to remain as open to new identities as possible, avoiding premature evidentiary closure. One is under constant pressure to render anomalies as outliers or to jam them into emergent theoretical categorizations. As Bourdieu (1990: 10–11) confessed, it is "hard to accept and really take into account in my analysis the objective ambiguity of a whole set of symbols and practices [and] to classify them as unclassifiable." One's sampling strategy, then, assumes extraordinary importance. If one has sampled too narrowly, spurious patterns of predominance may emerge. It is best, therefore, not to analyze a collection of texts from a single genre but rather to make a list of genres and sample across them.

At the end of the inductive recovery of this list of contextualized identities, one must evaluate which ones predominate. This exercise is mostly quantitative. As in most such cases, it is easy to grade the two extremes. Those with vanishingly small numbers are dropped; those with impressively high numbers are included. What to do with the intermediate category involves cutting with remorse, but without forgetting that these identities still existed, if only below the bar.

Intertextualizing Identities

Intertextualization is the process of rendering the contextualized identities meaningful across genres.[29] One wants to find out whether a particular identity, say Russian Orthodoxy, means the same thing across novels, textbooks, military newspapers, writers' congress proceedings, and other categories. If so, then this is a very powerful finding of intertextual consensus for this particular identity. If not, it is just as important a finding of difference in meaning across genres. The question then arises as to whether the different meanings of Russian Orthodoxy are systematically distributed across different genres of texts. Perhaps, for example, Orthodoxy is understood as antithetical to a true Soviet identity in *Pravda* but neutrally treated as background reality in popular novels. This finding signals the possible emergence of a predominant discourse and a competitor.

---

[29] On intertextualization, see Greenblatt 1990; Ashley 1989: 280–284; and its productive application in Etkind 2001: 416–471. On ethnographic and interpretivist approaches, more generally, see Geertz 1973b; Clifford and Marcus 1986; and Rabinow and Sullivan 1987.

Intertextualization may merely reinforce one's prior understanding of what the contextualized identities meant or, instead, may provide alternative under-standings of the nominally same identity. If one begins to relate identities across texts, it may occur that the contextualized identities become reinterpreted in light of the broader findings across genres. For example, one might have contextual-ized Orthodoxy in the novels as a neutral aside indicating background, which already is a far cry from *Pravda*'s rendering of Orthodoxy as a most undesirable Other for the Soviet self. But, upon reading the speeches of the writers at the Congress, it turns out that, far from being neutral, unremarked asides are under-stood more broadly as a positive evaluation of the church, and therefore there is no incompatibility between being Soviet and being a believer. In this instance, then, one must revise one's original interpretation of the merely contextualized nominal identity of Orthodoxy found in the novels, because, in the broader audience, these findings are not meaningless background noise at all.

From Intertextualization to Discourses of Identity

The move from intertextualized identities to discourses of identity is the most theory-laden step in the process of discourse analysis. It is one thing to enumerate contextualized identities and another to fashion them into an intertextualized, intersubjective social structure of identities. But it is still far more ambitious, and intrusive, to then assert that these collections of identities "hang together" in particular discourses, that is, to specify how the intertexutalized identities might relate to each other in creating a coherent account of the identity of interest – in this case, Soviet identity. I think about this process as a kind of qualitative factor analysis. For our purposes, a discourse of identity is a collection of intertextual-ized identities that consistently appears when the Soviet self is construed and which consistently excludes another collection of other identities. If we go back to the Orthodoxy example, a discourse should consistently include Orthodoxy as antithetical to Soviet identity, while simultaneously consistently having a number of other identities as necessary, say supranational, modern, or class-conscious.

In most cases, we will find a predominant discourse and at least one com-petitor. Establishing the relative predominance of a discourse is based on both quantity and variety. A discourse predominates to the extent that, numerically speaking with regard to competing discourses; it dwarfs its competitors in appearance in texts. But this is only necessary, but not sufficient, to count as dominance. The latter requires that this numerical preponderance be consistent across the range of genres of texts as well (Doty 1993: 305–306).[30] The

---

[30] A good example of scoring for discursive predominance is R. Hall 2003: 74–75.

counterhegemonic discourse is understood by the researcher necessarily in relationship to the predominant one, such that the challenger exists to the extent that it comprises a collection of intertextualized identities that counter those constituting the predominant view of the self.

Case Selection

While the Sino-Soviet split may not qualify as a crucial case for societal constructivism, it certainly is difficult. It is not easy because the Soviet Union at the time was hardly a democratic place, and therefore we should not expect that mass understandings of Soviet identity would have a significant effect on elite constructions of Soviet identity. Moreover, in the Soviet case, in particular, there is a regime committed to the ideological cultivation of its population. On the other hand, we might expect that elite understandings of identity, in such an authoritarian environment, would be systematically and comprehensively distributed among the mass public. This implies that if we find discourses of the Soviet self that are contrary to the predominant one authorized by the state and party, there is reason to speak about different, even competing, social constructions of identity, and so about the validity of applying societal constructivism to even this, seemingly hard, case.

If we find that social constructions of Soviet identity that are recovered in mass texts are evident in Soviet elite deliberations on foreign policy, then we surely should expect societal constructivism to account for more pluralist state-society relations in the rest of the world. It is also hard because of the serious strategic interests at stake. This is not a case of some trivial foreign policy choice. It is the single greatest shift in the balance of power during the Cold War. If neorealist claims that states balance against objective power are ever to operate, one might expect it to have occurred in this case.

Finally, while the interpretivist recovery of intersubjective reality through the analysis of texts may be necessary to collect evidence of what identity is, and what it means, in a given social context, it need not preclude other methodological approaches to its analysis. There is no reason why this kind of data cannot be analyzed from any number of other methodological perspectives: statistical, experimental, or agent-based modeling.[31] For example, it might be fruitful to specify focus group protocols or mass survey questionnaires based on the

---

[31] Wedeen (2002: 725–726) suggests the creation of interpretivist databases on crucial social and political identities, such as nation, ethnicity, religion, gender, and race, that then can be inventively accessed by statisticians and modelers. For examples of computerized simulation models, large-n surveys, and experiments applied to the constructivist problematique, see Cederman 1997; Rousseau 2006.

evidence gleaned from discourse analysis. This could be another test for both the reliability of the interpretation of the texts and the validity of the relationship between discourse and relations with other states. But noninterpretivist methods are most appropriate to the analysis of evidence that already has been collected through interpretivist, hermeneutic, ethnographic, or discourse analytic means.

EXPLAINING THE SINO-SOVIET SPLIT

How did China go from being a Soviet ally to a Soviet enemy? How did China become a threat worth balancing against? Prevailing theories of international politics treat this question as central and offer different answers. Neorealists argue that any great power must be treated as a potential threat. Systemic constructivists expect threat levels from great powers to range from acute to manageable to nonexistent, depending on which culture of anarchy – Hobbesian, Lockean, Kantian – predominates in a given epoch. Liberals expect democratic great powers to be threatened only by nondemocratic great powers.

None of these three theoretical approaches can account for the shift from amity to enmity, arguably the greatest shift in the global balance of power from 1949 to 1989. As a systemic theory that predicts only tendencies toward global balancing in a bipolar world, neorealism's predictions are indeterminate. Both abandoning China and maintaining an alliance with China are equally consistent with neorealism's claim that allies are desirable but not necessary.[32] Systemic constructivism also does not claim to be able to explain relations between any two states. So, the systemic Lockean culture of anarchy, which Wendt argues has prevailed from the seventeenth to the twenty-first century, like neorealism, can entertain both Sino-Soviet amity and enmity.[33] Finally, liberal theory, at least as read through the democratic peace, might imply the ultimate falling out among authoritarian allies but would not be able to explain why they were allies in the first place.[34]

Balance-of-threat theory provides a partial answer to the question and does so by abandoning neorealism's systemic and objectivist hard core (Hemmer and Katzenstein 2002: 586).[35] Instead of assuming that states balance against aggregations of objective power, they balance against power they perceive as subjectively threatening (Walt 1987). So, that is why the United States does not have targeting plans against the 400 or so British strategic nuclear warheads

---

[32] For neorealist claims, see Waltz 1979.
[33] For structural constructivism's claims, see Wendt 1999.
[34] For an overview of the findings of the democratic peace theory, see Rousseau 2006.
[35] The father of neorealism himself, Kenneth Waltz (1997: 916), wrote Steven Walt out of the neorealist church for this apostasy.

but does against a mere handful of inaccurate Chinese missiles. Walt's objective variables of offensive advantage, proximate military danger, and geographical proximity cannot explain this discrepancy, so he sensibly suggests that it is the subjective appreciation of threat that accounts for the unexplained variance. Walt is right that it is threat perception that matters but does not himself theorize threat (Katzenstein 1996: 27–28).

In the Sino-Soviet case, the objective variables of geography, offense-defense balance, and proximate military threat remained unchanged across time and so cannot explain a reversal of the dependent variable – from ally to enemy. Moreover, another objective variable – namely, the relative power of the common threat, the United States – points in precisely the wrong direction. As relative U.S. military power increased, as it did in the period, the USSR and China should have been more, not less, likely to ally together against the rising threat. Some indicators of the strategic balance moving against the Soviet Union in the period were West Germany's rearmament and membership in NATO in the mid-1950s, and the growing nuclear missile gap in favor of the United States, culminating in Khrushchev's decision to place his own intermediate range nuclear missiles on Cuba to address this imbalance in 1962. Still more, proximate U.S. military power, especially in Vietnam but also in East Asia more generally, grew appreciably. Therefore, it must be subjective threat perception that is doing all the theoretical lifting in this case. We need a theory that accounts for this. Social constructivism is such a theory, but its systemic variant cannot, and does not, claim to explain the identity relations between any two states.

Since Wendt's articulation of a systemic constructivist alternative to Waltz's structural realism, constructivist scholarship has roughly divided into two streams. Systemic constructivism has developed theoretical accounts of international politics at the global level of intersubjective structure (Wendt 1999; Reus-Smit 1997; Frederking 2003). A second body of scholarship has concentrated on why states do and do not adhere to particular norms of conduct in international affairs.[36] What is mostly missing from social constructivism, paradoxically enough, is society. This is not to say that constructivists have ignored domestic actors. But on the whole, these actors have been concentrated within the state, the legislature, interest groups, or, at best, in social movements mobilized around the adoption of a particular norm.[37] The public

---

[36] Finnemore 1996; Klotz 1995b; Tannenwald 1999; Price 1998; Keck and Sikkink 1998; Risse, Ropp, and Sikkink 1999; and Checkel 2001.

[37] Weldes (1999: 275–318) and the executive branch during the Cuban missile crisis; Kier (1997) and British and French military organizations; Tannenwald (1999) and foreign and military policy elites in postwar United States; Keck and Sikkink (1998) and human rights groups; Finnemore (1996) and state officials; Risse-Kappen (1995) and foreign policy elites.

at large, on the other hand, has been mostly ignored.[38] If constructivists assume that a state's identity is constructed in interaction with other states, then surely they must assume that its identity is formed in relationship with its own population as well. A social constructivist account of interstate relations should bring society back in.

John Ruggie (1998b), summarizing what constructivism has heretofore accomplished, pointed out that its practitioners are not "beginning with the actual social construction of meanings and significance from the ground up," but rather try to establish the existence of a particular collective social fact and its impact on behavior. Following Ruggie's advice, we would have to bring society back into constructivist accounts of international politics. At best, norm-centric constructivists describe the politics surrounding the contestation of a norm, politics being construed as the struggle among branches of government, bureaucracies, and interest groups, but without delving into the social construction of the meanings of the discursive instruments being used in these struggles.[39] I argue that "the social construction of meanings and significance from the ground up," as Ruggie put it, must begin with society writ large, not with decision-making political and social elites. By paying attention only to the politically engaged, social constructivism mistakenly truncates its own social ontology.

Societal constructivism concentrates on the domestic identity relationships between a state and its society and how these stand with regard to other states in the world. The Sino-Soviet split, in this view, was not caused by any changes in the material balance of power in the world, or by a change in how Moscow and Beijing acted toward each other, but instead was caused by changes in how the Soviet Union and China understood themselves and, therefore, each other. This does not mean, however, that societal constructivism is simply a "second-image," or domestic, version of social constructivism. There, after all, can be no identity relationship between the Soviet Union and China without interstate interaction. But the substantive content of these identities is impossible to specify a priori. For that, the discourses of identity that predominate in society must be investigated.

Systemic constructivism has focused exclusively on other states as significant others. Societal constructivism expects there to be domestic others as well. As a patently nonexhaustive list of domestic identities that might matter for the

---

[38] For notable exceptions, see Berger 1998; R. Hall 1999; and Katzenstein 1996.

[39] This is also where Milner (1997) and Moravcsik (1997) stop, perhaps indicating a common boundary for meaningful politics shared by liberals and norm-centric constructivists. This shared account of politics, in part at least, inspires Jennifer Sterling-Folker (2000) to lump the two research programs together. Some who are concerned with strategic culture also are constructivists at the elite or bureaucratic level, with no explicit concern with social discourse more deeply or international norms more systemically. For example, Kier 1996; Johnston 1995.

state, we might expect race, nation, ethnicity, religion, gender, region, class, wealth, tribe, and the like. Because of constructivism's partial origins in social psychology and sociology, significant others are mostly assumed to be other people, groups, or anthropomorphized agents, like states. But we must remain open to the fact that we also define ourselves in relationship to ideas, ideologies, theories, histories, and ideals.[40] One must resist a priori specification of the significant others of states in world politics. They have to be empirically recovered, not assumed.[41] As Milliken (1999: 247) warns, "one must forego a priori conceptualization in favor of studying how others have constituted their meanings."

Societal constructivism moves beyond the instrumentalist idea of societal identity as merely a political constraint for governing elites – that is, a source of costs if challenged or violated, and electoral or selectoral rewards if supported or unleashed (Price 1998: 631). Finnemore and Sikkink (1998: 903, n. 41), for example, consider domestic politics important because a government's desire for legitimacy at home might cause the choice of a particular international norm, thus implying that the domestic has no constitutive effect, "other than in relation to collective systemic interests" (see also Sterling-Folker 2000: 109; Zehfuss 2001: 316, 332–338). This move elides society as an agent in the construction of a state's identity, except in the very limited realm of normative appropriateness. What we need to recover is the constitutive aspect of any significant social identity – that is, the role it plays in constituting the available, imaginable, thinkable understandings of the self, in relationship to significant others. In this way domestic identities perform social cognitive functions – that is, they help delimit the representations and understandings available to elites. Of course, if elites do challenge these constraints, the punishments and rewards specified by the instrumentalists might ensue, but the variable that actually accounts for how the elite's actions will be apprehended – the prevailing social structure of societal identity – will have been omitted.

---

[40] Zehfuss (2001: 327–328), for example, writes about contemporary German identity being constructed in relationship to its very significant historical Other, Nazi Germany. Perhaps a potentially more generalizable way of putting this is done by assuming that social groups have narratives that are stories about their origins, defining events, and the future (M. Barnett 2002: 66).

[41] For example, Michael Barnett (2002: 63) finds four "constitutive strands" of Israeli identity: religion, nationalism, the Holocaust, and liberalism. It would be hard to imagine any general theory of identity from which one could deduce this particular list. See also Maloney 2002, where she finds three domestic identities of interest in Iran: antiimperialist, political Islamist, and Persian-historical nationalist. Ashish Nandy (1983) explains British imperial rule in India as a product of domestic Victorian conceptions of sex and age, such that a mature masculine Britain understands itself in relationship with a feminine childlike India, of course in need of paternal tutelage.

The conceptualization of discourses of identity as competitors in some rational-deliberative Habermasian debate, or public sphere, is not wrong (Risse 2000). But it continues to ignore the third logic of social order, the logic of habit. As Habermas himself put it, "communicative daily practice is embedded in a sea of cultural taking for grantedness, i.e., of consensual certainties."[42] It is in this ocean of naturalized normality that identities are produced and reproduced most of the time.

Societal constructivism fills the void between systemic and norm-centric constructivisms. It is more precise and determinant than systemic constructivism, able to furnish understandings of nontrivial foreign policy and strategic decisions by states. It is also more generalizable, and more generalizing, than norm-centric constructivism. By establishing what a state's identity is within a particular bounded context, it implies the kind of identity relations we can expect that state to have with a bounded collection of others across some medium range of time. This task cannot be accomplished if one limits one's constructivist account to a particular norm or to a particular institution within a state.

Other scholars have used a constructivist approach to link the identity of states to foreign policy and international relations.[43] Jutta Weldes (1999: 9) makes the boundaries of this task clear:

> Meanings . . . for states are necessarily the meanings . . . for . . . individuals who act in the name of the state . . . . And these . . . officials do not approach international politics with a blank slate onto which meanings are written as a result of interactions among states. . . . Their appreciation of the world, of international politics, and of the place of their states within the international system, is necessarily rooted in collective meanings already produced, at least in part, in domestic political and cultural contexts.

She goes on to suggest that pop culture, common sense, and quotidian practices as sites for the production of identity need more research (Weldes 1999: 242). Social constructivists should find out what is on that slate which decision makers are bringing with them in their interaction with external "Others." Just as Wendt explores the issue of systemic "cognitive structures," we need to pay as much attention to their domestic instantiations, if we wish to develop a constructivism able to account for the vast range of international politics that lies between systemic culture and norms.[44]

---

[42] Habermas 1995: 553 quoted in Risse 2000: 17. On the role of habit in the construction of identity, see Giddens 1991: 39–43.

[43] Katzenstein 1996; Reus-Smit 1997; Berger 1998; Ruggie 1997; Hall 1999; Nau 2002; Nandy 1983; and Neumann 1999.

[44] On cognitive structures, see Kratochwil 2000: 83.

But why should what society thinks of itself matter for how a decision maker regards another state? The first answer is that the decision maker herself has been socialized within that community. If we are to recover the logic of habit that predominates in a society, we need to see what taken-for-granted ways of understanding themselves are available in that society. In the Soviet case, for example, key elements of the predominant discourse that emerged after Stalin's death under Khrushchev – a modern Soviet Union atop and at the core of a premodern non-Russian periphery and a toleration for deviations from an idealized New Soviet Man – were already widely and deeply distributed in societal discourses under Stalin.[45] How do we know this? Not only did these alternative discourses appear in popular novels, but also the Stalinist state apparatus identified these challengers and tried to suppress them. The fact that they emerged in official discourse only after Stalin's death, of course, reveals the importance of agency as embodied in Khrushchev. But the fact that the contents were what they were underlines the importance of uncovering the discursive challengers in the first place. This is especially evident after Khrushchev's removal in 1964. If only agency mattered, then we should expect Brezhnev to choose some new Soviet identity, and that identity should lead to changes in relations with China. In fact, this is precisely what Chinese leaders expected to happen. Instead, the predominant discourse of difference persisted, not coincidentally in the absence of any Stalinist societal challenger.

Second, and related to the issue of continuity across leaders, a decision maker may not be socialized, as perhaps is the limiting case of Stalin and other autocrats, but one should start with the structuralist account for reasons of theoretical parsimony, as one might have an understanding of outcomes that travels across regimes, bureaucracies, and decision makers.

Third, it could very well be the case that on particular issues, say nuclear strategy, the intersubjective world of a particular bureaucracy, say the defense ministry, matters more than societal self-understandings. Or, alternatively, a transnational identity matters more than either society or institutions or decision makers, such as in the eighteenth-century European community of dynastic diplomacy. But I am dealing with a far broader question than military strategy or relations of enmity or amity between states, and if alternative identities matter for the outcome, they will appear in the empirical research.

What matters from the perspective of international relations theory is the fact that these identity differences antedated by years any objective material change in the balance of power or in relations between the two countries. The case discussed in the next section provides prima facie evidence in favor of a

---

[45] I elaborate on these elements in the next section.

societal constructivist approach to world politics and against any objectivist account of the Sino-Soviet split.

IDENTITY RELATIONS AND THE SINO-SOVIET SPLIT

What follows is an illustration of societal constructivism's potential to account for the Sino-Soviet split.[46] The short story is that Chinese-Soviet identity relations changed as a result of a post-Stalinist change of Soviet identity accompanied by a continued, and even deeper, Stalinization, if you will, of Chinese identity. The gap between these two identities became a chasm by 1958. Changes in Soviet interests in, and policies toward, China ensued.[47]

From 1945 to 1953, there was a predominant discourse with elements of societal discourse embedded in it. With the removal of Stalin in 1953, many previously repressed elements of societal discourse were empowered by the state. This is not to claim that society as an actor imposed these elements on the state or, contrariwise, that the state created the new predominant discourse independent of society. What the state chooses is already somewhat predetermined by what is already taken for granted by society. One might, for example, invoke John Steinbruner's cybernetic model of decision making here, where he argues that people satisfice from a finite menu of possibilities, rather than optimizing against a "rational" list of possibilities. It is that menu I take as being the socially taken-for-granted background I am trying to foreground here.

Uncovering what is repressed from 1945 to 1953 gives us clues as to what may become predominant from 1953 onward, and indeed what becomes predominant in 1985–1991 is partly predictable, on the basis of what was present in society but not propagated by the state, from 1956 to 1985, and what appears under Yeltsin was being constructed under Gorbachev. And what the present Russian state advances as the official discourse of Russian identity, and its societal challengers, gives us some purchase on future identity relations after Putin.

For Sino-Soviet relations from 1945 to 1953, the predominant Stalinist discourse was compatible with Mao's Stalinizing discourse for China; aspects of Soviet identity repressed under Stalin were precisely the elements that drove a wedge between their identities under Khrushchev. In that way, societal

---

[46] For an in-depth treatment of Soviet identity relations and foreign policy in 1955, see Hopf 2002.

[47] Constructivism's focus on interests is consistent with any conventional international relations theory that claims states maximize interests. This is considered to be trivially true, which is why constructivism problematizes what matters more: the social construction of these interests in the first place.

discourse in the Soviet Union was an underlying reason for the Sino-Soviet split that emerged in 1959–1960.

Critically, after 1964, the split continued and deepened, despite some people's (including Mao's) expectations that the split was just Khrushchev's personal agency. This shows the importance of locating a discourse of official identity beyond the leader or state itself. Identity differences continued until the 1980s, when Deng's renunciation of Mao combined with Gorbachev's empowerment of previously repressed discourses of Soviet identity as a normal social democratic European great power, instead of the vanguard of socialism, made normalization of relations possible.

The evidence presented in the chapter is largely of elites, because elites are the instruments through which the dependent variable of identity relations manifests itself. State-to-state identity relations are the outcome that societal discourses of identity are trying to explain. This is the connection between a novel that is penetrated by a discourse of difference about what it means to be Soviet and the outcome of Khrushchev or Suslov declaring Mao to be Stalin reborn. In the novel, one finds the habitual ways in which typical Soviets understand themselves. In private elite exchanges about relations with China, one finds out whether, and how much, these taken-for-granted logics manifest themselves in Soviet understandings of China.

What is critical here is the process tracing that goes on between the identities appearing in novels and the words to describe China that appear in Khrushchev's comments during Politburo meetings in the Kremlin. If an element of Soviet identity previously repressed under Stalin subsequently ends up in Khrushchev's understanding of China, then it demonstrates the value of having paid attention to societal constructions of Soviet identity in the first place.

But this does not mean we should necessarily be looking for societal understandings of China per se. I want to capture discourses of Soviet identity, which may or may not refer to China explicitly, and so create a broader collection of expectations for a wider array of states in the world. Second, as a matter of empirical reality, China is rarely if ever mentioned in mass texts, unless they are officially produced, as in textbooks or articles in the party press. Third, and related, once one includes the latter texts, one risks tautology, in that there is very little distance between a *Pravda* editorial and state-to-state identity relations, because both may be the product of the very same person, let alone institution. In order to demonstrate the constitutive power of social texts, one must find texts that are not about the dependent variable of interest, if one can. (And it is not always possible; for example, separating societal discourse from the United States or the West in the period is virtually impossible; both play large constitutive roles at both state and societal levels.)

In sum, societal discourses of identity are likely repositories of the taken-for-granted background knowledge I am hypothesizing informs most decisions most of the time. Sampling popular texts is one way of getting at these identities, and archival research on how decision makers understood another state is one way to assess whether these taken-for-granted habits of mind have found their way into the identity relations between states.

Soviet Identity

The identities in Table 10.1 are derived from the texts listed in the Appendix. The table divides these identities according to the elements about which the official and societal discourses disagree (conflictual elements) and the elements they have in common (reinforcing elements) The official discourse of the NSM was predicated on the danger of the slightest deviation from the idealized model of socialism, the danger of the bourgeois overthrow of the revolution itself. In this sense, the discourse of danger, as one might fairly characterize it, is filled with insecurity, a conviction that real conflict with dangerous reactionary forces is always possible at home and that consequently a paternalistic attitude toward the average naive Soviet common person must be maintained. The danger of difference manifested itself in a veneration of clear-cut us-them, black-white dichotomies, with no room for grays or ambiguities. This discourse of danger left little room for meaningless or innocuous private life; instead, all actions were deemed politically consequential and hence public.

Meanwhile, in novels, plays, and films of the period appeared identities that were in conflict with this predominant model, identities whose presence in texts often led to the suppression of these texts, if not the repression of their authors. Most importantly, societal discourses understood the Soviet project as secure, not in danger; after all, it had just proved itself in the most harrowing of circumstances against Hitler's Germany. The Soviet people had demonstrated its maturity, its commitment to a socialist future; it could therefore enjoy a more expansive notion of a private life and could be reliably Soviet without having to conform to the ideals of the New Soviet Man. Ambiguities, gray areas, and abstractions were all both natural and innocuous, given how secure socialism was in the country. This was a discourse of difference, not danger, a discourse that identified tolerated differences as evidence of Soviet power, not vulnerability.

The official and societal discourses of Soviet identity were not only in conflict; they also shared many common elements. To summarize, from the list of reinforcing elements in Table 10.1, they shared an understanding of the Soviet Union as a modern, developed vanguard for the world, Russia as the center and

TABLE 10.1. *Official and Societal Discourses of Soviet Identity, 1945–1953*

A. Conflictual Elements: Official/New Soviet Man vs. Societal
    Optimistic vs. realistic
    Infallible vs. fallible
    Conflict vs. contradictions
    Clarity vs. ambiguity
    Literalism vs. abstraction
    Dichotomies vs. continua
    Public vs. private
    Collective vs. individual
    Unique vs. normal/common
    Insecure vs. secure
    Danger vs. difference
    Paternalism vs. maturity

B. Reinforcing Elements
  1. Modernity
    Modern vs. premodern
    Center vs. periphery
    Russian vs. non-Russian
    Moscow vs. non-Moscow
    Russia vs. Central Asian/North
    Vanguard vs. mass
    Developed vs. underdeveloped
  2. The Russian Nation
    Taken-for-granted Soviet nation
    Atop the hierarchy
    Modern
    Vanguard
    Elder brother
    Non-Russian significant others
    Postbourgeois nation
    Identified with Russian Orthodoxy

apex of the Soviet Union with premodern developing peripheries subordinate to it. They also shared a taken-for-granted attitude toward Russia as the implicit nation leading the Soviet Union, an elder brother for other, non-Russian peoples, a vanguard for the premodern Central Asian and "northern" peoples, a nation farther on the road to socialism than the rest.

Until Stalin's death in March 1953, the NSM was the single predominant Soviet identity (Spechler 1982). Stalin's death buried the NSM and ushered in the Thaw. While many elements of the ideal Soviet Self remained intact, the discourse of danger was replaced by a discourse of difference. The possibility of a "private" self appeared, an individual personality unconnected to the public performance of being Soviet. The recognition of the possibility of irrelevant and innocuous difference entailed as well the acknowledgment of fallibility, of the possibility that errors might be made by even good Soviets. Tolerance for both mistakes and difference spoke of a new level of security and confidence felt by the post-Stalin generation of political elites in Moscow.

The Soviet Union remained the apex and the center of the world communist community, and the teleological end point for all modern humanity. Within the Soviet Union, Russia was the vanguard for all other republics and peoples, with Central Asians deemed the most peripheral and needful of a vanguard in Russia and Moscow. The Russian nation was the surrogate nation for a putatively supranational Soviet man (Hopf 2002: 39–82; Zubkova 1998: 169–172; Condee 2000; English 2000: 85).

The foreign policy consequences of the Thaw in Hungary and Poland in 1956 reverberated through the Soviet identity terrain at home. While the boundaries of allowable difference never advanced beyond the point achieved in 1956, they never were seriously reduced either. At a May 1957 Kremlin meeting, Khrushchev warned members of the intelligentsia that if they ever tried to create a "Petofi circle" of reformist intellectuals like they had in Budapest the year before, we "will grind you into dust."[48] Khrushchev's fulminations were characteristic of the rest of his rule: support for pushing the boundaries of difference with periodic eruptions of vitriol against what he deemed transgressive. Khrushchev charged Pasternak and others with a lack of patriotism after he was awarded the Nobel Prize for Literature in October 1958. But in May 1960 Khrushchev approved the publication, in *Pravda* no less, of an anti-Stalinist poem by Andrei Tvardovsky. Two years later, Khrushchev was railing at the Manezh exhibit of contemporary Soviet art about "all this shit" they were producing. But almost simultaneously he was approving, along with the Politburo, which met twice over the manuscript, the publication of Aleksandr Solzhenitsyn's path-breaking anti-Stalinist novel, *One Day in the Life of Ivan Denisovich* (Taubman 2003: 384–388, 527–528, and 594–602).

The removal of Khrushchev from power in October 1964 did not narrow the boundaries of permissible difference. The fact that Soviet identity did not change with Khrushchev's removal underlines the advantages of a societal constructivist approach over its more subjectivist decision-making competitors. Social structure outlives leadership change, even in a most authoritarian

---

[48] "Plenum, TsK KPSS, Iiun 1957. Stenograficheskii Otchet," *Istoricheskii Arkhiv* 3 (1993), 73.

society – where one would most expect different autocrats to be, well, different.[49] Indeed, Mikhail Suslov, in reading the bill of particulars before the Central Committee, praised "Khrushchev's positive role in unmasking the cult of personality of Stalin" and agreed with the ouster of Molotov in 1957.[50] Demonstrating the continuity of Soviet identity and its main competitor, a 1979 KGB report on avant-garde artists could have been written in 1955: "They produce individualistic works . . . based strictly on personal perceptions" (Andrew and Mitrokhin 1999: 330).

Soviet-Chinese Identity Relations

The relatively normal allied relations between Stalin's Soviet Union and Mao's China from 1949 to 1953 are consistent with the predominant discourse of the New Soviet Man. Stalinist fear of difference did not extend to China because the Stalinist hierarchy of center and periphery, modernity and premodernity, were projected onto China. China was the Soviet Union's oldest little brother, a revolutionary comrade-in-arms who aspired to become just like its elder and better. In the summer of 1949, Stalin met six times in Moscow with Liu Shaoqui, one of Mao's closest colleagues. At one meeting, Liu presented a six-hour report on China's political realities in which China was repeatedly described as on the road to becoming the Soviet Union. On Stalin's personal copy are a dozen "Da!"s written in Stalin's hand after passages that acknowledge China's subordinate position.[51] During these meetings an international division of revolutionary labor emerged. Stalin delegated to China leadership of the anticolonial movements of Asia, while reserving for Moscow overall leadership of the world communist movement, including Eastern Europe, and the working classes of modern North America and Western Europe. China would be the surrogate vanguard for revolutions in places like Vietnam and Indonesia, while the Soviet Union would be China's vanguard. Mao agreed to this hierarchy in his December 1949 meeting with Stalin in Moscow (Goncharov, Lewis, and Xue 1993: 46–74; Chen 2001: 50, 120; Gaiduk 2003: 2).

---

[49] It is interesting to point out that Soviet elites and U.S. intelligence analysts expected a change in Sino-Soviet relations after Khrushchev's ouster. If only they paid more attention to social cognitive structures! In addition, Soviet expectations highlight the fact that those within a social structure are often least capable of perceiving it. This is why Paul Ricoeur (1984: 129–130) suggests the method of a "hermeneutics of suspicion."

[50] "Plenum, TsK KPSS, Oktyabr 1964. Stenograficheskii Otchet," *Istoricheskii Arkhiv* 1 (1993), 7–9. See also Arbatov 1992: 134; English 2000: 108.

[51] Jun in Westad 1998: 305. The original is in Arkhiv Prezidenta Rossiiskoi Federatsii, fond 45, opus 1, delo 328.

At the dawn of the Thaw, China was the other state in world politics that came closest to being the Soviet Union. China's size, revolutionary and anti-imperialist history, devotion to Marxism-Leninism, and appeal to other revolutionary movements around the world gave China features that resonated with Soviet identity. But the closest "Other" is often the most threatening identity for oneself (Norton 1988: 11–49; Berger and Luckmann 1966). This is so because, as differences are erased and distance is closed, expectations for similarity grow. Difference that once could be ignored as trivial would now be a challenge to one's claims of authenticity if left uncorrected. As Soviets came to see China as a great power building socialism, just as they were, the questions about the identity boundaries between them became increasingly problematic. Differences that could easily be countenanced, as they were in East European countries, or, even more so, in Yugoslavia, could be tolerated only at much higher cost. The more China was the Soviet Union, the less China could deviate from the Soviet model. This tension was alleviated by the Soviet understanding of China as still underdeveloped, akin to Soviet Central Asia. To the extent that Soviets understood China as premodern, its deviations were attributed to its less developed status in the hierarchy. But this was a remedy that forced an uncomfortable trade-off between Chinese equality and Chinese underdevelopment, Chinese progress on the road to socialism and Chinese subordination to its older Soviet brother.

Consistent with being the Soviet Union's Closest Other, Khrushchev referred to the two countries as if they were partly each other. He told Burma's prime minister U Nu that "with friends like China, we have even greater possibilities to become more independent."[52] In other words, mutual dependence, or interdependence, between two socialist powers such as China and the Soviet Union produces independence with respect to the rest of the world. Such a conceptualization of relations between states made possible the seemingly counterintuitive position that dependence is actually the road to independence. Such an achievement is possible only if one understands the self and other as if they are partly each other. Khrushchev, at the July 1955 Central Committee Plenum, referred to China and the Soviet Union as heading the socialist camp together.[53] Moreover, during the relentless attack on Molotov over the latter's "Stalinist" approach to Yugoslavia, Khrushchev interrupted the proceedings to question why Molotov thought the Chinese could not correct the Communist Party of the Soviet Union in matters

---

[52] Tsentr Khranenie Sovremennoi Dokumentatsii (TsKhSD), f. 5, op. 30, d. 116, 230. These are the archives of the Central Committee, CPSU.

[53] CC Plenum, 9 July 1955, morning session, 19. Suslov used the same formulation at the 11 July 1955, evening session, 29.

of Marxism-Leninism. Khrushchev answered his own question before Molotov could reply: "they can."[54]

China was given equal billing as an exemplar for those pursuing "agrarian, anti-feudal, and anti-imperialist revolutions," while Moscow was the vanguard for the industrialized world (Tropkin 1955: 108). Soviet aid to China, including military aid, including the sharing of secrets necessary for the production of atomic and nuclear weapons, was not regarded purely as aid to another state but as aid to oneself.[55] As Khrushchev (1997: 346) later related in his memoirs, the Soviets regarded the strengthening of China as the strengthening of the socialist camp and as "the securing of our eastern borders."[56]

China nonetheless remained simultaneously a premodern periphery in need of a vanguard in Moscow. The Soviet discourse on modernity construed China as a primitive, rural, agricultural periphery in comparison to the industrialized modern Soviet center. In its hierarchy of socialist allies, the most common location for China was between the Soviet Union and Eastern Europe.[57] While China was on the path of "socialist construction," the USSR alone was building communism. Like all socialist states in the world, China was on the road to becoming the Soviet Union.

But in the hierarchy of modernity, China was beneath East Germany. Khrushchev ridiculed Molotov's request to take twenty-five buses with him to the GDR. Molotov responded by pointing out that Khrushchev had brought tractors to China. Khrushchev's response illuminated China's position: "Dear Viacheslav Mikhailovich! China is a destroyed peasant country. We are ambassadors of an industrially developed country. ... In giving these tractors to our Chinese friends . . . they will learn from us. ... But imagine if you take buses with you to Germany. ... After all, we learned how to build buses from the Germans. What will they say?"[58]

---

[54] CC Plenum, 11 July 1955, morning session, 18.

[55] For just a small example of the comprehensiveness of the military cooperation between Soviet agencies and Chinese colleagues, see deputy head, Far Eastern department, Ministry of Foreign Affairs (MFA), Kurdiukov's instructions to Ambassador Iudin pursuant to the council of ministers decisions on these matters in March. Archives of the Ministry of Foreign Affairs of the Russian Federation (AVPRF), f. 100, op. 48, d. 61, 16–18.

[56] I use Khrushchev's memoirs only because they are corroborated by other sources. The MFA archives contained dozens, if not hundreds of Chinese aid requests, including for military equipment, training, and advisers, all handled by the ministry in the most routine and automatic of fashions, implying a most natural relationship of material power flowing out of the Soviet Union and into China. See, in particular, AVPRF, ff. 100, 179, 243, 253, 270, 275, 312, and 313.

[57] While East European allies commonly received telegrams "en bloc," China got a personalized message (TsKhSD, f. 5, op. 30, d. 119, p. 53).

[58] CC Plenum, 12 July 1955: 35.

Chinese were seen as less developed intellectually and technically as well. All progress in agronomy was attributed to Chinese visits to Soviet institutes or the appearance of Soviet lecturers in China (Fedorenko 1955).[59] This resonates with the hierarchy at home between senior Russian brothers to the lesser developed, but beloved, non-Russian republics. This evolutionary understanding of China as on its way to where the Soviet Union already was found a place in an official secret history of Chinese-Soviet relations. The decision to close the joint-stock companies imposed on China by Stalin was explained as "the young China" finally "acquiring the necessary expertise to manage these enterprises."[60]

Consistent with the view that it is interaction that produces identity, China's daily practical behavior toward the Soviet Union reproduced its subordinate status. A typical letter to the Soviet embassy in Beijing from the Chinese foreign ministry would begin: "Taking into account the absence of people capable of operating the Iliushin-14s [we] ordered, the Chinese Civil Aviation Ministry appeals to the Soviet government to send six Iliushin-14 crews."[61] Through the daily identification of itself as the Soviet Union's dependent, China created for Moscow the identity that the Soviet Union was already applying to Beijing. In a conversation with Bulganin and Mikoyan in March 1955, Chinese ambassador Liu Xiao requested that Soviet economic advisers in China should "prompt their Chinese comrades, and not be embarrassed to point out their inadequacies and give advice."[62]

But an Other regarded very much like oneself, as the Soviet Union regarded China, is then expected to manifest very little difference from the model self. As Khrushchev told his colleagues at the July 1955 plenum, pursuing good state-to-state relations with Yugoslavia would be "more difficult, of course, than with bourgeois states like Austria or India whose leaders do not say they are Marxist-Leninists."[63] Because China was much farther along the socialist road than even peoples' democracies in Eastern Europe, let alone Yugoslavia, Khrushchev's sentiment went double for China. Similarity can promote discord, as disputes over authenticity are possible from actors who grant each other legitimate identities. Not similarity, but difference, can promote good relations, as claims about fundamental constitutive principles of each other's

---

[59] For additional expressions of fulsome gratitude to "older Soviet brothers," see Tan-Chiu 1955: 13–14.

[60] The history was drawn up by Fedorenko and Kapitsa. AVPRF, f. 100, op. 48, d. 39, 9.

[61] AVPRF, f. 100, op. 42, d. 5, p. 110. For similar self-situating language, see AVPRF, f. 100, op. 48, d. 1, 3 and 15. I say typical because I saw many dozens such letters, from all different Chinese government and party entities, in the Soviet foreign ministry archives, for just one year alone.

[62] AVPRF, f. 100, op. 48, d. 5, 82 and 83.

[63] CC Plenum, 9 July 1955, morning session: 14.

identities are moot. China was close enough to Soviet understandings of itself that Chinese differences from the ideal were the object of the closest official Soviet attention.

The Soviets saw China's class identity as problematic, given the level of class conflict still under way in China. While antagonistic class relations had been eliminated in the Soviet Union, they persisted in China, positioning China as subordinate. At their March 1955 party conference, Chinese leaders "smashed" the Gao Gang–Rao Shushi bloc. In commenting on this, Soviets noted they themselves had no class contradictions of this magnitude any more.[64] Soviet diplomatic personnel in China sent back a steady stream of reports attesting to the domestic political weakness of China relative to the Soviet Union. In an August 1955 report from the Soviet embassy in Beijing to Moscow, it was reported that Chinese security organs had registered more than one million people suspected of ties with the Kuomintang. Molotov blue-penciled this entire section of the report.[65]

Soviet observers understood Chinese economic reforms as if they were being carried out within the Soviet Union.[66] Chinese political deviations drew upon Soviet understandings of less developed parts of the Soviet self: individualism, conceit, daily moral degradation of communists, aspirations to a bourgeois way of life, selfishness, inadmissible relations with women, and various state crimes.[67] Chinese agricultural reforms were understood through the Soviet experience of the 1930s.[68]

One might expect that the post-Stalinist discourse of difference would have soured relations with a Stalinist China. This prediction is inaccurate but only in timing. While national roads to socialism violated Chinese adherence to a single Stalinist model, and China opposed treating the deviant Tito's Yugoslavia as a socialist country, Soviet admissions of past mistakes compensated for the toleration of deviance. Moreover, Khrushchev's decision to use force in Hungary, sanctioned and urged by the Chinese leadership at the time, reassured Beijing that there were some limits Khrushchev would thankfully not tolerate (Chen 2001: 150–156).

Mao cautiously supported Khrushchev's campaign against Stalin, though not the discourse of difference more generally. As Mao told Soviet ambassador

---

[64] The Chinese report about the conference was published in *Pravda*, 6 April 1955, 3. Soviet Ambassador Iudin's analysis of the conference is in AVPRF, f. 100, op. 48, d. 127, 15.

[65] AVPRF, f. 100, op. 48, d. 128, 91.

[66] AVPRF, f. 100, op. 48, d. 127, 6.

[67] AVPRF, f. 100, op. 48, d. 127, 274. This is from a Soviet embassy officer in Beijing who wrote a forty-two-page report on the internal party work of the CCP for Kuznetsov, Fedorenko, and Kurdiukov. It is dated 9 July 1955.

[68] AVPRF, f. 100, op. 48, d. 127, 398–401.

Iudin in May 1956, if he "had always followed Stalin's advice, he would be dead by now" (Westad 1998: 15). Mao was dissatisfied with the ambiguity created by the ongoing debates in the Soviet Union between difference and orthodoxy. In April 1956 Mao published his own interpretation of the Twentieth Party Congress, crafting the 70:30 rule of thumb about Stalin: he was 70 percent right (about the economic and political development model) and 30 percent wrong (on treatment of China and murder of colleagues) (Chen 2001: 65). Mao fashioned his own Thaw, the Hundred Flowers campaign launched in January 1957. But it was aimed not at expanding the boundaries of difference but at flushing out "rightists" who would then be arrested (Chen 2001: 69).

The struggle over difference and deviation heated up after the unrest in Hungary and Poland in the second half of 1956. The ouster of Molotov in 1957 marked not only the triumph of difference over the NSM at home but also the irreversible turn toward alienation from China. China's Stalinist model helped proponents of difference in Moscow point out what restoration of the NSM would mean for socialism in the Soviet Union. Soviet identity was publicly contested in the discourse of permissible difference in relationship to Chinese dogmatism. The Soviet identity of difference, unchallenged after Molotov's removal, contradicted the Chinese identity of Stalinist orthodoxy. The discourse between China and the Soviet Union after 1957 is almost identical to that between Molotov and Khrushchev the previous four years (Westad 1998: 20). "Each country defined the image of its partner according to whether or not it corresponded to its own ideas about the criteria of socialism" (Kulik 2000: 300; Zubok and Pleshakov 1996: 215). If Hungary fixed the limits of difference in 1956, then China in the 1960s empowered Soviet proponents of difference by giving them an example of orthodox Stalinism against which the Soviet Union was officially struggling (Shakhnazarov 2001: 105–106; Arbatov 1992: 97–101).

Meanwhile, China's identity over this period did not undergo any "Thaw." Even had Chinese identity just remained constant, identity difference would have emerged between the two socialist powers. Only the arrest of the Thaw through Soviet military intervention in Hungary in 1956, an action that China vigorously lobbied for within the counsels of the Presidium in Moscow itself, suspended the opening gap between Soviet and Chinese identities. But China's adoption of a still more Stalinist identity in 1958 with the Great Leap Forward made the gap a chasm and made tolerable difference into dangerous deviance.

Identity Relations and Policy Outcomes

The move from amity to enmity in Soviet-Chinese identity relations is reflected in real policy choices made by Soviet leaders. As China increasingly becomes the Stalinist identity the Soviets have just replaced by a discourse of difference, Soviet decision makers increasingly understand China in these terms and wind down the Soviet alliance relations with Beijing.

Soviet aid in the construction of industrial and defense plants accelerated after Stalin's death. In May 1953 the Soviet Union agreed to an additional 91 enterprises and to the replacement of fighter aircraft and tanks with newer models (Kulik 2000: 95).[69] During Khrushchev's first visit to China in October 1954, Mao asked to acquire nuclear weapons. Khrushchev suggested China concentrate on economic reconstruction, pledging it could rely on the Soviet deterrent, but did offer a civilian nuclear reactor. In March 1955 Moscow agreed to build another 166 industrial enterprises and help China build an atomic reactor and cyclotron. Seventy percent of China's foreign trade in the 1950s was with the Soviet Union (Shu Guang Zhang 2001: 110–166).

In October 1957 the Soviets agreed to give China a model of an atomic bomb. But only three months later, the identity gap became a chasm with Mao's announcement in January 1958 of the Great Leap Forward, a neo-Stalinist modernization program. In March, Mao told his colleagues that the Soviet model was no longer appropriate (Chen 2001: 72–73). In July 1959 Khrushchev declared the Great Leap Forward to be a leftist error. In August the Soviet Union remained neutral on the border clashes between Indian and Chinese forces, the first foreign policy manifestation of identity difference (Taubman 2003: 392; Chen 2001: 79). Remaining neutral was thinkable only given Soviet identity relations with China and India. India was exhibit A of the benefits yielded by the post-Stalinist discourse of tolerated difference. A country once consigned to the imperialists, the Thaw's toleration of difference made India an available alliance partner for the Soviet Union, and so the lack of support for Stalinist China against it in war.

The same month, the Soviet Union informed China that nuclear cooperation was over because it was inconsistent with Soviet efforts to get a comprehensive ban on testing nuclear weapons with the United States (S. Khrushchev 2000: 271; Chen 2001: 78). A month later, after his trip to the United States, Khrushchev traveled to Beijing where Mao accused him of "right opportunism," not coincidentally one of the charges made by Stalin in his purges in the 1930s against Bukharin, Tomsky, and Rykov (Taubman 1996–1997: 245; Taubman 2003: 394; Shu Guang Zhang 2001: 229; Zimianin 1995/1996: 356–359).

[69] I must single out this book for its extraordinary scholarship. Kulik was both a Soviet foreign ministry official in China in the 1940s and 1950s and then a Central Committee International Department worker responsible for China for twenty years thereafter. His book is based on nonpareil access to both Chinese and Soviet archives. It should be translated from Russian immediately.

Suslov, in his report to the December 1959 Central Committee Plenum, wrote that Mao had created a cult of personality, parroting Twentieth Party Congress charges against Stalin (Hershberg 1996–1997: 248–260; Gaiduk 2003: 103).[70] Just as the Stalinist NSM had been rejected at home, China's Stalinist identity was similarly treated as a dogmatic deviation.

In June 1960, at the Romanian party congress, Khrushchev publicly declared Mao to be an "ultra-leftist, ultra-dogmatist, indeed a Left revisionist," echoing the 1957 charges against Molotov (Westad 1998: 25; Taubman 2003: 470). He announced, upon returning to Moscow, the withdrawal of all Soviet advisers from China. Khrushchev reported to a 1960 Central Committee Plenum that "when he talks to Mao, he gets the impression he is listening to Stalin" (Prozumenschikov 1996–1997: 252; Zubok and Pleshakov 1996: 232).

By 1962, economic activity between the two countries had been reduced to 5 percent of 1959's level (Kulik 2000: 357). From September 1963 to July 1964, the Chinese Communist Party published a nine-part open letter in which it developed its case against the Soviet bourgeois deviant (Kulik 2000: 334–335). As Kulik (2000: 298–299) put it, relations between the two were now based "on generally accepted norms, [not] on the principles of socialist internationalism." From 1965 to 1973, the Soviets engaged in a sustained and massive military buildup in the Far East, punctuated by the armed clashes on the Amur River in 1969.

The identity conflict with China affected Soviet policy all over the world. Challenged by China for leadership of revolutions in the decolonizing world, the Soviet Union redoubled its efforts there to counter these charges and establish its credentials as the true socialist vanguard, which had sanguinary consequences for how the rest of the Cold War was to be played out with the United States in the Third World. Criticized for sacrificing the world revolutionary movement on the altar of détente with the United States, Khrushchev was increasingly constrained in making concessions to the West. Moreover, détente with the West increased Soviet interests in supporting national liberation movements in the developing world, to compensate for the softer line with the imperialists on the issues of Germany and nuclear weapons.

The change in identity relations with China implied Soviet interests in proving its vanguard identity in the decolonizing world (Shakhnazarov 1993: 24; Arbatov 1992: 101, 170; Kulik 2000: 336–347, 375; and Westad 1998: 386). At the December 1960 meeting of communist and workers' parties in Moscow, the communist parties from Latin America, Southeast Asia, and India all sided with China against the Soviet position of appreciating difference and of collaborating with bourgeois nationalists in decolonizing countries. The next

[70] For Suslov, see Kulik 2000: 336.

month Khrushchev gave a speech at the Institute of Marxism-Leninism in which he distinguished between just wars of national liberation and local and colonial wars that were both unjust and fraught with the risk of escalation to nuclear war. Soviet reluctance to arm resistance fighters in Algeria and Laos was overcome by the Chinese threat to supplant Moscow as the revolutionary vanguard (Richter 1994: 137–138). In August 1961 Khrushchev approved an unprecedented level of military aid to revolutionary groups in Latin America and Africa (Zubok and Pleshakov 1996: 254). At a 1964 meeting of Latin American communist parties in Havana, Moscow agreed to more military aid for local rebels on the condition that none of it ended up with factions enjoying Chinese support (Anderson 1993: 164; Zubok and Pleshakov 1996: 268–269). An April 1970 KGB memo to the Central Committee International Department advocating a more aggressive Soviet policy in Africa justified doing so by citing competition with China for leadership of revolutionary movements on that continent (Westad 1996–1997: 22, 30, n. 8). Identity relations with China kept Soviet vanguard identity alive throughout the Cold War and pushed Moscow to a series of military interventions there to vindicate that identity.[71]

In sum, the growing identity gap with the Soviet Union's very Closest Other resulted in a transformation of Soviet interests in China and elsewhere in the world. The policy consequences included a withdrawal of Soviet aid in the acquisition of nuclear weapons, lack of support for China in its war with India, a drastic decline in trade and complete cutoff of economic and military aid, and finally, military deployments and armed conflict. Critically, the change in identity relations preceded and foreshadowed all the material, objective indicators of balance of power and threat. Indeed, dare we say it, the changes in identity predicted the changes in interests, policy, and alliance choice.

In closing, let me situate societal constructivism's explanation of the Sino-Soviet split with the best available scholarship. In his classic work, Zagoria (1962) argues, as I do, that material differences and conflicts occurred after ideological conflict. But I argue that these ideological conflicts are rooted in a taken-for-granted social structure and accompanying incompatible identities. For this reason, I predict or assume that the conflict will continue until identity relations change or independent leadership changes. Zagoria, on the other hand (like Mao), expected that a change in Soviet leadership, the retirement of Khrushchev, for example, would allow material interests in balancing against the United States to trump ideological desiderata. In the event, Zagoria was proved wrong, as is, suggesting the greater productivity of looking at deeper societal discourses of identity.

---

[71] On Cuba, see Fursenko and Naftali 1997: 167–168; on Vietnam, see Chen 2001: 231–235 and Gaiduk 2003: 132–133; on Angola, see Kornienko 1994:166–168 and Westad 1996–1997: 21–27; and on Ethiopia, see Abebe 1996–1997: 40–42.

Lorenz Luthi's argument is consistent with my own, namely, that ideas matter more than matter. But he, too, does not delve into the deeper societal roots of identity differences or make any kind of causal claims about the continuity of the conflict after Khrushchev's disappearance from the Kremlin.

Finally, the work most consistent with my own argument is that of Boris Kulik (2000), which unfortunately remains untranslated from Russian. Kulik is a self-avowed "cultural materialist," arguing that the Sino-Soviet split has a material basis: unequal stages of economic development that are accompanied by particular ideological justifications. His explanation for the split is that Soviet and Chinese economic progress is "out of phase" with each other, so Stalinist capital accumulation in China is mismatched with Soviet consumer goods production, and so forth. Kulik expects persistent conflict until China "catches up" with the level of socialist development achieved in the Soviet Union. I would predict no such outcome, as identity relations are not parasitic on material factors, but instead make them meaningful in the first instance. At any rate, because the Soviet Union collapsed before China caught up, Kulik's hypothesis remains untested (Zagoria 1962; Luthi 2008; and Kulik 2000).

CONCLUSIONS

This chapter tries to demonstrate the utility of combining an intersubjectivist ontology with an interpretivist epistemology and method, while fashioning a research design that allows for normal conventional positivistic social scientific theory testing to proceed. A theory of identity that privileges its intersubjectivity, relationality, habitual reproduction, and societal foundations implies particular empirical methods. I am certainly not suggesting that the kind of discourse analysis performed here is the only approach permissible, given the theoretical constraints. Ethnography, as I have already argued, would in fact have been a superior method. Other approaches that privilege language, rhetoric, performance, narrativity, or daily social practices would also be appropriate.

But what would not have been possible would be the a priori specification of which identities should be present, and the consequent development of a research design to elicit these identities from the data. So survey instruments or computerized word searches would not be desirable. But these might very well be appropriate once the evidence has been gathered in ways more consonant with interpretivist standards. In fact, one of the very purposes of this volume is to get readers (and authors) thinking about how to fruitfully combine methodological approaches in ways that not only advance the study of identity but also remain true to explicitly specified epistemological and ontological claims.

APPENDIX: TEXTUAL SOURCES IN RUSSIAN USED FOR THE
EMPIRICAL RECOVERY OF SOVIET IDENTITY, 1945–1966

Journals

Sovetskaia Etnografiia (N = 36 articles read)
Kommunist (N = 89)
New Times (N = 207)

Memoirs

Fyodor Burlatsky
Aleksei Adzhubei

Textbook

Fedor F. Sovetkin, *Textbook of the Russian Language for the Young Who Do Not Know Russian*

Novels

Elena Panova, *Vremena Goda* (Span of Time)
Ilya Ehrenburg, *Ottepel* (The Thaw)
Leonid Leonov, *Russkii Les* (Russian Forest)
Valentin Ovechkin, *Trudnaia Vesna* (Hard Spring)
Vladimir Dudintsev, *Ni Xlebom Edinym* (Not by Bread Alone)
Boris Pasternak, *Doctor Zhivago*
Mikhail Sholokhov, *Sudba Cheloveka* (The Fate of a Man)
Aleksandr Solzhenitsyn, *Odin Den Zhizni Ivan Denisovicha* (One Day in the Life of Ivan Denisovich)

Newspapers

Pravda (N = 1,079)
Literaturnaia Gazeta (N = 156)
Krasnaia Zvezda (N = 711)

Conference Proceedings

Second Congress of All-Union Soviet of Writers

Archives

TsKhSD, Center for the Preservation of Contemporary Documents, former Central Committee, CPSU

GARF, State Archive of the Russian Federation, Presidium special files

RTsKhIDNI, Russian Center for the Preservation and Documentation of Latest History, former Institute of Marxism-Leninism

AVPRF, Archive of the Russian Ministry of Foreign Affairs

Techniques for Measuring Identity in Ethnographic Research

Laura L. Adams

IDENTITY IN ETHNOGRAPHIC RESEARCH

In anthropology and sociology, as in much of clinical and social psychology, the question of identity is so central that it would be an overwhelming task to review the literature or to try to summarize how ethnographers "define" identity. However, for the purposes of this chapter, I will put forth a working definition that is shared by many social scientists and review the way that identity has been measured in a select but diverse group of ethnographic studies. As many of the authors in this book have pointed out, the foundation of the concept of identity is that it is inherently a relational phenomenon: "self" is primarily defined in relation to "other." The definition I use for collective identity is *a reflexive self-understanding of group belonging*. The modifier "reflexive" draws our attention to the mutable nature of identity, which can be reevaluated at any time without being inauthentic. I explicitly contrast identity with categorization, a definition that is externally applied to a group, which becomes identity only when it is internalized. An understanding of "groupness" that is not reflexive, such as a division of humanity into three racial types, is a categorization rather than an identity.[1] Reflexivity also brings an element of self-awareness and agency into the definition of identity, recognizing that identities require at least some degree of conscious reproduction. None of this is to deny the role of inherited definitions and structural influences on the way that this understanding comes to be, but reflexivity is key to understanding the difference between identity and other collective phenomena such as practices or social structures.

---

[1] For an elaboration on the distinction between identification and categorization in relation to the term "groupness," see Brubaker 2004: 41–42.

A second key term that needs to be defined for the purposes of this chapter is ethnography. Anthropology and sociology have somewhat different understandings of what constitutes ethnographic research, but on the most general level ethnography involves the researcher directly interacting with people in situ in order to gain an understanding of that particular social world from an insider's perspective. Although the term comes from the root *ethno* and in common usage denotes the study of a particular ethnic group, in most social science disciplines the term has come to mean the study of any kind of group through frequent and sustained participation in the setting in which a group interacts.[2] Some researchers use the term ethnography to describe any research that involves spending time with people in a particular location, but true ethnographic research is actually quite rare outside of the discipline of anthropology, and most ethnographic fieldwork is actually much more superficial and less intensive than true ethnography. However, this distinction is not as important to other disciplines as it is to anthropology and qualitative sociology, so I will continue to use the term ethnographic research to describe the research I refer to in this chapter, which includes participant-observation, interviews, and other research methods that require sustained interaction with informants in situ.

In ethnographic research, the researcher generally selects a research setting on the basis of both theoretical and practical considerations, gains entry to the research setting (usually overtly presenting herself as a researcher), and receives at least tacit permission from those she is studying to be present as a participant or an observer. Then the researcher spends an extended time in the research setting watching, listening, and taking extensive field notes about what is happening, conducting formal or informal interviews, and perhaps working with other kinds of documentation such as sketches, genealogies, video, photos, audio recordings, and documents produced by the group being studied. These forms of documentation constitute the data that the ethnographer uses to construct her analyses. Ethnographic analysis is generally interpretive, seeking to explicate meanings rather than make verifiable predictions, or, as Clifford Geertz (1973b: 9) put it, "that what we call our data are really our own constructions of other people's constructions of what they and their compatriots are up to."

Unlike more structured methods of data gathering such as surveys and experiments, ethnographers are not required to develop hypotheses before

---

[2] A number of general introductions to these kinds of methods exist. Good sources to start with include Bernard 1998, Denzin and Lincoln 2000, and Lofland and Lofland 1995. For a good handbook on conducting qualitative interview research, see Weiss 1994.

entering the field, and many ethnographic studies use inductive reasoning to generate theories from the field research in addition to testing existing theories against the fieldwork data. Ethnography also has the advantage of being recursive, that is, as new data come in challenging existing theories and hypotheses, the researcher's questions can be refined and immediately tested against the reality of the field setting. Again, to quote Geertz (1973b: 20), ethnography "guess[es] at meanings, assess[es] the guesses, and draw[s] explanatory conclusions from the better guesses." Ethnography is thus a very flexible method, though it does not have the built-in rigor of more deductive methods.

The point of the ethnographic method is to uncover the explicit and implicit cultural knowledge that guides behavior in that group. The ethnographer comes very close to experiencing what is experienced by members of the group she is studying, thereby gaining a deeper understanding of what unspoken rules they might be responding to. It is an important research technique for anyone studying issues of identity because it gives you access to the self-understandings of the group in a variety of contexts, allowing you to experience the reflexivity of group identity as well as what the identity means in practical terms. Doing ethnographic research allows you to get beyond your preconceived notions about the content of identity and to see how people themselves talk about and enact their identities. Furthermore, you can ask people about what they think and do, and why, thereby getting at the reflexive element of identity, while at the same time grounding your questions in concrete examples you have seen and checking to see whether their answers match their actions later. This is why ethnographic research can get at the "cognitive content" of identity better than most other methods (see Abdelal et al., Chapter 1 in this volume).

Ethnographic research can stand on its own, but it also serves as a valuable component of other research strategies. For example, it is often a good idea to conduct participant-observation fieldwork with a population before constructing a survey instrument for them, so that you can determine in advance which issues or questions will be most fruitful to explore in a more structured way. Ethnography can serve as a very useful auxiliary method in order to check on the results that another technique is generating. Even if your primary data collection consists of surveys or structured interviews with a particular population, you may want to conduct fieldwork with this population as well, in order to check on the veracity of their answers or to see whether the reality diverges from their perception of it. Finally, ethnographic fieldwork is often the only way to study populations that are not likely to answer honestly to impersonal interview or survey questions. Persecuted minority groups, for example, are much more likely to share truthful information in the kinds of face-to-face, everyday interactions that ethnographic fieldwork encourages.

Ethnography also has its downsides, which go beyond its limited external validity (generalizability). Ethnographic research requires a much higher degree of commitment of the researcher's time and energy than other methods. Anthropologists often spend up to two years at a time, all day every day, "in the field." Sociologists and political scientists usually spend less time in the field but are still in the position of living in a context very different from their "normal" lives for long stretches of time. Thus, fieldwork can be psychologically draining, because every waking moment is a potential opportunity to learn something about the field setting. Ethnographic research requires a kind of commitment that other "day job" methods of research do not. Often ethnographers find there is no place for them to escape back to a more "authentic self," and that the psychological pressures of being in the field are upon them twenty-four hours a day (Adams 1999a). Depending on the group you are studying, fieldwork may also be stressful or even dangerous, requiring you to spend time in places where you are not welcome, where violence is prevalent, or where you become the victim of random crime (Raymond Lee 1995). If you will be doing research in another country, then fieldwork can also be demanding in terms of the time it takes to master another language. In short, ethnographic fieldwork is not for everyone, but it can produce results with very high internal validity (precision and accuracy of measurement).

APPROACHES TO MEASURING IDENTITY IN ETHNOGRAPHIC STUDIES

Ethnographers often look for three kinds of indicators when researching identity: boundaries (what's inside or outside as well as the boundary's permeability); changes in and contestation over boundaries and the content they encapsulate; and narratives that express implicit or explicit cognitive content of a group's identity. One fairly common empirical manifestation of boundaries can be found in the ways that a group seeks to defend its identity against impurity caused by cultural pollution coming from outside the group or against appropriation by asserting its rights of ownership over shared culture against the rights of those outside the group (Harrison 1999). Another way that boundaries serve as an indicator for identity in ethnographic research is to be found in implicit descriptions of how a group sees other groups, that is, how a group defines *itself* in relation to that other group. In his study of "modern clan politics" in Kazakhstan, Edward Schatz (2004) uncovered rich data about Kazakh identity through the triangulation of ethnographic, interview, and focus group research in different regions and in both urban and rural locations. Schatz showed that Kazakh identity is defined mainly in relation to two groups: the supraclan and the Russians. Looking inward, Kazakh identity is relationally and explicitly defined by the three large descent groups called *juz* (a term that Schatz translates as "umbrella clan") and *ru* (clan). Looking outward, Kazakh identity is implicitly defined largely in relation to Russians, who are almost as numerous in Kazakhstan as the Kazakhs.

Schatz found that while one's *juz* and *ru* were commonly exchanged pieces of information, they held little significance for further interaction in most contexts. In each kind of data collected by Schatz, the core of Kazakh identity is described by Kazakhs themselves as the ability to recite one's genealogy seven generations back (presumably a way to identify clan, though he also found that stating one's ancestral village was also a common clan identity marker). What has become important for Kazakhs is less the content of that identity (i.e., what clan and supraclan you belong to) but the ability to recite seven generations.

What appears at first to be a significant internal component of relational identity in fact is actually used as a way to define identity in relation to non-Kazakhs. Kazakhs define other Kazakhs on a spectrum that puts the ideal-typical Kazakh in the middle between the identities of Kazakhstan's neighbors to the north and south. Drawing on his fieldwork, Schatz (2004: 142) wrote, "among ordinary people in the 1990s, southerners would frequently deride northern Kazakhs as 'Russified,' and northerners would label southerners as 'Uzbeks.'" In one of his focus groups, a participant described urban Kazakhs as having "taken on Russian behaviour. . . . In the city, parents teach their genealogy, but they don't give it much significance" (Schatz 2004: 158). In this example, as in most of the identity talk Schatz discussed, identities are often defined through contrast, especially the opposition between Kazakh (meaning true Kazakh) and Russian (meaning not Russian but some other kind of less authentic Kazakh). Schatz's data also illustrate the contested nature of contemporary Kazakh identity, a contestation that revolves primarily around Russian or Kazakh oppositions.

It is important not to reify these boundaries that serve as indicators of identity, especially when members of the same community can pass between identities in the course of their lifetimes. In these cases, it is important to look for indicators of what boundaries are permeable, when one can transgress them and remain a member of the group, whether the return of exiles or refugees to the group is possible and for whom, and so on. In his ethnographic study of an impoverished Philadelphia neighborhood, *Code of the Street* (1999), Elijah Anderson showed that the residents of this neighborhood claimed two different identities, with most residents seeing themselves and others as either "decent" or "street." These identities did not only inhere in individual members of the group; they were attributes of entire families in that identity category, though a decent family may have had a kid who goes bad, or, occasionally, a kid from a street family turned out decent. Anderson used group norms as an indicator of identity in this study and showed how the identity of group members was tied up in their respect for or transgression of these boundaries.

The norms that identified "decent" families included behaviors such as churchgoing, parental sacrifice, and a traditional breadwinner role for the "man of the house" (E. Anderson 1999: 38–39). "Street" families, on the other hand, had norms that are governed by the "code of the street . . . a set of informal rules governing interpersonal public behavior, particularly violence" (E. Anderson 1999: 33). Anderson (1999: 63) characterized the norms of street families as consisting of a set of behaviors that indicate one has "juice" (respect) and can take care of oneself. These behavioral norms were oriented toward maintaining a particular personal bearing and involved clothing style and "posturing, abusive language, and the ready use of violence to settle disputes." In the cases of both decent and street identity, the failure to behave appropriately could result in a loss of respect, but the expected behavior of the two groups was often quite opposite. Here we have a clearly measurable continuum of identity, ranging from the tightly controlled behavior of decent-identified people to the disorderly (but not unpredictable) behavior of street-identified people. Anderson measured the internal content and boundaries of this identity in two ways: by observing interactions in everyday settings and by interviewing people about how they experience their identities. In the preceding example, the norms that distinguish "decent" from "street" families are not just a means of reproducing identity; they are also part of a larger strategy of achieving group goals, such as becoming middle class, living in a safe, clean neighborhood, and fighting racism. Anderson's study shows that in addition to looking at boundaries, we have to understand how permeable those boundaries are, whether it is possible to cross and return, and when those boundaries are contested by group members.

Another way that boundaries are constructed is through what Bourdieu (1977) calls *habitus*, a person's socially conditioned beliefs and dispositions that guide and limit a person's tastes and preferences. Ethnographic research is a good way to study the way that membership in a group shapes preferences, for example, how class identity shapes goals and tastes ("what do we want? what do people like us typically want?"). In his classic study of working-class youth in Britain, *Learning to Labor*, Paul Willis (1977: 96) examined how the working class reproduces itself, in part by socializing young people to desire a certain kind of work environment. A "lad" wants a job where he can "be open about his desires, his sexual feelings, his liking for 'booze' and his aim to 'skive off' as much as reasonably possible. . . .The future workplace has to have an essentially masculine ethos. It has to be a place where people are not 'cissies' and can 'handle themselves,' where 'pen-pushing' is looked down on in favor of really 'doing things.'" In Willis's study, working class identity was defined, in part, by a distaste for jobs that would lead to upward mobility.

Too much focus on boundaries can lead us to an overly homogenized or static view of group identity, so it is also important when looking for indicators of identity to examine changes in and the contestation within groups about where those boundaries lie and what exactly is enclosed within them. Contestation in this case does not have to mean an upheaval within a group; it can also describe the process by which the group negotiates its own identity in relation to other groups. It is not always clear which aspects of identity are more or less important for defining groupness, but through the course of doing fieldwork, the terrain often maps itself. Asking a number of Jews a question like, "What makes someone a Jew?" will generate a variety of different answers that will point to areas of conflict as well as areas of consensus. If the researcher samples a variety of settings and groups during the course of fieldwork, the consensual as well as the contested aspects of identity should show up in the field notes. Another technique is to run focus groups, or attend naturally occurring "focus groups" such as meetings of the group members, to see what areas of contestation emerge. Under such conditions, though, it is actually harder to measure consensus because the common sense about the group's identity often goes unremarked upon, whereas the contested areas are likely to show themselves quickly.

An example of contestation over gay and lesbian identity is *Families We Choose*, by Kath Weston (1991) who conducted ethnographic fieldwork in San Francisco in the mid-1980s, when collective action over family issues was just beginning to emerge in the gay community. Weston's book is filled with extended quotations from both her field notes and the formal interviews she conducted, which are of course carefully selected by Weston but nonetheless give the reader a feel for the "thick description" inscribed by her notes. She found that the community's discourse about gays being "exiles from kinship" was, during the 1980s, being transformed into a discourse about gays belonging to "families we choose." The problems encountered by gays and lesbians in receiving societal and legal recognition of their partners and children, not to mention the rejection from their natal families faced by many of them, caused a significant shift in what it meant to be gay. By the time Weston entered the field, to be a lesbian no longer meant that you could not have children; to be gay no longer meant that you could not talk about your life partner as your family.

The gay community's interest in redefining family and marriage to include their relationships was not without controversy, as some felt that their distinct identity was threatened by the new discourse about families. Weston (1991: 198) noted that "those who fear assimilation into a predominantly heterosexual society tend to identify 'the family' solely with procreation and heterosexuality." This debate as it evolved into the twenty-first century clearly illustrates the contestation of gay identity. Does being gay mean rejecting heterosexual culture? Does claiming the label of "family" or advocating for the legalization of gay marriage equal assimilation to straight culture? Although ethnography lacks true replicability, Weston's research could certainly be repeated twenty years later to give a longitudinal view of the changing discursive and structural elements of gay identity.[3] The subject of Weston's research could also be studied by combining ethnographic research in a particular locale with a discourse analysis of a diverse sample of gay and lesbian community newspapers, for example, to situate the ethnographic research in a broader context.

Different research methods can be employed to investigate the nature of intergroup boundaries and how identity is contested, but ethnography in particular is a good choice for understanding the "cognitive content" of identity (see Abdelal et al., Chapter 1 in this volume), the aspect of identity that structures the story of the group, how they see themselves in the world and how they see the world in relation to themselves. Good ethnography deals with cognitive content in depth and with skill, measuring identity in context through richly textured narratives. The classic example of how an anthropologist profoundly characterized a group's cognitive identity content through a highly contextualized analysis of symbols is Clifford Geertz's "Deep Play: Notes on the Balinese Cockfight" (1973c). Geertz analyzed what cockfights mean to the Balinese not by asking people why they engage in cockfighting but by reading the cockfight itself as a story the Balinese tell themselves about themselves. The cockfight orders themes of Balinese culture (death, masculinity, pride, chance) into an interpretive structure. "Attending cockfights and participating in them is, for the Balinese, a kind of sentimental education. What he learns there is what his culture's ethos and his private sensibility . . . look like when spelled out externally in a collective text" (Geertz 1973c: 449). Furthermore, these are not just representations of Balinese sensibilities; they are one of the agents in the creation and maintenance of these sensibilities (Geertz 1973c: 451).

As brilliant as these kinds of analyses can be, this kind of thick description of cognitive content is highly dependent on the ability of the researcher to correctly interpret the event. For this reason, measurement of cognitive content

---

[3] Although replicating a fieldwork study makes little sense methodologically, and would no doubt produce a book that publishers would spurn as being too similar to its predecessor, it is possible to build closely on previous fieldwork. See, for example, Carrington 1999, which is also a field study of gay and lesbian kinship in the Bay Area.

may be more subject to internal validity problems in fieldwork than other indicators. One way to get around the possibility of subjective bias is to examine cognitive content through explicit narratives that are recognized as such by the group you are studying, and which are therefore the subject of commentary by informants rather than just the interpretation of the researcher. An example of this kind of narrative is what I called in my dissertation a "trope of subordinate identity," which my Uzbek informants would regularly invoke in their discussions of the Soviet period (Adams 1999a: 126–134). Tropes of subordinate identity narrate the history of a group in a way that pits the wily in-group against the foolish but powerful dominant group, describing the horrible things "they" did to "us" and the clever ways "we" got around "their" rules. They are a way a group can control the objectification of their culture by self-objectification and project themselves as social equals of the dominant group without having to address actual inequalities between the groups (see also Dominguez 1989: 151–152). In this case, the in-group consisted of ethnic Uzbeks who supported national traditions and the dominant group was made up of Soviet loyalists, some of whom were Uzbeks. The pattern of the story became quite clear to me through hearing it in a variety of settings, and through it I was able to assess a number of aspects of contemporary Uzbek identity and its relationship to the Soviet past.

Another way to approach the measurement of cognitive content is by doing comparative research. For example, in her study of women who had recently adopted Orthodox forms of Judaism, Lynn Davidman (1991) found that even among this population of women who defined their Jewish identities in rather strict religious terms, there were two different worldviews that emerged from the conversion process of women at different life stages, with different educational backgrounds. Davidman found that the women going through the conversion process at a mainstream Orthodox synagogue had a very different interpretation of what the Orthodox tradition meant to them than the women undergoing conversion at a Lubavitch congregation. Though all of the women expressed the idea that they were responding to the dilemmas of modern life by choosing a strict form of religious practice, some of the women joining the mainstream Orthodox congregation did not even believe in God and saw their religious practice as a choice that made sense for them. Others, especially among the more conservative Lubavitch sect, understood their new religious practice as God controlling their fate.

METHODOLOGICAL CONCERNS IN ETHNOGRAPHIC RESEARCH

The methods of ethnography are eclectic, and some might say haphazard. As Michael Burawoy (2000: 25) puts it, "You learn ethnography through practice, and perhaps a little bit of apprenticeship. There are guidelines, but few rules. More or less anything goes." Of course, it is possible to receive a generalized set of instructions, to brush up on a repertoire of data-gathering techniques, and to plan out the stages of the research process, but it is not possible here to provide an adequate overview of ethnography as a method. Handbooks on research methods often boil down the steps of conducting ethnographic research to the following: selecting a field site, gaining access, introducing yourself and establishing rapport with your informants, identifying key informants, establishing a role for yourself in the field, moving back and forth between taking field notes and doing preliminary analysis, refining your analysis and collecting more data, exiting the field, and writing a report that makes a contribution to theory. In this section, I outline the strengths and weaknesses of ethnographic methods and explore the ways that ethnographers deal with the challenges of their research process.

Validity and Reliability

A persistent methodological dilemma in this interpretive process is the reactivity of ethnographic research. Unlike research on historical documents or the analysis of census data, ethnographic research is conducted in an environment where the data are likely to be affected by the researcher's presence. The ethnographer's observations may be tainted by her presence, as in the case where a "typical" household meal becomes transformed when an unexpected guest arrives. This is especially relevant in studies of identity, when the way an informant perceives the researcher has a potent effect on his own identity. Zanca (2000: 155), for example, in his discussion of the dilemmas of fieldwork in postsocialist societies, points out how the appearance of young, well-dressed, laptop-equipped graduate students from the West in the offices of Uzbekistani academics forces them to confront a paradox in their professional identity between "the unremitting hubris invoked by scholars who were scientifically inspired by socialism to commanding heights of pride and the depressing postsocialist recognition that in many ways their societies have a far lower standard of living and quality of life (especially for scholars) than is true of their colleagues from the West."

Furthermore, ethnographic research entails multiple levels of subjectivity, and often the researcher is interpreting the interpretation someone else gave of an event that happened to a third party. Some of these problems of subjectivity can be overcome by triangulation (conducting multiple observations or using multiple methods), but an equally important methodological issue is that the researcher recognizes this subjectivity, including her own subjectivity, and attempts to account for it as part of the data collection process. The approach to ethnographic fieldwork that I advocate (Adams 1999b) is to recognize and take into account *in one's analysis* the problematic relationship of the researcher to the people she is studying (Clifford and Marcus 1986; Haraway 1991: chap. 9; Marcus and Fischer 1986; D. Smith 1987). This approach emphasizes that the relationship between the knower and the object of her knowledge is a socially organized practice (D. Smith 1987: 72). The researcher-informant relationship brings into play dynamics of race, gender, class, nation, age, etc. that give both the researcher and the informant a permanently partial perspective of reality (Haraway 1991: chap. 9). The approach advocated by Haraway and others (e.g., Bhavnani 1993) stresses that each researcher must answer not for the impartiality or replicability of her research but for the *situated knowledge* she has collaborated with her informants to produce.

The concept of situated knowledge implies that the data do not simply exist "out there," being hidden or revealed by informants in response to the researcher's presentation of self, but rather that the data themselves are a product of the relationship between the researcher and her informants. Researchers need to recognize the informants' agency in the research relationship and how their reactions to us fundamentally affect the knowledge we are able to glean (Wolf 1992: 135). Whether or not collective identity is a focus of research, the identity of the researcher, especially the identification of the researcher by others in the field, has to be taken into account as part of the data. In the language of variables, one of the independent variables influencing whatever dependent variables the researcher examines has to be at least a crude estimation of the reflexive understanding of who the researcher is. The role a fieldworker adopts – that is, seeing and being seen in a certain way – affects the knowledge that the fieldworker eventually produces about the informants.

Sampling

For her study of gay and lesbian kinship, *Families We Choose*, Kath Weston (1991) conducted ethnographic fieldwork and eighty in-depth interviews in San Francisco in the mid-1980s. For her interviews, she used the most common sampling method in ethnographic research, "snowball sampling": working through a network of contacts, she conducted interviews with an equal number of men and women whose self-identification as gay, lesbian, or bisexual determined their inclusion in her sample. There are several ways that snowball sampling can bias data, and good ethnographic researchers do what they can to mitigate the most common biases.

Self-selection can be a problem in snowball sampling, so Weston went out of her way to find people who were reluctant to be interviewed. She also used "theoretical sampling" (the deliberate recruitment of people representing theoretically important categories) to keep her sample diverse in terms of race, ethnicity, and class background. These kinds of samples are nonprobability samples and therefore Weston cannot claim representativeness for her research, nor does she want to claim, for example, that her African American interviewees "represent" gay African Americans. Rather, she uses these sampling techniques to help her say something about how these other identities are meaningful to the interviewees themselves. As Weston (1991: 12) says, "I concentrate here on the interpretive links participants made (or did not make) between sexual identity and other aspects of who they considered themselves to be, always with the awareness that identical symbols can carry very different meanings in different contexts." These sampling methods are considered good research practices in ethnographic work as long as the author explains to the reader the selection process and the biases that it reflects.[4] Weston (1991: 9–17), for example, acknowledges that San Francisco is a rarefied field site for studying questions of gay and lesbian identity, that she neglected a theoretically important sampling category (age), and that her sample had a disproportionate number of well-educated people and people without children.

Gaining Access and Establishing Rapport

There are as many ways of gaining access to a field site as there are field sites, but generally there are two preferred strategies for conducting ethnographic research. The first is to go through official channels, requesting permission from a government or a community organization to study a particular locale or group. This method has the advantage of giving your actions legitimacy and giving you some immunity from police scrutiny or the resistance of lower-level authorities, but in some situations, official sanction can also compromise your research, if, for example, you are seen as a spy sent by the higher-ups or if your presence is associated with a despised administrator or government. The second way to gain access is through a key informant, someone whose knowledge of the field site is especially pertinent to your research, who can introduce you to the people you need to approve of your presence and who can explain a bit about what's going on behind the scenes. The disadvantage of working too closely with a single key informant is that you end up adopting his biases as your own, so after access has been gained, it is prudent to expand your network

---

[4] For an ethnographic study that uses probability sampling, see Sánchez-Jankowski 1991.

of key informants to include people with different perspectives on and positions in the field site.

Once you have gained access, the next task the ethnographer faces is establishing rapport with the people she is studying so that they will answer your questions and feel comfortable enough around you to act naturally. Again, you will probably have to figure out for yourself what methods of building rapport work best given your personality and the norms of the community you are studying. Working on interpersonal relations while gathering data can be stressful. The tricky thing about fieldwork is that you have to plunk yourself down and *be* there. But how can you be yourself and be a good research instrument at the same time? Are you the same multifaceted self that you are back home, or do you adapt to the conditions of the field? Do you find yourself trying to manipulate people through your presentation of self? Do you find yourself being coerced into acting in ways that you are not comfortable with?

In the field, I tend to carefully manage my presentation of self in an attempt to have some control over the way I am perceived by my informants. This adaptation involved dressing conservatively and through my behavior invoking an image of a "good girl" who was respectful of Uzbek culture and generally did not express her sexuality or challenge anyone's beliefs beyond asking about them. If I had behaved as I do among my friends in the United States, casually swearing, dressing casually, and asserting my feminist beliefs, I have no doubt that I would have irreparably damaged my relationships with my informants, most of whom were middle-aged men in a modern but sexist society. I also could not have been entirely successful behaving as I would among my colleagues at home, where I speak well, dress professionally, and assert myself as an expert in my field. I was not an expert and almost any handbook on field research will tell you that you will learn much more from your informants if you assume an "attitude of strangeness," expressing curiosity about the most ordinary things, as well as playing the "acceptable incompetent" (Lofland and Lofland 1995), who does not understand the first thing about how to operate in the field setting, yet behaves in a way that does not offend or alienate anyone.

Data Collection and Analysis

Ethnographers collect data in a variety of forms and use a wide range of techniques, including formal quantitative and qualitative analysis (with the help of software programs that facilitate qualitative data coding such as NVivo, Atlas.ti and The Ethnograph) to assist in the interpretation of their data. However, nothing defines the ethnographic method as much as does the concept of "thick description." A thick description goes beyond relaying empirical observation by interpreting the meaning that is subjectively attributed to the observed objects or practices. The ethnographic object of analysis lies in between the observation and the researcher's eventual interpretation, in the context in which the production, perception, and interpretation of a particular object or action takes place (Geertz 1973b: 7). Through the attentive observation of practices, the accumulation of highly detailed field notes,[5] and the persistent questioning of informants about the meanings of the observations contained in those notes, the researcher first tries to grasp and then render "a multiplicity of complex conceptual structures, many of them superimposed upon or knotted into one another, which are at once strange, irregular and inexplicit" (Geertz 1973b: 10).

Writing Up the Research

The topic of writing up ethnographic research has been subject to an intense debate that taps into concerns about power inequalities in fieldwork relationships and postmodern deconstructions of the author (van Maanen 1988). Inspired by Michel Foucault's (1984) critique of the idea of "the author," social scientists have increasingly become reflexive about their own role in the creation of knowledge through narrative. The argument for treating ethnographic narratives as embodying power dynamics got widespread attention in the 1980s (Clifford and Marcus 1986; Marcus and Fischer 1986), and many researchers doing ethnography have now assimilated these assumptions into their research practices and view their own narratives with a critical eye. An example of an experimental form of narrative that removes the researcher's authorial voice almost entirely is Susan Krieger's study of identity in a women's community, *The Mirror Dance* (1983). After a brief introduction, Krieger's only authorial moves are to edit the narratives from in-depth interviews with members of the community and group them into chapters. She does not offer her own commentary or analysis. Whereas raw survey data, for example, would be both difficult to interpret and uninteresting to read, ethnographic and interview data allow a wide range of analytical techniques to be imposed, from formal statistical analysis to a mode of analysis that puts the full burden of interpretation on the reader.

More practically, ethnographic writing relies on vivid descriptions and evocative language in the way that statistical analysis relies on tables and graphs. An example of how ethnographic writing has its own style comes from Elijah

---

[5] For a good introduction to anthropological methods, with an especially detailed section on recording field notes, see Bernard 2006.

Anderson's work that we discussed earlier. Having witnessed the way numerous interactions between street-identified people escalated into violence, Anderson (1999: 78–79) constructed a typical scenario of how in a "staging area" (hangout) a "statement" (insult) provokes a "beef" (challenge), which can result in a fight, which might end when the police are called or when an "equalizer" (gun) is employed. By translating both the event and how participants talk about it, Anderson gives us a detailed insight into the norms governing the behavior of members of this group. Anderson (1999: 54–63) also employed a technique of quoting extensively and in full from his ethnographic interviews, allowing us to evaluate and interpret his evidence for ourselves. With good ethnographic writing, we do not just learn what the ethnographer and his informants experienced but get a sense of how we ourselves would experience the same situation, giving us a much more sophisticated under-standing of the data the author is relaying to us than we would get from a narrative that tried for reasons of objectivity or academic style to distance the reader from the social milieu being described.

Theorizing

The relationship of ethnographic data to theory is somewhat more problematic than with other data collection methods precisely because the ethnographic process is often inductive. It is all too easy to find that the meanings extracted from the research setting are particular to that setting and that one's research not only is ungeneralizable but does not make a contribution to broader theoretical questions. Often, ethnographic research is used to make an argument that the research setting is a "microcosm" of some broader social world or a testing ground for a particular theory. While neither of these approaches is inherently flawed (depending on their assumptions), Geertz (1973b: 23) argues that the real value of ethnographic data is that they give social science theories and concepts "the sort of sensible actuality that makes it possible to think not only realistically and concretely *about* them, but, what is more important, creatively and imaginatively *with* them." This bridging work is important in any ethnographic study. In Brubaker et al.'s (2006: 167) work on ethnicity and nationalism in a Transylvanian town, they argue that while it is important to establish the contexts that result from large-scale and long-term processes, this "fosters a kind of optical illusion. National claims and counter-claims, easily 'legible' from afar, stand out in bold relief, and the path of least resistance, for the analyst, is to take them at face value." The solution, they argue, is to test the face value of claims and categories by examining them at the level of everyday life.

One method that links theory to ethnography quite rigorously is Burawoy's (1998: 5) extended case method that "applies reflexive science to ethnography in order to extract the general from the unique, to move from the 'micro' to the 'macro,' and to connect the present to the past in anticipation of the future, all by building on preexisting theory." This method, which Burawoy argues is emblematic of an alternative ("reflexive" as opposed to "positive") science, is based on several key processes that reflect much of what I have been arguing about ethnography thus far. The first "extension" in the extended case method is the extension of the observer to participant – the recognition of power relations inherent in field research and the embracing of the distortion of the social situation introduced by the researcher. "Even the most passive observer produces ripples worthy of examination, while the activist who seeks to transform the world can learn much from its obduracy" (Burawoy 1998: 17). The second extension is of observations over space and time in order to compile situational knowledge into theories of social process. The third extension is out from process to force, a comparative strategy "tracing the source of small difference to external forces . . . to causally connect the cases. Instead of reducing cases to instances of a general law, we make each case work in its connection to other cases" in order to contribute to the theorization of broader social forces (Burawoy 1998: 19). The final extension is of theory.

Our first three "extensions" – intervention, process, and structuration – all call for prior theory. But our stance toward theory is kamikaze. In our fieldwork, we do not look for confirmations but for theory's refutations. We need first the courage of our convictions, then the courage to challenge our convictions, and finally the imagination to sustain our courage with theoretical reconstruction. If these reconstructions come at too great a cost, we may have to abandon our theory altogether and start afresh with a new, interesting theory for which our case is once more an anomaly. (Burawoy 1998: 20)

The extended case method is a rigorous and extremely challenging form of ethnographic research to undertake in its fully realized form, which requires years, if not decades, of dedication to exploring a particular set of theoretical issues in a variety of contexts. However, it provides us with important insights into ethnography's possibilities to be much more than a case study or a travelogue.

Burawoy's description of the extended case method also hints at some of the more radical goals that ethnographers may have. While most of us are interested in a scientific program of research involving the elaboration of theory and the enrichment of our knowledge of the empirical world, ethnography is also conducive to some of the more explicitly political goals that scholars and activists might have. One example of this is participatory (or emancipatory) action research (e.g., Naples 1998). This method emerges out of a critical approach to social science where the goal is to gain scientific knowledge that reveals hidden power dynamics. While critical social science can certainly undertake a program of research that contributes to "normal" science (striving for "objective" knowledge), action research is conducted not just to understand a social setting but with the goal of empowering the group being studied.

DOING ETHNOGRAPHIC RESEARCH ON NATIONAL IDENTITY IN POST-SOVIET UZBEKISTAN

I spent most of 1996 conducting field research in Tashkent, Uzbekistan. My dissertation (Adams 1999a) was to be about national identity in the post-Soviet period. Fortunately, national identity was practically all everyone talked about. "Laura, have you seen our Uzbek national dances?" "Do you like *pilau*? It's our national dish." "Which do you like better: living in an Uzbek house or in an apartment?" "We Uzbeks are good at trade." "We Uzbeks are like puppets on a string. Our leaders are cowards." "Do you mind using an Uzbek toilet? We don't have a European toilet." It seemed like I had chosen the right topic, because the Uzbeks were obsessed with their own national identity.

Or maybe they were not. Fortunately, before I started writing a dissertation about how self-absorbed the Uzbeks are, I considered the possibility that what I was seeing was not so much a reflection of an everyday preoccupation with national identity but rather a response to me. In any interactive fieldwork method, be it interviews or ethnography, the researcher herself is a variable. The data produced by these methods are a product of the *relationship* between the researcher and those she is interacting with (in fieldwork terminology, her "informants.") When I showed up, an American who was interested in their culture, it shifted my informants' attention to the sharpest difference between us: our nationality.

I traveled around the country and went to villages where some people were wearing traditional clothing and others wearing a mixture of Uzbek and European style clothing. This probably was unremarkable to them – until I showed up. Then they would point out to me the one girl wearing a multicolored, waistless silk dress and colorfully contrasting pants, saying, "this is our national costume, do you like it?" Numerous such incidents gave me the impression that Uzbeks have a heightened sense of their "otherness." In part, this may have been due to the very ethnically self-conscious nature of Soviet subjectivity (Grant 1996; Slezkine 1994a, 1994b). As in the United States where the assimilationist principle of the "melting pot" never really overcame people's identification with their largely imagined ethnic homelands, daily life in the Soviet Union involved frequent references to the multiethnic nature of the Soviet Union and inculcated a sense of being a member of a particular ethnicity in its citizens. For example, the Soviet Union bragged of being a state with more than 100 nationalities; "the friendship of the peoples" was a cornerstone of Soviet ideology; and culture production in the non-Russian regions frequently involved "ethnic color," especially in the supposedly exotic southern reaches of Soviet space. The villagers I met in post-Soviet Uzbekistan were responding, through this ethnic subjectivity, to a situation in which I was defined all too clearly as a foreigner. People were showing off their nationality for me because of who I was and what I was studying. While this introduced one kind of bias into my work, I believe that this particular slant cut cleanly to some important issues. The data I was able to gather were incredibly rich precisely because national identities are defined in comparison to other nations and other kinds of identities. My presence offered a situation for the performance of national identity (Brubaker 2004: 10).

Even after I came to understand that my presence was likely to trigger a national identity performance, I had no way of telling if the performances I was seeing were authentic to the performers or if they were mainly for my benefit. Either way, these kinds of identity performances are integral to the experience of a collective identity. They are part of the practice of identity. What's more, they are readily accessible and easy to measure because they are so ritualized. However, extensive and carefully structured fieldwork is required to look beyond these stereotyped performances in order to understand issues related to the measurement of identity in these contexts.

The goal of my research was to understand, in a conceptual framework laid out by Benedict Anderson (1991), how Uzbekistan's cultural elites were imagining their national community in the post-Soviet era. In pursuit of mapping and analyzing this national imagining, my fieldwork took me to a variety of locations where this national identity was being produced. I focused mainly on public locations and on the culture being produced in Uzbekistan's capital, Tashkent. However, I made an effort to sample other locations in order to get a sense of the diversity and contestation of national imaginings. Furthermore, as I was living in Tashkent for ten months in 1996, and for another month in 1998, I encountered data on national identity across time and in a wide variety of contexts that I encountered both on purpose and by chance.

The primary focus of my research was on the production of national holiday concerts in Tashkent. The national holiday concerts were a concentrated form of the national imagination of Tashkent's cultural elites, produced to enhance the patriotism of the masses and to project an image of the newly independent Uzbekistan to audiences both at home and abroad. I focused on two holidays in particular, each with a different theme: Navro'z, a Zoroastrian spring equinox holiday, was a holiday specifically celebrating and reviving traditions of Central Asian culture; Independence Day was a holiday devoted to celebrating Uzbekistan's identity as a modern and multiethnic state. These holidays together gave a picture of the elite's ideas about Uzbek national identity as being rooted in both ethnic and civic conceptions of the nation. I could have analyzed these themes through a straightforward content analysis of the symbols present in holiday concerts, but by conducting fieldwork (attending planning meetings and rehearsals, interviewing the artists during and after the concerts) I was able to understand why those symbols were chosen, and I also knew which symbols had been considered and rejected. My analysis of the elite imagination was enhanced by seeing the elite's decisions unfold, seeing where there was consensus or conflict, and understanding how the production of these concerts was affected by the relationships among different groups of the elite (artists, bureaucrats, and others).

Museums, an archetypical repository of national imaginings, were another valuable data source. Museums tend to be official interpretations of local history and culture, locations that express consensus and exclude contestation. One of the interesting things that was taking place in Uzbekistan's museums in the mid-1990s was the reinterpretation of history in accordance with the government's new agenda of nation building. One example of this agenda was the content of the National History Museum, which revealed the essence of what the government defined as the geographical, historical, and cultural scope of Uzbek identity. Looking not just at the content of the museums but at what kinds of museums were being built was also an interesting source of data about national identity. In 1998 a new museum dedicated to Amir Timur, the medieval conqueror whose capital was located in Samarkand, was opened as part of a larger campaign to promote Timur as the national hero. During another visit in 2002, the Museum of the Victims of Repression opened, signaling the official rewriting of Uzbekistan's experience of Russian and Soviet domination. One of the advantages of fieldwork is being able to observe the same variable (e.g., museum content) across time and in different contexts, in order to measure identity dynamically.

One of my particular interests was in the performing arts not as an expression of individual creativity but as a channel for the expression of collective identities, national and otherwise. Therefore, one of the activities of my fieldwork was attending plays in order to understand what themes were important to Tashkent's cultural elite, how those themes were treated in drama and comedy, and how people in the audience reacted to these productions. I also used in-depth interviews to understand from the perspective of the directors, and sometimes of the playwrights and actors, what they wanted to express about collective identity through these performances. Again, rather than just analyzing the content of plays, I spoke to the producers of culture and heard about what they could and could not express regarding national identity, what restrictions the state placed on their expression, and their own interpretations of Uzbek identity, which were often at odds with what they were allowed to express in the public sphere.

Many ethnographers do not conduct their research in specifically targeted sites, like meetings, museums, or theaters; they simply live among people and see what they do. Though it is possible to do fieldwork in a more targeted way, it is still good to find ways to be a part of the everyday life of the people you are studying. A site of my fieldwork in Uzbekistan was the Ministry of Cultural Affairs, in the "Department of Public Creativity." I was there to analyze documents contained in its archives related to amateur folk music and dance groups, the general activities of Soviet and post-Soviet "houses of culture," and to investigate the way that Uzbek national identity was expressed through amateur culture during the Soviet era and early years of independence. While those data were all useful, it was also valuable to be sitting in the office working day after day with a group of people who gradually got used to my being around. As in other situations, naturally they responded to my being an American and my interest in Uzbek culture, but I also got to see their interactions with each other. As happened during the planning meetings for the holiday spectacles as well, my presence was sometimes ignored and I was able to see how people talked among themselves about issues of identity and their imaginings of the nation. This habituation to the presence of the researcher, which can be accomplished only through sustained interaction, is one of the ways the researcher can try to assess her own influence on what her informants say or do. She can then evaluate the data she gathers when informants are responding directly to her against the data she gathers when they seem to be unaware of her presence.

Ethnographic fieldwork is also useful for encountering a wide range of random, unexpected data coming from everyday life, such as what is being sold at newspaper kiosks, how people interact with each other in stores, what kinds of shows are being broadcast on television, and so on. While I did not consciously seek out these sources of information about national identity, nonetheless they would present me with confirmations (or disconfirmations) of my hypotheses or provide me with ideas of other topics to investigate. The internal validity of fieldwork comes in part from not focusing one's attention on questions determined a priori but instead being open to the whole range of contexts that you might encounter and seeing what emerges. As Brubaker et al. (2006: 15) point out, to study categories such as ethnicity by asking questions about ethnicity automatically imposes an analytical frame that almost guarantees that you will find what you are looking for. To study how identity works in everyday life, it is better to go into a research site without drawing attention to your own schemas and categories. To the extent that the ethnographer can refrain from imposing her own assumptions on the data she is gathering, ethnography allows for a much more rich and nuanced picture of the empirical world than other methods.

SCHEMAS OF NATIONAL AND ETHNIC IDENTITY IN POST-SOVIET UZBEKISTAN

My main claims about national identity are based as much on the methods of discourse analysis as they are on ethnography, and the two methods have many points of similarity.[6] As I said in the previous section, my empirical task was to map and analyze the (discursive) national imagining of cultural elites in Uzbekistan. The overall conclusion I have come to about national identity in Uzbekistan is that culture producers hope to propagate a national identity that expresses both "national" and "universal" values. The message is that citizens of Uzbekistan are part of a rich cultural heritage encompassing the Great Silk Road and the empire of Amir Timur, that they should be proud to be part of a multiethnic nation that celebrates friendship between all peoples, and that they have a bright future as a "normal" nation-state in the world from which they were isolated during the Soviet period. So what indicators of national imagining did I use to reach these conclusions, and how did I use ethnographic data to derive indicators of this national identity? I have already mentioned the way that national identity was narrativized through the trope of subordinate identity and in this section, I focus on three brief examples from my previously published work on this subject to link up with other parts of the earlier discussion of indicators of identity: cognitive content, contestation over boundaries, and contestation over content.

The first indicator of the national imagining that I focused on was the imagination of Uzbek identity through cognitive schemas of local or ethnic versus global or cosmopolitan. I encountered both kinds of discourse in my research, but somewhat unsurprisingly, among the Tashkent cultural elite, the cosmopolitan discourse was just as prevalent as the ethnic one. For example, the Uzbeks I worked with often expressed that they were honored that an "American" had gone to the trouble of learning their language and studying

---

[6] See, for example, Laffey and Weldes 2004 for an overview of discourse analysis as a method and its similarities to how I have presented ethnography here.

their culture. In addition to being proud of their "traditional culture," they were eager to impress upon me their nation's right to play a role in the modern world community. In an interview in Tashkent in April 1996, a theater director noted, "I hope you've seen that we're basically modern people. I hope that consciousness, as they say, national identity, is going in the right direction. Because we can see from the examples of other governments how civilization is moving forward, how democratization is proceeding in the other countries of the CIS."

Many elites wanted to bring back "forgotten" elements of their culture without destroying or neglecting the positive developments of the Soviet period. The hybrid Soviet Uzbek identity contained aspects of cosmopolitan culture as well as national culture; the Uzbek elites were as proud of their ballet as they were of their national music ensembles. The Independence Day spectacle in particular was used to convey a national identity that went beyond a narrowly defined traditional ethnic culture. Many people I interviewed echoed this chor-eographer's sentiments: "Navro'z is a folk holiday so it should have more national music and instruments. . . . It should be pure folk. Independence Day is an entirely different matter. . . . We should say, here's what we are, Uzbekistan! Orchestral music is also part of our accomplishments, classical ballet is an accomplishment, our young military men, these are our accomplish-ments" (interview conducted in Tashkent, June 1996).

The producers of holiday spectacles hoped to make an impression not just on the citizens of Uzbekistan, but on the larger world: "we want to show the representatives of other governments the art of Uzbekistan . . . [and] we want to express the ideas of friendship, Uzbekistan's place in the world, and the closening of east and west" (field notes of staff meeting, August 1996). Uzbe-kistan wanted to see itself as a legitimate member of the world community, as a normal nation. The *estrada* block of song and dance in the holiday spec-tacles, with its parade of pop stars singing Uzbek lyrics in musical styles ranging from syntho-ballad to techno-rap, was a perfect example of the way Uzbek elites manage to show that their culture is normal, modern, and yet still their own.

A second indicator is of the way that the national imagining was contested in terms of boundaries, specifically the tensions between ethnic boundaries and a desire to portray Uzbekistan as a civic, multiethnic nation. Producers of Uzbekistan's national holiday spectacles were interested in imposing a partic-ular order on the ways that identity in Uzbekistan was portrayed, but at the same time, my ethnographic observations showed the conflict and contestation that this organization of identity entailed. Holiday spectacles always contained blocks of song and dance representing a conceptual mapping of the cultures of the peoples of Uzbekistan and of the nations of the world. Here I focus on cases of conflict between the ways that elites wanted to categorize various ethnic groups and those who were to represent the categorized. The first example relates to the "Turkistan" block, reserved for the now-independent nations of the Central Asian region, and the "regions" block, which is used to display the internal diversity of Uzbekistan defined largely in ethnic terms. The second example comes from the production of the "friendship of the peoples" block, which showed off the variety of Uzbekistan's ethnic cultures, from Ukrainian to Tatar to Korean. In this block, the elites wanted to draw on Uzbekistan's multiethnic population in order to portray itself as having a civic-national as well as an ethnic national identity.

Uzbekistan's holiday performances clearly show the staying power of the Soviet definition of nationality, which set up a strict hierarchy of nations, nationalities, and peoples, along with creating objective definitive boundaries between ethnic groups. Kyrgyz and Kazakhs, for example, are at the same level in the hierarchy as Uzbeks because they are both independent countries, whereas Tatars and Uighurs rank a notch lower because they are among the many "peoples of Uzbekistan." Because holiday spectacles are divided up into different thematic blocks, these differences place differently ranked ethnic groups in different blocks. Thus, the organization of the holiday spectacle forces a distinction between ethnic groups that belong in the "friendship" block, such as Tatars and Uighurs, and those that belong in the "Turkestan, our common home" block, such as Kyrgyz and Kazakhs.

The boundaries between regional and national identities that exist in the minds of Tashkent cultural elites showed up several times in discussions of numbers that had elements that "didn't belong" in a particular block. For example, the Sirdaryo region incorporated Kyrgyz performers in Kyrgyz costume into their original program for Independence Day but were told by the Orgkom (the organizational committee of cabinet-level government officials overseeing the holiday) to "lose the Kyrgyz," who belong in the Turkistan block, not the regional block. Even though the director of the Sirdaryo ensemble said he was just fulfilling the instructions to "express regional character," by showing the importance in his region of citizens of Uzbekistan who happen to be ethnic Kyrgyz, this did not fit with the Orgkom's paradigm of homogeneous "regional character." Similarly, in the Navro'z holiday concert for 1996, the folk ensemble from Bukhara wanted to do a song with Tajik lyrics because much of the population of the Bukhara region speaks Tajik as a mother tongue. At a seminar for the directors of the folk ensembles from the regions of Uzbekistan, the director of the ensemble got into an argument with the lead directors over whether a song with Tajik lyrics could be allowed to represent one of Uzbekistan's regions. The Tashkent lead director suggested they just translate the lyrics into Uzbek, to which the ensemble director replied with exasperation, "but it's a *Tajik* song!" In the end, the ensemble director was forced to choose an Uzbek song instead. Diversity is allowed in the representation of regions, but it must be intra-Uzbek diversity. Ethnic diversity goes somewhere else.

But sometimes even the directors of the holiday spectacles get tripped up as to which group belongs where. During the Independence Day spectacle, a group of dances is devoted every year to "friendship of the peoples," a familiar Soviet trope. Representatives of the ethnic cultural centers are supposed to participate in this event, which means that sometimes, for example, although Tajik ethnic culture apparently was not allowed in the "regions" block, it can wind up being represented in both the "Turkistan" block (representing a "national" culture) and the "friendship" block (representing an ethnic culture of the peoples of Uzbekistan). The tension over "who goes where" in the categorization of ethnicity can highlight the ways that ethnic nationalism is the default position, whereas civic nationalism has to be crafted. For example, one of the lead organizers of Independence Day '96 embarrassed himself as well as the representatives from the Tajik cultural center when he said, "your holiday [Tajikistan's Independence Day] is coming up soon, too!" There was an awkward silence before one of the Tajiks icily replied, "it's not our holiday." At which point the man, a city government official, chuckled nervously and said, "well, of course, you're one of us. I wasn't, er, you know, our government, uh, not to say that . . ." (field notes from staff meeting, August 1996).

Although discrimination against non-Uzbeks was a feature of daily life in Uzbekistan, people from a wide variety of ethnic backgrounds worked together in Tashkent, and since 1989 there have been relatively few incidents of inter-ethnic conflict in Uzbekistan. In other cases related to the "friendship of the peoples" block, the resistance came from practical concerns and a lack of interest in the official nation-building project on the part of representatives of non-Uzbek ethnic groups. There were several large ethnic groups in Tashkent with cultural centers and enough active and talented community members to put together a spectacle number, but most of them resisted inclusion in the holiday because of time and budget constraints (the government funds for these centers are largely symbolic). The Korean cultural center had a very active amateur ensemble and was called on several times a year to perform at public cultural events. Likewise, the Tatar and Uighur cultural centers had fairly good talent available, but other centers (Latvian, Lithuanian, and German, to name a few) did not have the same talent pool to draw on and considered the "invitation" to participate in holiday concerts an unfair burden. Even though the ethnic cultural centers that were charged with the responsibility of putting together a number for the holiday show did not particularly want to devote their time and energy to the spectacle, they were more or less commanded to participate by the Organizational Committee of the holiday.

Holiday organizers described both an outward and an inward face to the friendship of the peoples block: the outward face presented a unified, multiethnic Uzbekistan to international guests, and the inward face encouraged members of various ethnic groups to participate in their national holiday (Independence Day). In his instructions to representatives from Tashkent's ethnic cultural centers, one holiday organizer explained how he wanted them to put together numbers for the 1996 Independence Day spectacle:

> He wants to have people from the cultural centers up on stage performing, too, because "it's their homeland. Let the people themselves participate." He wants peace, friendship, and festivity in the songs. He emphasized that it's important, this being a multinational republic, to include all of them in the celebration: "your participation is obligatory," he said. And, implying what was in it for them, he said, "you all know your own, right? They'll be recognized on TV." (Field notes from staff meeting, August 1996)

In spite of this pep talk and the commands from both city government and the Ministry of Cultural Affairs to participate in the "friendship" block, I observed a great reluctance and passive resistance on the part of these groups to participate in the holiday concerts. Perhaps ironically, there was a greater reluctance on the part of these groups than there was on the part of the regional folk ensembles, for example, to devote time and energy to the state's civic nationality project.

The final kind of indicator I discuss in terms of my own findings has to do with a case that illustrates the conflict between cultural elites and government elites, who have differing agendas for the portrayal of the content of Uzbek ethnic identity. An example of this happened after the dress rehearsal for the 1996 Navro'z spectacle, when the representatives from the cabinet of ministers canceled a dance representing fire, one of the key symbols of Navro'z. The official parameters of Uzbek national identity were much more friendly toward Islamic practices than Zoroastrian practices, and in the minds of the political elites, the dance looked too much like fire worship. This was frustrating to the dance's creators, who saw an opportunity to engage their creative vision in a genuine exploration of their people's heritage:

> In my opinion, you can't erase history, good, bad or average, it's all ours. At one time, in the ancient past, there weren't Uzbeks or Turks, there were some kinds of tribes here and they were fire worshippers. But in general, Navro'z is considered a Muslim holiday even though that's all relative, since it wasn't originally Muslim but was adopted by the

Muslims. But our [pauses] boys in politics decided that wasn't allowed. . . . They explained that "this isn't ours." (Interview with a theater director, Tashkent, April 1996)

This incident was also frustrating for them because it demonstrated the power of bureaucrats over the creative vision of the artists. The response of cultural elites in Uzbekistan to this friction between political and creative interests is usually resignation and rationalization rather than rebellion. The same director said later in the interview:

I don't think that anything terrible would have happened if it [the fire dance] had been left in, but it's not like it was a great loss, either. As a director, as an artist, it simply would have been interesting: how to communicate the idea, the theme, of fire worship . . . through the arts, you know? It was interesting in and of itself. But, since different viewers would see it, since it would be transmitted by television and tapes would go to different countries, it was an issue of Uzbekistan being a Muslim country, a Muslim state, and then "there's something about a fire . . . what are they up to there anyway?" You get it? There are these political nuances . . . it's obvious that there are politics that we can't fully comprehend.

Because my research on national identity in Uzbekistan focused primarily on the way that elites projected their imagination of the nation, I could have done a fairly successful discourse analysis project without ever having to set foot in Uzbekistan. I could have gotten the video tapes of the holiday concerts and coded them, for example, and made some of the same arguments I made here, about the mixing of cosmopolitan and local identities, the modern and the traditional in national identity, and about the way that the concerts schematize national, ethnic, and regional cultures. However, because I did ethnographic work as well, I was able to put this discourse analysis into a larger framework that also included contingency and conflict. I was able to see what was considered and discarded, and I was often able to find out why. Thus ethnographic methods should be seen as an important component of any study that seeks to understand identity on the level of meaning or in terms of contestation.

V

EXPERIMENTS

12

Psychological Approaches to Identity

Experimentation and Application

Rose McDermott

What is an identity? Does it refer only to some concrete category to which individuals believe they belong, like white, female, or Catholic? Does it instead refer to a particular kind of social relationship, such as daughter, wife, or sister? Or is it a kind of internal personal characteristic, like smart, witty, or perceptive? Assessment measures in clinical psychology, for instance, consider identity statements that stress the last of these formulations to represent the healthiest and most mature conceptualizations. Obviously, the colloquial meaning and understanding of identity is broad and loose enough to encompass all of these meanings. And when a single concept can refer to so many different notions, and mean so many different things, it can prove difficult to define, measure, and test.

The field of psychology has been interested in the notion of identity almost since its inception in the late nineteenth century. One of the earliest and most influential of neo-Freudian thinkers, Erik Erikson (1950), remained particularly fascinated with the meaning of ego identity and its development. Other early developmental psychologists also showed great interest in the process of identity formation as well. Most of these early investigations into the concept of identity focused on the creation and maintenance of a stable personal identity or a sense of self. Those who investigated the notion of identity from this perspective concentrated on the formation of individual ego identity in particular.

Yet, as noted, identity can also refer to a particular kind of social relationship. Those who have investigated the notion of identity from this angle have focused on the nature of the relationship between the self and the group. One of the leading figures in this area, Henri Tajfel, developed social identity theory and instigated the use of a minimal group paradigm to experimentally manipulate and test his model's predictions. This theory has spawned the most robust series of experimental research agendas in identity theory to date; in addition, most of the applications of psychological work on identity to political science topics and themes have utilized this model.

This chapter begins with a substantive discussion of the experimental work that has been conducted on social identity. This work deals almost exclusively with the implications, ramifications, and limitations of social identity theory. Limitations of this work for applications to political science will be addressed. The final section of this chapter examines some of the ways in which the method of experimentation might be expanded to investigate other realms of social identity and its progeny, social categorization theory within a political context. Social categorization (J. Turner, 1985, 1999; J. Turner and Oakes, 1986) adds a more cognitive element to social identity theory by introducing the importance of self-perception and self-selection into constructions of identity. Self-categorization assumes that individuals can place themselves into numerable and overlapping social categories.

EXPERIMENTAL EXPLORATIONS OF SOCIAL IDENTITY THEORY

Experimentation

In the larger identity project of which this chapter is a part, several methods of investigation have been presented as relevant to work on identity. Along with discourse analysis, content analysis, cognitive mapping, and surveys and interviews, experimentation offers one of those methods. Within political science, experimentation certainly has not taken hold as a common method of inquiry, although it is gaining ground in studies of voting behavior. However, experimentation has a long and successful history of utility in social psychology and the hard sciences, and increasingly in behavioral economics as well. Within the discipline of social psychology, experiments have been used extensively to examine identity in general and social identity theory in particular.

In a well-designed experiment, the experimenter develops a protocol that tests the particular hypothesis under investigation. For an experiment to produce reliable and accurate results, subjects must be randomly assigned to at least one experimental condition and one control condition. In this way, the experimenter attempts to control for the influence of all extraneous factors in order to examine only the impact of the variable or variables of interest. When a manipulation produces a significantly consistent effect on subjects in one condition and not in another, observers can become confident that the manipulated variable was indeed responsible for the measured effect. In this way, experiments offer a particular advantage that no other method can match;

when they are done well, they can establish a causal relationship between variables by controlling for the effect of all extraneous factors and manipulating only the variable of interest. In addition, aggregations of experiments can begin to tease out some of the dynamic ways in which related variables interact and exert effects on each other. Needless to say, limitations on the external validity of at least some experimental findings to broader political contexts exists; further discussion of the specifics related to social identity follows this section.

Social Identity Theory

As noted, most experimental tests of notions of identity have concentrated on social identity theory. Social identity theory began to be developed in the late 1970s by Henri Tajfel and his colleague John Turner (1970, 1981a, 1982; J. Turner, Brown, and Tajfel 1979). Social identity theory presented two important insights, which have continued to drive research into the relationship between individuals and groups. First, social identity theory rested on the foundation of social categorization. The idea here is that people quickly and easily divide themselves and others into basic categories. Tajfel argued that the social identity of intergroup relations was based on the categorization of the social environment. He suggested that the composition of an individual's social identity results fundamentally from a process of social comparison: people ask themselves how they are like other people and how they are different from them. Tajfel believed that the manifestations of in-group favoritism remain sensitive to both comparative aspects and specific cultural norms within given social contexts.

In-Group Identification

Social categories constitute the basis for collective identities. Tajfel argued that the distinction between one's in-group and the out-group was based fundamentally on the nature and feeling of belonging and that individuals used several processes to relate themselves to a group, including categorization, personal identity, comparison, and psychological distinctiveness. Psychological distinctiveness between groups, in particular, can strengthen high-status, insecure group identification when enhanced. In other words, if group members remain insecure in their identification to a high-status group, heightening the perceived differences between groups can increase group attachment. Because individuals are naturally aware of the existence of categories, this recognition, in and of itself, generates in-group favoritism. From this perspective, objective reasons for conflict or preexisting hostility remain superfluous; social identity alone remains sufficient for intergroup conflict to occur (Tajfel 1974).

Thus, social categorization can lead to in-group favoritism in and of itself. Once people divide the universe into "us" versus "them," the most basic of perceptual divisions, certain assumptions readily follow. Individual group members assume that out-group members are more similar to each other than those in the in-group, that they are different from the in-group, and that they are different from the in-group in ways that are bad and wrong. It is a short leap from the belief that others are bad and wrong to a feeling that we are good and right. Such processes occur even when people understand that their group has been formed on an arbitrary basis, or when the previous associations between individual members are nonexistent. It seems that all that is required for a group to form is for someone to tell the individual members that they are, in fact, a group (Billig and Tajfel 1973). The consequences that follow from such a label appear nothing short of amazing; members now believe that their constituents possess better personalities and better looks. In addition, members want to reward other in-group members more than out-group members. One of the most interesting manifestations of in-group favoritism is the emergence of the so-called self-serving attributional bias, whereby members understand their group successes to result from their own skills and talents and their failures to result from external circumstances beyond their control, while simultaneously assuming that the out-groups successes result from chance and luck and their failures from their own incompetence (for a review, see Brewer and Kramer 1985).

Self-Esteem and Motivation

The second insight of social identity theory came from an appreciation of the fact that the groups to which individuals belong mean something to them. People derive important satisfactions and gratifications from their group memberships. Everyone uses their various group memberships to help define who they are along important categories that include factors such as age, sex, race, religion, sexual orientation, occupation and so on. The idea here is that once a person sees himself or herself as part of a group, he or she will be able to derive important self-esteem from that group membership by enhancing the advantages of the in-group while simultaneously derogating the out-group.

This implication deserves particular attention because it demands a motivational aspect to social identity theory. While social categorization may result from a purely cognitive process, and that process may by itself exacerbate between-group differences, the desire to see oneself as not only different from but also better than others requires motivation. Because social identity theory has been used to explain some of the potential sources for prejudice and discrimination, motivation becomes critical because it means that mere cognitive processes of social categorization remain insufficient for racism or sexism, for example, to occur.

This motivational aspect of social identity theory provides the most direct theoretical linkage to the earlier neo-Freudian theories, which require motivation for the creation and establishment of identity. Although the forms of and sources of motivation may differ, both sets of models assume an intrinsically affective element to the constitution of identity and the behavior that flows from the recognition of the self as part of a group. The way in which these models differ remains equally significant. Fundamentally, Erikson's model, and that of other neo-Freudians, presents an essentially individualistic notion of identity. Freud viewed identity as a form of self-identification, a process whereby a child develops and internalizes a sense of self on the basis of a process involving interactions with the parents and internalization of parental values. Erikson (1950) was the first of the neo-Freudians to move this process of identity formation out beyond childhood. Erikson straddled the intrapsychic definition of identity provided by psychologists and the environmental one offered by sociologists. He argued that in selecting an identity, an individual child thereby engages in important ego differentiation from the parents. While espousing a multifaceted notion of identity, Erikson fundamentally constructed identity as a bipolar dimension from synthesis to confusion, representing the degree of comfort and integration an individual has been able to establish both within him and with the outside world.[1] Tajfel and his colleagues present a definition of identity that requires a similar interaction between psychological and social processes (for a discussion of these approaches, see J. Turner and Oakes 1986). In this regard, social identity theory offers a much more *social* understanding of the creation, nature, and function of identity than other psychological models.

Out-Group Denigration

The reason social identity theory has been used to try to explain discrimination is because one of the most important consequences of the process of social identification lies in the fact that people seem to want to see themselves and their own group members, the in-group, as being superior to excluded others,

---

[1] For a wonderfully accurate, rich and comprehensive review of this literature, see Seth Schwarz 2001.

or the out-group, on whatever relevant dimension group inclusion is assessed. In particular, when allocating resources across groups, individuals are prone to give more to members of their own group and less to members of the out-group. They do so when they do not personally benefit from this system of allocation and even when doing so proves personally disadvantageous for them (J. Turner, Brown, and Tajfel 1979; Brown, Schmidt, and Collins 1988). People appear to allocate resources in this way not simply to provide an advantage for the in-group but rather to create an explicit relative advantage for the in-group over the out-group (Tajfel et al. 1971; Brewer and Silver 1978).

In order to test his theory of social identity, Tajfel developed an experimental method often referred to as the minimal-group paradigm. Minimal groups are so called because extremely minimal effort is required to create a sense of groupness or cohesion among subjects in such experiments. Originally, Tajfel sought to facilitate the discovery of those conditions that were both necessary and sufficient for producing in-group favoritism. In his early work, it quickly became clear that simply grouping people in and of itself proved sufficient to create discrimination against the out-group. This experimental paradigm has been used extensively to manipulate and test various implications and ramification of social identity theory.

Tajfel's earliest work on social identity theory was experimental in nature. Note that in this work, and much of the work on social identity theory that followed, social identity is defined experimentally in the most minimal of terms. People are assumed to be part of a group once they are told by the experimenter that they are a group. By and large, individuals in these experiments do not possess a long history of being members of the same particular religious or political organizations, for example, which might have served to bond them together before the experiment. Neither are they classified according to readily acceptable and easily observable categories, such as race or sex. In this way, social identity is defined in terms of a minimal group membership, and what is then measured is not the strength of individual association to the group but rather the effects of this group membership on certain, usually behavioral outcomes, such as the allocation of money across individuals or groups.

While investigating the effect of social categorization on intergroup behavior in the early 1970s, Tajfel and others noticed that the discrimination between groups that he witnessed in his subjects could not be readily or easily explained away by their rational calculations of self-interest or by any previously existing hostility against the out-group. In these experiments, subjects were divided into groups on the basis of extremely trivial grounds. For example, in one study, Tajfel et al. (1971) asked students for their impression of paintings by Paul Klee and Wassily Kandinsky. They were then divided on the basis of their expressed preference for impressionist art. Another experiment had subjects toss a coin and divided them according to whether their coins landed heads or tails (Billig and Tajfel 1973). In a later experiment conducted in the Netherlands, subjects were separated on the basis of color. One group was called "green" and the other "blue" and asked to write on either green or blue paper (Rabbie 1981).[2]

Yet in all these examples, even when individuals were divided into groups on the basis of irrelevant classifications, in-group members favored their own members in individual allocations of real rewards and punishments. Further, Tajfel and his colleagues found that people allocated real resources in ways that maximized the differences between the in-group and the out-group, even when such an allocation strategy cost the individual in objective terms (Tajfel et al. 1971). Wilder (1981) sums up the typical differences in outcome allocation in these kinds of "minimal group" studies nicely: "When given the opportunity to divide 15 points (worth money) subjects generally award 9 or 10 points to their own group and 5 or 6 points to the other group." While there do not appear to be differences in these tendencies based on sex or age, these preferences do seem somewhat mitigated among individuals from communal cultures.

Experimental Tests of Mediating Factors

Accountability, or having to justify one's preferences to others, does appear to provide a key mediating factor for the mitigation of in-group favoritism and out-group discrimination in a variety of contexts. Marques et al. (1998), using the minimal group paradigm in four separate experiments, tested the notion that judgments that group members make of themselves and others reflect separate but simultaneous evaluations of the in-group and the out-group. In a series of four different experimental studies, subjects were assigned to either in-group or out-group membership status. Their status as either a modal or deviant member of their group was also manipulated. In a final manipulation, the salience of their personal accountability changed, with one group held accountable to in-group members and the second held accountable to out-group members. The authors found that increasing accountability and the salience of group norms increased derogation of out-group normative (meaning both in-group deviant and out-group modal members) and validation of in-group normative members (meaning out-group deviant and in-group modal

---

[2] For an example of how forty-five seconds of exposure to the names of other people can induce implicit liking and identification, and attraction to the group, see Greenwald, Pickrell, and Farnham 2002 and Pinter and Greenwald 2004. They call this the "implicit partisanship effect."

members). This is one of few studies that examine the interaction between small-group dynamics and social identity, demonstrating that such group tasks and constraints can strengthen social identity when individuals judge others both inside and outside their reference group. In a further examination of accountability processes, Dobbs and Crano (2001) find that out-group accountability, operationalized as requiring justification of the allocation of awards, alleviated out-group discrimination. This finding proved particularly prominent when the allocator came from the majority, as opposed to minority, group.

Evaluation, like accountability, can influence in-group identification. In one examination of this phenomenon, Simon and Stürmer (2003) examined the effect of performance evaluation on collective identification as well. These authors manipulated whether a subject was treated by other in-group members with respect or not, as well as whether he received a positive or negative performance evaluation. Not surprisingly, these authors found that respectful treatment increased collective identification and willingness to help the group regardless of the tenor of the performance evaluation.

Interestingly, this investigation has been extended to criticism that comes from out-group members as well. Critical feedback from members of one's group typically prompts a different response than similar negative evaluations from outside the group. The notion that criticism from one's own in-group is received less defensively than chiding from the out-group has been referred to as the intergroup sensitivity effect. Hornsey and colleagues have investigated this work in innovative ways. In one experiment, Hornsey, Trembath, and Gunthorpe (2004) used Australians and non-Australians to investigate the perception of criticism. In this experiment, Australians received criticism either from other Australians or from non-Australians. In this case, subjects accepted in-group criticism more favorably than out-group criticism only when the critic seemed to have a great deal of psychological investment in the group. In a second experiment, out-group critics in the form of Asian Australians were able to overcome sensitivity and defensiveness on the part of Anglo-Australians when they self-identified within the larger, shared category of "Australian." This implies that out-group members can overcome in-group defensiveness by identifying themselves in a larger superordinate category. Other work by Hornsey and Imani (2004) indicates that while experience with the in-group has no effect on out-groups' criticism, lack of experience can hurt the effect of in-group criticism. Constructive criticism helps to overcome defensiveness regardless of the source.

Cadinu and Rothbart (1996) began to explore some of the mechanisms by which social identity may create in-group favoritism within the context of a minimal-group paradigm. They hypothesized that in-group favoritism reflects the tendency to base assessments of in-group others on the self and to base judgments of the out-group on the opposite. In a series of four experiments, they manipulated the order in which subjects received information about the self and the target group. Some subjects had been categorized into minimal groups, while others had not. Subjects were then given ratings of particular traits about one group and asked to estimate the level of that trait in the other groups. In-group judges tended to base group rankings on the self, whereas out-group and uncategorized judges simply judged groups to be opposite to one another on the trait of interest. A fourth experiment gave feedback about the self or in-group concerning unfamiliar traits to subjects and, interestingly, found that subjects were more willing to make the leap from self to in-group than the reverse, from in-group to self. It seems that people have an easier time assuming that others are like them than that they are like others. In other words, individuals tend to think, "They are like me, but I am not necessarily like them."

Further experimental research might be able to profitably explore this relationship between self and other as a potential wedge by which to reduce the impact of in-group favoritism by manipulating subject empathy for other individuals' similar identification with, and distinctness from, ostensible group values or beliefs. If the fact that others resemble oneself can be highlighted in such a way as to make others' differences from their group identifications more salient, perhaps stereotyping can begin to diminish.

One of the key factors in in-group favoritism appears to be individual members' level of identification with the group. Marilynn Brewer (1991), arguing that social identities constitute forms of inclusive self-definition, found that lack of personalization and group size interacted in ways that affected the strength of social identification. In particular, she believed that individuals seek social identity as a mechanism by which to reconcile their conflicting needs for assimilation with, and separation from, others. In conceptualizing social identity as a dependent variable, instead of the independent variable it traditionally represented in the earlier studies by Tajfel and others, Brewer discovered that the intensity of group loyalty and social identity was strongest when people were simultaneously able to conceptualize themselves in ways that were both conjoined to others and unique.

Ellemers, Spears, and Doosje (1997) used a bogus pipeline technique to examine how in-group identification varies with levels of group commitment. The bogus pipeline technique (Jones and Sigall 1971) was originally devised to overcome subjects' tendency toward giving socially desirable but false accounts of their attitudes concerning socially sensitive topics like race. In a bogus pipeline, subjects are hooked up to what appear to be electrodes of some kind and told that these measure "skin conductance," "muscle contraction," or some other bogus measure of physiological response. In reality, these electrodes are not linked to anything at all. These studies indicate that when people believe they will be found out for not telling the truth they are more likely to offer their real attitudes and beliefs. This technique can be expensive to implement, in that it requires the purchase of realistic looking hardware and needs precision to administer realistically. Using this technique, the authors examined how in-group identification affected a group member's desire to move to other groups of either higher or lower status. They found that low identifiers see the group as less homogeneous, remain less committed to the group, and show a stronger desire to leave the group for a higher status group than high identifiers. This was true regardless of whether it was easy or hard to leave the group. Of course, this experimental research leaves aside the important predetermining question of what makes one individual more likely to identify more strongly with one particular group than another. In addition, a person may identify much more with certain of their multiple group identities than others. Perhaps certain categories of ethnic or gender identification demand stronger loyalty from group members than political or religious organizations because individuals cannot change these personal characteristics in the same way; however, this speculation remains an empirical question yet to be fully explored.

Additional work by Van Vugt and Hart (2004) examines the relationship between group identification and group loyalty. By manipulating individual levels of identification with the group, as well as the presence of an attractive or unattractive opportunity for escape from the group, these authors found that high identifiers demonstrate a stronger desire to stay in the group, even in the presence of an attractive exit option. Through further experimentation, these authors were able to determine that this effect is caused by the extremely positive association that high identifiers have for the group. This finding is not explained either by subjects' self-perception of previous investments that they have made in the group or by their desire not to abandon the group. From this perspective, social identity serves to promote group stability even when times get rough, which makes sense from an evolutionary perspective, where individual motivation to join social groups is based on mutual goals of cooperation and would not necessarily be affected by experience with the group or norms concerning group membership.

This study raises the interesting issue of how groups deal with imposters, or those who pretend to be in-group members when they are really out-group members. In one study involving vegetarians, in-group members showed more negative feelings toward those who ate meat occasionally. Further, high identifiers demonstrated this effect more strongly than low identifiers or non-identifiers. Interestingly, those who said publicly that they were vegetarians but were seen to eat meat were evaluated more negatively than those who kept their claims to be a vegetarian secret. However, vegetarians who tried to keep their meat-eating habits secret but were subsequently exposed for their meat-eating behavior were evaluated more negatively than those who admitted to their meat-eating sins openly (Hunter et al. 2004). This suggests that an in-group member is better off keeping out-group behavior secret so long as he does not get caught; once caught, open confession is more likely to produce a sympathetic response from in-group members than continued denial. Perhaps such dynamics help underlie the on-air confession of extreme societal deviants on television; once a sinner admits to her limitations, in-group members appear more likely to evaluate that person less negatively than if she continues to illegitimately claim in-group status.

Various work has attempted to distinguish the effect of interpersonal attractiveness from social identification more broadly. Such attachments are easily distinguished in multiuser dungeon communities, which are virtual groups. Typically played on the Web, such communities involve multiplayer computer games, often involving fantasy, linking many people throughout the world. Experimentalists can utilize existing game settings or design their own for particular purposes, but the latter strategy often takes a great deal of time and can cost a lot of money. Utz (2003) found both sources of attachment in her subjects within these communities but located different sources for their occurrence. Interpersonal attraction increased with length of group membership and physical life contacts. Social identification, in addition to predicting the expected in-group biases, appeared to be related to cognitive indicators of self-categorization and various aspects of the situational context. Perhaps automatic cognitive processes set up and define social categorization and identification, but learned behavior and processes that encompass the length, depth, and breadth of association strengthen the intensity of ties over time.

Further work by Ellemers, Kortekass, and Ouwerkerk (1999) argues for the importance of distinguishing processes of self-categorization from commitment to the group and self-esteem in examining social identity. They suggest that each concept provides an independent contribution to the process of members' development of social identity. In this experiment, they manipulated in-group size (majority or minority), structure (self-selected or assigned), and status (high or low). The authors found that each process exerted an independent effect on social identity. Not surprisingly, group status did influence group self-esteem. Both group status and group structure affected emotional attachments to the group. These findings hold important implications for those who seek to understand the emotional basis of group attachment; seemingly one way to increase emotional attachment to a group is to increase its status. Finally, only group structure influenced expressions of in-group favoritism. Again, the implications of this result offer sober instruction to those who seek to mediate the impact of in-group favoritism on out-group discrimination. In other words, in-group favoritism appears relatively impervious to the external manipulation of characteristics that might be easy to change, such as size. When groups form from the self-selection, choice, and definition of individual members, in-group favoritism remains remarkably robust.

Emotional factors appear intriguingly nuanced in their effect on group perception. For example, most work on group perception shows that individuals perceive members of the outgroup in homogeneous ways, seeing everyone in the group as similar to each other, while perceiving members of their own group as distinctly heterogeneous on various personality dimensions. Yet this perception can be altered when faces in the outgroup are manipulated to look angry. Ackerman et al. (2006) presented 192 white subjects with white faces and black faces that were either neutral or angry in expression. Later recognition tests in which subjects were asked if they had seen the face previously demonstrated typical outgroup homogeneity biases for neutral faces. However, surprisingly, this bias was completely eliminated when subjects were asked to recall the angry black faces. In fact, subjects showed more accurate recall for angry black than angry white faces, reversing the typical out-group homogeneity effect.

One of the most interesting applications of work on social identity to the political environment lies in the arena of leadership studies. Haslam and his colleagues (2001) examined the nature of charismatic leadership from a social identity perspective. They suggested that a leader's behavior serves to affirm and promote in-group identification among followers. In an experimental manipulation, they found that leaders who engage in identity-affirming behavior were perceived as more charismatic than those who exhibited more neutral or identity-negating behavior. In fact, identity-affirming leaders appeared to be protected from negative attributions, even in the context of a bad crisis.

Further work on leadership endorsement by Platow and van Knippenberg (2001) experimentally manipulated leader in-group prototypicality and leader fairness in distribution across groups. Interestingly, leader endorsement differed by levels of group identification. Low identifiers provided stronger endorsement for leaders who demonstrated fair distribution policies. High identifiers were more likely to endorse a leader who was perceived as high in in-group prototypicality regardless of his distribution strategies. For high identifiers to endorse a leader who was seen as not typical of the in-group, the leader had to make distributions that favored the in-group. Obviously, this finding raises important political implications. If leaders can engage in unfair distribution as long as they demonstrate characteristics of dominant in-group members, then they can garner support from those whose interests they thwart. One can imagine leaders manipulating patriotism for this effect in particular. Similarly, leaders who may offer policies that provide benefits to a large segment of society but who do so in an identity-negating manner are likely to lose support no matter how objectively popular their policies may seem.

In a further exploration of subjects' evaluations of leaders based on their treatment of various groups, Duck and Fielding (2003) manipulated the group status of the leader and the leader's behavior in the context of two subgroups within a larger superordinate group. The group leader was either an in-group or out-group member. The experimenters varied whether the leader favored the in-group or the out-group and also whether the comparative context took place within the group or outside the group. They found that members viewed in-group leaders more positively than out-group leaders regardless of the leader's allocation of benefits across groups. An in-group leader who favored the in-group improved his evaluation, as did an out-group leader who unexpectedly benefited the in-group. However, out-group leaders who favored their own group not only were seen as less fair and more biased but also generated less support for the superordinate group, leading to a less unified perception of the overall larger group. These findings pose obvious implications for partisan political politics. To the extent that leaders can appear to be a member of the in-group, they can reliably count on member support even when they do not further their members' direct interests. However, when they obviously play to their in-group members, they can alienate the larger constituency in ways that may make it more difficult to govern the larger polity as effectively or with as great a degree of legitimacy.

Clearly, a central aspect of leadership relates to power and its perceived legitimacy. In a study conducted by Matthew Hornsey et al. (2003), these effects were manipulated. In this experiment, math-science subjects were told they had either a high or a low level of representation relative to social science majors; they were also informed that this relative power position was either legitimate or illegitimate. They found that both high- and low-power groups proved more biased when power was illegitimate. Further, groups expected more discrimination from illegitimate power sources.

Finally, and interestingly, sex differences do appear to exist in in-group bias, at least with regard to sexual groups (Rudman and Goodwin 2004). Specifically, women's positive in-group bias (toward other women) remains remarkably stronger than male in-group bias. The authors undertook four experiments to examine the underpinnings of this ostensible sex difference in in-group bias; these experiments relied on self-reporting, implicit survey instruments designed to get at attitudes through indirect means. They found that women, but not men, demonstrated cognitive balance between in-group bias, identity, and self-esteem. They suggest that subjects show a pro-female bias to the extent that they favor their mothers over their fathers or associate male identity with violence. In addition, they found that *men* who demonstrated a more positive attitude toward sex showed more implicit favoritism toward women. The authors suggest that these findings indicate that gender presents a unique group for social identity.

APPLICATIONS OF SOCIAL IDENTITY TO POLITICAL SCIENCE

Expanding Experimental Paradigms

Psychological work on social identity theory has found some application within political science. This work has typically appeared in one of three different types of formats: international relations; negotiator behavior; and race and ethnic behaviors, which constitute by far the majority of such applications.

Tests of Conflict Resolution: "Us" versus "Them" into "We"

One of the insights for solving group conflict that grew out of Tajfel's paradigm was that groups that shared a common enemy could sometimes create or discover a new larger group identity and thus avoid intergroup hostility. This finding was consistent with Muzafir Sherif's earlier seminal studies called the Robber's Cave experiments (Sherif et al. 1961). In these studies, Sherif was able to generate conflict between two groups of boy campers who had been divided on relatively trivial grounds, such as which building they slept in. He was then able to overcome the prejudices that developed between the groups by creating situations where boys from both groups had to work together for common goals that were equally important to both. For example, a bus carrying both groups drove into a ditch, and boys had to work together to push it out.

Aronson's (1978) famous jigsaw classroom provided a profound demonstration of how superordinate goals can overcome established in-group prejudices and discrimination. Working in grammar school classrooms in Texas and California, Aronson divided students into racially and academically diverse groups of six. Each lesson was then divided into six parts, so that one student in each group learns a particular section. Students then report on their findings to their home group. In order to complete the group project, students have to learn and work together to integrate the parts. This strategy overcomes even entrenched prejudice to generate students who like themselves, each other, and school in general better.

Other people extended this work on intergroup bias to explore experimentally the ways in which members can transform the cognitive representations of their group to include members who might previously have been excluded; the idea here is that once two groups come to see themselves as both part of one larger group, conflict between them will be vastly mitigated as everyone comes to see each other as being part of the new in-group. Gaertner, Dovidio, and Bachman (1996) tested this notion of shifting members' notions from "us" versus "them" to "we" using a variety of methods, including an experiment, two surveys, and a field experiment. Drawing on Allport's (1954) contact hypothesis, they found that factors such as equal status between members, cooperative interdependence, self-revealing interactions, and egalitarian norms appear to be important prerequisites for the successful induction of a common group identity among previously separate groups. This explains, for instance, why mere contact between certain groups, such as majority and minority racial groups, is not successful in and of itself in garnering cooperation and understanding. Other features such as equal status must be present before attempts at cooperation are likely to prove effective in overcoming established prejudice and discrimination in real-world settings.

In another exploration of the effect of inducing a broader sense of social identity on the outcome of conflict processes, Kramer, Pommerenke, and Newton (1993) examined the effect of social identity in the context of negotiator decision making. They manipulated the salience of individual identification with the group to be high or low and also varied the level of interpersonal accountability that each individual had to the group to be high or low. They found that making shared social identity salient resulted in greater equity in outcomes, as negotiators gained a heightened concern for the other side's position. In this way, individuals who felt a sense of shared identity with their opponents were able to incorporate the other's desires into their own hierarchy of preferences. In addition, they showed that increased negotiator accountability similarly increased the preference for equal outcomes.

Another study of negotiating teams compared the performance of individuals and teams in negotiation (Polzer 1996). This study pitted cognitive and intergroup relations approaches to determine the effect of negotiating size on performance. Cognitive approaches would assume that teams work best by maximizing the number of ideas and perspectives brought to bear on a problem and reduce pressure on any given individual. Intergroup relations models suggest the possibility that team performance might be impeded by competitiveness and low levels of trust and cooperation. Polzer manipulated the structure of negotiations in an experimental design that included interindividual, intergroup, and mixed dyads. He found that teams do indeed increase competitiveness and decrease cooperation and trust between negotiating parties. In mixed negotiations between individuals and groups, however, groups did outperform individuals and, not surprisingly, were perceived to possess both more power and more alternative resolutions. Interestingly, teams decreased the performance of novices and increased the performance of experts in negotiation. This finding remains consistent with general findings in social efficacy, such that people and animals perform overlearned behavior better in the presence of others, but performance for novel tasks remains highest in solitude. For example, students do better taking a test with others when they know the material well but do better taking a test alone when they are relatively unfamiliar with the material.

Race and Ethnic Conflict

Not surprisingly, this area has received the most attention and application of social identity theory to political science. Most scholars have looked to social identity theory for an empirically based explanation for phenomena such as prejudice, discrimination, and nationalism. Some of the most sophisticated analyses of the impact of race on attitudes have been done in the context of experiments embedded in nationally representative samples, such as the National Election Survey (Kuklinski et al. 1997; see also Taeku Lee, Chapter 4 in this volume). However, these experiments have not typically explored social identity as a causal mechanism in attitudes toward race.

Most applications of social identity theory to race take race as a particularly powerful basis of in-group bias. In one study, white dyads were placed in either competitive or interdependent dyads, which were experimentally manipulated to interact with confederate pairs who were either black or white (D. A. Taylor and Moriarty 1987). In-group bias was determined by the level of attraction the subjects had toward their confederate partners. Results found that in-group bias was greater when groups were competitive rather than interdependent and when the confederate out-group was black rather than white.

Other scholars have attempted to investigate whether pride and prejudice naturally co-occur in the real world as commonly as in the laboratory. In a nationally based study of African Americans, Herring, Jankowski, and Brown (1999) found that the strength of black identity was most strongly defined around a sense of common fate for the group. The investigators did not locate this identity in terms of opposition to whites, necessarily, but rather through the socialization provided by both informal and formal networks of other blacks. In a theoretically similar study of the relationship between patriotism and nationalism, de Figueiredo and Elkins (2003) investigated the relationship between in-group pride and out-group prejudice in the context of immigration policy. They found that, while pride can be measured in terms of two distinct dimensions of patriotism and nationalism, each of these factors appears to have a different relationship with prejudice. Patriots do not appear to harbor prejudice toward immigrants, whereas nationalists demonstrate hostility toward this out-group. Druckman (1994) argues that social identity theory can provide a useful psychological perspective on the origins of nationalism precisely because individuals develop loyalty to groups that can produce hostility toward outside groups. He suggests that such hostility can provide the basis for collective stereotypes held by members of one group toward members of other groups and that these perceptions can affect group behavior. He posits that such behavior can differentiate groups that operate within any given political context.

In a clever design intended to look at the impact of out-group salience on political evaluations, Valentino (1999) experimentally manipulated U.S. media stories about crime in which the race of the suspect was varied. Support for the U.S. president, at the time Bill Clinton, declined with the report of any crime. But, significantly, his support proved lowest when the crime suspect came from a minority group. Further, when minority suspects were implicated in crime, subjects' evaluation of President Clinton's performance on crime was greatest. This effect also appeared to spread to other race-related issues, such as his performance on welfare. In a further demonstration of the wide-ranging impact of race on evaluations of political candidates, the importance of President Clinton's support as a predictor of overall support was increased for whites who were exposed to minority criminals. These findings are illuminated by similar work that examines the relationship between social identity and mass-media reports of conflict between social groups (Price 1998). Price argues that such reports induce listeners to think about certain issues from within the perspective of their particular social identity and that this process, in turn, leads to polarized perceptions of group identity. This leads to personal opinions that reflect the exaggerated sense of group opinions. Experimental tests of these hypotheses support the notion that media portrayal of group conflict can affect the substance of public opinion. The recent election of Barack Obama provides a fascinating real-world experiment on the ability of an interethnic leader to create and establish a superordinate social identity in American political discourse.

Seul (1999) argues that religion provides a particularly powerful arena of identity competition because religion serves to provide comprehensive worldviews, including systems of ethics, traditions, rituals, and other institutions that support individual needs for belonging, self-esteem, and identity. These religious factors provide especially powerful identity content and thus help to explain why religious conflict remains so endemic and uncompromising. Indeed, Monroe (2001) finds an explanation for morality in identity, noting that, although processes of social categorization appear universal, people do feel a need to grant equal status to all members within a given group. She therefore locates the drive for morality in the human psychological propensity for empathy.

Other scholars have examined the impact of social identity within other political contexts as well. Ewa Golebiowska (1996, 2001) investigated the relationship between individuals and groups as the target of political intolerance. She found experimental support for the notion that individuals from negatively stereotyped political groups are tolerated to the extent that they deviate from the dominant stereotypes of their group. In particular, she finds that individuals from unpopular groups are tolerated more than the groups themselves, and that this tolerance appears particularly pronounced when more information individuates the person from the group. Elizabeth Kier (1998), for one, has turned the implications of social identity theory on its head in arguing for the inclusion of gays in the military. Citing John Turner's work on social categorization and group behavior, she (1998: 21) argues that, "group membership leads to in-group favoritism even where members of a group dislike one another. In other words, it is not interpersonal attraction (or shared values and attitudes) that leads to a group identity, but group membership that leads to interpersonal attraction." In this regard, it is possible to see how the implicit psychological pressures toward in-group identification and aggrandizement can supplant and alleviate long-standing antipathies based on other domains of social identity when such camaraderie is enforced.

HOW TO CONDUCT EXPERIMENTS

In most experimental work on social identity theory within psychology, investigators seek to document and interpret the impact of social identity on important outcomes, such as the distribution of resources across groups by individuals within them. To understand the impact of social identity on such outcomes, various contextual factors of the situation, such as the number of people in a given group or the amount of resources, were kept constant in order to examine the impact of the manipulated variable on the outcome of interest. The purpose in this kind of strategy is to uncover the causal effect of social identity. As a result, some of the situations in which these studies take place may appear highly stylized and unrealistic. This does not diminish the utility of such exercises, however, because they help locate the causal factors of import. If such forces exert an impact on behavior in a controlled laboratory situation, the next step becomes an attempt to explore the extent to which these causal variables motivate, reinforce, or intensify outcomes in real-world contexts with countervailing pressures. Such applications of experimental findings to diverse populations and alternative environments serve to refine theoretical understanding.

One of the benefits of an experimental paradigm is that it requires investigators to specify the measures that are being manipulated. In research on identity, such definition remains central to experimental design. For example, identity can be conceptualized in a wide variety of ways. It can represent a pretreatment background variable, as when people systematically vary on ethnic identification; it can offer a variable to be manipulated experimentally; or it can remain a variable that is assessed only after an independent experimental manipulation has taken place. Random assignment of subjects to conditions typically handles issues related to pretreatment variation in identity, or anything else, successfully. As a treatment variable, experimenters can manipulate identity directly, where possible and appropriate; this is what takes place in the creation of a minimal group around trivial divides, as with the original Tajfel experiments where people were divided randomly according to an ascribed color, toss of a coin, or trivial art preference. When identity results as a posttreatment variable, it emerges as a product of changes in values, incentives, or other factors that have been manipulated in the actual experiment itself. To the extent that identity shifts as a result of these effects, the causal variables lie in the other interventions, not in identity itself. This point highlights the importance of avoiding a tautological design; the effects of various factors in an experiment should result from the independent variables, and not derive from any inherent aspect of the dependent variables, as may easily occur when the impact of racial or sexual identity is being assessed.[3]

Conducting experimental work can seem a daunting enterprise for those who have not undertaken such work before, but the challenges need not overwhelm the interested novice. In psychology, most students learn to conduct experiments through an apprenticeship process of working closely with faculty advisers or more advanced graduate students on experiments they conduct. This remains probably the simplest and the best way to learn both the informal and formal rules and strategies for experimentation. Most laboratories in psychology departments welcome free labor if an interested person wants to

---

[3] I am grateful to Kevin Quinn for helpful comments clarifying this point.

offer research assistance services in exchange for experience and knowledge. I offered my services free for years to various professors in the psychology department at Stanford as an undergraduate and graduate student and learned many of the tricks of the trade from the best in the business, including luminaries such as Philip Zimbardo, Lee Ross, and Amos Tversky. But this route is not open to all and certainly constitutes a tremendous time investment.

There are many other ways to learn the practice of experimentation. Even with limited amounts of money and laboratory space, an interested investigator can conduct a very respectable experiment. For those whose experimental tests can be framed in the context of surveys, or experiments embedded in surveys, Time Sharing Experiments in Social Science (TESS), funded by the National Science Foundation, offers a wonderful opportunity to run experiments for free on a nationally representative sample. While not all proposals are funded, the feedback that an investigator can receive on her proposal can prove invaluable, even if the project is rejected. If accepted, TESS runs the study for the experimenter through a Web-based system whereby subjects participate in exchange for free Internet connections. For those who wish to gain such access without the time-consuming vetting process, private organizations like Knowledge Networks or Polimetrix can provide the same services for a fee.

For those who wish to conduct studies with a more behavioral dimension, many universities offer space that can be used for free as long as it is reserved in advance. Such space can take the form of classrooms, offices, or other facilities. Subjects often need to be paid, but occasionally one can generate subject participation through course credit. Remember that in any experiment involving human subjects, investigators must obtain prior permission from their university's institutional review board. Without such permission, individual researchers have no protection from an unhappy subject who decides to sue the researcher for any reason.

Many useful resources exist for those who wish to study experimentation. My personal favorite for clarity, accuracy, and brevity is *Methods of Research in Social Psychology* (1990) by Elliot Aronson, Phoebe Ellsworth, J. Merrill Carlsmith, and Marti Gonzalez. While the examples in this book focus on psychology and not politics, many of the topics relate to identity, and its scope is comprehensive and very accessible. But many other helpful volumes exist as well.

The main principles of experimentation are simple and basic. Once a person knows what he or she wants to study and has a fair idea of what the causal mechanisms may be, the most important thing is to do the best job possible in controlling for every other conceivable factor, while systematically manipulating the putative causal variable. Design the experiment from the perspective of the subject, imagining what that person's experience will be like, and not from the viewpoint of what you as the experimenter hope to get out of the study. Subjects should be assigned randomly across conditions, and every subject should be administered the same experimental protocol the same way, as much as possible. Start small, and aggregate findings across studies, using past results to inform future manipulations.

It is very easy to get discouraged early when conducting experiments that do not turn out as planned the first time, given that they often require a lot of work to set up. That is why it is very helpful to conduct small pilot tests on willing friends and relatives before undertaking a full-scale experiment to make sure things will work as planned. An astute experimentalist can learn a great deal from debriefing subjects after an experiment to find out what the person was thinking or feeling while doing the required tasks, and this can help improve later variants on the experiment immeasurably. Finally, failure remains simply inevitable and endemic, but very helpful. A good experimentalist learns a great deal from failed experiments. Many skilled, clever, and practiced psychologists consider a 50 percent success rate on experiments to be very good.

EXPANDING EXPERIMENTAL PARADIGMS

Tremendous opportunity exists to expand upon the original social identity paradigms to further explore various aspects of social identity within wider and more representative political contexts. Several issues and topics appear most likely to integrate the psychological findings with political applications, and remain worthy of further highlighting and independent attention.

One of these topics is related to self-esteem. In traditional social identity theory, self-esteem retains a central causal role in the creation of in-group bias and out-group denigration. Yet self-esteem works to sharpen these tendencies, not mitigate them. Just as California's attempt to introduce self-esteem education failed to reduce aggression in schools, higher self-esteem, especially without commensurate accomplishments to justify it, may backfire, thereby inducing greater hostility toward out-groups. Understanding the mechanism by which self-esteem can induce or alleviate out-group hostility deserves greater attention. Self-esteem can be manipulated in experimental settings through false feedback on various tasks, allowing an investigation of its impact on out-group prejudice and discrimination.

Norms of fairness offer another potential avenue of investigation. Can preference for equality be enhanced by making shared and common interests more salient? Does empathy work to create greater equality in bargaining and negotiation? Can attempts to find overarching identities overcome race- and sex-based prejudice and discrimination? Many opportunities for applications in various subfields of political science exist. For example, how can governments shift from an "us" versus "them" mentality when former enemies become allies, as Germany and Japan did after World War II? Central to this shift in alliance and allegiance were these countries' explicit endorsement of democratic values, market institutions, and nonaggressive foreign policies. Adopting more pacifist identities served to reduce the sense of perceived threat on the part of former adversaries.

Within the context of domestic politics, how might increasing identification with victims in one's own group increase empathy with victims in other outgroups? Jews, for example, appear more liberal on racial and political issues than other whites, even when education and ideology are controlled (Glaser 1997). Further experimental and survey studies can examine the extent to which other minority groups support greater freedoms and institutional protections for members of other outcast groups than majority groups might, and whether such attitudes result from empathy and shared identity as an out-group or derive from other sources.

Normative arguments, such as those presented by Kristen Monroe (2001: 491), can help explain how support for equal treatment in one's in-group can promote attempts to extend such tolerance to members of the out-group if we are to "honor the humanity of others in order to claim it for ourselves."

Further experimental studies might easily examine the extent to which leaders can engage in biased distribution policies while maintaining important group support through maintaining evidence of in-group typicality on other dimensions. Particularly in light of the 2000 and 2004 presidential elections, where many wondered how low-income people could support a Republican Party that did not appear to have their best economic interests at heart, studies of this nature may prove particularly relevant and insightful. For instance, it might be possible to manipulate the extent to which subjects received various payments from leaders who either did or did not conform to in-group characteristics on particular social dimensions. In this way, it would be possible to determine both the tipping point of support for similar individuals who shortchange supporters financially and the nature of in-group typicality that can overwhelm financial self-interest. Such studies might employ computer-aided technology to shift vocal intonation, facial expressions, and other important leadership identity cues.

Experimental studies could also manipulate the level of uncertainty surrounding the support, or likelihood of success, for particular leaders or policies. The psychological literature demonstrates that uncertainty raises group identification, but how much uncertainty is needed to generate such identification can prove a worthy subject of investigation. This topic holds particular relevance for those interested in studying the pervasiveness of conflict, either within a given governmental agency (Kaarbo and Gruenfeld 1998) or between countries. Conflict can endure even when it undermines the goals of all concerned parties, at least partly because uncertainty persists, especially in secretive cultures, such as intelligence, military strategy or novel product development.

Finally, experiments that examine the impact of group size on group identification may prove fruitful, especially in the context of multiple overlapping individual identities. Clear-cut experiments that vary group size, and group salience, can begin to uncover the mechanisms by which group loyalty is created and sustained. Such work can begin to uncover the microfoundations of the intense in-group identifications associated with terrorists' cells, suicide bombers, and other groups that believe that out-group violence provides the most direct route to in-group power.

Interest in identity development began essentially with the birth of psychology as an independent science and continues into modern psychological theory. Early models began by stressing the social aspect of identity development and consolidation. Tajfel's original social identity model, with its experimental operationalization involving the minimal group paradigm, produced a remarkably robust research agenda, which continues to this day within psychology. In some ways, social identity theory has been eclipsed theoretically by self-categorization theory not because social identity failed to generate interesting and important experimental results but because the emphasis in social psychology continues to prefer the agency of the individual over the group. When a person chooses his or her own identities and group associations actively and consciously through a process of self-categorization, the choice and agency remain with the individual, not the collective. To introduce the possibility that the group may define the identity of the individual risks moving agency out of the realm of psychology and into that of sociology.

Tremendous opportunity exists to extend and expand upon the original social identity paradigms to further explore various aspects of social identity, its creation and maintenance, forms of persuasion within groups, and practices that encourage conflict or cooperation within them. While a few aspects have been presented here, many others appear possible. With persistence and creativity, such research can continue to inform and enlighten the study of such important group processes as ethnic conflict, civil war, and leadership and followership.

Bibliography

Aarelaid-Tart, Aili. 1996. "Eesti Kodanikualgatuse Ajaloolised Juured." In *Kodani-kualgatus ja Seltsid Eesti Muutuval Kultuurimaastikul*, edited by Aili Aarelaid-Tart. Tallinn: Jaan Tõnissoni Instituut.

Abdelal, Rawi. 2001. *National Purpose in the World Economy: Post-Soviet States in Comparative Perspective*. Ithaca: Cornell University Press.

Abdelal, Rawi, Yoshiko M. Herrera, Alastair Iain Johnston, and Rose McDermott. 2006. "Identity as a Variable." *Perspectives on Politics* 4, no. 4 (December): 695–711.

Abebe, Ermias. 1996–1997. "The Horn, the Cold War, and Documents from the Former East-Bloc: An Ethiopian View." *Cold War International History Project Bulletin* 8–9(Winter): 40–45.

Abrams, Dominic, and Michael A. Hogg, eds. 1990. *Social Identity Theory: Constructive and Critical Advances*. New York: Springer-Verlag.

1999. *Social Identity and Social Cognition*. Oxford: Blackwell.

Acemoglu, Daron, and James Robinson. 2005. *Economic Origins of Dictatorship and Democracy*. Cambridge: Cambridge University Press.

Ackerman, Joshua, Jenessa Shapiro, Steven Neuberg, Douglas Kenrick, Vaughn Becker, Vladas Griskevicius, Jon Maner, and Mark Schaller. 2006. "They All Look the Same to me (Unless They Are Angry): From Out-Group Homogeneity to Out-Group Heterogeneity." *Psychological Science* 17, no. 10: 836–840.

Adams, Laura L. 1999a. "Celebrating Independence: Arts, Institutions and Identity in Uzbekistan." Ph.D. thesis, University of California, Berkeley.

1999b. "The Mascot Researcher: Identity, Power, and Knowledge in Fieldwork." *Journal of Contemporary Ethnography* 28, no. 4: 331–363.

Adams, Josh, and Vincent J. Roscigno. 2005. "White Supremacists, Oppositional Culture and the World Wide Web." *Social Forces* 84, no. 2: 759–778.

Adler, Emanuel. 1992. "The Emergence of Cooperation: National Epistemic Communities and the International Evolution of the Idea of Nuclear Arms Control." *International Organization* 46, no. 1 (Winter): 101–146.

2002. "Constructivism and International Relations: Sources, Contributions, Debates, and Future Directions."In *Handbook of International Relations*, edited by Walter

Carlsnaes, Thomas Risse, and Thomas Simmons, 95–118. London: Sage Publications.

Adler, Emmanuel, and Michael Barnett, eds. 1998. *Security Communities.* Cambridge: Cambridge University Press.

Ahuvia, Aaron. 2001. "Well-Being in Cultures of Choice: A Cross-Cultural Perspective." *American Psychologist* 56, no. 1 (January): 77–78.

Alba, Richard D. 1990. *Ethnic Identity: The Transformation of White America.* New Haven: Yale University Press.

Alba, Richard, and Victor Nee. 2003. *Remaking the American Mainstream: Assimilation and Contemporary Immigration.* Cambridge, MA: Harvard University Press.

Alesina, Alberto, Arnaud Devleeschauwer, William Easterly, Sergio Kurlat, and Romain Wacziarg. 2003. "Fractionalization." *Journal of Economic Growth* 8, no. 2 (June): 155–194.

Alexa, Melina, and Cornelia Zuell. 2000. "Text Analysis Software: Commonalities, Differences and Limitations: The Results of a Review." *Quality and Quantity* 34, no. 3 (August): 299–321.

Alexander, Jeffrey C., and Philip Smith. 2003. "The Strong Program in Cultural Sociology: Elements of a Structural Hermeneutics." In *The Meanings of Social Life: A Cultural Sociology,* edited by Jeffrey C. Alexander, 11–26. Oxford: Oxford University Press.

Allison, Graham T. 1971. *Essence of Decision; Explaining the Cuban Missile Crisis.* Boston: Little, Brown.

Allport, Gordon W. 1954. *The Nature of Prejudice.* Cambridge, MA: Addison-Wesley.

Anderson, Barbara A., and Brian D. Silver. 1983. "Estimating Russification of Ethnic Identity among Non-Russians in the USSR." *Demography* 20, no. 4 (November): 461–489.

      1984. "Equality, Efficiency, and Politics in Soviet Bilingual Education Policy: 1934–1980." *American Political Science Review* 78, no. 4 (December): 1019–1039.

      1990. "Some Factors in the Linguistic and Ethnic Russification of Soviet Nationalities: Is Everyone Becoming Russian?" In *The Nationalities Factor in Soviet Politics and Society,* edited by Lubomyr Hajda and Mark Beissinger, 95–130. Boulder: Westview Press.

Anderson, Benedict. 1991. *Imagined Communities: Reflections on the Origin and Spread of Nationalism.* Rev. ed. London: Verso.

Anderson, Elijah. 1999. *Code of the Street: Decency, Violence, and the Moral Life of the Inner City.* New York: W. W Norton.

Anderson, Margo. 1988. *The American Census.* New Haven: Yale University Press.

Anderson, Margo, and S. Feinberg. 1999. *Who Counts.* New York: Russell Sage Foundation.

Anderson, Richard D., Jr. 1993. *Public Politics in an Authoritarian State: Making Foreign Policy during the Brezhnev Years.* Ithaca: Cornell University Press.

Andersson, Camilla M., Gunilla E. M. Bjärås, Per Tillgren, and Claes-Göran Östenson. 2003. "Health Promotion Activities in Annual Reports of Local Governments: 'Health for all' Targets as a Tool for Content Analysis." *European Journal of Public Health* 13, no. 3 (September): 235–239.

Andrew, Christopher, and Vasili Mitrokhin. 1999. *The Sword and the Shield: The Mitrokhin Archive and the Secret History of the KGB*. New York: Basic Books.

Anheier, Helmut K., Friedhelm Neidhardt, and Wolfgang Vortkamp. 1998. "Movement Cycles and the Nazi Party: Activities of the Munich NSDAP, 1925–1930." *American Behavioral Scientist* 41, no. 9 (June–July): 1262–1281.

Appiah, Kwame Anthony. 2005. *The Ethics of Identity*. Princeton: Princeton University Press.

Arbatov, Georgi. 1992. *The System: An Insider's Life in Soviet Politics*. New York: Times Books.

Arends-Tóth, Judit, and Fons J. R. van de Vijver. 2004. "Domains and Dimensions in Acculturation: Implicit Theories of Turkish-Dutch." *International Journal of Intercultural Relations* 28, no. 1 (February): 19–35.

Arnesen, Eric. 1994. "Like Banquo's Ghost, I Will Not Down: The Race Question and the American Railroad Brotherhoods, 1889–1920." *American Historical Review* 99, no. 5 (December): 1601–1633.

Aronson, Elliot, Phoebe Ellsworth, Merrill Carlsmith, and Marti Hope Gonzalez. 1990. *Methods of Research in Social Psychology*. 2nd ed. New York: McGraw-Hill.

Aronson, Elliot, N. Blaney, C. Stephan, J. Sikes, and M. Snapp. 1978. *The Jigsaw Classroom*. Beverly Hills: Sage Publications.

Arutiunian, Iu. V. 1992. *Russkie: ethno-sotsiologicheskie ocherki*. Moscow: Nauka.

Ashley, Richard K. 1989. "Living on Border Lines: Man, Poststructuralism and War." In *International/Intertextual Relations: Postmodern Readings in World Politics*, edited by James Der Derian and Michael J. Shapiro, 259–321. Lexington: Lexington Books.

Ashmore, Richard D., Kay Deaux, and Tracy McLaughlin-Volpe. 2004. "An Organizing Framework for Collective Identity: Articulation and Significance of Multidimensionality." *Psychological Bulletin* 130, no. 1 (January): 80–114.

Atlas Narodov Mira. 1964. Moscow: Miklukho-Maklai Ethnological Institute of the Department of Geodesy and Cartography of the State Geological Committee of the Soviet Union.

Axelrod, Robert. 1976. *Structure of Decision*. Princeton: Princeton University Press.

Axelrod, Robert, and Ross A. Hammond. 2003. "The Evolution of Ethnocentric Behavior." Paper presented at the Midwest Political Science Convention, Chicago, 3–6 April.

Azzam, Maha. 1991. "The Gulf Crisis: Perceptions in the Muslim World." *International Affairs* 67, no. 3 (July): 473–485.

Babbie, Earl R. 1998. *The Practice of Social Research*. 8th ed. Belmont: Wadsworth.

Bailey, Robert. 1999. *Gay Politics, Urban Politics: Identity and Economy in the Urban Settings*. New York: Columbia University Press.

Bailey, S. R. 2002. "The Race Construct and Public Opinion: Understanding Brazilian Beliefs about Racial Inequality and Their Determinants." *American Journal of Sociology* 108, no. 2: 406–439.

Bargh, John A., and Tanya L. Chartrand. 1999. "The Unbearable Automaticity of Being." *American Psychologist* 54, no. 7 (July): 462–479.

Barnett, George A. 2002. "A Longitudinal Analysis of the International Telecommunication Network: 1978–1999." Paper presented to the conference at Beijing Broadcast Institute, National Centre for Radio and Television Studies, Beijing, April.

2004. "The Role of the Internet in Cultural Identity." Paper presented to the Internet Communication in Intelligent Societies conference, Chinese University of Hong Kong, July.

Barnett, George A., and Han Woo Park. 2004. "The Structure of International Internet Hyperlinks and Bilateral Bandwidth." Paper presented to the Association of Internet Research, Toronto, June.

Barnett, Michael N. 1999. "Culture, Strategy, and Foreign Policy Change: Israel's Road to Oslo." *European Journal of International Relations* 5, no. 1 (March): 5–36.

2002. "Israeli Identity and the Peace Process: Re/creating the Un/thinkable." In *Identity and Foreign Policy in the Middle East*, edited by Shibley Telhami and Michael N. Barnett, 58–87. Ithaca: Cornell University Press.

Barone, Michael. 2001. *The New Americans: How the Melting Pot Can Work Again.* New York: Regnery Press.

Barr, R., A. Dowden, and H. Hayne. 1996. "Development Changes in Deferred Imitation by 6- to 24-Month-Old Infants." *Infant Behavior and Development* 19: 159–170.

Bartelson, Jens. 1998. "Second Natures: Is the State Identical with Itself?" *European Journal of International Relations* 4, no 3: 295–326.

Bateson, Gregory. 1958. *Naven, a Survey of the Problems Suggested by a Composite Picture of the Culture of a New Guinea Tribe Drawn from Three Points of View.* 2nd ed. Stanford: Stanford University Press.

Baudrillard, Jean. 1994. *Simulacra and Simulation.* Ann Arbor: University of Michigan.

Bauer, Martin, and George Gaskell, eds. 2000. *Qualitative Researching with Text, Image and Sound.* Thousand Oaks, CA.: Sage Publications.

Bell, David A. 2001. *The Cult of the Nation in France: Inventing Nationalism, 1680–1800.* Cambridge, MA: Harvard University Press.

Bem, Daryl J. 1972. "Self-Perception Theory." In *Advances in Experimental Social Psychology*, vol. 6, edited by Leonard Berkowitz, 1–62. New York: Academic Press.

Benjamin, Walter. 1969. *Illuminations.* New York: Schocken Books.

Bennion, Layne, and Gerald Adams. 1986. "A Revision of the Extended Version of the Objective Measure of Ego Identity Status: An Identity Instrument for Use with Late Adolescents." *Journal of Adolescent Research* 1, no. 2 (Summer): 183–197.

Berelson, Bernard. 1952. *Content Analysis in Communication Research.* New York: Hafner.

Berger, Peter L., and Thomas Luckmann. 1966. *The Social Construction of Reality.* New York: Doubleday.

Berger, Thomas U. 1998. *Cultures of Antimilitarism: National Security in Germany and Japan.* Baltimore: Johns Hopkins University Press.

Beriker, Nimet, and Daniel Druckman. 1996. "Simulating the Lausanne Peace Negotiations, 1922–1923: Power Asymmetries in Bargaining." *Simulation and Gaming* 27, no. 2 (June): 162–183.

Berinsky, Adam. 2004. *Silent Voices.* Princeton: Princeton University Press.

Bernard, H. Russell. 1998. *Handbook of Methods in Cultural Anthropology.* Walnut Creek, CA: Alta Mira Press.

2006. *Research Methods in Anthropology: Qualitative and Quantitative Approaches.* Lanham, MD: AltaMira Press.

Berry, John W. 1980. "Acculturation as Varieties of Adaptation." In *Acculturation: Theory, Models, and Some New Findings*, edited by Amando M. Padilla, 9–25. Boulder: Westview Press.

Bhavnani, Kum-Kum. 1993. "Tracing the Contours: Feminist Research and Feminist Objectivity." *Women's Studies International Forum* 16, no. 2: 95–104.

Billig, Michael, and Henri Tajfel. 1973. "Social Categorization and Similarity in Intergroup Behavior." *European Journal of Social Psychology* 3, no. 1 (March): 27–52.

Birnir, Johanna. 2004. *The Ethnic Effect.* Cambridge: Cambridge University Press.

Bishop, Yvonne M. M., Stephen E. Fienberg, and Paul Holland. 1975. *Discrete Multivariate Analysis.* Cambridge, MA: MIT Press.

Blee, K. M. 2002. *Inside Organized Racism: Women in the Hate Movement.* Berkeley and Los Angeles: University of California Press.

Blumer, Herbert. 1961. "Race Prejudice as a Sense of Group Position." In *Race Relations: Problems and Theory*, edited by Jitsuichi Masuoka and Preston Valien, 66–72. Chapel Hill: University of North Carolina Press.

Bobo, Lawrence D. 2004. "Inequalities that Endure? Racial Ideology, American Politics, and the Peculiar Role of Social-Science." In *The Changing Terrain of Race and Ethnicity*, edited by Maria Krysan and Amanda E. Lewis, 13–42. New York: Russell Sage Foundation.

Bobo, Lawrence D., and Vincent L. Hutchings. 1996. "Perceptions of Racial Group Competition: Extending Blumer's Theory of Group Position to a Multiracial Social Context." *American Sociological Review* 61, no. 6 (December): 951–972.

Boix, Carles. 2003. *Democracy and Redistribution.* Cambridge: Cambridge University Press.

Bourdieu, Pierre. 1977. *Outline of a Theory of Practice.* Cambridge Studies in Social Anthropology, no. 16. Cambridge: Cambridge University Press.

1990. *The Logic of Practice.* Stanford: Stanford University Press.

Bourret, Pascale, Andrei Mogoutov, Claire Julian-Reynier, and Alberto Cambrosio. 2006. "A New Clinical Collective for French Cancer Genetics: A Heterogeneous Mapping Analysis." *Science Technology Human Values* 31, no. 4: 431–464.

Brady, Henry E. 2004a. "Conceptualizing and Measuring Ethnic Identity." Paper presented at the Harvard Identity Project Conference, Harvard University, Cambridge, Massachusetts, October.

2004b. Introduction to Symposium on "Two Paths to a Science of Politics." *Perspectives on Politics* 2, no. 2 (June): 295–300.

Brady, Henry E., and Cynthia S. Kaplan. 2000. "Categorically Wrong? Nominal versus Graded Measures of Ethnic Identity." *Studies in Comparative International Development* 35, no. 3 (Fall): 56–91.

Brady, Henry E., and Paul Sniderman. 1985. "Attitude Attribution: A Group Basis for Political Reasoning." *American Political Science Review* 79, no. 4 (December): 1061–1078.

Brass, Paul R. 1974. *Language, Religion and Politics in North India.* Cambridge: Cambridge University Press.

1991. *Ethnicity and Nationalism: Theory and Comparison.* New Delhi: Sage Publications.

Brewer, Marilynn B. 1991. "The Social Self: On Being the Same and Different at the Same Time." *Personality and Social Psychology Bulletin* 17, no. 5 (May): 475–482.

1999. "Multiple Identities and Identity Transition: Implications for Hong Kong." *International Journal of Intercultural Relations* 23, no. 2 (March): 187–197.

2001a. "Ingroup Identification and Intergroup Conflict: When Does Ingroup Love Become Outgroup Hate?" In *Social Identity, Intergroup Conflict and Conflict Resolution,* edited by Richard D. Ashmore, Lee Jussim, and David Wilder, 17–41. New York: Oxford University Press.

2001b. "The Many Faces of Social Identity: Implications for Political Psychology." *Political Psychology* 22, no. 1: 115–125.

2003. *Intergroup Relations.* 2nd ed. Philadelphia: Open University Press.

Brewer, Marilynn B., and W. Gardner. 1996. "Who Is This 'We'?: Levels of Collective Identity and Self-Representations." *Journal of Personality and Social Psychology* 71, no. 1: 83–93.

Brewer, Marilynn B., and Roderick Kramer. 1985. "The Psychology of Intergroup Attitudes and Behavior." *Annual Review of Psychology* 36: 219–243.

Brewer, Marilynn B., and Norman Miller. 1996. *Intergroup Relations.* Pacific Grove: Brooks/Cole Publishing.

Brewer, Marilynn B., and Sonia Roccas. 2001. "Social Complexity." Unpublished manuscript, Ohio State University.

Brewer, Marilynn B., and Madelyn Silver. 1978. "Intergroup Bias a Function of Task Characteristics." *European Journal of Social Psychology* 8, no. 3 (September): 393–400.

Briggs, Charles. 1986. *Learning How to Ask: A Sociolinguistic Appraisal of the Role of the Interview in Social Science Research.* Cambridge: Cambridge University Press.

Brimelow, Peter. 1995. *Alien Nation: Common Sense about America's Immigration Disaster.* New York: Random House.

Brown, Jonathon D., Gregory W. Schmidt, and Rebecca L. Collins. 1988. "Personal Involvement and the Evaluation of Group Products." *European Journal of Social Psychology* 18, no. 2 (April–June): 177–179.

Brown, Roger. 1986. *Social Psychology.* 2nd ed. New York: Free Press.

Brubaker, Rogers. 2004. *Ethnicity without Groups.* Cambridge, MA: Harvard University Press.

Brubaker, Rogers, and Frederick Cooper. 2000. "Beyond 'Identity.'" *Theory and Society* 29, no. 1 (February): 1–47.

Brubaker, Rogers, Margit Feischmidt, Jon Foy, and Liana Grancea. 2006. *Nationalist Politics and Everyday Ethnicity in a Transylvanian Town.* Princeton: Princeton University Press.

Brubaker, Rogers, Maria Loveman, and Peter Stamatov. 2004. "Ethnicity as Cognition." *Theory and Society* 33, no. 1 (February): 31–64.

Bruland, Peter, and Michael Horowitz. 2003. "Research Report on the Use of Identity Concepts in Comparative Politics." Unpublished manuscript, Harvard Identity Project, Cambridge, Massachusetts, April.

Buchan, Nancy R., Rachel T. A. Croson, and Robyn M. Dawes. 2002. "Swift Neighbors and Persistent Strangers: A Cross-Cultural Investigation of Trust and

Reciprocity in Social Exchange." *American Journal of Sociology* 108, no. 1 (July): 168–206.

Budenheim, Thomas L., David A. Houston, and Stephen J. DePaola. 1996. "Persuasiveness of In-Group and Out-Group Political Messages: The Case of Negative Campaigning." *Journal of Personality and Social Psychology* 70, no. 3 (March): 523–534.

Budge, Ian, and Richard I. Hofferbert. 1996. "Comparative Textual Analyses of Government and Party Activity: The Work of the Manifesto Research Group." In *Comparing Government Activity*, edited by Louis M. Imbeau and Robert D. McKinlay, 82–100. New York: St. Martin's.

Bull, Hedley. 1977. *The Anarchical Society: A Study of Order in World Politics*. New York: Columbia University Press.

Burawoy, Michael. 1998. "The Extended Case Method." *Sociological Theory* 16, no. 1: 4–33.

———. 2000. *Global Ethnography: Forces, Connections, and Imaginations in a Postmodern World*. Berkeley: University of California Press.

Burke, Peter J. 1997. "An Identity Model for Network Exchange." *American Sociological Review* 62, no. 1 (February): 134–150.

Burke, Peter J., and Donald C. Reitzes. 1981. "The Link between Identity Theory and Role Performance." *Social Psychology Quarterly* 44, no. 2 (June): 83–92.

Burke, Peter J., and Judy C. Tully. 1977. "The Measurement of Role Identity." *Social Forces* 55, no. 4 (June): 881–897.

Buvac, Vanja, and Philip J. Stone. 2001. *The General Inquirer User's Guide*. Cambridge, MA: Harvard University. Available online at http://www.wjh.harvard.edu/~inquirer.

Cadinu, Maria R., and Myron Rothbart. 1996. "Self-Anchoring and Differentiation Processes in the Minimal Group Setting." *Journal of Personality and Social Psychology* 70, no. 4 (April): 661–677.

Callero, Peter L. 1985. "Role-Identity Salience." *Social Psychology Quarterly* 48, no. 3 (September): 203–215.

Canning, Kathleen. 1996. *Languages of Labor and Gender: Female Factory Work in Germany, 1850–1914*. Ithaca: Cornell University Press.

Carley, Kathleen. 1994. "Extracting Culture through Textual Analysis." *Poetics* 22, no. 4 (June): 291–312.

Carmines, Edward G., and Richard A. Zeller. 1979. *Reliability and Validity Assessment: Quantitative Applications in the Social Sciences*. Beverly Hills: Sage Publications.

Carrington, Christopher. 1999. *No Place like Home: Relationships and Family Life among Lesbians and Gay Men*. Chicago: University of Chicago Press.

Castano, Emanuele, Vincent Yzerbyt, David Bourguignon, and Eléonore Seron. 2002. "Who May Enter? The Impact of In-Group Identification on In-Group/Out-Group Categorization." *Journal of Experimental Social Psychology* 38, no. 3 (May): 315–322.

Cederman, Lars-Erik. 1997. *Emergent Actors in World Politics*. Princeton: Princeton University Press.

Cederman, Lars-Erik, and Christopher Daase. 2003. "Endogenizing Corporate Identities: The Next Step in Constructivist IR Theory." *European Journal of International Relations* 9, no. 1 (March): 5–35.

Chan, S. F. 2000. "Formal Logic and Dialectical Thinking Are Not Incongruent." *American Psychologist* 55, no. 9 (September): 1063–1064.

Chandra, Kanchan. 2001. "Cumulative Findings in the Study of Ethnic Politics." *APSA-CP* 12, no. 1 (Winter): 7–11.

——— 2004a. *Why Ethnic Parties Succeed: Patronage and Ethnic Headcounts in India.* Cambridge: Cambridge University Press.

——— 2004b. "What Is Ethnicity?" Paper presented at the Harvard Identity Project Conference, Cambridge, Massachusetts, 9–11 December.

——— 2005a. "Ethnic Parties and Democratic Stability." *Perspectives on Politics* 3, no. 2 (June): 235–252.

——— 2005b. "Ethnic Diversity and Democratic Stability." Unpublished manuscript, New York University.

Chandra, Kanchan, and David Laitin. 2002. *"A Constructivist Framework for Thinking about Identity Change."* LICEP 5 Conference at Stanford University, Stanford, California, 11 May.

Chandra, Kanchan, Rachel Gisselquist, Daniel Metz, Chris Wendt, and Adam Ziegfeld. 2005. "The Weakness of Explicit Ethnic Appeals." Paper prepared for presentation at the meeting of the American Political Science Association, Washington, DC, 1–4 September.

Chang, Tsan-Kuo. 1998. "All Countries Not Created Equal to Be News: World System and International Communication." *Communication Research* 25, no. 5 (October): 528–563.

Charlick-Paley, Tanya, and Donald A. Sylvan. 2000. "The Use and Evolution of Stories as a Mode of Problem Representation: Soviet and French Military Officers Face the Loss of Empire." *Political Psychology* 21, no. 4 (December): 697–728.

Checkel, Jeff. 2001. "Why Comply? Social Learning and European Identity Change." *International Organization* 55, no. 3 (Summer): 553–588.

Chen, Jian. 2001. *Mao's China and the Cold War.* Chapel Hill: University of North Carolina Press.

Chinn, Menzie D., and Robert W. Fairlie. 2004. *The Determinants of the Global Digital Divide: A Cross-Country Analysis of Computer and Internet Penetration.* Cambridge, MA: National Bureau of Economic Research.

Chon, Bum Soo, George A. Barnett, and Young Choi. 2004. "Clustering Local Tastes in Global Culture: The Reception Structure of Hollywood Films." Unpublished manuscript, Munwha Broadcasting Corporation, Kyunggido, Korea.

Chun, Kevin M., Pamela B. Organista, and Gerardo Marin, eds. 2003. *Acculturation: Advances in Theory, Measurement, and Applied Research.* Washington, DC: American Psychological Association.

Chwe, Michael Suk-Young. 2001. *Rational Ritual: Culture, Coordination and Common Knowledge.* Princeton: Princeton University Press.

Citrin, Jack, Beth Reingold, and Donald P. Green. 1990. "American Identity and the Politics of Ethnic Change." *Journal of Politics* 52, no. 4 (November): 1124–1154.

Citrin Jack, Ernst B. Haas, Christopher P. Muste, and Beth Reingold. 1994. "Is American Nationalism Changing? Implications for Foreign Policy?" *International Studies Quarterly* 38, no. 1 (March): 1–31.

Citrin, Jack, Amy Lerman, Michael Murakami, and Kathryn Pearson. 2007. "Testing Huntington: Is Hispanic Immigration a Threat to American Identity?" *Perspectives on Politics* 5, no. 1 (March): 31–48.

Citrin, Jack, David O. Sears, Christopher P. Muste, and Cara Wong. 2001. "Multiculturalism in American Public Opinion." *British Journal of Political Science* 31, no. 2 (April): 247–273.

Citrin, Jack, Cara Wong, and Brian Duff. 2001. "The Meaning of American National Identity: Patterns of Ethnic Conflict and Consensus." In *Social Identity, Intergroup Conflict and Conflict Resolution*, edited by Richard D. Ashmore, Lee Jussim, and David Wilder, 71–100. New York: Oxford University Press.

Citro, Constance F., Daniel L Cork, and Janet L Norwood, eds. 2004. *The 2000 Census*. Washington, DC: National Academy Press.

Clifford, James, and George E. Marcus, eds. 1986. *Writing Culture: The Poetics and Politics of Ethnography*. Berkeley: University of California Press.

Cohen, Cathy J. 1999. *The Boundaries of Blackness: AIDS and the Breakdown of Black Politics*. Chicago: University of Chicago Press.

Collier, Paul. N.d. "Implications of Ethnic Diversity." Working Paper, Oxford University.

Collier, Paul, and Anke Hoeffler. 2001. "Greed and Grievance in Civil War." Typescript, World Bank, Washington, DC.

Condee, Nancy. 2000. "Cultural Codes of the Thaw." In *Nikita Khrushchev*, edited by William Taubman, Sergei Khrushchev, and Abbott Gleason, 160–176. New Haven: Yale University Press.

Copeland, Dale. 2000. "The Constructivist Challenge to Structural Realism: A Review Essay." *International Security* 25, no. 2 (Autumn): 187–212.

Corn, Wanda M. 1999. *The Great American Thing: Modern Art and National Identity, 1915–1935*. Berkeley: University of California Press.

Costa, Janeen A., and Gary J. Bamossy. 1995. "Perspectives on Ethnicity, Nationalism, and Cultural Identity." In *Marketing in a Multicultural World: Ethnicity, Nationalism and Cultural Identity*, edited by Janeen A. Costa and Gary J. Bamossy, 3–25. Thousand Oaks, CA: Sage Publications.

Cox, Robert W. 1981. "Social Forces, States, and World Orders: Beyond International Relations Theory." *Millennium* 10, no. 1: 126–155.

———. 1986. "Social Forces, States, and World Orders." In *Neorealism and Its Critics*, edited by Robert Keohane, 204–254. New York: Columbia University Press.

de Cremer, David, and Eric van Dijk. 2002. "Reactions to Group Success and Failure as a Function of Identification Level; A Test of the Goal-Transformation Hypothesis in Social Dilemmas." *Journal of Experimental Social Psychology* 38, no. 5 (September): 435–442.

Crawford, Neta. 2004. "Understanding Discourse: A Method of Ethical Argument Analysis." *Qualitative Methods: Newsletter of the American Political Science Association Organized Section on Qualitative Methods* 2, no. 1: 22–25.

Cross, William E., Jr. 1991. *Shades of Black: Diversity in African-American Identity*. Philadelphia: Temple University Press.

Cross-National Time-Series Data Archive. N.d. Binghamton: State University of New York at Binghamton. Available online at http://www.databanks. sitehosting.net/.

Custen, George F. 1992. *Bio/Pics: How Hollywood Constructed Public History*. New Brunswick: Rutgers University Press.

Dahl, Robert. 1956. *A Preface to Democratic Theory*. Chicago: University of Chicago Press.

    1971. *Polyarchy*. New Haven: Yale University Press.

Darwin, Charles. 1874. *The Descent of Man*. E-book from the Classic Literature Library. http://charles-darwin.classic-literature.co.uk/the-descent-of-man/.

Davidman, Lynn. 1991. *Tradition in a Rootless World: Women Turn to Orthodox Judaism*. Berkeley: University of California Press.

Dawson, Michael C. 1994. *Behind the Mule: Race and Class in African-American Politics*. Princeton: Princeton University Press.

    2001. *Black Visions: The Roots of African-American Political Ideology*. Chicago: University of Chicago Press.

    2005. "Black and Blue: Black Public Opinion in an Era of Conservative Triumph." The First Leonard White Lecture delivered to the Political Science Department, University of Chicago, 11 March.

    Forthcoming. *Black Politics in the Early 21st Century*. Book manuscript in preparation, University of Chicago.

Dawson, Michael C., and Michael G. Hanchard. N.d. "Toward a Theory of Black Civil Society." Unpublished manuscript, University of Chicago.

Dawson, Michael C., and Rovana Popoff. 2004. "Reparations: Justice and Greed in Black and White." *Du Bois Review* 1, no. 1 (March): 47–92.

de Figueiredo, Rui J. P., and Zachary Elkins. 2003. "Are Patriots Bigots? An Inquiry into the Vices of In-Group Pride." *American Journal of Political Science* 47, no. 1 (January): 171–188.

Denzau, Arthur T., and Douglass C. North. 1994. "Shared Mental Models: Ideologies and Institutions." *Kyklos* 47, no. 1 (February): 3–31.

Denzin, Norman K., and Yvonna S. Lincoln. 2000. *The Handbook of Qualitative Research*. Thousand Oaks, CA: Sage Publications.

Deutsch, Karl W. 1953. *Nationalism and Social Communication*. Cambridge, MA: MIT Press.

    1954. *Political Community at the International Level*. New York: Doubleday.

    1963. *The Nerves of Government: Models of Political Communication and Control*. New York: Free Press.

    1968. *Political Community and the North Atlantic Area: International Organization in the Light of Historical Experience*. Princeton: Princeton University Press.

Devos, Thierry, and Mahzarin R. Banaji. 2005. "America = White?" *Journal of Personality and Social Psychology* 88, no. 3 (March): 447–66.

Dewey, John. 1957. *Human Nature and Conduct: An Introduction to Social Psychology*. New York: Modern Library.

Diener, Ed, Shigehiro Oishi, and Richard E. Lucas. 2003. "Personality, Culture, and Subjective Well-Being: Emotional and Cognitive Evaluations of Life." *Annual Review of Psychology* 54, no. 1: 403–425.

Dobbs, Michael, and William D. Crano. 2001. "Outgroup Accountability in the Minimal Group Paradigm: Implications for Aversive Discrimination and Social Identity Theory." *Personality and Social Psychology Bulletin* 27, no. 3 (March): 355–364.

Dominguez, Virginia R. 1989. *People as Subject, People as Object: Selfhood and Peoplehood in Contemporary Israel*. Madison: University of Wisconsin Press.

1997. *White by Definition*. New Brunswick: Rutgers University Press.

Doty, Roxanne Lynn. 1993. "Foreign Policy as Social Construction: A Post-Positivist Analysis of US Counterinsurgency Policy in the Philippines." *International Studies Quarterly* 37, no. 3: 297–320.

Druckman, Daniel. 1994. "Nationalism, Patriotism, and Group Loyalty: A Social Psychological Perspective." *Mershon International Studies Review* 38, no. 1 (April): 43–68.

Du Bois, W.E.B. 1984. *Dusk of Dawn: An Essay toward an Autobiography of a Race Concept*. New Brunswick, NJ: Transaction.

Duck, Julie M., and Kelly S. Fielding. 2003. "Leaders and Their Treatment of Subgroups: Implications for Evaluations of the Leader and the Superordinate Group." *European Journal of Social Psychology* 33, no. 3 (May): 387–401.

Durkheim, Emile. 1982. *The Rules of Sociological Method*. Edited by Steven Lukes. New York: Free Press.

Eilders, Christiane, and Albrecht Luter. 2000. "Germany at War: Competing Framing Strategies in German Public Discourse." *European Journal of Communication* 15, no. 3 (September): 415–428.

Elbadawi, Ibrahim A., and Nicholas Sambanis. 2000. "Why Are There So Many Civil Wars in Africa? Understanding and Preventing Violent Conflict." *Journal of African Economies* 9, no. 3 (October): 244–269.

Ellemers, Naomi, Paulien Kortekass, and Jaap W. Ouwerkerk. 1999. "Self-Categorization, Commitment to the Group and Group Self-Esteem as Related but Distinct Aspects of Social Identity." *European Journal of Social Psychology* 29, no. 2–3 (March): 371–389.

Ellemers, Naomi, Russell Spears, and Bertjan Doosje. 1997. "Sticking Together of Falling Apart: In-Group Identification as a Psychological Determinant of Group Commitment versus Individual Mobility." *Journal of Personality and Social Psychology* 72, no. 3 (March): 617–626.

English, Robert D. 2000. *Russia and the Idea of the West: Gorbachev, Intellectuals, and the End of the Cold War*. New York: Columbia University Press.

Erikson, Erik H. 1950. *Childhood and Society*. New York: Norton.

Estes, W. K. 1991. "Cognitive Architectures from the Standpoint of an Experimental Psychologist." *Annual Review of Psychology* 42 (January): 1–29.

Etkind, Aleksandr. 2001. *Tolkovanie Puteshestvii: Rossiia i Amerika v Travelogakh i Intertektstakh*. Moscow: Novoe Literaturnoe Obozrenie.

Fanis, Maria. Forthcoming. *Imaginable War, Unimaginable Peace: The Moral Economy of British and American Relations in the Nineteenth Century*. Ann Arbor: University of Michigan.

Farley, Reynolds. 1999. "Racial Issues: Recent Trends in Residential Patterns and Intermarriage." In *Diversity and Its Discontents*, edited by Neil Smelser and Jeffrey Alexander, 85–128. Princeton: Princeton University Press.

Fearon, James. 1999. "What Is Identity (as We Now Use the Word)?" Unpublished manuscript, Stanford University, 3 November.

———. 2003. "Ethnic Structure and Cultural Diversity by Country." *Journal of Economic Growth* 8, no. 2 (June): 195–222.

Fearon, James, and David Laitin. 2003. "Ethnicity, Insurgency and Civil War." *American Political Science Review* 97, no. 1 (February): 75–90.

Featherstone, Mike, ed. 1990. *Global Culture: Nationalism, Globalization and Modernity.* London: Sage Publications.

Fedorenko, Nikolai. 1955. "Peking Diary." *New Times* 10 (6 March): 21–25.

Feng, Chongyi. 1999. "Seeking Lost Codes in the Wilderness: The Search for a Hainanese Culture." *China Quarterly* 160: 1036–1056.

Fetterman, David M. 1998. *Ethnography: Step by Step.* Thousand Oaks, CA: Sage Publications.

Field, Les. 1999. *The Grimace of Macho Raton: Artisans, Identity and Nation in Late-Twentieth Century Western Nicaragua.* Durham, NC: Duke University Press.

Fierke, Karin. 1996. "Multiple Identities, Interfacing Games." *European Journal of International Relations* 2, no. 4 (December): 467–498.

———. 2004. "World or Worlds? The Analysis of Content and Discourse." *Qualitative Methods: Newsletter of the American Political Science Association Organized Section on Qualitative Methods* 2, no. 1: 36–39.

Fink, Arlene, ed. 2003. *The Survey Kit.* 2nd ed. Thousand Oaks, CA.: Sage Publications.

Finnemore, Martha. 1996. *National Interests in International Society.* Ithaca: Cornell University Press.

Finnemore, Martha, and Kathryn Sikkink. 1998. "International Norm Dynamics and Political Change." *International Organization* 52, no. 4 (Fall): 887–917.

Fiske, Susan T., and Shelley E. Taylor. 1991. *Social Cognition.* 2nd ed. New York: McGraw-Hill.

Fortner, Michael. 2009. "Must Difference Divide? The Institutional Roots of Racial Politics." Ph.D. dissertation, Department of Government, Harvard University.

Foucault, Michel. 1971. *The Order of Things: An Archaeology of the Human Sciences.* New York: Pantheon Books.

———. 1984. "What Is an Author?" In *The Foucault Reader*, edited by Paul Rabinow, 101–120. New York: Pantheon Books.

Franklin, John Hope. 1994. *From Slavery to Freedom.* 7th ed. New York: Knopf.

Frederking, Brian. 2003. "Constructing Post–Cold War Collective Security." *American Political Science Review* 97, no. 3 (August): 363–378.

Froelich, Josh. 2000. "Tutorial: TextAnalyst Introduction." Bloomington: Megaputer Intelligence Inc. Available online at http://www.megaputer.com/products/ta/tutorial/textanalyst_tutorial_1.html.

Furia, Peter. 2002. "Patriotism, Nationalism and International Politics." Paper presented at the annual meeting of the American Political Science Association, Boston, September.

Fursenko, Aleksandr, and Timothy Naftali. 1997. *One Hell of a Gamble: Khrushchev, Castro and Kennedy, 1958–1964.* New York: W. W. Norton.

Gaertner, Lowell, and Chester A. Insko. 2001. "On the Measurement of Social Orientations in the Minimal Group Paradigm: Norms as Moderators of the Expression of Intergroup Bias." *European Journal of Social Psychology* 31, no. 2 (March): 143–154.

Gaertner, Samuel L., John F. Dovidio, and Betty A. Bachman. 1996. "Revisiting the Contact Hypothesis: The Induction of a Common Ingroup Identity." *International Journal of Intercultural Relations* 20, nos. 3–4(Summer–Autumn): 271–290.

Gaiduk, Ilya V. 2003. *Confronting Vietnam: Soviet Policy toward the Indochina Conflict, 1954–1963*. Stanford: Stanford University Press.

Gaines, Kevin K. 1996. *Uplifting the Race: Black Leadership, Politics, and Culture in the Twentieth Century*. Chapel Hill: University of North Carolina Press.

Gamson, William A., and Andre Modigliani. 1989. "Media Discourse and Public Opinion on Nuclear Power: A Constructionist Approach." *American Journal of Sociology* 95, no. 1 (July): 1–37.

Geertz, Clifford. 1973a. "The Integrative Revolution: Primordial Sentiments and Civil Politics in the New States." In *The Interpretation of Cultures*, 255–311. New York: Basic Books.

1973b. *The Interpretation of Cultures*. New York: Basic Books.

1973c. "Deep Play: Notes on the Balinese Cockfight." In *The Interpretation of Cultures*, 412–454. New York: Basic Books.

Gellner, Ernest. 1983. *Nations and Nationalism*. Ithaca: Cornell University Press.

Gerner, Deborah J., Philip A. Schrodt, Ronald A. Francisco, and Judith L. Weddle. 1994. "Machine Coding of Event Data Using Regional and International Sources." *International Studies Quarterly* 38, no. 1 (March): 91–119.

George, Alexander L., and Andrew Bennett. 2005. *Case Studies and Theory Development in the Social Sciences*. Cambridge, MA: MIT Press.

Gibadullin, Rustam Mursel'evich. 1993. *Tatarskoe naselenie Naberezhnykh Chelnov*. Naberezhnye Chelny: Mag'rifat.

Gibson, James L., and Amanda Gouws. 2000. "Social Identities and Political Intolerance: Linkages within the South Africa Mass Public." *American Journal of Political Science* 44, no. 2 (April): 278–292.

Giddens, Anthony. 1984. *The Constitution of Society: Outline of the Theory of Structuration*. Berkeley: University of California Press.

1991. *Modernity and Self-Identity*. Stanford: Stanford University Press.

Gilroy, Paul. 1996. "One Nation under a Groove: The Cultural Politics of 'Race' and Racism in Britain." In *Becoming National*, edited by Geoff Eley and Ronald Grigor Suny, 352–369. New York: Oxford University Press.

Gitlin, Todd. 1979. "Prime Time Ideology: The Hegemonic Process in Television Entertainment." *Social Problems* 26, no. 3 (February): 251–266.

Glaser, James M. 1997. "Toward an Explanation of the Racial Liberalism of American Jews." *Political Research Quarterly* 50, no. 2 (June): 437–458.

Glazer, Nathan. 1997. *We Are All Multiculturalists Now*. Cambridge, MA: Harvard University Press.

2001. "American Diversity and the 2000 Census."*Public Interest* 144 (Summer): 3–18.

2002. "Do We Need the Census Race Question?" *Public Interest* 145 (Fall): 21–31.

Glazer, Nathan, and Daniel Moynihan. 1975. Introduction to *Ethnicity: Theory and Experience*, edited by Nathan Glazer and Daniel Moynihan, 1–26. Cambridge, MA: Harvard University Press.

Gleason, Philip. 1983. "Identifying Identity: A Semantic History." *Journal of American History* 69, no. 4 (March): 910–931.

Goffman, Erving. 1974. *Frame Analysis: An Essay on the Organization of Experience.* London: Routledge.

Golder, Mathew. 2005. "Democratic Electoral Systems around the World, 1946–2000." *Electoral Studies* 24, no. 1 (March): 103–121.

Goldmann, Kjell, Ulf Hannerz, and Charles Westin, eds. 2000. *Nationalism and Internationalism in the Post-Cold War Era.* London: Routledge.

Goldstein, Joshua, and Ann Morning. 2000. "The Multiple-Race Population of the United States: Issues and Estimates." *Proceedings of the National Academy of Sciences* 97, no. 11 (November): 6230–6235.

Goldstein, Judith, and Robert O. Keohane, eds. 1993. *Ideas and Foreign Policy: Beliefs, Institutions, and Political Change.* Ithaca: Cornell University Press.

Golebiowska, Ewa A. 1996. "The 'Pictures in Our Heads' and Individual-Targeted Tolerance." *Journal of Politics* 58, no. 4 (November): 1010–1034.

2001. "Individual-Targeted Tolerance and Timing of Group Membership Disclosure." *Journal of Politics* 63, no. 4 (November): 1017–1040.

Goncharov, Sergei N., John W. Lewis, and Litai Xue. 1993. *Uncertain Partners: Stalin, Mao, and the Korean War.* Stanford: Stanford University Press.

Goodman, B. 2000. "Improvisation on a Semi-Colonial Theme, or, How to Read a Celebration of Transnational Urban Community." *Journal of Asian Studies* 59, no. 4: 889–926.

Goodman, David S.G. 2002. "Structuring Local Identity: Nation, Province and County in Shanxi during the 1990s." *China Quarterly* 172: 837–862.

Gordon, Milton M. 1964. *Assimilation in American Life: The Role of Race, Religion and National Origins.* New York: Oxford University Press.

Gordy, Laurie L., and Alice M. Pritchard. 1995. "Redirecting Our Voyage through History: A Content Analysis of Social Studies Textbooks." *Urban Education* 30, no. 2 (May): 195–218.

Goskomstat RSFSR. 1991. *Nekotorye pokazateli, kharakterizuiushchie natsional'nyi sostav naseleniia RSFSR: Po dannym Vsesoiuznoi perepisi naseleniia 1989 goda,* vol. 1. Moscow: Respublikanskii informatsionno-izdatel'skii tsentr.

Gottschalk, Louis A. 1995. *Content Analysis of Verbal Behavior: New Findings and Clinical Applications.* Hillsdale, NJ: Lawrence Erlbaum.

Gramsci, Antonio. 1971. *Selections from the Prison Notebooks.* New York: International Press.

Granato, Jim, and Frank Scioli. 2004. "Puzzles, Proverbs, and Omega Matrices: The Scientific and Social Significance of Empirical Implications of Theoretical Models (EITM)." *Perspectives on Politics* 2, no. 2 (June): 313–323.

Grant, Bruce. 1996. *In the Soviet House of Culture: A Century of Perestroikas.* Princeton: Princeton University Press.

Greenblatt, Stephen Jay. 1990. *Learning to Curse.* New York: Routledge.

Greenwald, Anthony G., Jacqueline E. Pickrell, and Shelly D. Farnham. 2002. "Implicit Partisanship: Taking Sides for No Reason." *Journal of Personality and Social Psychology* 83, no. 2 (August): 367–379.

Gubrium, Jaber F., and James A. Holstein, eds. 2002. *Handbook of Interview Research: Context and Method*. Thousand Oaks, CA: Sage Publications.

Guinier, Lani. 1994. *The Tyranny of the Majority: Fundamental Fairness in Representative Democracy*. New York: Free Press.

Gurin, Patricia, Shirley Hatchett, and James S. Jackson. 1989. *Hope and Independence: Blacks' Response to Electoral and Party Politics*. New York: Russell Sage Foundation.

Gurung, R.A.R. 2003. "Comparing Cultural and Individual Learning Tendencies." *American Psychologist* 58, no. 2 (February): 145–146.

Gutmann, Amy. 2003. *Identity in Democracy*. Princeton: Princeton University Press.

Guzzini, Stefano. 2000. "A Reconstruction of Constructivism in International Relations." *European Journal of International Relations* 6, no. 2 (June): 147–182.

Habermas, Juergen. 1995. *Replik auf Einwande in Habermas, Vorstudien und Ergaenzungen zur Theorie des kommunikativen Handelns*. Frankfurt am Main: Suhrkamp.

Hacking, Ian. 1999. *The Social Construction of What?* Cambridge, MA: Harvard University Press.

Hall, Rodney Bruce. 1999. *National Collective Identity. Social Constructs and International Systems*. New York: Columbia University Press.

2003. "The Discursive Demolition of the Asian Development Model." *International Studies Quarterly* 47, no. 1 (March): 74–75.

Hall, Stuart. 1996. "Introduction: Who Needs Identity?" In *Questions of Cultural Identity*, edited by Stuart Hall and Paul du Gay, 1–17. London: Sage Publications.

Halle, David. 1993. *Inside Culture: Art and Class in the American Home*. Chicago: University of Chicago Press.

Hanchard, Michael G. 1994. *Orpheus and Power*. Princeton: Princeton University Press.

Haney-Lopez, Ian F. 1996. *White by Law: The Legal Construction of Race*. New York: New York University Press.

Haraway, Donna J. 1991. *Simians, Cyborgs, and Women: The Reinvention of Nature*. New York: Routledge.

Hardy, Cynthia, Bill Harley, and Nelson Phillips. 2004. "Discourse Analysis and Content Analysis: Two Solitudes?" *Qualitative Methods: Newsletter of the American Political Science Association Organized Section on Qualitative Methods* 2, no. 1 (Spring): 19–22.

Harris, Cheryl I. 1993. "Whiteness as Property." *Harvard Law Review* 106, no. 8 (June): 1709–1795.

Harris, David R., and Jeremiah J. Sims. 2002. "Who Is Multi-racial? Assessing the Complexity of Lived Race." *American Sociological Review* 67, no. 4 (August): 614–627.

Harris-Lacewell, Melissa V. 2004. *Barbershops, Bibles, and BET: Everyday Talk and Black Political Thought*. Princeton: Princeton University Press.

Harrison, Simon. 1999. "Cultural Boundaries." *Anthropology Today* 115, no. 5: 10–13.

Hart, Rod P. 2000. *The Text-Analysis Program: Diction 5.0*. Austin: Digitext.

Haslam, S. Alex, Michael J. Platow, John C. Turner, Katherine J. Reynolds, Craig McGarty, Penny Oakes, Susan B. Johnson, Michelle K. Ryan, and Kristine Veenstra. 2001. "Social Identity and the Romance of Leadership: The Importance of Being Seen to Be 'Doing It for Us.'" *Group Processes and Intergroup Relations* 4, no. 3 (July): 191–205.

Hemmer, Christopher, and Peter Katzenstein. 2002. "Why Is There No NATO in Asia? Collective Identity, Regionalism, and the Origins of Multilateralism." *International Organization* 56, no. 3 (Summer): 575–607.

Henry, Charles P. 1992. "Clarence Thomas and the National Black Identity." *Black Scholar* 22, no. 1–2 (Winter–Spring): 40–41.

Herrera, Yoshiko M. 2005. *Imagined Economies: The Sources of Russian Regionalism.* Cambridge: Cambridge University Press.

Herrera, Yoshiko M., and Bear F. Braumoeller. 2004. "Symposium: Discourse and Content Analysis." *Qualititative Methods: Newsletter of the American Political Science Association Organized Section on Qualitative Methods* 2, no. 1: 15–18.

Herring, Mary, Thomas B. Jankowski, and Ronald E. Brown. 1999. "Pro-black Doesn't Mean Anti-white: The Structure of African-American Group Identity." *Journal of Politics* 61, no. 2 (May): 363–386.

Herrmann, Richard K., J. Voss, T. Schooler, and J. Ciarrochi. 1997. "Images in International Relations: An Experimental Test of Cognitive Schemata." *International Studies Quarterly* 41, no. 3: 403–433.

Hershberg, James G., ed. 1996–1997. "More New Evidence on the Cold War in Asia." *Cold War International History Project Bulletin* 8–9 (Winter): 220–269.

Hertog, James K., and David P. Fan. 1995. "The Impact of Press Coverage on Social Beliefs: The Case of HIV Transmission." *Communication Research* 22, no. 5 (October): 545–574.

Higgins, John, ed. 2001. *The Raymond Williams Reader.* Oxford: Blackwell.

Hint, Mati. 1988. "Eesti Vabariik ja Eesti Keel." *Looming* 5: 679–682.

Hirschman, Charles, Richard Alba, and Reynolds Farley. 2000. "The Meaning and Measurement of Race in the U.S. Census: Glimpses into the Future." *Demography* 37, no. 3 (August): 381–394.

Ho, D. Y. F. 2000. "Dialectical Thinking: Neither Eastern nor Western." *American Psychologist* 55, no. 9 (September): 1064–1065.

Hochschild, Jennifer. 2003. "Multiple Racial Identifiers in the 2000 Census, and Then What?" In *The New Race Question: How the Census Counts Multiracial Individuals,* edited by Joel Perlmann and Mary C. Waters, 340–353. New York: Russell Sage Foundation.

Hoffman, Rose Marie. 2001. "The Measurement of Masculinity and Femininity: Historical Perspective and Implications for Counseling." *Journal of Counseling and Development* 79, no. 4 (Fall): 472–485.

Hogg, Michael A., and Dominic Abrams. 1986. *Social Identifications: A Social Psychology of Intergroup Relations and Group Processes.* London: Routledge.

Hogg, Michael A., and Sarah C. Hains. 1998. "Friendship and Group Identification: A New Look at the Role of Cohesiveness in Groupthink." *European Journal of Social Psychology* 28, no. 3 (May): 323–341.

Hogg, Michael A., Deborah J. Terry, and Katherine M. White. 1995. "A Tale of Two Theories: A Critical Comparison of Identity Theory with Social Identity Theory." *Social Psychology Quarterly* 58, no. 4: 255–269.

Hollinger, David. 1995. *Post-Ethnic America: Beyond Multiculturalism.* New York: Basic Books.

  2003. "Amalgamation and Hypodescent: The Question of Ethnoracial Mixture in the History of the United States." *American Historical Review* 108, no. 5 (December): 1363–1390.

Holt, Thomas C. 1995. "Reconstruction in United States History Textbooks." *Journal of American History* 81, no. 4 (March): 1641–1651.

  2000. *The Problem of Race in the Twenty-first Century.* Cambridge, MA: Harvard University Press.

Hooper, Michael. 1976. "The Structure and Measurement of Social Identity." *Public Opinion Quarterly* 40, no. 2: 154–164.

Hooson, David J. M., ed. 1994. *Geography and National Identity.* Oxford: Blackwell.

Hopf, Ted. 1998. "The Promise of Constructivism in IR Theory." *International Security* 23, no. 1 (Summer): 171–200.

  2002. *Social Construction of International Politics: Identities and Foreign Policies, Moscow, 1955 and 1999.* Ithaca: Cornell University Press.

  2004. "Discourse and Content Analysis: Some Fundamental Incompatibilities." *Qualitative Methods: Newsletter of the American Political Science Association Organized Section on Qualitative Methods* 2, no. 1 (Spring): 31–33.

Hornsey, Matthew J., Mark Trembath, and Sasha Gunthorpe. 2004. "'You Can Criticize Because You Care': Identity Attachment, Constructiveness, and the Intergroup Sensitivity Effect." *European Journal of Social Psychology* 34, no. 5 (September–October): 499–518.

Hornsey, Matthew J., and Armin Imani. 2004. "Criticizing Groups from the Inside and the Outside: An Identity Perspective on the Intergroup Sensitivity Effect." *Personality and Social Psychology Bulletin* 30, no. 3 (March): 365–383.

Hornsey, Matthew J., and Jolanda Jetten. 2003. "Not Being What You Claim to Be: Imposters as Sources of Group Threat." *European Journal of Social Psychology* 33, no. 5 (September): 639–657.

Hornsey, Matthew J., Russell Spears, Iris Cremers, and Michael A. Hogg. 2003. "Relations between High and Low Power Groups: The Importance of Legitimacy." *Personality and Social Psychology Bulletin* 29, no. 2 (February): 216–227.

Horowitz, Donald. 1975. "Ethnic Identity." In *Ethnicity: Theory and Experience,* edited by Nathan Glazer and Daniel Moynihan. Cambridge, MA: Harvard University Press.

  1985. *Ethnic Groups in Conflict.* Berkeley: University of California Press.

Horowitz, Michael. 2002. "Research Report on the Use of Identity Concepts in International Relations." Unpublished manuscript, Harvard Identity Project, Cambridge, Massachusetts, July.

Horton, Carol A. 2005. *Race and the Making of American Liberalism.* New York: Oxford University Press.

Hsieh, Raymond. 2004. "Comparison across Reference Frames: Rotation of Galileo Space with Inconsistent Objects – an Example of Comparison of User's Perception

and Online Legal Policy." Ph.D. dissertation, State University of New York at
     Buffalo.
Huddy, Leonie. 2001. "From Social to Political Identity: A Critical Examination of
     Social Identity Theory." *Political Psychology* 22, no. 1: 127–156.
Hunter, John A., Kypros Kypri, Natalie M. Stokell, Mike Boyes, Kerry S. O'Brien, and
     Kathleen E. McMenamin. 2004. "Social Identity, Self-Evaluation and In-Group
     Bias: The Relative Importance of Particular Domains of Self-Esteem to the In-
     Group." *British Journal of Social Psychology* 43, no. 1 (March): 59–81.
Huntington, Samuel. 2000. "Reconsidering Immigration: Is Mexico a Special Case?"
     Backgrounder. Washington, DC: Center for Immigration Studies.
     2004. *Who Are We? Challenges to American National Identity*. New York: Simon
     and Schuster.
Hurd, Ian. 1999. "Legitimacy and Authority in International Politics." *International
     Organization* 53, no. 2 (Spring): 379–408.
Hymans, Jacques E.C. 2006. *The Psychology of Nuclear Proliferation: Identities,
     Emotions, and Foreign Policy*. Cambridge: Cambridge University Press.
Inglehart, Ronald, and Wayne E. Baker. 2000. "Modernization, Cultural Change, and
     the Persistence of Traditional Values." *American Sociological Review*, 65, no. 1
     (February): 19–51.
Iskhaki, Gaiaz. 1991. *Idel' Ural*. Kazan: Tatarskoe knizhnoe izdatel'stvo.
Iyengar, S., and D. R. Kinder. 1987. *News That Matters*. Chicago: University of
     Chicago Press.
Jacob, Philip E., and James V. Toscano, eds. 1964. *The Integration of Political
     Communities*. Philadelphia: Lippincott.
James, William. 1981. *The Principles of Psychology*. Vol. 1. Cambridge, MA: Harvard
     University Press.
Jencks, Christopher. 2001. "Who Should Get In?" *New York Review of Books* 48,
     no. 19 (29 November): 94–101.
Jepperson, Ronald, Alexander Wendt, and Peter J. Katzenstein. 1996. "Norms, Iden-
     tity, and Culture in National Security." In *The Culture of National Security:
     Norms and Identity in World Politics*, edited by Peter J. Katzenstein, 33–75.
     New York: Columbia University Press.
Johnston, Alastair I. 1995. *Cultural Realism: Strategic Culture and Grand Strategy in
     Chinese History*. Princeton: Princeton University Press.
Jones, Edward E., and Harold Sigall. 1971. "The Bogus Pipeline: A New Paradigm for
     Measuring Affect and Attitude." *Psychological Bulletin* 76: 349–364.
Jones-Correa, Michael, and David L. Leal. 1996. "Becoming 'Hispanic': Secondary
     Panethnic Identification among Latin American-Origin Populations in the United
     States." *Hispanic Journal of Behavioral Sciences* 18, no. 2: 214–254.
Jun, Niu. 1998. "The Origins of the Sino-Soviet Alliance." In *Brothers in Arms: The
     Rise and Fall of the Sino-Soviet Alliance, 1945–1963*, edited by Odd Arne
     Westad, 47–89. Stanford: Stanford University Press.
Junn, Jane. 1999. "Participation in Liberal Democracy: The Political Assimilation
     of Immigrants and Ethnic Minorities in the United States." *American Behavioral
     Scientist* 42, no. 9 (June–July): 1417–1438.

Kaarbo, Juliet, and Deborah H. Gruenfeld. 1998. "Whither the Study of Governmental Politics in Foreign Policymaking? A Symposium." *Mershon International Studies Review* 42, no. 2 (July): 226–233.

Kaasik, Tõnis. 1995. *Ida-Virumaa: Man, Economy, Nature.* Tallinn: Stockholm Environment Institute.

Kabanoff, Boris, and Paul Nesbit. 1997. "Metamorphic Effects of Power as Reflected in Espoused Organizational Values: Implications for Corporate Governance." *Australian Psychologist* 32, no. 1 (March): 62–70.

Kaplan, Cynthia. 2006. "Setting the Political Agenda: Cultural Discourse in the Estonian Transition." In *Empire to Nation: Historical Perspectives on the Making of the Modern World,* edited by Joseph W. Esherick, Hasan Kayali, and Eric Van Young, 340–372. Boulder, CO: Rowman and Littlefield Publishers.

Kaplan, Cynthia S., and Henry E. Brady. 1999. "Issue Framing, Elite Actions, and Estonian Mobilization for Independence: 1988–1993." Paper presented at the meeting of the Midwest Political Science Association, Chicago, 17 April.

——— 2002. "Russian Identity at the Time of Independence: Media Choice and Cognitive Worlds." Paper presented at the special convention on "Nationalism, Identity and Regional Cooperation: Compatibilities and Incompatibilities," Forli, Italy, 4–9 June.

Kaplinski, Jaan. 1989. "Püha riik ja revolutsioon." *Looming* 2: 1669–1672.

Kasfir, Nelson. 1976. *The Shrinking Political Arena.* Berkeley: University of California Press.

——— 1979. "Explaining Ethnic Political Participation." *World Politics* 31, no. 3 (April): 365–388.

Katzenstein, Peter J. 1996. *Cultural Norms and National Security: Police and Military in Postwar Japan.* Ithaca: Cornell University Press.

Keck, Margaret, and Kathryn Sikkink. 1998. *Activists beyond Borders: Advocacy Networks in International Relations.* Ithaca: Cornell University Press.

Keefer, Philip. 2002."DPI Database of Political Institutions: Changes and Variable Institutions." Typescript, World Bank, Washington, DC.

Kelam, Tunne. 1989. "Eesti Vabariik kui reaalsus: Intervjuu Toomas Haugile." *Looming* 5: 646–653.

Kelley, Robin. 1994. *Race Rebels: Culture, Politics, and the Black Working Class.* New York: Free Press.

——— 2002. *Freedom Dreams.* Boston: Beacon Press.

Kellner, Douglas. 1990. *Television and the Crisis of Democracy.* Boulder: Westview Press.

Kelly, Caroline. 1988. "Intergroup Differentiation in a Political Context." *British Journal of Social Psychology* 27, no. 4 (December): 319–332.

——— 1989. "Political Identity and Perceived Intergroup Homogeneity." *British Journal of Social Psychology* 28, no. 3 (October): 239–250.

Kelman, Herbert C. 1969. "Patterns of Personal Involvement in the National System: A Social-Psychological Analysis of Political Legitimacy." In *International Politics and Foreign Policy: A Reader in Research and Theory,* rev. ed., edited by J. N. Rosenau, 276–287. New York: Free Press.

——— 1997. "Negotiating National Identity and Self-Determination in Ethnic Conflicts." *Negotiation Journal* 13, no. 4: 327–340.

1999. "The Interdependence of Israeli and Palestinian National Identities." *Journal of Social Issues* 55, no. 3: 581–600.

2001. "The Role of National Identity in Conflict Resolutions." In *Social Identity, Intergroup Conflict, and Conflict Reduction*, edited by Richard D. Ashmore, Lee Jussim, and David Wilder, 187–212. Oxford: Oxford University Press.

Kertzer, David, and Dominique Arel. 2002. *Census and Identity*. Cambridge: Cambridge University Press.

Key, Vladimer Orlando. 1949. *Southern Politics in State and Nation*. New York: Knopf.

Khrushchev, Nikita S. 1997. *Vospominaniia: Izbrannye Fragmenty*. Moscow: Vagrius.

Khrushchev, Sergei N. 2000. *Nikita Khrushchev and the Creation of a Superpower*. University Park: Pennsylvania State University Press.

Kier, Elizabeth. 1996. "Culture and French Military Doctrine before World War II." In *The Culture of National Security: Norms and Identity in World Politics*, edited by Peter J. Katzenstein, 186–215. New York: Columbia University Press.

1997. *Imagining War: French and British Military Doctrine between the Wars*. Princeton: Princeton University Press.

1998. "Homosexuals in the U.S. Military: Open Integration and Combat Effectiveness." *International Security* 23, no. 2 (Autumn): 5–39.

Kim, Claire Jean. 2000. *Bitter Fruit: The Politics of Black-Korean Conflict in New York City*. New Haven: Yale University Press.

King, Gary, James Honaker, Anne Joseph, and Kenneth Scheve. 2001. "Analyzing Incomplete Political Science Data: An Alternative Algorithm for Multiple Imputation." *American Political Science Review* 95, no. 1 (March): 49–69.

King, Gary, Michael Tomz, and Jason Wittenberg. 2003. "Clarify: Software for Interpreting and Presenting Statistical Results." *Journal of Statistical Software* 8, no. 1 (January): 245–246.

Kionka, Riina. 1990. "Estonians." In *The Nationalities Question in the Soviet Union*, edited by Graham Smith, 40–53. London: Longman.

Kirch, Marika. 1997. "Mass Media and Integration of the Russian Population." In *The Integration of Non-Estonians into Estonian Society: History, Problems, and Trends*, edited by Aksel Kirch, 94–105. Tallinn: Estonian Academy Publishers.

Klandermans, Bert. 1997. *The Social Psychology of Protest*. Cambridge, MA: Blackwell.

Klotz, Audie. 1995a. *Norms in International Relations: The Struggle against Apartheid*. Ithaca: Cornell University Press.

1995b. "Norms Reconstituting Interests: Global Racial Equality and U.S. Sanctions Against South Africa." *International Organization* 49, no. 3 (Summer): 451–478.

Knowles, E. D., and K. Peng. 2005. "White Selves: Conceptualizing and Measuring a Dominant-Group Identity." *Journal of Personality and Social Psychology* 89, no. 2: 223–241.

Kornienko, Georgii M. 1994. *Kholodnaia Voina: Svidetelstvo ee Uchastnika*. Moscow: Mezhdunarodnye otnosheniia.

Kramer, Roderick M., Pamela Pommerenke, and Elizabeth Newton. 1993. "The Social Context of Negotiation: Effects of Social Identity and Interpersonal Accountability on Negotiator Decision Making." *Journal of Conflict Resolution* 37, no. 4 (December): 633–654.

Kratochwil, Friedrich V. 2000. "Constructing a New Orthodoxy? Wendt's 'Social Theory of International Politics' and the Constructivist Challenge." *Millennium* 29, no. 1 (January): 73–101.

Krieger, Susan. 1983. *The Mirror Dance: Identity in a Women's Community.* Philadelphia: Temple University Press.

Krippendorff, Klaus. 2004. *Content Analysis: An Introduction to Its Methodology.* 2nd ed. Thousand Oaks, CA: Sage Publications.

Krosnick, J. A., and D. R. Kinder. 1990. "Altering the Foundations of Support for the President through Priming." *American Political Science Review* 84, no. 3: 497–512.

Kruskal, Joseph B. 1983. "An Overview of Sequence Comparison." In *Time Warps, Strings Edits and Macromolecules: The Theory and Practice of Sequence Comparison,* edited by David Sankoff and Joseph B. Kruskal, 1–44. Reading, MA: Addison-Wesley.

Kuhn, Manford H., and Thomas S. McPartland. 1954. "An Empirical Investigation of Self-Attitudes." *American Sociological Review* 19, no. 1: 68–76.

Kuklinski, James, Paul Sniderman, K. Knight, T. Piazza, Philip Tetlock, L. Gordon, and Barbara Mellers. 1997. "Racial Prejudice and Attitudes toward Affirmative Action." *American Journal of Political Science* 41: 402–419.

Kulik, Boris T. 2000. *Sovetsko-Kitaiskii Raskol: Prichiny i Posledstviia.* Moscow: Institut Dal'nego Vostoka RAN.

Laar, Mart, Urmas Ott, and Sirje Endre. 1996. *Teine Eesti: Eesti iseseisvuse taassünd 1986–1991.* Tallinn: Meedia- ja Kirjastuskompanii.

Laffey, Mark, and Jutta Weldes. 2004. "Methodological Reflections on Discourse Analysis." *Qualitative Methods Newsletter* 2, no. 1 (Spring): 28–31.

Lagerspetz, Mikko. 1993. "Social Problems in Estonian Mass Media, 1975–1991." *Acta Soiologica* 36, no. 4: 357–369.

   1996. "Constructing Post-Communism: A Study in the Estonian Social Problems Discourse." *Turun Yliopiston Julkaisuja Ser. B Osa-tom.* 214 Humaniora. Turun Yliopisto, Turku.

Lagerspetz, Mikko, and Rein Raud. 1997. *Cultural Policy in Estonia.* Strasbourg: Council of Europe.

Laitin, David D. 1998. *Identity in Formation: The Russian-Speaking Populations in the Near Abroad.* Ithaca: Cornell University Press.

   2000. "What Is a Language Community?" *American Journal of Political Science* 44, no. 1 (January): 142–155.

   2002. "Culture and National Identity: 'The East' and European Integration." *West European Politics* 25, no. 2: 56–80.

Laitin, David, and Kanchan Chandra. 2002. "A Constructivist Framework for Thinking about Identity Change." Unpublished Manuscript, Stanford University and New York University, December.

Laitin, David, and Daniel Posner. 2001. "The Implications of Constructivism for Constructing Ethnic Fractionalization Indices." *APSA-CP* 12, no. 1 (Winter): 13–17.

Lallukka, Seppo. 1990. "The East Finnic Minorities in the Soviet Union: An Appraisal of the Erosive Trends." *Suomalaisen Tiedeakatemian Toimituksia Ser. B.,* vol. 252. Helsinki: Suomalainen Tiedeakatemia.

Lamont, Michèle. 2001. "Culture and Identity." In *Handbook of Sociological Theory,* edited by Jonathan H. Turner. New York: Kluwer-Plenum.

Lazarevska, Elena, Jayne M. Sholl, and Michael D. Young. 2006. "Links among Beliefs and Personality Traits: The Distinctive Language of Terrorists." In *Beliefs and Leadership in World Politics: Methods and Application of Operational Code Analysis*, edited by Mark Schafer and Stephen G. Walker, 171–185. New York: Palgrave Macmillan.

Lazarus, Neil. 1999. *Nationalism and Cultural Practice in the Postcolonial World*. Cambridge: Cambridge University Press.

Lee, Jennifer, and Frank D. Bean. 2004. "America's Changing Color Lines: Immigration, Race/Ethnicity, and Multiracial Identification." *Annual Review of Sociology* 30 (August): 221–242.

Lee, Raymond M. 1995. *Dangerous Fieldwork*. Newbury Park, CA: Sage Publications.

Lee, Richard M., and Hyung Chol Yoo. 2004. "Structure and Measurement of Ethnic Identity for Asian American College Students." *Journal of Counseling Psychology* 51, no. 2 (April): 263–269.

Lee, Taeku. 2004. "Between Social Theory and Social Science Practice: Towards a New Approach to the Survey Measurement of Race." Paper presented at the Harvard Identity Project Conference, Cambridge, Massachusetts, 9–11 December.

Lee, Yueh-Ting. 2000. "What Is Missing in Chinese-Western Dialectical Reasoning?" *American Psychologist* 55, no. 9 (September): 1065–1067.

Lehman, Fritz, ed. 1992. *Semantic Networks in Artificial Intelligence*. New York: Pergamon Press.

Levine, Robert A., and Donald T. Campbell. 1971. *Ethnocentrism: Theories of Conflict, Ethnic Attitudes, and Group Behavior*. New York: Wiley.

Lewin, Kurt, Ronald Lippitt, and Ralph White. 1939. "Patterns of Aggressive Behavior in Experimentally Created 'Social Climates.'" *Journal of Social Psychology*, 10 (May): 271–299.

Li, Jin. 2003. "The Core of Confucian Learning." *American Psychologist* 58, no. 2 (February): 146–147.

Lieberson, Stanley, and Mary C. Waters. 1993. "The Ethnic Responses of Whites: What Causes Their Instability, Simplification, and Inconsistency?" *Social Forces* 72, no. 2 (December): 421–450.

Lien Pei-Te, Margaret Conway, and Janelle Wong. 2004. *The Politics of Asian Americans*. New York: Routledge.

Lijphart, Arend. 1977. *Democracy in Plural Societies*. New Haven: Yale University Press.

Lind, Michael. 1995. *The Next American Nation*. New York: Free Press.

Lipsitz, George. 1998. *The Possessive Investment in Whiteness*. Philadelphia: Temple University Press.

Liu, James H, Ken'ichi Ikeda, and Marc Stewart Wilson. 1998. "Interpersonal Environmental Effects on Political Preferences: The 'Middle Path' for Conceptualizing Social Structures in New Zealand and Japan." *Political Behavior* 20, no. 3 (September): 183–212.

Lofland, John, and Lyn H. Lofland. 1995. *Analyzing Social Settings: A Guide to Qualitative Observation and Analysis*. Belmont, CA: Wadsworth.

Lombard, Matthew, Jennifer Snyder-Duch, and Cheryl Campanella Bracken. 2002. "Content Analysis in Mass Communication: Assessment and Reporting of Intercoder Reliability." *Human Communication Research* 28, no. 4 (October): 587–604.

Lowe, Will. 2002. "Software for Content Analysis: A Review." Unpublished paper. http://people.iq.harvard.edu/~wlowe/Publications/rev.pdf.

    2004a. "Content Analysis and Its Place in the (Methodological) Scheme of Things." *Qualitative Methods: Newsletter of the American Political Science Association Organized Section on Qualitative Methods* 2, no. 1 (Spring): 25–27.

    2004b. *Software for Content Analysis–A Review*. Unpublished manuscript, Harvard University, Cambridge, Massachusetts.

Luhtanen, Riia K., and Jennifer Crocker. 1992. "A Collective Self-Esteem Scale: Self-Evaluation of One's Social Identity." *Personality and Social Psychology Bulletin* 18: 302–318.

Luthi, Lorenz. 2008. *The Sino-Soviet Split*. Princeton: Princeton University Press.

Maloney, Suzanne. 2002. "Identity and Change in Iran's Foreign Policy." In *Identity and Foreign Policy in the Middle East*, edited by Shibley Telhami and Michael Barnett, 88–116. Ithaca: Cornell University Press.

March, James G., and Johan P. Olsen. 1989. *Rediscovering Institutions: The Organizational Basis of Politics*. New York: Free Press.

    1995. *Democratic Governance*. New York: Free Press.

    1998. "The Institutional Dynamics of International Political Orders." *International Organization* 52, no. 4 (Fall): 943–969.

Marcia, James E. 1993. *Ego Identity: A Handbook for Psychosocial Research*. New York: Springer-Verlag.

Marcus, George E., and Michael M. J. Fischer, eds. 1986. *Anthropology as Cultural Critique: An Experimental Moment in the Human Sciences*. Chicago: University of Chicago Press.

Markus, Hazel. 1977. "Self-Schemata and Processing Information about the Self." *Journal of Personality and Social Psychology* 35: 63–78.

Marks, Jonathan. 1994. "Black, White and Other: Racial Categories Are Cultural Constructs Masquerading as Biology." *Natural History* 103, no. 12 (December): 32–35.

Mar-Molinero, Clare. 2000. *Politics of Language in the Spanish-Speaking World*. London: Routledge.

Marques, José M., Dominic Abrams, Dario Páez, and Michael A. Hogg. 2001. "Social Categorization, Social Identification, and Rejection of Deviant Group Members." In *Blackwell Handbook of Social Psychology: Group Processes*, edited by Michael A. Hogg and R. Scott Tindal, 400–424. Oxford: Blackwell.

Marques, José, Dominic Abrams, Dario Paez, and Cristina Martinez-Taboada. 1998. "The Role of Categorization and In-Group Norms in Judgments of Groups and Their Members." *Journal of Personality and Social Psychology* 75, no. 4 (October): 976–988.

McCarthy, John D., Clark McPhail, and Jackie Smith. 1996. "Images of Protest: Dimensions of Selection Bias in Media Coverage of Washington Demonstrations, 1982 and 1991." *American Sociological Review* 61, no. 3 (June): 478–499.

McCracken, Grant. 1988. *The Long Interview*. Thousand Oaks, CA: Sage Publications.

McDermott, Rose. 2004. "Psychological Approaches to Identity: Definition, Measurement and Experimentation." Paper prepared for the Harvard Identity Project Conference, Cambridge, Massachusetts, 9–11 December.

Mead, George Herbert. 1934. *Mind, Self, and Society*. Chicago: University of Chicago Press.

Mearsheimer, John J. 1990. "Back to the Future: Instability in Europe after the Cold War." *International Security* 15, no. 1: 5–56.

———. 1994–1995. "The False Promise of International Institutions." *International Security* 19, no. 3 (Winter): 5–49.

Meeus, Wim, Jurjen Iedema, and Gerard Maassen. 2002. "Commitment and Exploration as Mechanisms of Identity Formation."*Psychological Reports* 90, no. 3 (June): 771–785.

Mendelberg, Tali. 2001. *The Race Card: Campaign Strategy, Implicit Messages and the Norm of Equality*. Princeton: Princeton University Press.

Mercer, Jonathan. 1995. "Anarchy and Identity." *International Organization* 49, no. 2 (Spring): 229–252.

Merritt, Richard L. 1966. *Symbols of American Community, 1735–1775*. New Haven: Yale University Press.

Metskas, Amanda K., Amy Horowitz, and Donald A. Sylvan. 2006. "Identity, Music, and the Politics of Mizrahi Jews in Israel." Unpublished manuscript, Ohio State University.

Mill, John Stuart. [1861] 1991. *Considerations on Representative Government*. Reprint, New York: Prometheus Books, 1991.

Miller, J. M., and J. A. Krosnick. 2000. "News Media Impact on the Ingredients of Presidential Evaluations." *American Journal of Political Science* 44, no. 2: 301–315.

Milliken, Jennifer. 1999. "The Study of Discourse in International Relations: A Critique of Research and Methods." *European Journal of International Relations* 5, no. 2 (June): 225–254.

Milner, Helen V. 1997. *Interests, Institutions, and Information: Domestic Politics and International Relations*. Princeton: Princeton University Press.

Mitrany, David. 1944. *A Working Peace System: An Argument for the Functional Development of International Organization*. London: Royal Institute of International Affairs; New York: Oxford University Press.

Mitzen, Jennifer. 2005. "Ontological Security in World Politics: State Identity and the Security Dilemma." Unpublished Manuscript, Ohio State University, April.

Monroe, Kristen R. 2001. "Morality and a Sense of Self: The Importance of identity and Categorization for Moral Action." *American Journal of Political Science* 45, no. 3 (July): 491–507.

Monroe, Kristen R., James Hankin, and Renée Bukovchik van Vechten. 2000. "The Psychological Foundations of Identity Politics." *Annual Review of Political Science* 3: 419–447.

Moravcsik, Andrew. 1997. "Taking Preferences Seriously: A Liberal Theory of International Politics." *International Organization* 51, no. 4 (Autumn): 513–553.

Morning, Ann. 2003. "New Faces, Old Faces: Counting the Multi-racial Population Past and Present." In *New Faces in a Changing America: Multiracial Identity in the 21st Century*, edited by Loretta I. Winters and Herman L. DeBose, 41–67. Thousand Oaks, CA: Sage Publications.

Morrison, Toni. 1992. "Introduction: Friday on the Potomac." In *Race-ing Justice, En-gender-ing Power: Essays on Anita Hill, Clarence Thomas and the Construction of Social Reality*, edited by Toni Morrison, vii–xxx. New York: Pantheon Books.

Mozaffar, Shaheen, and James Scarritt. 2003. "Electoral Institutions, Ethnopolitical Cleavages, and Party Systems in Africa's Emerging Democracies." *American Political Science Review* 97, no. 3 (August): 379–390.

Mueller, Carol. 1997. "International Press Coverage of East German Protest Events, 1989." *American Sociological Review* 62, no. 5 (October): 820–832.

Mullin, Barbara-Ann, and Michael A. Hogg. 1998. "Dimensions of Subjective Uncer-tainty in Social Identification and Minimal Intergroup Discrimination." *British Journal of Social Psychology* 37, no. 3 (October): 345–365.

Murphy, Gregory L., and Douglas L. Medin. 1985. "The Role of Theories in Concep-tual Coherence." *Psychological Review* 92, no. 3: 289–316.

Nadler, A., and S. Halabi. 2006. "Intergroup Helping as Status Relations: Effects of Status Stability, Identification, and Type of Help on Receptivity to High Status Group's Help." *Journal of Personality and Social Psychology* 91: 97–110.

Nadler, A., and I. Liviatan. 2006. "Intergroup Reconciliation: Effects of Adversary's Expressions of Empathy, Responsibility, and Recipients' Trust." *Personality and Social Psychology Bulletin* 32: 459–470.

Nagel, Joanne. 1995. "American Indian Ethnic Renewal: Politics and the Resurgence of Identity." *American Sociological Review* 60, no. 6 (December): 947–965.

Nandy, Ashish. 1983. *The Intimate Enemy: Loss and Recovery of Self under Colonialism*. Delhi: Oxford University Press.

Naples, Nancy A. 1998. *Community Activism and Feminist Politics: Organizing across Race, Class, and Gender*. New York: Routledge.

Nau, Henry R. 2002. *Identity and Power in American Foreign Policy*. Ithaca: Cornell University Press.

Neuendorf, Kimberly A. 2002. *The Content Analysis Guidebook*. Thousand Oaks, CA: Sage Publications.

———. 2004a. "Content Analysis: A Contrast and Complement to Discourse Analysis." *Qualitative Methods: Newsletter of the American Political Science Association Organized Section on Qualitative Methods* 2, no. 1 (Spring): 33–36.

———. 2004b. "Quantitative Content Analysis Options for the Measurement of Identity." Paper presented to the Harvard Identity Project Conference, Harvard University, Cambridge, Massachusetts, 9–11 December.

Neuendorf, Kimberly A., Brian F. Blake, and Colin Valdiserri. 2003. "Acculturation in the Global Marketplace." Paper presented to the Midwest Association for Public Opinion Research, Chicago, November.

Neumann, Iver B. 1996. "Self and Other in International Relations." *European Journal of International Relations* 2, no. 2 (June 1996): 139–174.

———. 1999. *Uses of the Other: "The East" in European Identity Formation*. Minneapolis: University of Minnesota Press.

Nobles, Melissa. 2000. *Shades of Citizenship: Race and the Census in Modern Politics*. Stanford: Stanford University Press.

Nordenstreng, Kaarle, and Herbert I. Schiller, eds. 1993. *Beyond National Sovereignty: International Communications in the 1990s*. Norwood: Ablex Publishing.

North, Douglass. 1990. *Institutions, Institutional Change, and Economic Performance.* Cambridge: Cambridge University Press.

Norton, Anne. 1988. *Reflections on Political Identity.* Baltimore: Johns Hopkins University Press.

Noyes, Dorothy. 2003. *Fire in the Plaça: Catalan Festival Politics after Franco.* Philadelphia: University of Pennsylvania Press.

Nutt, Mart. 1990. "Kollaboratsionism." *Looming* 9: 1269–1273.

Oetting, Gene, and Fred Beauvais. 1990–1991. "Orthogonal Cultural Identification Theory: The Cultural Identification of Minority Adolescents." Special issue: "Use and Misuse of Alcohol and Drugs: Ethnicity Issues." *International Journal of the Addictions* 25 (May): 655–685.

Okihiro, Gary. 2001. *Common Ground: Reimagining American History.* Princeton: Princeton University Press.

Oliver, Carl R. 2004. "Impact of Catastrophe on Pivotal National Leaders' Vision Statements: Correspondences and Discrepancies in Moral Reasoning, Explanatory Style, and Rumination." *Dissertation Abstracts International: Section B: The Sciences and Engineering* 64 (12-B): 6359.

Oliver, Pamela E., and Gregory M. Maney. 2000. "Political Processes and Local Newspaper Coverage of Protest Events: From Selection Bias to Triadic Interactions." *American Journal of Sociology* 106, no. 2 (September): 463–505.

Oliver, Pamela E., and Daniel J. Myers. 1999. "How Events Enter the Public: Conflict, Location, and Sponsorship in Local Newspaper Coverage of Public Events." *American Journal of Sociology* 105, no. 1 (July): 38–87.

Omi, Michael. 2000. "The Changing Meaning of Race." In *America Becoming: Racial Trends and Their Consequences,* vol. 1, edited by Neil J. Smelser, William Julius Wilson, and Fay Mitchell, 243–263. Washington, DC: National Academy Press.

Omi, Michael, and Howard Winant. 1994. *Racial Formation in the United States.* Rev. ed. New York: Routledge.

Oshiba, Ryo. 2002. "National Symbols, History Textbooks and Neo-nationalism in Japan." In *"We the People" in the Global Age: A Re-examination of Nationalism and Citizenship,* edited by Ryo Oshiba, Edward Rhodes, and Chieko Kitagawa Otsuru, 125–135. Osaka: Japan Center for Area Studies.

Oshiba, Ryo, Edward Rhodes, and Chieko Kitagawa Otsuru, eds. 2002. *"We the People" in the Global Age: A Re-examination of Nationalism and Citizenship.* Osaka: Japan Center for Area Studies.

Ownbey, Shiretta, and Patricia Horridge. 1998. "The Suinn-Lew Asian Self-Identity Acculturation Scale: Test with a Non-student, Asian-American Sample." *Social Behavior and Personality* 26, no. 1: 57–68.

Padilla, Amado M., ed. 1980. *Acculturation: Theory, Models and Some New Findings.* Boulder: Westview.

Peng, Kaiping, and R. E. Nisbett. 1999. "Culture, Dialectics, and Reasoning about Contradiction." *American Psychologist* 54, no. 9 (September): 741–754.

———. 2000. "Dialectical Responses to Questions about Dialectical Thinking." *American Psychologist* 55, no. 9 (September): 1067–1068.

Pennington, Nancy, and Reid Hastie. 1986. "Evidence Evaluation in Complex Decision Making." *Journal of Personality and Social Psychology* 51, no. 2 (August): 242–258.

Perlmann, Joel, and Mary C. Waters, eds. 2003. *The New Race Question: How the Census Counts Multiracial Individuals*. New York: Russell Sage Foundation.

Petersen, Lars-Eric, and Hartmut Blank. 2003. "Ingroup Bias in the Minimal Group Paradigm Shown by Three-Person Groups with High or Low State Self-Esteem." *European Journal of Social Psychology* 33, no. 2 (March): 149–162.

Phillips, Nelson, and Cynthia Hardy. 2002. *Discourse Analysis: Investigating Processes of Social Construction*. Thousand Oaks, CA.: Sage Publications.

Pinter, Brad, and Anthony G. Greenwald. 2004. "Exploring Implicit Partisanship: Enigmatic (but Genuine) Group Identification and Attraction." *Group Processes and Intergroup Relations* 7, no. 3 (July): 283–296.

Platow, Michael J., and Daan van Knippenberg. 2001. "A Social Identity Analysis of Leadership Endorsement: The Effects of Leader Intergroup Prototypicality and Distributive Intergroup Fairness." *Personality and Social Psychology Bulletin* 27, no. 11 (November): 1508–1519.

"Plenum, TsK KPSS, Iiun 1957. Stenograficheskii Otchet." 1993. *Istoricheskii Arkhiv* (3).

"Plenum, TsK KPSS, Oktyabr 1964. Stenograficheskii Otchet." 1993. *Istoricheskii Arkhiv* (1).

Polzer, Jeffrey T. 1996. "Intergroup Negotiations: The effects of Negotiating Teams." *Journal of Conflict Resolution* 40, no. 4 (December): 678–698.

Popping, Roel. 2000. *Computer-Assisted Text Analysis*. London: Sage Publications.

Portes, Alejandro, and Ruben Rumbaut. 1996. *Immigrant America: A Portrait*. Los Angeles: University of California Press.

Posner, Daniel. 2004. "Measuring Ethnic Fractionalization in Africa." *American Journal of Political Science* 48, no. 4 (October): 849–863.

——— 2005. *The Institutional Origins of Ethnic Politics in Africa*. Cambridge: Cambridge University Press.

Postmes, Tom. 2003. "A Social Identity Approach to Communication in Organizations." In *Social Identity at Work: Developing Theory for Organizational Practice*, edited by S. Alexander Haslam, Daan Van Knippenberg, Michael J. Platow, and Naomi Ellemers, 81–97. New York: Psychology Press.

Powell, Walter W., and Paul J. DiMaggio, eds. 1991. *The New Institutionalism in Organizational Analysis*. Chicago: University of Chicago Press.

Prewitt, Kenneth. 2003. "Race in the 2000 Census: A Turning Point." In *The New Race Question: How the Census Counts Multiracial Individuals*, edited by Joel Perlmann and Mary C. Waters, 354–361. New York: Russell Sage Foundation.

Price, Richard. 1998. "Reversing the Gun Sights: Transnational Civil Society Targets Land Mines." *International Organization* 52, no. 3 (Summer): 613–644.

Price, Richard, and Nina Tannenwald. 1996. "Norms and Deterrence: The Nuclear and Chemical Weapons Taboos." In *The Culture of National Security: Norms and Identity in World Politics*, edited by Peter J. Katzenstein, 114–152. New York: Columbia University Press.

Price, Vincent. 1989. "Social Identification and Public Opinion: Effects of Communi-
    cating Group Conflict." *Public Opinion Quarterly* 53, no. 2 (Summer): 197–224.
Prizel, Ilya. 1998. *National Identity and Foreign Policy: Nationalism and Leadership
    in Poland, Russia, and Ukraine.* Cambridge: Cambridge University Press.
Prozumenschikov, Mikhail Iur'evich. 1996–1997. "The Sino-Indian Conflict, the
    Cuban Missile Crisis, and the Sino-Soviet Split, October 1962: New Evidence from
    the Russian Archives." *Cold War International History Project Bulletin* 8–9
    (Winter): 251–258.
Przeworski, Adam, Michael E. Alvarez, Jose Antonio Cheibub, and Fernando Limongi,
    eds. 2000. *Democracy and Development.* Cambridge: Cambridge University
    Press.
Puddifoot, John E. 1995. "Dimensions of Community Identity." *Journal of Community
    and Applied Social Psychology* 5, no. 5 (December): 357–370.
Rabbie, J. 1981. "The Effects of Intergroup Competition and Cooperation on Intra-
    and Intergroup Relationships." In *The Psychology of Intergroup Relations*, edited
    by Stephen Worchell and William Austin, 25–48. Chicago: Nelson Hall.
Rabinow, Paul, and William M. Sullivan, eds. 1987. *Interpretive Social Science: A
    Second Look.* Berkeley: University of California Press.
Rabushka, Alvin, and Kenneth Shepsle. 1972. *Politics in Plural Societies.* Columbus:
    Charles E. Merrill.
Rajasingham-Senanayake, Darini. 1999. "Democracy and the Problem of Represen-
    tation: The Making of Bi-polar Ethnic Identity in Post/Colonial Sri Lanka."
    In *Ethnic Futures*, edited by Joanna Pfaff-Czarnecka, Darini Rajasingham-
    Senanayake, Ashis Nandy, and Edmund Terence Gomez, 99–134. New Delhi:
    Sage Publications.
Raun, Mait. 1989. "Ühiskonnavastane ühiskond." *Looming* 11: 1545–1550.
Raun, Ott. 1990. "Eesti idée." *Looming* 4: 567–568.
Raun, Tovio U. 1991. *Estonia and the Estonians.* 2nd ed. Stanford: Hoover Institution
    Press.
Rebane, Iaan. 1988. "Bolevye tochki' iazykovoi situatsii." *Tallinn* 4: 80–89.
Reed, Adolph, Jr. 1999. *Stirrings in the Jug: Black Politics in the Post-Segregation
    Era.* Minneapolis: University of Minnesota Press.
Reeves, Keith. 1997. *Voting Hopes or Fears: White Voters, Black Candidates, and
    Racial Politics in America.* New York: Oxford University Press.
Reicher, Stephen D., and Nick Hopkins. 2001. *Self and Nation.* London: Sage
    Publications.
Reiter, Dan. 1995. "Exploding the Powder Keg Myth: Preemptive Wars Almost Never
    Happen." *International Security* 20, no. 2 (Autumn 1995): 5–34.
Reus-Smit, Christian. 1997. "The Constitutional Structure of International Society and
    the Nature of Fundamental Institutions." *International Organization* 51, no. 4
    (Autumn): 555–590.
    1999. *The Moral Purpose of the State.* Princeton: Princeton University Press.
Reyes Schramm, Adelaida. 1979. "Ethnic Music, the Urban Area and Ethnomusicology."
    Sociologus 29, no. 1: 1–21.
Reykowski, Janusz. 1994. "Collectivism and Individualism as Dimensions of Social
    Change." In *Individualism and Collectivism: Theory, Method, and Applications*,

edited by Uichol Kim, Harry C. Triandis, Cigdem Kagitcibasi, Sang-Chin Choi, and Gene Yoon, 276–292. Thousand Oaks, CA: Sage Publications.

Richter, James. 1994. *Khrushchev's Double Bind: International Pressures and Domestic Coalition Politics*. Baltimore: Johns Hopkins University Press.

Ricoeur, Paul. 1984. *Time and Narrative*. Vol. 1. Chicago: University of Chicago Press.

Riffe, Daniel, Stephen Lacy, and Frederick G. Fico. 2005. *Analyzing Media Messages: Using Quantitative Content Analysis in Research*. 2nd ed. Mahwah, NJ: Lawrence Erlbaum.

Ringrose, Marjorie, and Adam J. Lerner, eds. 1993. *Reimagining the Nation*. Buckingham: Open University Press.

Risse, Thomas. 2000. "'Let's Argue!': Communicative Action in World Politics." *International Organization* 54, no. 1 (Winter): 1–39.

Risse, Thomas, Daniela Engelmann-Martin, Hans-Joachim Knopf, and Klaus Roscher. 1999. "To Euro or Not to Euro? The EMU and Identity Politics in the European Union." *European Journal of International Relations* 5, no. 2 (June): 147–187.

Risse, Thomas, Steve C. Ropp, and Kathryn Sikkink, eds. 1999. *The Power of Human Rights: International Norms and Domestic Political Change*. Cambridge: Cambridge University Press.

Risse-Kappen, Thomas. 1995. *Cooperation among Democracies: The European Influence on U.S. Foreign Policy*. Princeton: Princeton University Press.

1996. "Collective Identity in a Democratic Community: The Case of NATO." In *The Culture of National Security: Norms and Identity in World Politics*, edited by Peter Katzenstein, 357–399. New York: Columbia University Press.

Roberts, Carl W., ed. 1997. *Text Analysis for the Social Sciences: Methods for Drawing Statistical Inferences from Texts and Transcripts*. Mahwah, NJ: Lawrence Erlbaum Associates.

Robertson, Roland. 1997. "Social Theory, Cultural Relativity and the Problem of Globality." In *Culture, Globalization and the World-System: Contemporary Conditions for the Representation of Identity*, edited by Anthony D. King, 69–90. Minneapolis: University of Minnesota Press.

Roccas, Sonia. 2003. "The Effects of Status on Identifications with Multiple Groups." *European Journal of Social Psychology* 33, no. 3: 351–366.

Rodden, Jonathan. 2004. "Comparative Federalism: Meaning and Measurement." *Comparative Politics* 36, no. 4 (July): 481–500.

Rodden, Jonathan, and Eric Wibbels. 2002. "Beyond the Fiction of Federalism: Macroeconomic Management in Multitiered Systems." *World Politics* 54, no. 4 (July): 494–531.

Rodriguez, Clara E. 2000. *Changing Race: Latinos, the Census and the History of Ethnicity in the United States*. Philadelphia: Temple University Press.

Rogin, Michael. 1997. *Ronald Reagan, the Movie, and Other Essays in Political Demonology*. Berkeley: University of California Press.

1998. *Blackface, White Noise: Jewish Immigrants in the Hollywood Melting Pot*. Berkeley: University of California Press.

Ropp, Stephen C., and Kathryn Sikkink, eds. 1999. *Power of Human Rights*. Cambridge: Cambridge University Press.

Rosch, Eleanor, and Barbara B. Lloyd, eds. 1978. *Cognition and Categorization.* Hillsdale: Halsted Press.

Rothì, Despina M., Evanthia Lyons, and Xenia Chryssochoou. 2005. "National Attachment and Patriotism in a European Nation: A British Study." *Political Psychology* 26, no. 1 (February): 135–154.

Rousseau, David L. 2006. *Identifying Threats and Threatening Identities: The Social Construction of Realism and Liberalism.* Stanford, CA: Stanford University Press.

Rubin, Herbert J., and Irene S. Rubin. 1995. *Qualitative Interviewing: The Art of Hearing Data.* Thousand Oaks, CA.: Sage Publications.

Rudman Laurie A., and Stephanie A. Goodwin. 2004. "Gender Differences in Automatic In-Group Bias: Why Do Women Like Women More than Men Like Men?" *Journal of Personality and Social Psychology* 87, no. 4 (October): 494–509.

Ruggie, John Gerard. 1997. "The Past as Prologue? Interests, Identity, and American Foreign Policy." *International Security* 21, no. 4 (Spring): 89–125.

——— 1998a. "Interests, Identity, and American Foreign Policy." In *Constructing the World Polity,* edited by John G. Ruggie, 203–228. New York: Routledge.

——— 1998b. "What Makes the World Hang Together? Neo-utilitarianism and the Social Constructivist Challenge." In *Constructing the World Polity,* edited by John G. Ruggie, 1–40. New York: Routledge.

Rustow, Dankwart. 1970. "Transitions to Democracy: Towards a Dynamic Model." *Comparative Politics* 2, no. 3 (April): 337–364.

Ruutsoo, Rein. 1988. "Kuida mäletada ühte ajastut?" *Looming* 5: 674–676.

Sambanis, Nicholas. 2001. "A Review of Recent Advances and Future Directions in the Quantitative Literature on Civil War." Working paper, Yale University.

Sánchez-Jankowski, Martín. 1991. *Islands in the Street: Gangs and American Urban Society.* Berkeley: University of California Press.

Satterfield, Jason M. 1998. "Cognitive-Affective States Predict Military and Political Aggression and Risk Taking: A Content Analysis of Churchill, Hitler, Roosevelt, and Stalin." *Journal of Conflict Resolution* 42, no. 6 (December): 667–690.

Sawyer, Mark Q. 2005. *Racial Politics in Post-Revolutionary Cuba.* Cambridge: Cambridge University Press.

Scaritt, James R., and Shaheen Mozaffar. 1999. "The Specification of Ethnic Cleavages and Ethnopolitical Groups for the Analysis of Democratic Competition in Africa." *Nationalism and Ethnic Politics* 5, no. 1 (Spring): 82–117.

Schafer, Mark. 1999. "Cooperative and Conflictual Policy Preferences: The Effect of Identity, Security and Image of the Other." *Political Psychology* 20, no. 4 (December): 829–844.

Scharl, Arno. 2004. "Web Coverage of Renewable Energy." In *Environmental Online Communication,* edited by Arno Scharl, 25–34. London: Springer.

Schatz, Edward. 2004. *Modern Clan Politics: The Power of "Blood" in Kazakhstan and Beyond.* Seattle: University of Washington Press.

Schelling, Thomas C. 1960. *The Strategy of Conflict.* Cambridge, MA: Harvard University Press.

Schreer, George E., and Jeremy M. Strichartz. 1997. "Private Restroom Graffiti: An Analysis of Controversial Social Issues on Two College Campuses." *Psychological Reports* 81: 1067–1074.

Schrodt, Philip A. 1998. "Kansas Event Data System, K-E-D-S." Department of Political Science, University of Kansas, Lawrence. Available online at http://www.ku.edu/~keds/software.

———. 2005. "TABARI: Text Analysis by Augmented Replacement Instructions." Department of Political Science, University of Kansas, Lawrence. Available online at http://www.ku.edu/~keds/software.dir/tabari.

Schuman, Howard, and Stanley Presser. 1996. *Questions and Answers in Attitude Surveys.* Thousand Oaks, CA: Sage Publications.

Schuman, Howard, Charlotte Steeh, Lawrence D. Bobo, and Maria Krysan. 1998. *Racial Attitudes in America.* Rev. ed. Cambridge, MA: Harvard University Press.

Schutz, Alfred. 1973a. "Common-Sense and the Scientific Interpretation of Human Action." In *Collected Papers,* vol. 1, edited by Alfred Schutz, 3–47. The Hague: M. Nijhoff.

———. 1973b. *Collected Papers. Vol. 2.* The Hague: M. Nijhoff.

Schwartz, S.J. 2001. "The Evolution of Eriksonian and Neo-Eriksonian Identity Theory and Research: A Review and Integration." *Identity: An International Journal of Theory and Research* 1: 7–58.

Schwartz, Shalom H. 1992. "Universals in the Content and Structure of Values: Theoretical Advances and Empirical Tests in 20 Countries." In *Advances in Experimental/Social Psychology* 25, edited by Mark P. Zanna, 1–65. Orlando: Academic Press.

———. 1994. "Beyond Individualism/Collectivism: New Cultural Dimensions of Values." In *Individualism and Collectivism: Theory, Method, and Applications,* edited by Uichol Kim, Harry C. Triandis, Cigdem Kagitcibasi, Sang-Chin Choi, and Gene Yoon, 85–119. Thousand Oaks, CA: Sage Publications.

Scott, James. 1998. *Seeing Like a State: How Certain Schemes to Improve the Human Condition Have Failed.* New Haven: Yale University Press.

Searle, John. 1995. *Construction of Social Reality.* New York: Free Press.

Sears, David O. 1986. "Symbolic Politics: A Socio-Psychological Theory." In *Explorations in Political Psychology,* edited by Shanto Iyengar and William J. McGuire, 113–149. Durham: Duke University Press.

Sears, David O., Jack Citrin, Sharmaine V. Cheleden, and Colette van Laar. 1999. "Cultural Diversity and Multicultural Politics: Is Ethnic Balkanization Inevitable?" In *Cultural Divides: Understanding and Overcoming Group Conflict,* edited by Deborah A. Prentice and Dale T. Miller, 35–79. New York: Russell Sage Foundation.

Sears, David O., and Victoria Savalei. 2006. "The Political Color Line in America: Many 'Peoples of Color' or Black Exceptionalism?" *Political Psychology* 27, no. 6 (December): 895–924.

Sen, Amartya. 2000. "Other People." *New Republic,* 18 December.

Sending, Ole Jacob. 2002. "Constitution, Choice and Change: Problems with the 'Logic of Appropriateness' and Its Use in Constructivist Theory." *European Journal of International Relations* 8, no. 4 (December): 443–470.

Seul, Jeffrey R. 1999. "'Ours Is the Way of God': Religion, Identity and Intergroup Conflict." *Journal of Peace Research* 36, no. 5 (September): 553–569.

Sewell, William H., Jr. 1992. "A Theory of Structure: Duality, Agency, and Transformation." *American Journal of Sociology* 98, no. 1 (July): 1–29.

Shabad, Goldie, and Kazimierz M. Slomczynski. 1999. "Political Identities in the Initial Phase of Systemic Transformation in Poland: A Test of the Tabula Rasa Hypothesis." *Comparative Political Studies* 32, no. 6: 690–723.

Shakhnazarov, Georgii. 1993. *Tsena Svobody: Reformatsiia Gorbacheva Glazami ego Pomoshchnika.* Moscow: Rossika/Zevs.

2001. *S Vozhdiami i Bez Nikh.* Moscow: Vagrius.

Shelby, Tommie. 2002. "Foundations of Black Solidarity: Collective Identity or Common Oppression?" *Ethics* 112, no. 2 (January): 231–266.

Sherif, Muzafer, O. J. Harvey, B. J. White, B. W. R. Hood, and C. W. Sherif. 1961. *The Robber's Cave Experiment: Intergroup Conflict and Cooperation.* Middletown, CT: Wesleyan University Press.

Shiloah, Amnon, and Erik Cohen. 1985. "Major Trends of Change in Jewish Oriental Music in Israel." *Popular Music* 5: 199–223.

Shils, Edward. 1957. "Primordial, Personal, Sacred and Civil Ties." *British Journal of Sociology* 8, no. 2: 130–145.

Shklar, Judith N. 1991. *American Citizenship: The Quest for Inclusion.* Cambridge, MA: Harvard University Press.

1998. *Redeeming American Political Thought.* Ed. Dennis F. Thompson. Chicago. University of Chicago Press.

Sidanius, Jim, and Felicia Pratto. 1999. *Social Dominance: An Intergroup Theory of Social Hierarchy and Oppression.* Cambridge: Cambridge University Press.

Sidanius, Jim, and John R. Petrocik. 2001. "Communal and National Identity in a Multiethnic State: A Comparison of Three Perspectives." In *Social Identity, Intergroup Conflict and Conflict Resolution,* edited by Richard D. Ashmore, Lee Jussim, and David Wilder, 101–131. New York: Oxford University Press.

Sidanius, Jim, Seymour Feshback, Shana Levin, and Felicia Pratto. 1997. "The Interface between Ethnic and National Attachment: Ethnic Pluralism or Social Dominance?" *Public Opinion Quarterly* 61, no. 1 (Spring): 102–133.

Simon, Bernd, and Stefan Stürmer. 2003. "Respect for Group Members: Intergroup Determinants of Collective Identification and Group-Serving Behavior." *Personality and Social Psychology Bulletin* 29, no. 2 (February): 183–193.

Simon, Herbert A. 1947. *Administrative Behavior.* New York: Macmillan.

Singer, Eleanor, and Stanley Presser, eds. 1989. *Survey Research Methods: A Reader.* Chicago: University of Chicago Press.

Sirgy, M. Joseph, Dong-Jin Lee, Rustan Kosenko, H. Lee Meadow, Don Rahtz, Muris Cicic, Guang Xi Jin, Duygun Yarsuvat, David L. Blenkhorn, and Newell Wright. 1998. "Does Television Viewership Play a Role in the Perception of Quality of Life?" *Journal of Advertising* 27, no. 1 (Spring): 125–142.

Skalski, Paul D. 2002. "Computer Content Analysis Software." In *The Content Analysis Guidebook,* edited by Kimberly A. Neuendorf, 225–239. Thousand Oaks, CA: Sage Publications.

Skerry, Peter. 2000. *Counting on the Census: Race, Group Identity, and the Evasion of Politics.* Washington, DC: Brookings Institution.

Slezkine, Yuri. 1994a. *From Savages to Citizens: Russia and the Small Peoples of the North.* Princeton: Princeton University Press.

1994b. "The USSR as a Communal Apartment, or How a Socialist State Promoted Ethnic Particularism." *Slavic Review* 53, no. 2 (Summer): 414–452.

Smith, Ann Marie. 1999. "Girls on Film: Analysis of Women's Images in Contemporary American and 'Golden Age' Hollywood Films." M.A. thesis, Cleveland State University.

Smith, Anthony D. 1986. *The Ethnic Origins of Nations*. Cambridge: Blackwell.

———. 1990. "Towards a Global Culture?" In *Global Culture: Nationalism, Globalization and Modernity*, edited by Mike Featherstone, 171–191. London: Sage Publications.

———. 1991. *National Identity*. Reno: University of Nevada Press.

———. 1992. "National Identity and the Idea of European Unity." *International Affairs* 68, no. 1 (Winter 1992): 55–76.

———. 1993. "The Nation: Invented, Imagined, Reconstructed?" In *Reimagining the Nation*, edited by Marjorie Ringrose and Adam J. Lerner, 9–28. Buckingham: Open University Press.

Smith, C.E., and R. Hopkins. 2004. "Mitigating the Impact of Stereotypes on Academic Performance: The Effects of Cultural Identity and Attributions for Success among African American College Students." *Western Journal of Black Studies* 28, no. 1: 312–321.

Smith, Dorothy. 1987. *The Everyday World as Problematic: a Feminist Sociology*. Boston: Northeastern University Press.

Smith, Edward E., and Douglas L. Medin. 1981. *Categories and Concepts*. Cambridge, MA: Harvard University Press.

Smith, Rogers M. 1997. *Civic Ideals: Conflicting Visions of Citizenship in U.S. History*. New Haven: Yale University Press.

———. 2002. "Identity, Interests, and the Future of Political Science." *Perspectives on Politics* 2, no. 2 (June): 301–312.

———. 2003. *Stories of Peoplehood*. Cambridge: Cambridge University Press.

Smith, Tom W. 2001."Aspects of Measuring Race: Race by Observation vs. Self-Reporting and Multiple Mentions of Race and Ethnicity." *GSS Methodological Report, no. 93*. Chicago: National Opinion Research Center.

Smith, Tom W., and L. Jarkko. 2001. *National Pride in Cross-National Perspective*. Chicago: University of Chicago, National Opinion Research Center.

Sniderman, Paul M., Louk Hagendoorn, and Markus Prior. 2004. "Predisposing Factors and Situational Triggers: Exclusionary Reactions to Immigrant Minorities." *American Political Science Review* 98, no. 1 (February): 35–49.

Snipp, C. Matthew. 2003. "Racial Measurement in the American Census: Past Practices and Implications for the Future." *Annual Review of Sociology* 29, no. 1: 563–588.

Spechler, Dina R. 1982. *Permitted Dissent in the USSR: "Novy Mir" and the Soviet Regime*. New York: Praeger.

Stapel, Diederik, Stephen D. Reicher, and R. Spears. 1994. "Social Identity, Availability and the Perception of Risk." *Social Cognition* 12, no. 1 (Spring): 1–17.

Starr, Paul. 1987. "The Sociology of Official Statistics." In *The Politics of Numbers (Population of the United States in the 1980s)*, edited by William Alonso and Paul Starr, 7–57. New York: Russell Sage Foundation.

Steinmetz, George, ed. 1999. *State/Culture: State-Formation after the Cultural Turn*. Ithaca: Cornell University Press.

Stephan, Cookie White, and Walter G. Stephan. 2000. "The Measurement of Racial and Ethnic Identity." *International Journal of Intercultural Relations* 24, no. 5 (September): 541–552.

Sterling-Folker, Jennifer. 2000. "Competing Paradigms or Birds of a Feather? Constructivism and Neoliberal Institutionalism Compared." *International Studies Quarterly* 44, no. 1 (March): 97–120.

Stets, Jan E., and Peter J. Burke. 2000. "Identity Theory and Social Identity Theory." *Social Psychology Quarterly* 63, no. 3: 224–237.

Stone, Philip J. 1997. "Thematic Text Analysis: New Agendas for Analyzing Text Content." In *Text Analysis for the Social Sciences: Methods for Drawing Statistical Inferences from Texts and Transcripts*, edited by Carl W. Roberts, 35–54. Mahwah, NJ: Lawrence Erlbaum.

Stratigaki, Maria. 2004. "The Cooptation of Gender Concepts in EU Policies: The Case of 'Reconciliation of Work and Family.'" *Social Politics* 11, no. 1 (Spring): 30–56.

Stryker, Sheldon. 1987. "Identity Theory: Development and Extensions." In *Self and Identity: Psychosocial Perspectives*, edited by Krysia Yardley, K.M. Yardley, and Terry Honess, 89–103. New York: John Wiley and Sons.

——— 2000. "Identity Theory." In *Encyclopedia of Sociology,* vol. 2, 2nd ed., edited by Edgar F. Borgatta and Rhonda J.V. Montgomery, 1253–1258. New York: Macmillan References USA.

Stryker, Sheldon, Timothy J. Owens, and Robert W. White, eds. 2000. *Self, Identity, and Social Movements.* Minneapolis: University of Minnesota Press.

Stryker, Sheldon, and Richard T. Serpe. 1994. "Identity Salience and Psychological Centrality: Equivalent, Overlapping, or Complementary Concepts?" *Social Psychology Quarterly* 57, no. 1: 16–35.

Suny, Ronald Grigor. 1993. *The Revenge of the Past: Nationalism, Revolution, and the Collapse of the Soviet Union.* Stanford: Stanford University Press.

Sutherland, Anne. 1975. *Gypsies: The Hidden Americans.* London: Tavistock Publications.

Sylvan, Donald A., Andrea Grove, and Jeffery Martinson. 2005. "Problem Representation and Conflict Dynamics in the Middle East and Northern Ireland." *Foreign Policy Analysis* 1, no. 3 (November): 279–299.

Sylvan, Donald A., Amy Horowitz, and Amanda K. Metskas. 2004. "Functionalism or Familiarity Breeding Contempt? Identity Development, Music, and the Politics of Mizrahi Jews in Israel." Paper presented at the annual meeting of the International Society of Political Psychology, Lund, Sweden, 15–18 July.

Sylvan, Donald A., and Arie Nadler. 2005. "The Role of Victimization and Identity in the Palestinian-Israeli Conflict: Experimental and Text Analytic Perspectives." Paper presented at the annual meeting of the International Studies Association, Hawaii, 1–5 March.

Sylvan, Donald A., and Jon C. Pevehouse. 2002. "Deciding Whether to Intervene: Problem Representations of US and French Elites Dealing with Central Africa." In *International Intervention: Sovereignty vs. Responsibility*, edited by Michael Keren and Donald A. Sylvan, 56–74. London: Frank Cass.

Sylvan, Donald A., and Stuart J. Thorson. 1992. "Ontologies, Problem Representation, and the Cuban Missile Crisis." *Journal of Conflict Resolution* 36, no. 4 (December): 709–732.

Sylvan, Donald A., and Nathan Toronto. 2004. "Empathy with Palestinians vs. Israelis: Examining U.S. Media Representations, Coverage, and Attitudes." Paper presented at the annual meeting of the International Society of Political Psychology, Lund, Sweden, 15–18 July.

Sylvan, Donald A., and J.F. Voss, eds. 1998. *Problem Representation in Foreign Policy Decision Making*. Cambridge: Cambridge University Press.

Taagepera, Rein. 1982. "Size and Ethnicity of Estonian Towns and Rural Districts, 1922–1979." *Journal of Baltic Studies* 13, no. 2 (Summer): 105–127.

Tafoya, Sonya M. 2003. "Mixed Race and Ethnicity in California." In *The New Race Question: How the Census Counts Multiracial Individuals*, edited by Joel Perlmann and Mary C. Waters, 102–113. New York: Russell Sage Foundation.

Tajfel, Henri. 1970. "Experiments in Intergroup Discrimination." *Scientific American* 223, no. 5: 96–102.

   1972. "The Devaluation by Children of Their Own National and Ethnic Group: Two Case Studies." *British Journal of Social and Clinical Psychology* 11, no. 3 (September): 235–243.

   1974. "Social Identity and Intergroup Behavior." *Social Science Information/sur les sciences sociales* 13, no. 2: 65–93.

   ed. 1978. *Differentiation between Social Groups: Studies in the Social Psychology of Intergroup Relations*. London: Academic Press.

   1981a. *Social Identity and Intergroup Behavior*. Cambridge: Cambridge University Press.

   1981b. *Human Groups and Social Categories: Studies in Social Psychology*. Cambridge: Cambridge University Press.

   1982. "Social Psychology of Intergroup Relations." *Annual Review of Psychology* 33, no. 1: 1–39.

Tajfel, Henri, Michael G. Billig, R. P. Bundy, and Claude Flament. 1971. "Social Categorization and Intergroup Behavior." *European Journal of Social Psychology* 1, no. 2 (June): 149–178.

Tajfel, Henri, and John C. Turner. 1986. "The Social Identity Theory of Intergroup Behavior." In *Psychology of Intergroup Relations*, edited by Stephen Worchel and William G. Austin, 7–24. 2nd ed. Chicago: Nelson-Hall.

Tambiah, Stanley. 1986. *Sri Lanka: Ethnic Fratricide and the Dismantling of Democracy*. Chicago: University of Chicago Press.

Tamm, Aksel', and Svetlan Semenenko. 1989. "V odnom dome, v obshchem kotle." *Tallinn* 4: 78–86.

Tan-Chiu, Lin. 1955. "Springtime in China." *New Times*, 30 April.

Tannenwald, Nina. 1999. "The Nuclear Taboo: The United States and the Normal Basis of Nuclear Non-Use." *International Organization* 53, no. 3 (Summer): 433–468.

Tate, Katherine. 1993. *From Protest to Politics: The New Black Voters in American Politics*. Cambridge, MA: Harvard University Press.

Taubman, William. 1996–1997. "Khrushchev vs. Mao: A Preliminary Sketch of the Role of Personality in the Sino-Soviet Split." *Cold War International History Project Bulletin* 8–9 (Winter): 243–248.

———. 2003. *Khrushchev: The Man and His Era*. New York: W.W. Norton.

Taylor, Dalmas A., and Beatrice F. Moriarty. 1987. "Ingroup Bias as a Function of Competition and Race." *Journal of Conflict Resolution* 31, no. 1 (March): 192–199.

Taylor, Donald M. 2002. *The Quest for Identity: From Minority Groups to Generation Xers*. Westport, CT: Praeger.

Taylor, Shelley, Letitia Peplau, and David O. Sears. 1997. *Social Psychology*. 9th ed. Princeton: Princeton University Press.

Telhami, Shibley, and Michael Barnett. 2002. "Introduction: Identity and Foreign Policy in the Middle East." In *Identity and Foreign Policy in the Middle East*, edited by Shibley Telhami and Michael Barnett, 1–25. Ithaca: Cornell University Press.

Terent'eva, I. V. 1993. *Politicheskie partii i obshchestvennye dvizheniia v Respublike Tatarstan*. Kazan: Apparat Prezidenta Respubliki Tatarstan: Otdel Mezhnatsional'nykh otnoshenii i sviazi s obshchestvenno-politicheskimi ob"edineniiami.

Tilly, Charles. 2003. "Political Identities in Changing Polities." *Social Research* 70, no. 3 (Summer): 1301–1315.

Tishkov, Valery. 1997. *Ethnicity, Nationalism and Conflict in and after the Soviet Union*. Thousand Oaks, CA: Sage Publications.

Titscher, Stefan, Michael Meyer, Ruth Wodak, and Eva Vetter. 2000. *Methods of Text and Discourse Analysis*. Thousand Oaks, CA: Sage Publications.

Tourangeau, Roger, Lance J. Rips, and Kenneth Rasinski. 2000. *The Psychology of Survey Response*. Cambridge: Cambridge University Press.

Triandis, Harry C. 1994. "Theoretical and Methodological Approaches to the Study of Collectivism and Individualism." In *Individualism and Collectivism: Theory, Method, and Applications*, edited by Uichol Kim, Harry C. Triandis, Cigdem Kagitcibasi, Sang-Chin Choi, and Gene Yoon, 41–51. Thousand Oaks, CA: Sage Publications.

Tronvoll, Kjetil. 1998. "The Process of Nation-Building in Post-War Eritrea: Created from Below or Directed from Above?" *Journal of Modern African Studies* 36, no. 3: 461–482.

Tropkin, N.. 1955. "O strategii i taktika leninizma." *Kommunist* 1.

Trosset, Carol, and Douglas Caulkins. 2002. "Cultural Values and Social Organization in Wales: Is Ethnicity the Locus of Culture?" In *British Subjects: An Anthropology of Britain*, edited by Nigel Rappaport, 239–258. Oxford: Berg.

Tuomela, Raimo. 2002. *The Philosophy of Social Practices: A Collective Acceptance View*. Cambridge: Cambridge University Press.

Turner, John C. 1985. "Social Categorization and the Self-Concept: A Social Cognitive Theory of Group Behavior." In *Advances in Group Processes,* vol. 2, edited by Edward J. Lawler, 77–121. New York: JAI Press.

———. 1988. *A Theory of Social Interaction*. Stanford: Stanford University Press.

———. 1999. "Some Current Issues in Research on Social Identity and Self-Categorization Theories." In *Social Identity*, edited by Naomi Ellemers, Russell Spears, and Bertjan Doosje, 6–34. Oxford: Blackwell.

Turner, John C., R. J. Brown, and Henri Tajfel. 1979. "Social Comparison and Group
Interest in Ingroup Favoritism." *European Journal of Social Psychology* 9, no. 2
(June): 187–204.

Turner, John C., Michael A. Hogg, Penelope J. Oakes, Stephen D. Reicher, and
M. S. Wetherell. 1987. *Rediscovering the Social Group: A Self-Categorization
Theory*. Oxford: Blackwell.

Turner, John C., and Penelope J. Oakes. 1986. "The Significance of the Social Identity
Concept for Social Psychology with Reference to Individualism, Interactionism,
and Social Influence." *British Journal of Social Psychology* 25, no. 3 (October):
237–252.

Turner, Stephen. 2002. *Brains, Practices, Relativism: Social Theory after Cognitive
Science*. Chicago: University of Chicago Press.

Utz, Sonja. 2003. "Social Identification and Interpersonal Attraction in MUDs." *Swiss
Journal of Psychology* 62, no. 2: 91–101.

Vahtre, Lauri. 1991. "Millal lõppes Eesti aeg?" *Looming* 1: 121–123.

Valentino, Nicholas A. 1999. "Crime News and the Priming of Racial Attitudes
during Evaluations of the President." *Public Opinion Quarterly* 63, no. 3
(Autumn): 293–323.

Valenzuela, J. Samuel, and Timothy R. Scully. 1997. "Electoral Choices and the Party
System in Chile: Continuities and Changes at the Recovery of Democracy."
Comparative Politics 29, no. 4: 511–527.

van Maanen, John. 1988. *Tales of the Field: On Writing Ethnography*. Chicago:
University of Chicago Press.

Van Vugt, Mark, and Claire M. Hart. 2004. "Social Identity as Social Glue: The Origins
of Group Loyalty." *Journal of Personality and Social Psychology* 86, no. 4
(April): 585–598.

Verkuyten, Maykel. 1991. "Self-Definition and Ingroup Formation among Ethnic
Minorities in the Netherlands." *Social Psychology Quarterly* 54, no. 3: 280–286.

Veroff, Joseph. 1992. "Power Motivation." In *Motivation and Personality: Handbook
of Thematic Content Analysis*, edited by Charles P. Smith, 278–285. Cambridge:
Cambridge University Press.

Vetik, Raivo. 1999. "Inter-Ethnic Relations in Estonia, 1988–1998." *Acta Universitatis
Tamperensis* 655. Tampere: University of Tampere.

Vihalemm, Peeter, and Marju Lauristin. 1997. "Political Control and Ideological Can-
onisation. The Estonian Press during the Soviet Period." In *Vom Instrument der
Partei zur "Vierten Gewalt" Die ostmitteleuropäische Presse als zeithistorische
Quelle. Sonderdruck as tagungen zur Ostmitteleuropa-Forschung*, edited by
Eduard Mühle, 103–109. Marburg: Verlag Hereder-Institut.

Wald, Kenneth D., and Samuel Shye. 1994. " Interreligious Conflict in Israel: The Group
Basis of Conflicting Visions." *Political Behavior* 16, no. 1 (March): 157–178.

Walt, Stephen. 1987. *The Origins of Alliances*. Ithaca: Cornell University Press.

Waltz, Kenneth N. 1979. *Theory of International Politics*. Boston: McGraw Hill.

    1997. "Evaluating Theories." *American Political Science Review* 91, no. 4
(December): 913–917.

Walzer, Michael. 1997. *On Toleration*. New Haven: Yale University Press.

Waters, Mary C. 1990. *Ethnic Options: Choosing Ethnic Identities in America*.
Berkeley: University of California Press.

2001. *Black Identities: West Indian Immigrant Dreams and American Realities.* Cambridge, MA: Harvard University Press.

Watzlawick, Paul, Janet Beavin Bavelas, and Don. D. Jackson. 1967. *The Pragmatics of Human Communication: A Study of Interactional Patterns, Pathologies, and Paradoxes.* New York: Norton.

Weaver, Vesla. 2005. "Linked Fate Annotated Bibliography." Unpublished manuscript, University of Chicago, compiled for Michael Dawson.

Weber, Max. 1968. *Economy and Society.* Vol. 1. New York: Bedminster Press.

Weber, Robert Philip. 1990. *Basic Content Analysis.* 2nd ed. Newbury Park, CA: Sage Publications.

Wedeen, Lisa. 2002. "Conceptualizing Culture: Possibilities for Political Science." *American Political Science Review* 96, no. 4: 713–728.

Weiss, Robert Stuart. 1994. *Learning from Strangers: The Art and Method of Qualitative Interview Studies.* New York: Free Press.

Weldes, Jutta. 1999. *Constructing National Interests: The United States and the Cuban Missile Crisis.* Minneapolis: University of Minnesota Press.

Weldes, Jutta, Mark Laffey, Hugh Gusterson, and Raymond Duvall, eds. 1999. *Cultures of Insecurity: States, Communities and the Production of Danger.* Minneapolis: University of Minnesota Press.

Wendt, Alexander. 1994. "Collective Identity Formation and the International State." *American Political Science Review* 88, no. 2 (June): 384–396.

1999. *Social Theory of International Politics.* Cambridge: Cambridge University Press.

Westad, Odd Arne. 1996–1997. "Moscow and the Angolan Crisis, 1974–1976: A New Pattern of Intervention." *Cold War International History Project Bulletin* 8–9 (Winter): 21–32.

ed. 1998. *Brothers in Arms: The Rise and Fall of the Sino-Soviet Alliance, 1945–1963.* Stanford: Stanford University Press.

Weston, Kath. 1991. *Families We Choose: Lesbians, Gays, Kinship.* New York: Columbia University Press.

Wetherell, Margaret. 1987. "How to Analyze Discourse." In Jonathan Potter and Margaret Wetherell, *Discourse and Social Psychology: Beyond Attitudes and Behaviour,* 158–187. Thousand Oaks, CA: Sage Publications.

White, Clovis L., and Peter J. Burke. 1987. "Ethnic Role Identity among Black and White College Students: An Interactionist Approach." *Sociological Perspectives* 30, no. 3: 310–331.

Wilder, David A. 1981. "Perceiving Persons as a Group: Categorization and Intergroup Relations." In *Cognitive Processes in stereotyping and intergroup behaviour,* ed. David Hamilton, 213–257. Hillsdale, NJ: Lawrence Erlbaum.

Wilkenfeld, Jonathan, interim director. 2004. "Minorities at Risk" Dataset. Integrated Network for Societal Conflict Research, University of Maryland at College Park. Available online at http://www.cidcm.umd.edu/inscr/mar/.

Wilkinson, Steven. 2008. "Which Group Identities lead to Conflict? Evidence from India." In *Order, Conflict and Violence,* edited by Stathis Kalyvas, Ian Shapiro, and Tarek Masoud. Cambridge: Cambridge University Press.

Williams, Kim. 2001. "Boxed In: The United States Multi-racial Movement." Ph.D. dissertation, Cornell University.

Williams, Raymond. 1970. *The English Novel from Dickens to Lawrence*. London: Chatto and Windus.

Willis, Paul E. 1977. *Learning to Labour: How Working Class Kids Get Working Class Jobs*. Farnborough, Eng.: Saxon House.

Willnat, Lars, and Jian-Hua Zhu. 1996. "Newspaper Coverage and Public Opinion in Hong Kong: A Time-Series Analysis of Media Priming." *Political Communication* 13, no. 2: 231–246.

Wilson, Barbara J., Dale Kunkel, Dan Linz, James W. Potter, Edward Donnerstein, S. L. Smith, E. Blumenthal, and T. Gray. 1997. "Violence in Television Programming Overall: University of California, Santa Barbara Study." *National Television Violence Study*, vol. 1, edited by M. Seawall, 3–184. Newbury Park, CA: Sage Publications.

Winters, Loretta I., and Herman L. DeBose. 2003. *New Faces in a Changing America: Multiracial Identity in the 21st Century*. Thousand Oaks, CA: Sage Publications.

Wittenberg, Jason. 2004. "Ethnic Diversity and Electoral Extremism in Interwar Eastern Europe." Paper presented at the Laboratory in Comparative Ethnic Processes, Columbia University, 8 March.

Wittgenstein, Ludwig. 1958. *Philosophical Investigations*. New York: Macmillan.

Wixman, Ron. 1993. "The Middle Volga: Ethnic Archipelago in a Russian Sea." In *Nations and Politics in the Soviet Successor States*, edited by Ian Bremmer and Ray Taras, 421–427. Cambridge: Cambridge University Press.

Wodak, Ruth. 2004. "National and Transnational Identities: European and Other Identities Constructed in Interviews with EU Officials." In *Transnational Identities: Becoming European in the EU*, edited by Richard K. Herrmann, Thomas Risse-Kappen, and Marilynn B. Brewer. Lanham, MD: Rowman and Littlefield.

Wodak, Ruth, and Michael Meyer. 2001. *Methods of Critical Discourse Analysis*. London: Sage Publications.

Woelfel, Joseph. 1993. "GalileoCATPAC: User Manual and Tutorial." Galileo Company, Amherst. Available online at http://www.galileoco.com.

Wolf, Margery. 1992. *A Thrice-Told Tale: Feminism, Postmodernism, and Ethnographic Responsibility*. Stanford: Stanford University Press.

Wong, Cara J. 2002. "Boundaries of Obligation, Racial, National and Geographic Communities in American Politics." Ph.D. dissertation, University of California at Berkeley.

Woodward, Comer Vann. 1966. *The Strange Career of Jim Crow*. Oxford: Oxford University Press.

World Values Survey. 2004. Stockholm: World Values Survey. Retrieved from http://www.worldvaluessurvey.org, accessed 12 November.

Worthington, Roger L., Holly Bielstein Savoy, Frank R. Dillon, and Elizabeth R. Vernaglia. 2002. "Heterosexual Identity Development: A Multidimensional Model of Individual and Social Identity." *Counseling Psychologist* 30, no. 4 (July): 496–531.

Yamada, Atsushi. 2002. "Going Local in the Global Age: Globalization and Techno-Nationalism. In *"We the People" in the Global Age: A Re-examination of Nationalism and Citizenship*, edited by Ryo Oshiba, Edward Rhodes, and Chieko Kitagawa Otsuru, 61–78. Osaka: Japan Center for Area Studies.

Yashar, Deborah J. 1998. "Contesting Citizenship: Indigenous Movements and Democracy in Latin America." *Comparative Politics* 31, no. 1: 23–42.

Young, Iris Marion. 1990. *Justice and the Politics of Difference*. Princeton: Princeton University Press.

2000. *Inclusion and Democracy*. Oxford: Oxford University Press.

Young, Michael D. 1996. "Cognitive Maps Meet Semantic Networks." *Journal of Conflict Resolution* 40, no. 3 (September): 395–414.

2001. "Building WorldViews with Profiler +." In *Applications of Computer Content Analysis*, edited by Mark D. West. Progress in Communication Sciences, 17. Westport, CT: Greenwood Publishing Group.

Zagoria, Donald S. 1962. *The Sino-Soviet Conflict, 1956–1961*. Princeton: Princeton University Press.

Zajonc, Robert Boleslaw. 1968. "Attitudinal Effects of Mere Exposure." *Journal of Personality and Social Psychology Monograph Supplement* 9, no. 2 (part 2): 1–27.

Zanca, Russell. 2000. "Intruder in Uzbekistan: Walking the Line between Community Needs and Anthropological Desiderata." In *Fieldwork Dilemmas: Anthropologists in Postsocialist States*, edited by Hermine G. De Soto and Nora Dudwick, 153–171. Madison: University of Wisconsin Press.

Zehfuss, Maja. 2001. "Constructivism and Identity: A Dangerous Liaison." *European Journal of International Relations* 7, no. 3 (September): 315–348.

Zhang, J. 1991. "The Interaction of Internal and External Representations in a Problem Solving Task." In *Proceedings of the Thirteenth Annual Conference of the Cognitive Science Society*, Chicago, 954–958. Hillsdale, NJ: Lawrence Erlbaum.

Zhang, Shu Guang. 2001. *Economic Cold War: America's Embargo against China and the Sino-Soviet Alliance, 1949–1963*. Washington, DC: Woodrow Wilson Center Press.

"Zimianin on Sino-Soviet Relations." 1995/1996. *Cold War International History Project Bulletin* 6–7 (Winter): 170–185.

Zuberi, Tukufu. 2001. *Thicker than Blood: How Racial Statistics Lie*. Minneapolis: University of Minnesota Press.

Zubkova, Elena. 1998. *Russia after the War: Hopes, Illusions, and Disappointments, 1945–1957*. Armonk: M.E. Sharpe.

Zubok, Vladislav, and Constantine Pleshakov. 1996. *Inside the Kremlin's Cold War: From Stalin to Khrushchev*. Cambridge, MA: Harvard University Press.

Zucker, Lynne G. 1991. "The Role of Institutionalization in Cultural Persistence." In *The New Institutionalism in Organizational Analysis*, edited by Walter W. Powell and Paul J. DiMaggio, 83–107. Chicago: University of Chicago Press.

Index